When Emancipation Came

When Emancipation Came

The End of Enslavement on a Southern Plantation and a Russian Estate

SALLY STOCKSDALE

McFarland & Company, Inc., Publishers
Jefferson, North Carolina

This book has undergone peer review.

ISBN (print) 978-1-4766-8198-6
ISBN (ebook) 978-1-4766-4632-9

LIBRARY OF CONGRESS AND BRITISH LIBRARY
CATALOGUING DATA ARE AVAILABLE

Library of Congress Control Number 2022031904

On the cover: Liberated Slaves at Hurricane Plantation Cottage,
Davis Bend, July 4, 1863, from the photograph collection of the Old Court
House Museum, Vicksburg, MS; photograph of the Emancipation Anniversary
of the Liberated Serfs at Undory Estate, Simbirsk Province, March 3, 1862
(Copyright © 2021 Literaturnyĭ muzeĭ "Dom Yazykovykh"; Literature
Museum "The House of Yazykovs," Ulyanovsk, Russia).

Printed in the United States of America

*McFarland & Company, Inc., Publishers
Box 611, Jefferson, North Carolina 28640
www.mcfarlandpub.com*

For Geoffrey and Aurora

Table of Contents

Acknowledgments

I would like to acknowledge a number of people and institutions without whom and which this project could not have been accomplished. This study began as a doctoral dissertation at the University of Delaware. I will be forever grateful for the wise counsel of my advisor, Peter Kolchin. I also greatly appreciate the grants that the University of Delaware provided, which enabled me to make several research trips to Mississippi and Ulyanovsk, Russia. I am indebted to Russell Zguta and William Hermann for their encouragement, as well as a host of other scholars and academics with whom I shared conversations about my work. Susan Barber and Charles Ritter have been the best of friends and mentors. My dear friend, Faina Vaynerman, one of Ulyanovsk's daughters, has an impact on this work, and I owe her my gratitude. It was through her that I was able to contact a number of people and scholars in Ulyanovsk, whose help and assistance were vital. These include (but are not limited to) Tamara Alekseeva, Sergei Gogin, Vladimir Gurkin, Natalya Kolobanova, Lyubov Kovalskaya, Oleg Moskalenko, Mira Savich, Ivan Sivoplias, Aleksei Sytin, Zhores Trofimov, Olga Turina, Tatiana Urentsova, and Larissa Yershova. I appreciate the archival and research help offered by the kind people at the Old Courthouse Museum in Vicksburg, the Mississippi Department of Archives and History, and the following in Ulyanovsk: the "Dvorets Knigi," Ulyanovskaya Oblastnaya Nauchnaya Biblioteka (Book Palace, Ulyanovsk Regional Scientific Library); Karamzinskaya Obshchestvennaya Biblioteka (Karamzin Public Library); Literaturniy Muzei "Dom Yazykovikh" (Literary Museum "The House of Yazykovs"); and OGBUK Ulyanovskiy Oblastnoy Kraevedcheskiy Muzei Imeni I.A. Goncharova (OGBUK Ulyanovsk Regional Museum of Local Lore named after I.A. Goncharov). The archivists at the Muzei "Usad'ba Yazykovykh" (Museum of "the Yazykov Estate"), Yazykovo Selo, Karsun District, Ulyanovsk Region, were most hospitable and helpful. A descendent of Caroline Couper Lovell, Hugh Stiles Golson, very kindly gave me her unpublished manuscript documenting the way of life at Palmyra Plantation and in Mississippi in general during the postbellum period. I also appreciate the careful reading and suggestions provided by the anonymous reviewers. Finally, I extend my heartfelt appreciation to my extended family and dear friends. Above all, I thank my husband, Matt, who has served as my best (though not severest!) critic and friend.

Maps

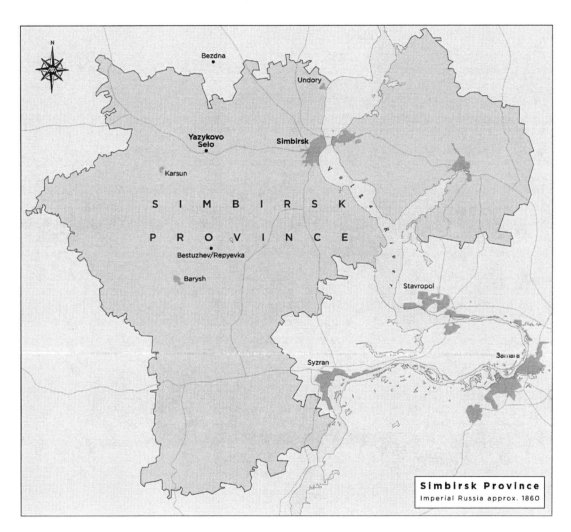

Simbirsk Province, approximately 1860 (Map Archive).

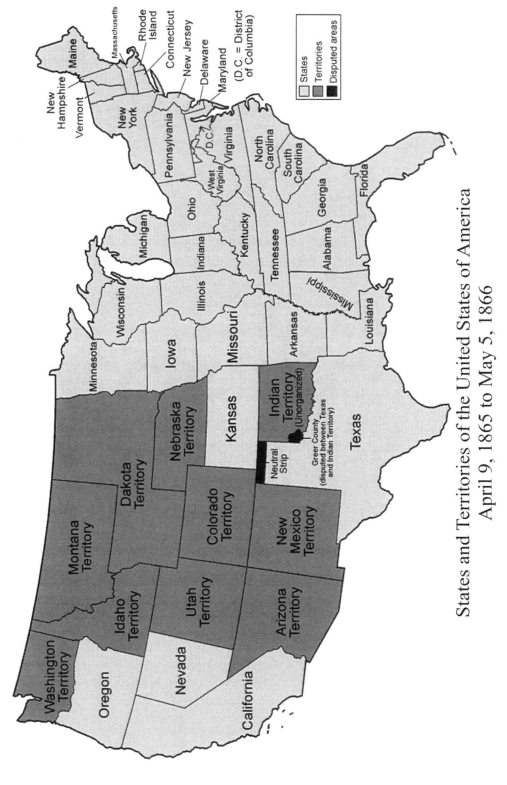

States and Territories of the United States of America
April 9, 1865 to May 5, 1866

States and Territories of the United States of America, April 9, 1865, to May 5, 1866 (by User: Golbez, Wikimedia Commons, CC BY-SA 3.0).

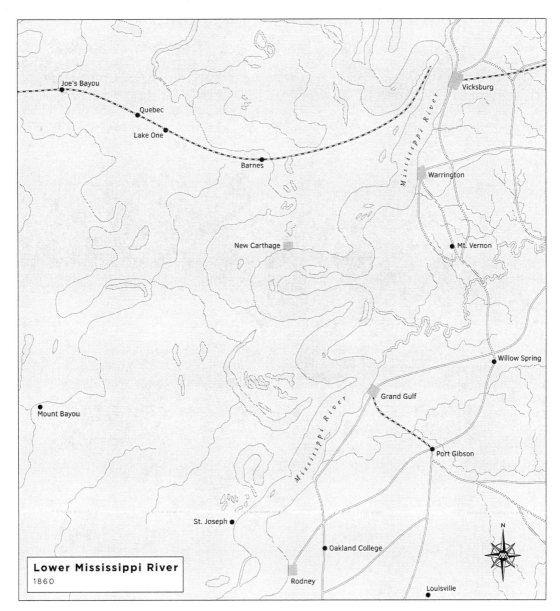

Map of the Mississippi River with following map callout (Map Archive).

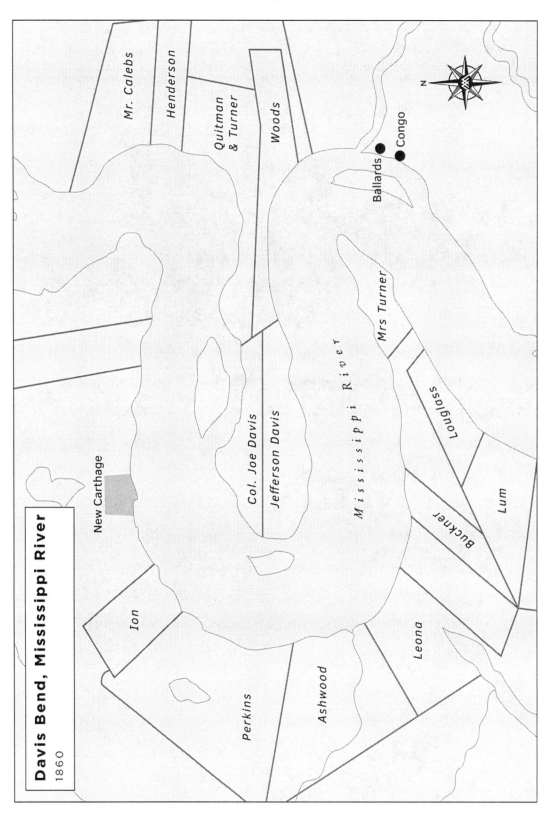

Davis Bend, Mississippi River

1860

Mr. Calebs

Henderson

Quitman & Turner

Woods

Ballards

Congo

N

New Carthage

Col. Joe Davis

Jefferson Davis

Mississippi River

Mrs Turner

Longlass

Buckner

Lum

Ion

Perkins

Ashwood

Leona

Notes on the Text

Note Regarding Dates

Until the Bolshevik Revolution in October 1917, Russia was on the Julian Calendar, which, in the 19th century, was twelve days behind the Gregorian Calendar; in the 20th century, that gap had extended to thirteen days. On January 1, 1918, the Bolsheviks adopted the Gregorian Calendar. Hence the occasional appearance of O.S. (old style) or N.S. (new style) abbreviations in this text.

Note Regarding the Name of Simbirsk, Russia

In 1924, Simbirsk Province and its capital city, Simbirsk, were renamed Ulyanovsk Region and Ulyanovsk, respectively, in honor of Simbirsk's most famous son and the Bolshevik Revolution's father, Vladimir Ilyich Ulyanov (known as Lenin). Lenin was born in Simbirsk in 1870. In 1860, the province consisted of six districts; by 1897, there were eight. The Russian estate featured in this study, Yazykovo Selo, was located in Simbirsk District of Simbirsk Province.

Note Regarding the Transliteration Scheme

I greatly appreciate the valued assistance of linguist Eugenia Vlasova. A modified version of the Library of Congress transliteration scheme has been utilized. Common English spellings for well-known Russian names, artists, and places are retained— hence Akademiya nauk instead of Akademiĩa nauk, Franciya instead of Frantsiĩa, Rossiya instead of Rossiĩa, Ulyanovsk instead of Ul'ianovsk, Usolye instead of Usol'e, Yatsenko instead of ĨAtsenko, Yazykov instead of ĨAzykov, and Yury instead of ĨUriĭ.

Preface

It is a staggering fact of global history that the abolition of Russian serfdom and American slavery coincided. After years of preparation, and triggered by Russia's defeat in the Crimean War (1853–1856), Tsar Alexander II emancipated roughly twenty-two million serfs in February 1861 (O.S.), ending the centuries-old institution. Almost two years later, in the cauldron of the American Civil War (1861–1865), President Lincoln issued the Emancipation Proclamation in January 1863, a weapon of war freeing only those slaves "beyond Union authority," totaling about three million African Americans. After the Confederacy's defeat, the United States ratified the Thirteenth Amendment to the Constitution, legalizing the de facto liberation that the Proclamation had set in motion. Arguably, more people were emancipated by government edicts in the 1860s than at any other time in global history. Despite the overarching differences between Russia and the United States in terms of political and economic systems, and the lack of geographic and cultural proximity, the coincidence of emancipation of this magnitude is compelling.

This work is a comparative examination of the experience of emancipation at a Russian estate and a Southern plantation from the moment of liberation through the end of the Reform period in Russia in 1881 and the end of Reconstruction in the United States in 1877.[1] A relatively brief (yet significant) period in global history, the "emancipation era" was a period when freedom incubated. While emancipation represented a marked break with the past, moving forward, the shape and parameters of freedom remained to be seen. Its meaning was not fixed; rather, it was subject to variegated, fluid, and raw contextual circumstances. Indeed, that which emerged in the emancipation era was, to borrow a phase put forward by Peter Kolchin, the "first of many freedoms."[2]

The Russian subject in this story is Yazykovo Selo, one of a number of estates owned and operated by a prominent noble family in Simbirsk Province, the Yazykovs. The estate was located approximately 450 miles east of Moscow on Russia's greatest water artery, the Volga River. During the pre- and post-emancipation periods, the estate was owned and managed by Vasili Yazykov. The Southern counterpart in this study is Palmyra Plantation, in the state of Mississippi. One of a number of properties owned during the antebellum period by "fire-eater"[3] and secessionist General John Quitman, Palmyra was managed after the Civil War by the latter's son-in-law, a Northern transplant, William Storrow Lovell. Similar to Yazykovo Selo, Palmyra was located on a great river artery—in this case, the Mississippi. Thus, each demesne in this study was located in its country's heartland and situated on a great river. Before emancipation, each was a fully functioning demesne in terms of economic productivity. Each was owned and operated by families who had historic roots and influence in their respective region. And each was the home and the workplace of generations of people held in servitude.

I contextualize this comparative, micro-case study within the grand arc of the emancipation era. This approach accommodates detail and nuance. It also fills in the contours of (and juxtaposes some historiographical debates about) both developments, as well as the meaning of freedom at the time. And it accommodates complexities, contingencies, and both certainties and uncertainties. Not only is this approach important for its focus on the richness of the local stories, but it also enables the historian to illustrate broader themes more effectively. Meaning is in the details.

Because historical stages are not closed to themselves, when appropriate I contextualize the emancipation era within a longer historical trajectory, in each country, and comparatively. To the extent that I examine how the various groups involved responded to freedom, it is a top-down as well as bottom-up analysis. Because both individuals' and social groups' behaviors and experiences are neither isolated from other individuals and groups nor alienated from the contexts in which they are situated, I consider the "lifeworld"[4] of each locale—that is, the phenomenological character of the place. The freed people were not divorced from their surroundings but were an organic part of them. The *place*, and all that goes into its making (such as the routine and the exceptional, the relationships, and the qualities and characteristics of the way of life for both elites and subalterns), made up the lifeworld. In this regard, it also means a comparative prosopographical discussion of the Yazykov family and the Quitman/Lovell family, as well as a study of each subaltern group's common, collective characteristics. Implicitly, this study is interdisciplinary: social, cultural, political, economic, and demographic history combine to produce a holistic story.

On one hand, what follows is an important story in and of itself. The emancipation of people who were formerly unfree and their comparative experiences at freedom's gate are compelling for their human interest and timeless appeal. On the other hand, I re-conceptualize both emancipation and the immediate aftermath in both Russia and the American South, from a history that approaches each as an isolated, self-contained story to one that presents an integrated common framework. Although state policies and the reactions to them in each country, and at each demesne, do not follow identical chronological trajectories, there were remarkable similarities, which I categorize under thematic headings. In addition to the "compare and contrast" methodology, which parses information in terms of similarities and differences, I consider the meaning of these. I identify and explain the topics, developments, and characteristics that transcend space and time, standing as phenomena associated with the context of emancipation and their manifestations at each demesne. This is important for expanding our knowledge about and reinterpreting "what happens" in an emancipation process in which freedom has been handed down from above, by the state.

Historiography

"Global history" continues to be a burgeoning field of study. It can mean many things and has great versatility in both methodology and subject matter. Among other things, it is concerned with comparing phenomena and tracking patterns across time and space and with searching for distinctions and similarities in order to identify exceptions and universals. It might utilize a category of analysis—such as capitalism, or institutions of unfree labor, or emancipation—in order to help our understanding of such a phenomenon in general or the way it manifested at regional or local levels. To the extent that this study utilizes "the emancipation era" as a category of analysis and compares two disparate places, it fits within the global studies paradigm.[5]

Historiography on comparative studies of both slavery and emancipation continues to be both a significant and an expansive subject area. Many studies consist of anthologies comprising chapters devoted to the experience of slavery and/or abolition in a nation-state or in regions. Others broadly compare the contours and nature of the themes between two or more locales within a region. Still others consist of thematic approaches, in which the various subjects under examination are juxtaposed.[6] While this study falls into the latter category, because it presents a comparative micro analysis of Russian and American emancipation of the serfs and slaves, respectively, it contributes to the corpus of work devoted to abolitions, as well as abolition as a globally shared experience.[7] It injects the comparison of a Russian subject and an American one into the body of work on societies undergoing emancipation and the immediate post-emancipation period.

The emancipation story in *each* country has been researched exhaustively, and the historiography is rich. Throughout this book I engage with some historiographical debates and trends with respect to a variety of topics. Although some of my findings fall into line with some established interpretations, others do not. For example, with respect to the Russian noble landowners, much debate has occurred regarding the impact of emancipation on their status, and even their identity. One mainstay is the notion that, because they could no longer count on their serf labor after emancipation, their fate was one of steady decline.[8] This "stagnation at the estate" (sometimes called the "declension of the nobility") paradigm was epitomized by the drama played out in Chekhov's *The Cherry Orchard*, in which a noblewoman, incapable of changing with the times and making decisions, sells her estate to a merchant who has the orchard chopped down in order to make way for the development of summer villas that he will rent for a profit. To the extent that the nobleman at Yazykov Selo sold the estate in 1881 to a merchant who developed it thereafter, it appears that the *Cherry Orchard* template could fit. However, appearances are not always as they seem. Yazykovo Selo's story suggests that when we discuss the "declension of the nobility" theme, perhaps more correctly we are describing a phenomenon that actually began after the period featured in this study, after 1881. Or perhaps it suggests that we are conflating expectations and assumptions about the behavior of the nobility with the Russian merchants, or even with the generic entrepreneurial ethos associated with Western capitalism. To be sure, history provides exceptions to norms. But evaluating a nobleman/noblewoman's behavior after emancipation according to whether he/she "flipped the switch" of his or her cultural *mentalité* not only demonstrates an inaccurate understanding of the Russian nobility but also seems to apply the characteristics of the prototypical Western capitalist to people who were neither capitalists nor entrepreneurs, at least in the Western sense (especially by which I mean profit driven).

In a number of ways, the historiographical genres of Russian history described as "regional studies" and/or "provincial studies" deal with this topic. Implicit in these approaches is an awareness of the relationship between the local or regional and the distant or central jurisdiction and/or establishment, along with the dynamics that accompany it. Related to this topic is an examination of the extent and nature of compliance, as well as the characteristics of adaptations and adjustments on the part of each locale to regional and distant dictates and trends. Important discoveries associated with these historiographical genres are that the provincial nobility was far from being passive and incapable of drive and initiative and that the provinces were regions with their own geographic and culturally distinct identities and histories. Scholarship in this area of study challenges what was primarily a literary construction of the Russian provinces, which lumped them together as homogeneous across time and space and as sleepy, dusty, and boring places.[9] The Russian portion of this study fits into these genres, especially with respect to the complicated issues surrounding the emancipation process at the local level and Vasili Yazykov's activities.

With respect to the Russian peasants after emancipation, implicit in both Western and Soviet historiography has been the interpretation that the "terms" of freedom were so crushing that the revolutions of 1905 and 1917 were indirect (if not direct) outcomes.[10] However, recent scholarship has challenged these views, with some historians discussing whether emancipation accelerated modernization and productivity.[11] In terms of economic progress and productivity, an evaluation of the situation at Yazykovo Selo can be tricky since defining "progress" itself is potentially problematic, given that it means different things to different people and different societies, at different places, and over time. "Progress" is also difficult to gauge since specific numbers for agricultural output on Russian estates is problematic in and of itself.[12] Both direct and circumstantial evidence suggest that, indeed, in terms of production, things did not appear to go well at Yazykovo Selo after emancipation. This was due, in part, to a number of general economic realities and developments in both Simbirsk Province specifically and Russia in general and, in part, to what I suggest was Yazykovo Selo's inhabitants' resistance to the "terms" of emancipation in the form of their labor performance (or lack thereof). On the one hand, it could be summarized as exhibiting ambivalence. On the other, it can be interpreted as an illustration of "strategic passive retreat."[13] It is this idea that, at best, does not get the attention it deserves or, at worst, gets conflated with the "emancipation as crushing defeat" thesis. Alternatively, it will be made clear that it was the revolutionary act of emancipation that gave the green light to the former serfs to resist working for their former masters. In addition, the evidence suggests that while the latter may be true, the peasants of Yazykovo Selo enjoyed social cohesiveness and cultural traditions and participated in a thriving shadow economy after emancipation.

The situation in the post–Civil War/post-emancipation American South was epitomized by the novel and the film *Gone with the Wind*, which romanticized the antebellum era as a bastion of order, chivalry, genteelism, idyll, and custom and lamented the demise of its civilization. The "old" historiography presented a picture of economic stagnation, political and social turmoil, slow adjustment, and racism.[14] While some recent historiography points out that after the war there was a zenith in the industrializing cotton economy, others assert that this development occurred *after* the immediate post-emancipation period—that is, in the decades following 1877 through the turn of the century and beyond.[15] A more recent turn in the historiography argues that slavery fed the Industrial Revolution and capitalism, and both of the latter in turn reinforced the former, which adapted and expanded in response to the demand for cotton. Then, the argument continues, the emancipation of American slaves internationalized capitalism, which, with its insatiable demand for cotton (and other raw products), hurled it into the global market, seeking coerced labor elsewhere.[16] In addition, notwithstanding the emancipation of slaves in the American South, capitalism's need for coerced labor meant that the cotton economy and its labor force adapted to the new legal or moral rejection of slavery and found alternative configurations of labor. (I address the new labor configurations at Palmyra Plantation in chapter 6.) Although it is true that in many ways William Storrow Lovell was typical of what historians have identified as the "new master" prototype and steered the cotton enterprise at Palmyra through the murky waters of adaptation in the post-emancipation era, this is not to suggest that there were no problems and recovery was even and certain.[17] A close analysis of Lovell's plantation journals and other evidence includes descriptions of constant struggles and much uncertainty. And with respect to labor, Lovell utilized a variety of modalities. After years of adjustments and fine-tunings, sharecropping did take hold, but that was well after 1880.

Finally, on the one hand, the long-standing narrative with respect to the American freed people is that, for a host of reasons (especially the fact that they did not receive land), they did not fare well in emancipation's aftermath. Indeed, in spite of the marked break with the past that abolition represented, many assert that slavery was replaced with another form of servitude, as exemplified by the institution of sharecropping.[18] On the other hand, with the rise of the modern civil rights movement and black consciousness studies, historiography since the 1950s increasingly demonstrated that former slaves showed great agency and incentive, forging cohesive and thriving social and economic communities.[19] An analysis of what played out at Palmyra Plantation demonstrates a far more nuanced conclusion on both counts, and why. For one thing, although sharecropping made its appearance as early as the Civil War, it did not become entrenched in Mississippi until after the end of Reconstruction in 1877.[20] This is true for Palmyra Plantation. As mentioned above, Lovell utilized a variety of compensationary methods during the period under review. The system of "squad labor" that emerged after 1865 meant that, among other things, there was a high turnover rate of seasonal labor there. Thus, while this development may well support the "macro-economic determinism" (my words) of the Sven Beckert thesis (see chapter 6), it also speaks to an interpretation that the freed people did have a role in both determining and defining themselves.

In a sense, both macro and micro narratives (or "macro-level" generalizations and "micro-realities," as one historian describes them) are two sides of the same coin: the former establishes grand narratives while the latter accounts for "irregularities" and nuance.[21] In combination, they equally contribute to historical understandings. My findings in the story that follows demonstrate that the understanding of both the emancipation process and outcomes in each region is enhanced by the comparative method. Comparison brings into sharper focus the distinguishing characteristics and experiences of emancipation in each country. It also delineates transnational phenomena associated with an emancipation experience spearheaded by the state. And it shows that the former serfs and slaves did have contingencies and acted, sometimes according to socially and/or historically prescribed roles, and other times with the tools (however limited) they had at their disposal at any given moment. The greatest tool in their toolbox was emancipation itself, for it armed them with a powerful, legal truth, on which they could base their negotiations (and resistance) in a variety of contextual circumstances.

Sources

I utilize and incorporate many Russian and American secondary sources that provide the general arc of the established history of emancipation era in each country. It is important to remember, however, that these sources are segregated. They stand alone, focusing on either the Russian or the American subject of emancipation and its related issues. While I utilize established narratives throughout the text, there are places where I do synthesize historiographies relating to emancipation in each country.

My research in both Ulyanovsk and Mississippi led me to a number of important primary and secondary sources. With respect to Yazykovo Selo, Vasili Yazykov's management, and the freed people there, I have utilized official government records as well as first- and secondhand and circumstantial accounts. These include, but are not limited to, the *Statutory Charter* (*Ustavnaya Gramota*) (see glossary) for Yazykovo Selo; the 1881 bill of sale of Yazykovo Selo; both national and local provincial reports and documentation; the censuses (*Reviizia*) (see glossary); and individual reports, both formal and informal, written by government officials and Yazykov relatives and acquaintances. No personal or autobiographical records of either the former master or the freed people exist for a number of reasons. First, the notorious 1864 fire in Simbirsk destroyed much of the main library there, which housed archival sources for the entire province. Also, many historical records were lost because of subsequent political and social upheaval that Russia experienced in the 20th century. Sometimes even official government accounts regarding the state of affairs on Russian estates in the 19th century are difficult to come by.[22] However, a number of sources documenting developments by Yazykov relatives, friends, and associates do exist. In their totality, these sources make it possible to reconstruct developments at the estate.

With respect to Palmyra Plantation, Lovell left detailed records in his plantation logs. In addition, there are numerous letters written by various members of the extended Quitman/Lovell family, as well as official and government records, including agricultural censuses and tax records, reportage and personal accounts left by members of the Freedmen's Bureau and other Union officials, along with a number of labor contracts.

With respect to the freed people at both Yazykovo Selo and Palmyra Plantation, firsthand accounts are practically nonexistent given that, by and large, they were illiterate and/or did not have the opportunity to leave written records of their experiences. When they did leave accounts, they were recorded by elites who interpreted their subjects' accounts through their own prisms. In some places, biases and patronizing, racist attitudes are evident. In other places, documentation shows prescience, compassion, and understanding.

In addition to utilizing such a great variety of sources to reconstruct developments at each demesne, one approach I use to gauge the freed people's consciousness (as well as their responses to emancipation and interpretations of freedom) is looking at what they *did* and *did not do*. Thematic topics include expressions of assertion and resistance; festivities, celebrations, and ceremonies; their attitudes toward education; their efforts to secure what they considered a "real" freedom rather than a nominal one (especially exemplified by their experiences with statutory and redemption agreements, as well as labor regulations and contracts); and their labor performance or, more correctly, the degree to which they worked, and for whom.

Themes

There are several thematic categories of analysis in this study. For example, the category of immobility versus mobility (and the implications that this dichotomy had on labor obligations, contracts, and performance) appears repeatedly. While the Russian Emancipation Manifesto attached the freed serfs to the land, it also preserved the integrity of their homes on the demesne. In addition, the Manifesto essentially replaced the master's authority over the male residents of a village with the commune authority. Therefore, while they did not have the de jure option of voting with their feet and permanently leaving the demesne in search of a new home and/or work, or for whatever reason, the freed serfs did have the security of tenure and could not be "evicted." In fact, as will be made clear, the peasants in the region were quite mobile in that they participated in a thriving shadow economy. In a sense, cottage industries and trade in markets and fairs proved to be strong elements of economic adaptability and pliability. Although the American freed people had great hopes of receiving land as part of the terms of their freedom, they were neither awarded nor attached to it. In a sense, at freedom's door they were homeless. However, in addition to the American theory of free labor—that it was more efficient than slavery and that it was *the* route to upward mobility—the fact that the former slaves were no longer "tied" to the land gave them a powerful tool to leverage when it came to negotiating work contracts in the post-emancipation period, when demand for their labor was great.

Another thematic category has to do with wage labor. In the Russian case, the terms of emancipation were rigid and perpetual. Only with a Redemption Law passed in 1881 is a shift in the labor performance at Yazykovo Selo discerned. The law mandated wage labor, and the merchant who purchased the estate in 1881 then began paying wages to the laborers there. Although it is not a part of this study, evidence shows that by 1900, Yazykovo Selo's production yields were among the highest in the province.[23] Conversely, the American emancipation legislation made no requirements with respect to labor obligations and, by proxy, made possible a pliable and evolutionary approach to contract and wage labor. In addition to signing seasonal labor contracts, Lovell frequently paid hired hands wages. The incentive of wage labor, at least in part, appears to have been a crucial variable in both outcomes.

Rumors and suspicion are frequent themes in this story, and they run in all directions at any given moment in time. For example, while the authorities in each context were fearful of a peasant/slave uprising for any possible reason at any given moment, both the former serfs and the one-time slaves were extremely suspicious of the authorities for a variety of reasons, including deep-seated fears of being tricked or reimpressed into servitude.

Modern war and armies are also salient features. Indeed, emancipation emerged in both Russia and the United States in the context of war. This fact is not surprising. Through the ages, history has taught us that often great social and political upheaval and/or reforms accompany (or are even brought about by) war. The presence of the armies in each context is impossible to downplay since the authorities, on the one hand, deemed these forces crucial for the maintenance of social control, the preservation of the integrity of labor on the demesne, and the "implementation" of freedom, and yet, on the other hand, they feared collaboration and/or collusion between soldiers and the emancipated. That is to say, in the Russian case, the rank-and-file solders were drawn from peasant communities across Russia, and, therefore, the authorities feared that they might cross over to the side of the freed people who resisted freedom's terms.[24] In the American case (and especially with respect to the African American soldiers who had joined the Union army), the white, Southern populace feared collaboration and collusion between these troops and the freed people, illustrating an atavistic fear of a "slave uprising."

Last but not least, another theme has to do with elites' and/or authorities' expectations versus those of the freed people with respect to freedom. For example, although the former acknowledged emancipation, they could conceive of no one other than the former serfs and slaves as *the* source for labor on the demesne after emancipation. Conversely, each set of people expected land gifts, with no strings attached, as part of emancipation.

Chapter Organization

Given that each demesne was in a rural location, its lifeworld was governed by an agrarian culture, and labor habits were determined by the seasonal calendar, I have divided this book into parts based on agricultural seasons. Indeed, emancipation is the thing that is being sown, grown, and gleaned. Therefore, there are four parts, each containing two chapters.

The first part, "The Pre-Treatment Period," contains chapters titled "Rural Muses, Unfree People, and the Abolitionist Impulse" and "Emancipation Comes to Russia and America." In the first, I comparatively explain the geographic and social character of each region, the development of the institutions of serfdom and slavery, and the abolitionist movements in each country. In the second, I explain the distinguishing characteristics of emancipation in each country, as it was mandated from the top down, as well as how each demesne in this study encountered emancipation at its inception.

The second part, "Planting and Plowing," contains chapters 3 and 4, respectively titled "Liberation: Conditions, Expectations, and Resistance" and "Regulating Freedom: Contracts and Agreements." In the former, I comparatively examine the themes of rumor, suspicion, and confrontation over the meaning and terms of freedom. In chapter 4, I comparatively explain the authorities' priorities of social control and protecting the demesnes' economic integrity. Here the authoritarian management of freedom via legal documents is significant.

The third part, "Tending and Reaping Freedom," comprises two complementary chapters. In chapter 5, "Understanding Contextual Realities: Background to the Post-Emancipation Story at Yazykovo Selo and Palmyra Plantation," I lay the groundwork for its counterpart, chapter 6, "Reaping Freedom: Management, Labor, and Productivity in the Midst of Liberation," by contextualizing each demesne in its respective regional and national economy. I also discuss the *mentalités* of both elite and subaltern groups in order to understand behavior, identity, and aspirations. In chapter 6, I explain the adjustments and adaptations that were made at each demesne with respect to labor, productivity, and the management styles of each landlord. In the midst of liberation, the key transitional issue had to do with labor. Nominally, coercion was a thing of the past. But what "free labor" would look like remained to be seen, even if (in the Russian case) there were de jure prescriptions for it, as well as de facto expectations in the American one. Here the work of Alessandro Stanziani is helpful. He challenges a traditional conceptualization of abolition, which, in short, considers an "either/or" contrast—that is, "unfree" versus "free." Instead, he offers a more nuanced approach that conceptualizes labor on a continuum, with the polar opposites being completely unfree and entirely free. I conclude that, ironically, there was a kind of convergence, or parallel progression, between Yazykovo Selo and Palmyra Plantation in that, after emancipation, each demesne entered a new stage in which there was a reconfiguration of labor obligations and contractual arrangements, as well as examples of "shadow" economic activities. Moreover, I discuss how freedom was "expressed" in their labor (or lack thereof). In this context, the differences between the two demesnes were in degrees, rather than contrasting profiles of "backward" versus "free."[25]

The fourth part, "Gleaning and Taking Stock," features a pair of concluding chapters. Chapter 7, "The Meaning of Freedom in Daily Life," discusses the number of ways each liberated group participated in the new, fresh context of freedom. Tangential to this is a recapitulation on *mentalités* and what was important to them (and why). In chapter 8, "The Meaning of Freedom in a Global Context," I review the phenomena replications identified in this study and suggest that the number and "types" of similarities highlighted are so striking that they carry implications for understanding emancipation as a category of analysis in global history. Notwithstanding the existence of nuance, agency, contingency, diversity, and difference, I argue that patterns and replications exist in pockets of history in specific contextual circumstances, the meaning of which points to a commonality of the human experience. The epilogue discusses the fate of each demesne.

Introduction

The Subjects in This Study

Yazykovo Selo was the nest of Simbirsk Province's famous noble family, the Yazykovs. It was also the home of generations of peasants. Indeed, like the majority of Russian estates in this region, the land on which Yazykovo Selo was built was one of a number of land grants awarded to an ancestor in the 17th century as part of the imperial strategy to expand Muscovy's control. And, like all estates in the area, Yazykovo Selo's lifeline was its proximity to the Volga River.

The Yazykov family was famous, rich, and, via marriage and custom, inextricably linked to a web of other prominent noble families in Simbirsk. One of many Yazykov properties, Yazykovo Selo was typical of large estates in the province. It boasted a mansion; a church; many outbuildings, including the estate administration office (in Russian known as the *kontora*); and about 800 enserfed peasants (see figure I.1). Its primary agricultural products included rye, oats, barley, and wheat. Significant to the post-emancipation story here was the presence of a wool factory built in 1851 in anticipation of government requisitions for the army, which the Crimean War confirmed. The patriarch of the estate at the time of emancipation, Vasili Yazykov, was a typical provincial nobleman in that service was central to his life. He served in the military during his formative years, and, after he inherited the estate on his father's death in 1851, he participated in a variety of civil service and philanthropic endeavors for the remainder of his life.

The Southern counterpart in this study, Palmyra Plantation, was one of a number of properties owned during the antebellum period by the "fire-eater" and secessionist General John Quitman. Originally from New York, Quitman acquired Palmyra Plantation from his wife's relations in the 1840s. In the postbellum period, Palmyra was owned and managed by Quitman's son-in-law, a Northern transplant, William Storrow Lovell. Via marriage, business, and politics, the Quitmans/Lovells were related to a collection of elite planters in the region, known as "Natchez nabobs."[1] Unlike Vasili Yazykov, Lovell was neither born into a master-class family nor raised with the idea that he would one day take over the management of a demesne. However, like his Russian counterpart, Lovell was a career military man in his formative years. Following his marriage to Antonia (Tonie) Quitman in June 1858, Lovell resigned his commission in May 1859 and retired to become a Southern planter. His management of the plantation was put on hold in 1861, when he re-entered the military, this time on behalf of the Confederacy. It was only with the Civil War's conclusion and his submission of an amnesty oath of allegiance to the United States that Lovell returned to his wife's family cradle. On the eve of the war, the plantation had registered 311 slaves. Organized around cotton production, the plantation comprised the main house and numerous outbuildings, including a gin and press, as well as a store (see figure I.2). The slave quarters included approximately thirty-five detached, whitewashed houses, arranged in uniform rows.[2]

To the extent that it contributes to an understanding of the situation at both Yazykovo Selo and Palmyra Plantation, there are places in this study where comparative comments are made with respect to each demesne's neighbors. For example, comparing the situation at Yazykovo Selo with other demesnes in its immediate neighborhood, in Simbirsk Province, and Russia in general (especially Vasili's brother's estate, Undory) is important for understanding its typicalities and exceptionalisms. Palmyra was one of four plantations located on a pear-shaped peninsula, Davis Bend, which jutted out into the Mississippi River just south of Vicksburg. The "Bend" was named after its most famous residents, the Davis brothers, Joseph and Jefferson— the latter being the president of the Confederacy during the Civil War. Because of its notoriety and relative geographic isolation, Union armies secured the Bend early in the war and, expropriating the plantations there, earmarked it as a "Home Colony." Tinged with elements of utopianism and didacticism, the idea was that it would be populated by former slaves who would build their community and benefit directly from their toil. Although it was founded on idealist principles, the Home Colony was also a powerful political symbol in a public relations campaign. The Union founded a community of freed people on confiscated property of the Confederacy's president, showcasing their accomplishments based on "free labor." It was also implemented as part of a strategic policy to line the banks of the Mississippi River with communities loyal to the Union.

Considering each demesne's "personality" is important for understanding why things played out as they did after emancipation. It is significant that Palmyra Plantation was incorporated into the Davis Bend experiment in social engineering. Because it was one of just a handful of settlements for former slaves that was spearheaded and overseen by Union officials, the freed people's experience at Palmyra during the war was not typical of most Southern plantations at that time. Yet, because the Davis Bend Home Colony was closely managed by Union overseers, it ironically shared a number of characteristics with Yazykovo Selo, whose experience was fairly typical of what transpired on many Russian estates, and certainly in Simbirsk Province—namely, an authoritarian management of freedom. The motivations behind this approach in each case included the goals of maintaining social order, controlling labor, and protecting the demesnes' economic integrity.

Herein lay a paradox of emancipation: on the one hand, it was about ending both coerced, unfree labor and barbaric, archaic social institutions that, according to the authorities, arrested modernization.[3] On the other hand, it did not solve the "problem" of the demand for cheap labor on the demesne. Therefore, "management" of the freed people in each context often focused on their labor. As a result, the form of labor after emancipation was crucial to the meaning of freedom in each context. Conversely, each set of freed people's expectations of freedom were frequently expressed in the context of labor. All this is important to understand when considering the crucial question, "What happened to labor on the demesne after emancipation?" In various ways, the chapters that follow answer this question.

Comparing and Contrasting

My aim is not to argue that 19th-century Russia and the American South, nor the estate and plantation under review, were identical. Indeed, there are many things that distinguish the two points of comparison in this study. The most glaring is that, whereas Imperial Russia was a bureaucratic autocracy with an absolute ruler in the tsar, the United States was a democratic republic, albeit with an intact institution of slavery. Another obvious difference is the geographic component of each institution. Whereas slavery was exclusive to the American South (and illegal in the North), Russian serfdom was scattered across European Russia, albeit more heavily concentrated in certain provinces, such as those in the "bread basket," which, in general, was located in the geographic area west, southwest, and south of Moscow, as well as Eastern Ukraine.

In addition, although Yazykovo Selo and Palmyra Plantation were located on the largest river arteries in their respective countries, participants in their respective region's economy, owned and managed by elite families, maintained by unfree labor prior to emancipation, and roughly self-sufficient, there were nuanced differences between the two. For example, while Vasili Yazykov would sell his estate outright to a local merchant in 1881, thus irrevocably cutting off the Yazykov family's ties to its noble nest, the Quitmans/Lovells would go to great lengths to preserve Palmyra in the years following the Civil War. When the plantation house went up in flames in 1894, Lovell's daughter-in-law demonstrated the family's attachment to the demesne in writing, "The dear old house! To think of it no longer in existence. To me it was consecrated by the happiness of my life there.... It is a real sorrow to think the dear old place is no more."[4] It is also worth noting that when Vasili sold the estate in 1881, a powerful source of continuity lay in the fact that most of the peasants still lived there. Indeed, to this day, most of the village's inhabitants are descendants of the estate's serfs. Contrast this enduring legacy with today's Davis Bend, Mississippi, which is a remote wilderness, devoid of any trace of its plantations and communities.

Another difference between Yazykovo Selo and Palmyra Plantation is that, unlike the latter, the former did not experience the tumult of war, occupation, confiscation, and reclamation. That said, there were military units posted in every province across Russia in anticipation of disturbances associated with the emancipation proceedings. As will be discussed in chapter 3, an army contingent was summoned to Yazykovo Selo in order to control disturbances associated with the decree's labor requirements. Furthermore, the crucial interim period of Union military occupation in the American South influenced how things played out after the Quitman/Lovell family recovered the plantation. Although Palmyra was ultimately recovered, William Storrow Lovell (unlike Vasili Yazykov) had not been the lord of the manor prior to emancipation. In other words, there was a strong element of continuity between the pre- and post-emancipation periods at Yazykovo Selo in terms of both ownership and stewardship, while the same did not hold true at Palmyra. Still, although he was an outsider, the fact that William Storrow Lovell was a Quitman in-law meant he represented a source of both continuity and legitimacy at Palmyra. To the extent that they also help explain why things played out as they did at each demesne after emancipation, the management styles and effectiveness of both Vasili and Storrow are important points of comparison in this study.

Still another difference between the two contexts has to do with the issue of race. While we recognize today that race is a construct, during the 19th century it was fully

Figure I.1. The estate mansion at Yazykovo Selo, approximately 1905 (copyright © 2020 M. Riabushkin, "Sud'ba yazykovskoĭ usad'by usad'by," *Pamiatniki Otechestva*, Nomer 41, Chast' 1 [1998], str. 129–134). The Yazykov mansion was made of wood, in the classic style, with the main façade decorated with four-column porticos and two wings flanking each side. The house towered over a stone terrace with a built-in grotto.

Figure I.2. Joshua Rushing's rendition of the main house at Palmyra Plantation, based on the account of Caroline Couper Lovell (copyright © 2020 Joshua Rushing). The house was built by Quitman in-laws, the Turners, who migrated to Mississippi from the Tidewater region of Virginia just after the turn of the century. Thus, the house is a replica of that region's architecture, with its dormer windows, two chimneys, and a breezeway down the middle.

accepted as both a scientific fact and a category of social distinction. Whereas in Russia the freed serfs were the same race as their former masters—over the centuries Russians had enserfed their fellow Russians—in the Southern United States, the enslaved people were primarily those with African ancestry.[5] But the *distinctions* between the noble, elite landowner and his/her former serfs in Russia and those between the former owner and the former slaves in the American South shared a number of similarities: down through the ages, both sets of subaltern groups were targeted for their labor in regions where there was an abundance of land and a shortage of hands. Both groups were viewed by the elites in their respective regions as intrinsically "lazy" and "childlike," requiring supervision, as well as potentially violent and prone to "idleness." To the extent that each group of subalterns was a distinct social category, set apart from social superiors, a strong sense of paternalism on the part of the masters also prevailed. In addition, both sets of subalterns could be viewed as "others" by the elites (and vice versa) *within* the country in which they lived. While the American slaves were distinct because of their skin color, it was routine for Russians to refer to the peasants as "dark people" (although this was more typically a reference to their perceived intellectual capacity). Some believed in the myth that peasants literally had "black bones." Russian philosopher Vissarion Belinski called the serfs "our white Negroes." Although literal differences in "race" were absent with respect to the nobleman and the serf, the differences in social station (and/or corporation, and/or class, and/or estate—*soslovie*) in Russia could function in the way that race did in 19th-century America. When de jure emancipation ended these legal distinctions in both Russia and America, often there could be a lag of culture; stereotypes and socially prescribed roles were frequently persistent. Furthermore, some characteristics of legislation pertaining to emancipation in each country reinforced and/or constructed new distinctions. Thus, the differences between each subaltern group's status in each country were of degree but not kind.[6] (To be clear, when discussing differences between the elites and the subalterns in each society, it is not to suggest that each set had no experience with each other or that the former perceived the latter in some kind of abstract or archetypal way. Both sets of elites and subalterns lived and worked in their societies simultaneously in separate spheres *as well as* in spheres that had great overlap. Instead, these groups were distinct because of their de jure and de facto identities in each society.)

There were also differences with respect to demography. In general, the roughly twenty-two million (privately owned) enserfed peasants in 1860 constituted approximately 30 percent of Russia's population, which was around seventy-four million at the time. Conversely, in 1860 the United States contained roughly four million people with African heritage and around twenty-three million white inhabitants in the North and approximately five million in the South. Making up 14 percent of the United States' population, the enslaved people constituted a much smaller minority than the percentage of peasants in Russia. (Actually, if all of the social and legal categories were combined in the pre-emancipation era, peasants made up roughly 80 percent of Russia's population.) But in some Southern states, the black-white ratio was almost equal, and in some counties, blacks were a majority (see figure I.3). Indeed, the 1860 census showed that Mississippi had 343,899 whites and 436,631 blacks. Out of the 63,015 households in Mississippi, 30,943 (or 49.1 percent) owned slaves. Of that percentage, only 8 households owned 300–499.[7] To be sure, far more people in Russia were enserfed than those who were enslaved in the United States. But, relative to population numbers, the percentage of Russians who owned serfs was smaller than the percentage of Americans who owned slaves.

While the Yazykovs were not part of the most elite echelon of the Russian nobility, neither were they in the lowest tier, which is often referred to as poverty stricken. When compared with the broad spectrum across Russia, the Yazykovs can be accurately categorized as in the middling echelon in terms of wealth and prestige.[8] Still, as members of the nobility, they were in the top 1.6 percent of the Russian population. And, to be sure, they were one of the most elite noble families in Simbirsk Province. They owned many properties there, and, if Yazykovo Selo's population of approximately 800 people is an indication, it would be a fair estimation that they owned upward of 5,000 serfs. Conversely, the Quitman/Lovell family was one of the wealthiest in the American South, with 300 slaves at Palmyra in 1860 and scores at the family's three other plantations (Belen, Live Oaks, and Springfield). In short, both the Quitmans/Lovells and Yazykovs were among the most the most privileged in their respective regions.[9]

Census of 1860.

No.	States.	Free Population.	Slave Population.	Total.	Per Centage of Slaves.
1	South Carolina	301,271	402,541	703,812	57.2
2	Mississippi	354,700	436,696	791,396	55.1
3	Louisiana	376,280	333,010	709,290	47.0
4	Alabama	529,164	435,132	964,296	45.1
5	Florida	78,686	61,753	140,439	43.9
6	Georgia	595,097	462,232	1,057,329	43.7
7	North Carolina	661,586	331,081	992,667	33.4
8	Virginia	1,105,192	490,887	1,596,079	30.7
9	Texas	421,750	180,682	602,432	30.0
10	Arkansas	324,323	111,104	435,427	25.5
11	Tennessee	834,063	275,784	1,109,847	24.8
12	Kentucky	930,223	225,490	1,155,713	19.5
13	Maryland	599,846	87,188	687,034	12.7
14	Missouri	1,067,352	114,965	1,182,317	9.7
15	Delaware	110,420	1,798	112,218	1.6
		8,289,953	3,950,343	12,240,296	32.2

Figure I.3. Callout from the NOAA Map Showing the Distribution of the Slave Population of the Southern States of the United States 1860.

After emancipation, the number of freed people at Yazykovo Selo generally remained constant in relation to the pre-emancipation period. During the Civil War, but *before* de jure emancipation, the numbers at Palmyra Plantation swelled because Union policy relocated hundreds, if not thousands, of refugee slaves there. Then, after the end of the war in 1865, and after the Quitman/Lovell family recovered the property, the population count stabilized at a level that resembled the antebellum numbers, with one qualification: there was a substantial element of fluidity in that Lovell regularly hired seasonal workers from labor factors, especially in New Orleans.[10]

All these differences aside, as the following chapters will demonstrate, the

similarities between the two subjects in this study are compelling and point to important historical lessons. First, both the rollout of emancipation and the ways in which
it proceeded thereafter were neither flawless nor seamless. The whole period under
study was "raw" or "uncooked," to borrow terms used by Claude Levi-Strauss. That
is, the recipients of emancipation were participants in a great social science experiment in which millions of people met freedom at the starting gate. Sometimes efforts
made by those who set freedom in motion from above produced results that were the
opposite of the goals for which they were originally designed. This study looks at the
actions (or inactions) of those charged with *implementing* the terms of freedom. What
the liberated "did" with freedom at its inception might not be what we, from a 21st-cen-
tury standpoint, would expect. This study takes into consideration the fluid circumstances with which the freed people at each demesne were confronted. At once, they
were unknowing trailblazers of freedom and actors who instinctively knew what freedom was because of their former condition. The freed people at Yazykovo Selo and
Palmyra Plantation, like millions across Russia and the American South, moved into
their future carrying vivid memories and firsthand experience of what it meant to be
unfree. They demonstrated agency *within* the societies in which they lived—places that
contained their own histories, culture, economies, traditional practices and norms, and
political characteristics. By "agency," I do not mean that I apply current criteria for (or
assumptions about) the freed people's aspirations, motivations, or actions. As Walter
Johnson has made clear, assuming that "beneath all history there lies a [classical or oth-
erwise] liberal individual subject waiting to be emancipated into the precise conditions
that characterize the lives of the" modern, middle class of the "twenty first century" not
only is ill advised but, indeed, borders on doing violence to history and to those individual actors under scrutiny.[11] No, these were real people with real lives, in *their* contextual
regions and eras. Rather, by agency, I mean that they acted when and if they could, and
when they did, not surprisingly, they may have done so in familiar ways from the past.
In other words, both the authorities and the freed people had tools at their disposal that
they brought with them from their past into the new era. Still, the new conditions and
realities ushered in by emancipation brought to the fore new opportunities and tools that
the freed people could and did utilize. But they also introduced new constraints.

Another important lesson is that both the shape and the meaning of freedom can
depend on the shape and extent of oppression/exploitation/"unfreedom" that preceded
it. Take one example: Whereas Russian serfs could marry and attend school, American slaves did not enjoy legally recognized marriages, and it was illegal to educate a
slave. After emancipation, the latter group seized on both as expressions of freedom,
whereas the former serfs did not need to, as these rights had never been denied them.
Alternatively, the Russian peasants were fixated on land that they had always considered theirs. This fixation was only reinforced by the terms of emancipation granted to
them. Above all, it will be clear that, while social control and protecting the integrity
of labor on the demesnes were paramount for both sets of elites, what both sets of freed
people desired in this first phase of freedom was that which they had always longed for
and been denied: autonomy.

PART I

The Pre-Treatment Period

1

Rural Muses, Unfree People, and the Abolitionist Impulse

Rural Muses

> The [Russian] steppe country is reached at last. You look from a hill-top; what a view! Round low hills ... are seen in broad undulations; ravines, overgrown with bushes, wind coiling among them; small copses are scattered like oblong islands; from village to village run narrow paths; churches stand out white; between willow bushes glimmers a little river, in four places dammed up by dykes; far off, in a field, in a line, an old manor house, with its out-buildings, orchard, and threshing-floor, huddles close up to a small pond ... there is scarcely a tree to be seen. Here it is at last—the boundless, untrodden steppe!
>
> From "The Forest and the Steppe"
> in *A Hunter's Sketches* by Ivan Turgenev (1852)

> [The lower Mississippi River country] ... lies flat ... [the] soil, very dark brown, creamy and sweet-smelling, without substrata of rock.... The land does not drain into the river ... but tilts back from it.... In the old days this was a land of unbroken forests. All trees grew there ... to enormous heights, with vast trunks and limbs, and between them spread a chaos of vines and cane and brush.... The roads [connected] ... plantation with plantation.... The real highway was the river. All life, social and economic, centered there.[1]

In the 13th century, the Mongol Horde swept westward across the Asian steppes toward Europe, disrupting communities and triggering a surge of human migration fleeing northward, seeking shelter in the woodlands. One of the groups driven from their homeland in the Gobi Desert was the Asian Tatars, who settled in the plains along the Volga River. The Tatars assimilated with the Muslim Bulgars, who had migrated there centuries earlier from what is now Turkey. To our own time, the region is famous for its archaeological splendor, bringing forth treasures of its ancient Bulgar capital (Kazan) and its Tatar, pagan Slav, and Mongol past. Over time, the Tatar presence among the Eastern Orthodox Christian Slavs would provide a significant "other" against whom Russians would unite. After the fall of the Horde in the 15th century and the rise of Russia's core—namely, Moscow—subsequent tsars, through a series of wars, official decrees, and land expropriations and gifts, used a system of concentric rings to expand Russia's line of defense to the Baltic in the north, the Crimean peninsula and Caucasus in the south, the Polish frontier in the west, and the Volga River and beyond to Siberia in the east, thus reversing the migratory trend set in motion by the Mongol invasion.

In 1648, Tsar Aleksei sent nobleman Bogdan Khitrovo 450 miles east of Moscow to the Middle Volga River region, to establish a capital city-fortress, Simbirsk, on the line of defense. Following Khitrovo were many noblemen who received land grants from the tsar as rewards for military service and incentives for loyalty. Around 1670, one of these men was a Yazykov ancestor, Vasili A. Yazykov, who was awarded 90 *desiatiny* outside of the city along the newly built road connecting Moscow and Simbirsk. There is an old Russian saying: "Scratch a Russian, and you'll find a Tatar." This was certainly true for the Yazykovs. Legend has it that Vasili was the descendent of a Tatar prince who was related to one of the 13th-century khans of the Golden Horde. Yazykov's peasants evidently had mixed feelings about leaving the Yazykov demesne in Vladimir Province, just northeast of Moscow. One, so the story goes, fell on his knees and begged, "Leave us here to die, on our native land." But others, citing the hard winters, hunger, malaria, and yellow fever, noted that "people are running away from this place, and our [lord] wants to take us ... so we don't have to cry about it. Be joyful."[2]

After the summer harvest and milling were finished, twenty-eight serf families set off for the Volga steppes. Along the way they encountered caravans of runaway serfs, debtors, adventurers, and a multitude of ethnic groups on the move. At several points they were met by military commanders who inquired about their status and purpose of travel. "Are you all serfs of Yazykov?" and "Among you are there any escapees?" were frequent questions. At the end of the journey, they came to learn about their new home. On the one hand, Yazykov's new land was fresh and unspoiled, punctuated by ravines, forests, and tall, thick, grassy fields. It was situated on a tributary of the Volga. On the other hand, the soil itself was a disappointment. While some parts consisted of rich, fertile black earth, others were full of stones, sand, and clay.[3]

Yazykov's descendants expanded the family's holdings over the next century and a half. Like many elite members of the region, the Yazykovs would become known for their numerous properties. Records from 1684 indicate that Yazykovo Selo consisted of 30 peasant homes and a one-story home for Master Yazykov, as well as one administrative office (the *kontora*). Here the serfs gathered every morning to receive their work orders for the day. This is where merchants and callers checked in, and where bills of sale and purchases were made. From the soil that was good, grains and hemp were produced. But for the most part, the sandy soil was used to make clay bricks and tiles. A pond was dug near the river, and two mills were constructed, one on a spring and the other on the river. By 1770, a wooden church was built, thus making the settlement an official village (or *selo*). In front of the manor house was a fountain, while around it were numerous flower beds, gazebos, groups of picturesquely located trees (including birch, linden, elm, pine, and spruce), and shrubbery, such as wild cherry, lilac, and willows.[4]

The village itself was a combination of the schemata that Mary Matossian long ago identified. It had clusters of houses scattered in several places, as well as in linear organization, where houses were set in one or more lines along the ponds' banks. Also, the houses were "built of weathered, unpainted logs" and were rectangular, with the short width of the house facing the street. They displayed both kinds of roofs: "saddleback" ("pitched with two slopes, to shed snow") and "hip" ("four slopes ... for protection against strong winds").[5]

In 1812, a government census indicated that the original holdings of 90 *desiatiny* had expanded to 3,744. This now included a city mansion in Simbirsk, at least ten other villages in the Simbirsk and Kazan Provinces, and a number of other estates through marriage. These holdings pale in comparison to those of the highest echelon of Russia's nobility. The Naryshkin family, for example, received in 1690 alone 79 land grants near Saratov just south of Simbirsk, totaling more than 20,000 *desiatiny*. But this was the exception. The typical number for the elite strata of the nobility was less than 500 *desiatiny*, with approximately 45 souls (that is, male serfs) each.[6]

By the mid–19th century, the Yazykovs were one of the premier noble families of the province. Illustrious family members and friends included a handful of Napoleonic War veterans; the famed Decembrists[7] Vasili Ivashev and Peter Bestuzhev; historian Nikolai Karamzin; Russia's most famous literary figure, Alexander Pushkin; the poet Nikolai Yazykov; the father of the Romantic movement in Russia, Vasili Zhukovsky; noted Slavophiles[8] Aleksei Khomiakov and the Kireevsky brothers; and one of the framers of the emancipation legislation, Slavophile Yuri Samarin. Like many members of the Russian nobility, these relatives and close associates shared a strong affinity for the principles of freemasonry. Indeed, freemasonry gave many elites in the post–Decembrist political atmosphere a place where they could associate and share ideas in private. Freemasonry was also appealing because it symbolically transmuted the literal work of construction to a metaphysical principle of building (or rebuilding) both society and the self. Moreover, these Yazykov family members and friends, in one way or another, were both touched by and constructed a particular form of nationalism associated with the Romantic era that was similar to that epitomized by the novels of Sir Walter Scott: namely, a belief that their nationalism was a product of its history—a unique and organic result of the Russian people and geographic setting, which set them apart from the "West."

Situated atop a 500-foot bluff overlooking the mighty Volga, the capital of the province, Simbirsk, had developed from a fortification to a rather typical provincial capital. The cityscape included masses of red brick buildings and tall white churches, bookended by suburbs of wooden houses, with poverty-stricken quarters on the fringe. Indeed, by 1900 Simbirsk had the largest number of churches in all of provincial Russia, including 29 Russian Orthodox churches and 2 monasteries, as well as mosques and synagogues.[9] Imagine the torrent of sounds provided by the hundreds of bells ringing on any given day!

Simbirsk was known as the "Jewel of the Russian Nile" since, after the two capitals of St. Petersburg and Moscow, it had the largest number of noble families and, therefore, power, prestige, and money, as well as libraries, museums, schools, charitable societies, merchants, and waterway trade. The bustling river trade made an interesting contrast with the wide, quiet streets, which were typically plagued by dusty spells kicked up by the strong winds blowing from both the river and the steppes. The census estimated that by 1900, the city had about 44,100 residents.[10]

Like Russia, America had a vast frontier and a long, complex history of migratory peoples, civilizations, and servitude. Paleoanthropologists have long established that the first inhabitants of the Americas migrated from Siberia across an ice bridge connected to present-day Alaska, resulting in hundreds of distinct nations and tribes established throughout the continents in the Western Hemisphere. One of these, the Natchez, was a branch of the Woodland or Mound Building Civilization. The only mound builders surviving after European migration to the Western Hemisphere began, the Natchez settled in the lower Mississippi River region. Characteristic features that the Natchez shared with their river woodland precursors included the great mounds built for burial, religious, and social purposes; permanent, urban settlements; horticulture, especially maize; a monotheistic religion; and complex social stratification, including slavery.[11] Indeed, the Natchez's huge Emerald Mound site (outside of what is today Natchez, Mississippi) is second only to Monk's Mound of Cahokia, near St. Louis. Archaeological remnants of a Natchez settlement were discovered and excavated on one of the Quitman properties in the 19th century.

On the eve of the American Revolution, the previous two centuries had witnessed the development of three great colonial empires: (1) the thirteen British colonies hugging the eastern coastline; (2) a French colony in the contoured shape of a great crescent that began at the mouth of the St. Lawrence River and made its way southwest to the Great Lakes region, then to the Ohio River Valley, and across to the Mississippi River, ending in present-day Louisiana; and (3) the northern borderland of Spain's colonial empire, which followed a route from present-day Florida across to the Southwest, ending along the California coastline. Over the course of the Colonial and the early Republic periods, these nations went to war over territorial ambitions. In the crosshairs of European conflict, colonization, and migration were the Native Americans. The latter would participate with the European newcomers in trade partnerships and cultural hybridization. But Native Americans would also resist European encroachment and defend their homelands and cultures. However, because of continued European encroachment and the fact that other tribes, such as the Choctaw, allied with the French to neutralize the Natchez, the latter gradually disappeared. For those who survived brutal confrontation, amalgamating with other tribes was their best remaining option to survive.[12]

The region that became the state of Mississippi in 1817 was at the crossroads of a struggle between the Natchez defending their homeland, the French who sought to establish both tobacco plantations and a waterway outlet to the Gulf of Mexico, and the Spanish, desperate to maintain the integrity of their northern borderlands. The latter would entice Americans with gifts of land in order to populate Mississippi, thereby anchoring its settlement. Spain would even make offers of $100,000 to anyone who would instigate Kentucky to secede from the United States and, presumably, join the Spanish territory. In addition, the state of Georgia would claim the Mississippi region on the basis of its 1732 colonial charter, passing a resolution in 1785 for the establishment of a western county named Bourbon.[13] At stake were furs, lucrative cash crops, land, and power.

But the greatest of these battles was the French and Indian War in the 1750s. For a century, English colonists had migrated beyond the thin strip of backcountry that had separated the British and French colonies. These squatters were both the spearhead of English expansionist policy and common people risking confrontation with the French and their Native American allies in search of a better life. When the English prevailed over the French in 1763, the western border of the colonial empire shifted to the Mississippi River. Like their colonial counterparts, Americans of the early Republic period would take to the footpaths, trails, and traces, migrating west to the Ohio Valley, in addition to following a crescent-shaped route arching down to the southwesternmost region of the territory. Indeed, Joyce Appleby has described this first generation of Americans after the Revolutionary War as the authors of the national culture. They were on the move, optimistic, ambitious, opportunistic, self-serving, individualistic, entrepreneurial, resilient, self-congratulatory, and "self-made." It is ironic that many of these migrants came from humble origins (if not downright poverty), and in moving to the South, buying cheap land, and obtaining slaves, they garnered a fast track to freedom and economic upward mobility. These people were also literate, representing themselves to themselves in didactic journals, newspapers, and pamphlets.[14] One of these was John A. Quitman.

Born in Rhinebeck, New York, in 1799, Quitman was the son of a gigantic, overbearing, strict Lutheran minister whose parents had emigrated from Cleves and a doting mother who was the daughter of the governor of Curacao.[15] Not terribly scholarly, John eschewed the idea of following in his father's footsteps. He did pursue a career in law, however, graduating in 1818. More important, John's formative years were spent immersed in the post–Revolutionary Romantic era zeitgeist. Drawn to the imaginative, literary world of Sir Walter Scott and Lord Byron, as well as the outdoors, hunting, and military maneuvers, John Quitman spent much of his spare time playing the flute and writing quippish, flowery prose. His biographer has described him as being driven by a "campaign of socializing." Indeed, Quitman was a professional social aspirant, running his life according to a maxim of utility to reach his goals. Perhaps this is why, in part, he chose to accept one Mrs. Griffiths' letter of introduction to Natchez, Mississippi's society in 1821. As a passenger on the steamer *Car of Commerce* en route down the River, Quitman would write in his diary, "My heart began to throb at the hopes and fears that alternately ran thro' my bosom." As he gazed at the changing character of the landscape, he wondered whether, perhaps in the South, his "ambition" would be "satiated."[16]

When Quitman disembarked at the notorious, crummy underbelly of Natchez, Under-the-Hill, he discovered the city was an odd mixture of sophisticates and rabble. In general, the former were "Nabobs," members of a close-knit, pseudo-aristocratic group that amounted to about forty families in the area, related by an intricate web of both marriages and business ventures.[17] They were also generally of Whiggish[18] principles, definitely pro-Union, and Federalists. Indeed, Quitman would never be comfortable with Jacksonian Democratic principles. Drawn to the ideas of freemasonry, like most nabobs, Quitman joined Natchez society. These affluent people made a stark contrast to the enslaved African American population as well as the lawless adventurers, boatmen, vagabonds, and runaways who had drifted downstream from points north. Originally famous for its "Natchez tobacco," Eli Whitney's invention of the cotton gin ensured the resuscitation of what, up until the 1790s, most thought would die a natural death—slavery. By 1821, Natchez's nabobs were already steeped in extending their holdings to include cotton and, to a lesser degree, sugar. When Quitman arrived, the graceful city on the bluff was undergoing a transformation from a frontier town to a thriving hub of river commerce. The old creditor-debtor rancor from both the Colonial and the early Republic periods persisted under the new labels of Federalist and Republican. As the antebellum period drew to a close, those old quarrels manifested themselves in a new format: union versus states' rights.[19]

After opening a law firm and acquiring land with a number of partners (most of whom were also Northern transplants), Quitman married the daughter of a nabob in 1824, Eliza Turner. They went on to have ten children. Soon he acquired a spacious city mansion, Monmouth, which served as his home, as well as four plantations and over 40,000 acres of land. These included the cotton plantations of Palmyra, Belen, and Springfield, as well as a sugar and molasses demesne, Live Oaks, with 311, 32, 39, and 85 slaves, respectively. As the federal census of 1850 listed only twenty-seven slave owners in Mississippi with more than two hundred slaves, Quitman certainly qualified as a Natchez nabob.[20]

Palmyra Plantation shared the peninsula with Joseph and Jefferson Davis' holdings, Hurricane and Brierfield, respectively. Cotton was so abundant on this approximately 7-mile-long and 2-mile-wide peninsula that one visitor doubted "very much whether the planters will be able to pick it all."[21] Cotton plowing alone required the use of 50 two-mule teams a year! Spreading over 2,500 acres of land, Palmyra was divided into three sections: Upper, Lower, and Palmyra Island. The massive cotton fields were punctuated by weeping willows, pecan groves, clusters of blackberry bushes, pastures for cattle and sheep, orangey-red flowering trumpet creepers, and the ubiquitous yellow sedge grass. In the center of the peninsula was a large swamp where massive cypress trees stood, their branches curving downward to the ground "under the heavy weight of gray moss." Turtles and snakes were everywhere, especially at night. The plantation had its own cotton gin, press, store, and sawmill, and the cash crop was marketed in bulk. It also provided copious amounts of food and supplies, such as chickens, eggs, cattle, dairy products, timber, and lumber, in exchange for sugar, molasses, corn, and pickled oysters (to name a few) from his other properties. Quitman often moved his slaves from one plantation to the next, depending on work needs.[22]

Quitman went on to become a Mississippi state delegate and senator, as well as both a chancellor and a governor of the state. Promoted to a major general in the U.S. Army during the war with Mexico in 1848, he participated in the notorious storming of Chapultepec, and General Winfield Scott appointed him provisional governor of Mexico City. After the war with Mexico, Quitman turned to filibustering (agitating for the annexation of Cuba), for which he was investigated unsuccessfully by the federal government. He was elected to Congress in 1854. Notwithstanding his Whiggish principles during his formative years, Quitman evolved into a states' rights "fire-eater," suggesting as early as 1851 the organization of a confederacy for the South. Similar to the defensive nationalism exemplified by the Slavophiles in Russia, over the course of the 1850s Quitman increasingly advocated Southern nationalism and secession from the union. As a result of the notorious food poisoning episode at one of President James Buchanan's inaugural dinners, Quitman suffered for more than a year, and his premature death in 1858 spared him the experience of the Civil War.

Geographically both Simbirsk Province and the state of Mississippi were situated on the greatest rivers in their respective countries. The Volga and the Mississippi were drifting, rolling, heartland rivers; geographic arteries of communication and supplies; borders, beyond which lay the frontier wilderness; and bound to the hearts and minds of those who both respected and were nourished by them. Each had an important role in history in terms of the rise of civilizations, serving as the source of great floods; ensuring fertile, alluvial soils; and being the sites of epic battles.

Each became reified as symbolic icons of nature in the consciousness of their respective inhabitants. Their mightiness and surrounding landscape would be aestheticized because of ideas in the 19th century about scenery, in and of itself, having picturesque, natural, wondrous beauty. However, because they came to be associated with the countries in which they were located, the rivers would become nationalized, epitomizing that which became quintessentially "Russian" or "Southern." Indeed, the lower Mississippi River valley has been described as the most "African part of America," the most "Southern Place on Earth," and the "South's South," while the Volga has been characterized as "Russia itself," just as the Nile is Egypt.[23]

Both rivers flowed along a north-to-south route, dividing their respective countries into two real and imagined sections that were viewed as "developed" and "wild," the former being geographically closer to Western Civilization's core (in the case of the Mississippi River) and to European Russia (in the case of the Volga River); while the "wild" section was off to the west beyond the right bank of the Mississippi, it extended off to the east of the left bank of the Volga. Flowing for approximately 2,300 miles each, both rivers were accompanied by monotonous, flat terrain, occasionally punctuated alternatively by high bluffs and wide meadows. While the Middle Volga River region was typically hot, dry, and windy in the summers and cold and snowy in winters, the lower Mississippi River region experienced scorching, humid summers and temperate, overcast winters. However, both rivers entered into the popular culture as formidable foes to be tamed with levies and dams, as well as for what, arguably, each region was most notorious: the Russian artist, Ilia E. Repin, portrayed the painfully grim life of inhumane labor in his painting *Barge Haulers on the Volga* (see figure 1.1), and photographs and songs, such as "Ol' Man River" from the musical *Show Boat* (albeit produced well after the time period in this study), captured the toil and pathos endured by African Americans (see figure 1.2). In this sense, each river symbolized a place of hard labor. However, because each river was often, literally, a conduit to freedom, the Volga and the Mississippi also represented to the unfree a refuge as well as an escape route from their condition. A gendered component also emerged over time, when the Volga came to be known as "Mother Volga," probably due, in part, to the fact that it is a feminine word in the Russian language (it is also due to the fact that Russians have historically and culturally interpreted the river as well as the great Russian land as feminine).[24] As in the aforementioned "Ol' Man River," the Mississippi has been characteristically male, the origins of which are thought to be in the Algonkin name for the river: Mississippi, or "Father of the Waters."[25]

Figure 1.1. *Barge Haulers on the Volga*, by Ilya Repin, 1870–1873.

Figure 1.2. Toil on the Mississippi, approx. 1910–1915 (Detroit Publishing Company).

Figure 1.3. *Harvest Time*, by Grigoriy Myasoyedov, 1887.

Figure 1.4. *A Cotton Plantation on the Mississippi*, **by William Aiken Walker (1838–1921), 1883, oil on mesonite, 20 × 30 in., 0126–1206 (Gilcrease Museum, Tulsa, OK).**

Unfree People

One state policy that accompanied the expansionist policies of both the Russian Empire and the United States was the respective institutionalization of serfdom and slavery. As Russia expanded, bodies were needed for agricultural production and military conquest, in addition to anchoring outpost settlements. Over time various legislative codes in one way or another mandated the peasants' subaltern status, permanent attachment to the land, and inherited condition.[26] Ironically, the more Russia expanded geographically, the greater was its labor shortage, thus reinforcing serfdom's institutionalization. Wars, famine, and pestilence also plagued Russia during tumultuous times. Dispersed settlements and the constant presence of threats forced a communal bond within widely scattered communities across Russia, with authority vested, first, in the older male in the household; next, in the village with the "elders"; then on the estate with the noble landlord; and so on up the chain to the ultimate source, the tsar.[27]

As European nations colonized the "new" old world, a shortage of laborers was also addressed with an evolving institutionalization of hereditary slavery. The Southern colonies (and, later, states) were major sources of labor-intensive, primary-source cash crops such as sugar, tobacco, rice, indigo, and, eventually, cotton. Like their Russian counterparts, the English would search for sources of more permanent and pliable labor, especially as indentured servitude became obsolete for reasons that included servants' increasing ability to survive their terms as well as courts recognizing their grievances. The demand for cheap labor, the emergence of English maritime power, and the coincidental decline of the great West African kingdoms combined to create an Atlantic slave trade that spanned four continents and several centuries. To be sure, from the moment they were accosted in their homeland, Africans would try to run away or even choose death rather than be impressed into slavery. However, as time passed, African Americans (especially the second generation and their descendants) went on to forge communities on the demesnes where they lived and worked. Even though the Mississippi Delta was stifling hot and humid in the summer months, and its cash crop fields were punctuated by thick forests and swamplands, in general the climate in the American South was better compared to that of the Caribbean islands. Furthermore, the fact that both men *and* women were brought to North America, and the workload (albeit brutal) was not necessarily the *immediate* death sentence that the sugar plantations of the Caribbean constituted, also meant that conditions were more conducive for those enslaved to forge "communities" on demesnes.

Nevertheless, the conditions of enslaved African Americans did not improve from a legal standpoint. Indeed, as institutionalization of serfdom occurred in the Russian case, over time both state and federal legal decisions served to fully entrench slavery structurally, politically, economically, and socially in the United States. Various legislative codes mandated slaves' permanent status and restricted movement and rights enjoyed by free members of society. Although the codes would vary from colony to colony, and later state to state, in general, there were certain universal restrictions, such as denying slaves the freedom to assemble, own firearms, be educated, and have legally recognized marriages (to name just a few). Above all, the codes were designed to deal with "deviations" from normative habits and were therefore enforced on an "as needed" (rather than uniform) basis. To be sure, American slavery was particularly entrenched and formed the "backbone" of the economy in places where the agricultural cash crops were tied to and geared toward a market economy.[28]

Russian peasants responded to these developments in a variety of ways. Countless thousands complied with the tsar's and, by proxy, noblemen's edicts. However, "vagabondage, theft, and brigandage" were common. In addition to spreading rumors, dissimulation, pilfering, arson, work slowdowns, and petitions, the most common form of noncompliance was flight, with many males joining marauding bands of Cossacks. Indeed, between 1678 and emancipation, there was a massive shift in the peasant population from the forest heartland in the north to the steppes in the southeast. After emancipation and the 1880s in particular, another mass migration occurred from the steppes to wild fields of Siberia.[29]

Lethal mass peasant uprisings were both rare and notorious. Indeed, Simbirsk Province was home to two of the most infamous uprisings in Russian history—namely, the Razin and Pugachev rebellions (discussed further in chapter 3). That said, throughout Russian history countless acts of violence erupted, both spontaneously and planned, and on both an individual/local level and a massive, widespread scale. As the old Russian saying went, "Be afraid of the people's rebellion; it's bloody and merciless."[30] The most common lethal weapon was fire. Arson was used not only to express anger, frustration, and aggression but also as a "crafty" tool intended to financially destroy the master, thereby resulting in one's own manumission.[31] Down through the ages, fire was at once a cultural symbol of warmth and sustenance and a weapon of destruction, defiance, and subversion. Indeed, a village elder once remarked that peasant "children are most sensitive to two things: village fires and stories about plots of land that once 'were ours.'"[32]

Both serf and slave communities had sources of survival and sustenance. The enserfed Russian peasant was attached to the land and lived in a rural world. Although, to be sure, enserfed peasants had experience participating in local markets and points of trade, festivals, and the like throughout their region, typically they would not venture beyond the local environment where they had been born and raised. Boris Mironov has stressed that the community was the peasant's very sustenance:

> The relationship between the peasant and commune may be called organic, voluntary conformism. This conformism was political, intellectual, moral, and social ... [and the commune exerted] social control that was so powerful that it was quite literally impossible for the peasants to exist—physically or psychologically—if they found themselves in a hostile relationship with the commune.[33]

The Russian serf's frame of mind included the belief that cultivated land was the property of the person who tilled it. In fact, their view of the land was similar to the air or the water, in that they believed it was provided by God for all. But the "who tills it, owns it" belief was particularly reinforced after Tsar Peter III freed the nobility in 1762 from state service obligations, which, incidentally, was a turning point in the cultural history of Russia:

> Relieved of their stately duties, many noblemen retired to the country and developed their estates. The decades following the emancipation of the nobility were the golden age of the pleasure palace, with galleries for art, exquisite parks and gardens, orchestras and theatres appearing for the first time in the Russian countryside. The estate became much more than just an economic unit or living space.[34]

Indeed, after his emancipation, Petr V. Yazykov began creating a park on the grounds of Yazykovo Selo, in the style of the English country garden model. In addition to acquiring an estate consciousness, emancipation from service allowed the nobility to devote time to developing social and cultural institutions and infrastructure, from libraries, theaters, and schools to hospitals, almshouses, and fire departments. But the larger point is that the serfs understood the connection between the elimination of the nobility's service obligations and their own. Thereafter rumors traveled like wildfire across the Russian land that Peter had also liberated the serfs and had given them land, but the nobility had suppressed the news.[35]

Russian serfs also lived within a religious culture that "directed all aspects of life and action and infused the world and events with meaning." Their understanding of causality was fatalistic. However, fatalism does not connote an absence of rational thinking or self-efficacy. Fatalism and free will thinking are not mutually exclusive. As Leonid Heretz has explained, fatalism preserves the "notion of God's sovereign power while disassociating Him from the harsh facts of existence." The peasants' religious belief system was known as a "dual faith," or a syncretization of Orthodox Christianity and pagan pantheism.[36] Nature was said to be alive in everything. Thus, Russian serfs' lives were determined by and closely adhered to the dictates of the state requiring service and obligations; the agricultural, seasonal calendar; the family life cycle; official religious holidays; and an informal paganism rich in ancient beliefs and practices including superstition, myths, rituals, and archetypes.

Sources of survival and sustenance for African American slaves included extralegal and/or surrogate extended kinship families comprising those who lived on the plantation as well as those who lived in the neighborhood. In this context, "neighborhood" carries both a geographic and a metaphysical meaning: vicinity, in the sense that there was a larger community, with clusters of relations, friendships, and acquaintances across plantation lines, as well as one of consciousness, as in having a collective identity.[37] Of course, the community was dominated by work, for which both the nature and the time of year mattered: the "gang system" (associated with tobacco, sugar, and later cotton) involved group, field work, while the "task system" (most often associated with rice) involved individual, assigned work. After the harvest, holidays and Sundays were typically times for rest and socializing. This meant coming together to eat, drink, talk, smoke tobacco, dance, sing, and play cards and dice, which, in turn, involved African artifactual antecedents such as preparing stews, okra, and yams; playing banjos, drums, and Mancala; plaiting hair; and making jewelry. Rest time, as well as, say, tending to their own private gardens, had several benefits. It provided ownership over some aspects of their lives and thus had a placating effect that, in turn, benefited the plantation master.[38] Another source of sustenance was religion, which was a blend of Christianity and African traditional beliefs and practices, such as talismanry, animism, myths, archetypes, rituals, superstition, and ancestor worship. Above all, Christianity gave them comfort in their condition (the strength to endure) and promised them freedom.

Enslaved African Americans would resist their condition in a variety of ways, including spreading rumors, arson, dissimulation, pilfering, work slowdowns, sullenness, and feigning sickness. Here the myth of the "crafty slave" (suggesting rational thought) applies. These examples are just some of what W.E.B. Du Bois referred to as the "double consciousness" of African Americans. That is, having a "two-ness" of being, which involved, in part, living according to one's own reflexive truths *as well as* giving the master and others the impression that you were living according to theirs.[39]

Enslaved African Americans also ran away, but typically this act was temporary and a way of withholding one's labor—indeed, a form of negotiation with the master for an improvement in conditions or a favor. However, "maroon" communities composed of runaways existed. Rarely did African Americans stage massive uprisings, because they were too few in number relative to the larger number of whites. That their communities were scattered geographically also worked against cohesive strategizing. But rebellions did exist. Perhaps the most notorious included the Stono Rebellion in South Carolina in 1739 and Nat Turner's movement in 1831. Arguably, the American and French Revolutions, and the uprising overthrowing slavery and the French in Haiti in 1804, had a greater impact in terms of spearheading the beginning of slavery's demise in the United States. The Haitian uprising proved to Americans that slave revolutions were real and not imagined.[40]

Thus, both serfs and slaves forged communities. Each had a conscious identity and sources of sustenance. And, in one way or another, each resisted and rebelled in ways that constituted forms of abolitionism. Well before emancipation, they were the ones on the front lines of freedom.

The Abolitionist Impulse

Just as the institutions of serfdom and slavery had become fully entrenched in their respective countries by the turn of the 19th century, an abolitionist impulse was emerging in each. To be sure, there were concrete events the historian can single out as either triggering or accelerating abolitionism in each country. For example, as mentioned above, Tsar Peter III's emancipation of the nobility from state service in 1762 set in motion an anticipatory expectation across Russian society for the abolition of serfdom. Another significant outcome of this edict is that it unintentionally redirected noblemen away from the service sector in the capitals to their estates in the countryside, where they would proceed to participate in local politics, cultural development, and personal introspection. In essence, they evolved into a cultural elite.[41] During roughly the same period, and beginning with the United States' independence from Britain in 1783, one by one, all the Northern states made slavery illegal, thus demarcating a geographic fissure along which the North and South sections would coexist for the next 77 years.

But there were intangibles that also influenced a consciousness about abolitionism. Both the American and the French Revolutions and their accompanying Enlightenment principles of universal, inalienable, and individual God-given rights, liberty, equality, fraternity, and representative government were powerful moral messages that were irresistible to thoughtful, contemplative activists and members of the intelligentsia in each country. (For example, a portrait of Benjamin Franklin hung in the mansion at Yazykovo Selo for decades.[42]) Indeed, even as Russians would increasingly become aware of the immorality of serfdom, a heightened level of discomfort with the existence of slavery burgeoned in the United States, whose origins were rooted in the concept of freedom. The fact that slavery was abolished in the Northern states after American independence set the country up for an inevitable showdown between the two sections.

The rise of print culture in the first half of the 19th century made the exchange and advocacy of abolitionist ideas possible. Arguably, the most notorious pieces of literature in both Russia and the United States included Alexander Radishchev's *Journeys from St. Petersburg to Moscow* (1792); Simbirsk Province's own Nikolai Karamzin's *Poor Liza* (1794); the serial abolitionist publication out of Boston, *The Liberty Bell* (1839–1858); and Harriet Beecher Stowe's *Uncle Tom's Cabin* (1852). These and other novels and tracts brought to the fore sentimentalism, empathy, and *feeling* for the unfree. *Uncle Tom's Cabin* had such an impact that when President Lincoln met Stowe on Thanksgiving Day in 1862, he purportedly greeted her with the line "So you're the little lady that caused this great war!"[43] Indeed, in Russia, it was illegal to translate *Uncle Tom's Cabin*. But Alexander Herzen's periodical *The Bell* (1857–1865) did pass the censor. Among other social justice goals, the magazine demanded emancipation of the serfs, *with* land.[44]

Another development had to do with nationalism. Immediately following (if not coinciding with) the Enlightenment and Napoleonic eras was the Romantic, idealist zeitgeist, which rejected rationalism, reason, and secularism, instead asserting emotion, feelings, the moral worth and freedom of the individual, and national heritage. In Russia and the American South, the particular brand of defensive nationalism that percolated up to the surface was known as Slavophilism for the former and Southern secessionism for the latter.

Although some sentiments associated with Slavophilism had been in the cultural bloodstream of Eastern Europe for centuries,[45] this "modern" manifestation in the 19th century sprouted out of the anti–Enlightenment and the Napoleonic Wars. It was then, especially during the War of 1812, that Russia experienced modern, national self-discovery. Routing Napoleon's army all the way back to Paris, the Russian officers, educated and from the upper-class ranks of society, were exposed to Western Europe's standard of living and enlightened principles of liberty, equality, and reason. Many of them would participate in the failed Decembrist uprising in 1825. Also discovered during the war was the moral worth of the patriotic peasant soldier, prepared to lay down his life for the motherland. For the rest of the imperial period, the tension would be palpable between those members of Russian society who espoused Western liberal principles and those who would both stress and laud the unique qualities of Slavic culture and the Russian autocracy. Those who defended Russia's "Russianness" viewed ideas imported from the West as germs of the French Revolution from which the country needed to be inoculated.

An important aspect of Slavophilism was its animus toward the West. Born out of a direct refutation of one Russian critic who declared that Russia was a "historic swampland," which had never contributed anything to civilization, the Slavophiles fixated on the criticism that Russia was "backward" and developed a national ideology that extolled the East and perceived some aspects of Western modernization (such as corruption, rationality, individualism, and decadence) as cultural contaminants. In fact, the Slavophiles viewed serfdom as a product of Tsar Peter the Great's Westernizing impulse in the 17th century and, therefore, an inorganic, alien institution grafted onto a pristine Russian culture. The Slavophiles came to believe that it was the Russian peasants who naturally embodied and were the repository of an authentic Russia. Indeed, they were the very spirit of the nation. Liberating the serfs, therefore, would be historically corrective.[46]

This idea was reinforced by a religious component of the zeitgeist of the day, which actually was a "new" installment of an age-old impulse associated with Christianity—namely, millenarianism. That is, in addition to the Slavophiles seeking emancipation as a historical corrective, they advocated abolition as a component of the Christian promise of peace and freedom here on earth. Abolitionists such as Afanasy Shchapov and Yazykov brother-in-law Alexei Khomiakov believed that the early Christian teachings had stressed millennialist expectations of freedom.[47] Thus, a romantic, nationalistic, and religious view of the peasants as being both *naturally* communal and the true harbingers of Russian national culture meant that emancipating the serfs would be culturally restorative. In this sense, emancipation took on both religious and historically messianic symbolism.[48]

Although not identical in sequence and composition, these phenomena were present in the United States. First, the United States also experienced modern, national self-discovery during the War of 1812. Also known as the "Second War of Independence," the War of 1812 lent elements of legitimacy and authenticity to the relatively new, fledgling, post–Enlightenment nation. Similar to the experience in Russia, the war also triggered a cultural dichotomy of sorts. Thomas Abernethy explained that, whereas in the North victory reinforced the desire for a strong central government by a "class in the interests of that class," in the South it triggered a powerful nationalism that would become a strident separatism (or secessionism) after 1850. In fact, before 1812 secessionism was intersectional. However, as the century progressed, Southern nationalism and secessionism merged, emerging concurrently with (and in response to) real and imagined Northern criticism, especially about its institution of slavery and the South's "backwardness." Beyond the foremost provocative issue of slavery lay a cultural divide in the United States that coalesced along sectional lines, which was similar to that between the Russian Slavophiles and Westerners: one favoring particularism and tradition, as well as anxiety about modernity, and the other embracing homogeneity, reform, development, and "progress."[49]

As happened in Russia, millenarianism in the United States also had a role in the abolitionist impulse. Like the Slavophiles, Northern abolitionists were driven by a religious commitment to ending slavery. For example, the biblical story of Exodus carried great symbolism and influence with respect to the emigrationist drive in the "back to Africa" movement. Reformers such as the Grimke sisters, James McCune Smith, and David Walker considered the mission of uplifting the enslaved as one and the same with the Christian duty to extend brotherly love and transform the hearts and minds of whites about the "African race." Only through emancipation could both American whites and America itself be redeemed. As in the Russian case, American abolitionism was an important part of a historical, religious, messianic correction.[50]

On the contrary, Southerners increasingly felt defensive about slavery. They argued that the Northern section participated in and benefited from slavery via the textile mills and other industries and that it was hypocritical in its criticism of the South's institution when its own treatment of the poor, working classes was appalling. They also argued that Southern society was ordered and tranquil *because* of slavery. As is commonly known, Southern defenders of slavery even found justification in the Bible, not to mention the pseudo-scientific ideas of the day.

What Russian Slavophilism and Southern nationalism appear to have shared was an apprehension or anxiety, or even alienation, about being confronted with a modernizing world that stood in contradistinction to what they perceived as their way of life. We see this theme reappear time and again in the literature explaining both Slavophilism and Southern nationalism.[51] To both assert and defend their way of life meant to both authenticate and redeem it. Interestingly, whereas Slavophilism found the source of Russia's redemption in a theology of culture—that is, a religious essence of culture—so, too, did defenders of the South find religious sanction for their nationalism.[52] In fact, both were modern responses to modernity.

Liah Greenfeld has defined nationalism as a "style of thought" that locates individual identity within a "people" and assumes homogeneity. Moreover, it is rooted in mimesis of an "other." In other words, nationalism is necessarily an indigenous development because every country or group that imports or comes into contact with an idea that is foreign to itself (Western Europe in the case of Russia, and the North in the case of the South) necessarily focuses on

> the source of importation which [is] the object of imitation, and react[s] to it. Because the model [is] more often than not superior to the imitator [in the latter's own perception], and the contact itself serve[s] to emphasize the latter's inferiority, the reaction more often than not assume[s] the form of "ressentiment."

Indeed, Greenfeld holds that nationalism cannot occur without a model. *Ressentiment* stems from unresolved envy or shame, which is rooted in the *belief* in fundamental equality as well as the *perception* of real or imagined inequality (or "backwardness"), which is then perceived as fundamental and exists to such a degree that it rules out practical achievement of equality. It triggers "transvaluation of values" of the object of imitation. That is, the imported or borrowed ideas are "reinterpreted and adjusted to the internal reality of the country [or group] that copies them." Greenfeld explains that the inconsistency between expectations and the reality that is either real or perceived as fact becomes unbearable and results in "anomie," or alienation. Finally, nationalism emerges at the moment when alienation and/or anxiety about status peaks. Above all, it is about securing dignity and expunging shame.[53]

Thus, while both *ressentiment* and religion led Slavophiles such as Alexei Khomiakov to call for emancipation, these forces influenced Southerners (including John Quitman) to defend the institution of slavery. And while both the Slavophiles and Northern abolitionists had in common a Christian religious influence behind arguments for emancipation, Southern nationalists defended slavery from a religious standpoint as well.

To be clear, this analysis does not reduce the multifaceted elements of both Russian and Southern nationalism to a one-dimensional portrait in which they both simply "hated" their perceived opponents due to some kind of irrational fear.[54] Nor does it neglect the political or economic reasons that influenced both abolitionists and defenders of serfdom and slavery. Indeed, as Peter Kolchin has explained, many historians attribute the *simultaneity* of Russian and American emancipation to the rise of capitalism. This overarching explanation includes the "natural limits thesis," which hypothesizes that both serfdom and slavery had become increasingly obsolete in economies where free, wage labor was far more productive and efficient, and each kept Russia and the South backward. This theory, however, has been countered by historians who hold that "serfdom and slavery were neither moribund nor unprofitable." Nevertheless, it is true that both Russia and the American South lagged far behind advanced Western European countries and the Northern region of the United States on practically every indicator of "modernization." In this regard, in the same way that the Romantic zeitgeist and millenarianism equally influenced abolitionism, so, too, did the ideals associated with economic modernization during the 19th century—namely, a modernizing humanism that questioned the institutions of serfdom and slavery and espoused a fundamental belief in freedom. The meaning of freedom in this sense had both abstract and concrete connotations, which included things like the freedom to exchange goods and make a contract; free, wage labor; and discomfort with humans as "property." It also meant the freedom to make choices about one's life path as well as limited restrictions on those choices. In short, it was a humanitarian sensibility that serfdom and slavery were morally reprehensible in a modernizing society.[55]

The one thing that ended all debate and set each nation on the inevitable course to abolition was war. In many ways, the Crimean and Civil Wars were comparable in that they were the first modern, industrial wars, producing high casualty rates, innovating military medical attention, and showcasing the gap between outdated battle plans and logistics, on the one hand, and modern technology, on the other. And like the American South, which would suffer defeat after four arduous years of resistance during the Civil War, the Russian loss in Crimea was a hard blow. Since the time of Peter the Great, Russia had not lost a war. Just as the series of wars on the American continent had taught the South that wars could be fought and won, so, too, did Russia's triumph over Napoleon in 1812 embolden Russians. In fact, for both Russia and America, the events of 1812 catapulted them onto the world stage of being "great powers."

The Crimean defeat challenged that claim for Russia. Furthermore, Russia's humiliation was far more serious than a 19th-century loss of honor. The Crimean War brought home Russia's lack of industrial capacity and especially the anachronism of having a huge standing army comprising more than a million peasant soldiers in peacetime alone. Such a force was costly to maintain in peacetime, and it was dangerous for a nation whose security depended on soldiers drawn from a servile population who were trained in the use of firearms. Indeed, Alexander Gerschenkron and Alexander Polunov explained emancipation as a proactive, preventative measure against peasant revolts. Bruce Lincoln and Jerome Blum placed weight on the shock of the Crimean defeat in 1856 as having convinced the tsar that reform was needed. If we are to turn to the tsar himself to explain emancipation, we need look no further than Alexander II's own words as he signed the peace ending the war: "It is better to begin to abolish serfdom from above than to await that time when it will begin to abolish itself from below." In this statement we see the powerful influence of fear. Furthermore, the tsar's decision to emancipate the serfs was at once revolutionary and conservative: it was a break with the past, and it loosened the grip of the estate (*soslovie*) system. But it was also forward looking in that it previewed a series of reform edicts ranging from regional self-government (*zemstvo* councils, discussed in chapter 7) to education, freedom of the press, and judicial and military changes (a.k.a. the Great Reforms). However, emancipation was conservative in that Alexander II acted in order to *preserve* the autocracy.[56]

In the United States, President Lincoln was also responsible for a revolutionary measure enacted for conservative reasons—namely, the preservation of the Union. Although both "free soiler" sentiment and an abolitionist movement in the United States had stressed economic as well as moral reasons for ending slavery, the Emancipation Proclamation in January 1863 was significant in that it was a weapon of war. As the president explained, "If I could save the Union without freeing any slave, I would do it; and if I could save it by freeing all the slaves, I would do it…. What I do about Slavery … I do because I believe it helps to save this Union." The Emancipation Proclamation was intended to both deprive the Southern home front of a crucial source of labor and deal a psychological blow to the enemy's morale. It was also at once a revolutionary, diplomatic, political, moral, and pragmatic measure in that it shifted the war's purpose from the Union's preservation to the abolition of slavery, targeted the favor of foreign powers, placated radical abolitionists such as Frederick Douglass, seized the moral high ground, and would, arguably, accelerate the North's victory. It would also save white lives since blacks would now presumably be available to fill the Union's military ranks. In addition, it was a response to what historians such as Ira Berlin, Steven Hahn, and Enrico Dal Lago have described as the self-emancipation of African Americans, which began when the first shots were fired. "Voting with their feet," African Americans seized the opportunity presented by the war's tumult, left their plantations by the thousands as Union army currents drew them in, and found community with other refugees in the armies' wakes. The Emancipation Proclamation was also forward looking in that it previewed constitutional amendments and congressional legislation that codified citizenship for African Americans.[57]

* * *

In this chapter, I integrated the background stories of each subject in this study using three general categories of analysis, and I identified a number of phenomena replications. Although the Yazykov and Quitman demesnes were worlds apart in terms of geographic proximity, language, and political culture, the situation, time, and condition rendered intriguing similarities. Geographically, each demesne was situated in its nation's main river corridor. The great rivers figured prominently in each nation's historical memory and cultural identity, serving simultaneously as geographic identifiers, critical trade and exchange routes, and life sustainers. The lifeworld in each place was similar in terms of spatial terrain and temporal rhythm. Both regions showcased large, agrarian societies, with rigidly defined social divisions and socially prescribed roles. Each had fully entrenched institutions of unfree labor that emerged as a result of "modernizing" impulses. And each region was marked by great ethnic and religious diversity, both historically and contemporaneously.

The Yazykovs and Quitmans had scores of enserfed and enslaved people. The Russian peasant serfs at Yazykovo Selo and African American slaves at Palmyra had in common their unfree condition. Their lives and lifestyles were shaped and held together by their regional lifeworld, their work, and their personal relationships, including those with their masters and local elites. Each had a rich, distinctly folk culture. And the Russian peasants' Orthodox Christianity was sprinkled with pagan beliefs and practices, while African Americans' Christianity was blended with vestiges of ancestor veneration, animism, and talismanry.

Yazykovo Selo and Palmyra were categories of what is arguably the most common and enduring organized form of settlement in the early modern era: the demesne. Like all Russian estates and Southern plantations, they were economic, cultural, and social entrêpots, with main houses surrounded by clusters of auxiliary buildings and servant quarters, and with their own orbits of influence. These were privately owned spaces where public and private spheres overlapped. They were at once self-contained, semi-autonomous places with part-societies and part-cultures. That is, they were inextricably linked politically, economically, socially, and culturally in the greater regions and/or nations where they were located. Each demesne was also at one end of a rural-urban nexus. The Russian noble master and Southern elite planter lived in rural worlds, but they could and did negotiate in a modernizing world beyond the boundaries of their demesnes. Both families had city mansions and multiple estates, and they were connected to the larger web of elites in their respective locales. The Russian serfs and African American slaves also lived in part-societies with part-cultures: they were neither tribal nor primitive, closed societies. Both the nobleman and planter *and* the serf and slave were cultural hybrids, in that the former pair simultaneously participated in a greater society or modernizing civilization while maintaining their own demesnes, and the latter pair concurrently traversed the requirements imposed by the demesne and larger societal order while crafting a way of life distinguished by its parochial traditions.

Both regions experienced tumultuous times, including famines, pestilence, episodic disturbances, rebellions, and wars. It is significant that the emancipation era coincided with destructive wars.

Each region shared some particular aspects of the zeitgeist of the times: Romantic idealism, defensive nationalism, and religious millennialism. All these were manifestations of a modernizing world order in the 19th century, albeit with esoteric or situational variables and sequential differences. One of those variables had to do with abolitionism. While Slavophile Russians pressed for the abolition of serfdom from the standpoint of a nationalistic, historical corrective, Southern secessionists were opposed to emancipation out of loyalty to *their* region and history. Ironically, both movements had their roots in the goal of preserving their respective "nations." Also ironic was the modernization impulse that set each country on a trajectory to end these anachronistic institutions. All these ingredients blended and contributed to the moment when emancipation became a reality. It is that abolition moment that the next chapter will address.

2

Emancipation Comes
to Russia and America

Though serfdom's sad conditions left behind,
Yet there be countless snares of varied kind!
Well! Although the people soon may rend thee,
Let me, oh Freedom, a welcome send thee!

From N.A. Nekrasov's poem "Freedom" (1861)

Not as we hoped, in calm of prayer,
The message of deliverance comes,
But heralded by roll of drums
On waves of battle-troubled air!

Not as we hoped; but what are we?
Above our broken dreams and plans
God lays, with wiser hand than man's,
The corner-stones of liberty.

From John Greenleaf Whittier's poem "Abolition
of Slavery in the District of Columbia" (1862)

The spring of 1861 was extraordinary in global history. The machinery of the liberation of millions was set in motion—in Russia, with the stroke of Tsar Alexander II's pen, and in the United States, with the ignition of cannon fire. In order to understand what unfolded at Yazykovo Selo and Palmyra Plantation, a brief discussion about the nature of emancipation in each country will be instructive.

The Nature of Emancipation in Russia and in the United States

Following the end of the Crimean War in 1856, the tsar set Russia on a deliberative course of reforms, the centerpiece of which was emancipation. Liberation came to the serfs from the top down. It was preemptive and carefully managed by the bureaucracy. The Emancipation Manifesto, issued on February 19, 1861 (O.S.), was accompanied by a complicated 400-page manual of sorts, the *Regulations* (*Polozheniĭa*). Anticipating peasant dissatisfaction with the terms of freedom, the tsar dispersed hundreds of army units across the country on the eve of the Manifesto's release to maintain order and enforce its stipulations. The appearance of military units across the land certainly signaled to the peasants that change was in the offing, and rumors were rampant. A

Figure 2.1. *Watch Meeting Dec. 31, 1862—Waiting for the Hour,* **by W.T. Carlton, 1863 (White House Collection/White House Historical Association).**

Department of Peasant Affairs was established to aid former serfs' transition to freedom and to address their grievances. Although the peasants were immediately liberated from their former masters, gained the right to engage in trade and other business activities, and could even join guilds, in an effort to preserve the supply of labor on estates and prevent the mobility of a landless class comprising millions of people, the legislation attached the peasants to the land. It also mandated that former masters would earmark a certain amount of land to the freed people. In addition, although the legislation broke the former master's authority over the serfs, it replaced it with the village "commune" (*obshchina*—that is, village community, or literally village society), which was directly supervised by the village elders and indirectly by a host of other government officials. Among other things, this arrangement meant that if an individual wanted to travel, they needed to obtain a "passport" from the village elders.

The crucial legal tool for implementing emancipation was a contract of sorts, known as the Statutory Charter (*Ustavnaya Gramota*). Within one year of the emancipation date, it was supposed to be drafted on every estate across Russia, and certainly by March 1863 the authorities expected that all charters would be completed. Ideally, both the former master and the former male serfs in toto (in the form of a few representatives) were to agree to it with their signatures. This charter defined the land allotments that the former serf owner was required to earmark for his/her former *male* serfs.

Figure 2.2. *Reading the Emancipation Act of 19 February 1861*, by G. Myasoedov, 1873 (in the collection of the State Tretyakov Gallery, Moscow).

Figure 2.3. Emancipation print by Thomas Nast, 1865 (Library of Congress).

Figure 2.4. *The Emancipation of the Serfs*, **by Boris Kustodiev, 1908–1909.**

The *Regulations* required that the allotted land fall within a range between a maximum and a minimum amount. This prescribed range varied from province to province, based on such calculations as the quality and productivity of the soil. A crucial player in the negotiation of the charter contract was the peace mediator (a.k.a. peace arbitrator), an official who was supposed to mediate differences and moderate negotiations between the noble landowners and their former serfs. No charter was legitimate without the mediator's approval.[1]

But the Manifesto also mandated that the former master be compensated for the land expropriated by the state on behalf of the freed people. The peasants were to pay their former master for the land that was allotted to them. Since they did not have the money to pay for it, the government was scheduled to advance most of the price of the land—about 80 percent—directly to each nobleman in the form of bonds. This process could become messy. For example, noblemen who were indebted to the government would have their reimbursement made net of a deduction for any amounts owed. The peasants were to reimburse the government with 6 percent interest in annual payments spread out over 49 years. They were also responsible for paying the remaining 20 percent to the noble landlord directly. Once the peasants and their former master entered into another legal document, the Redemption Agreement (a kind of payment plan for the land), the elaborate payment arrangement was set in motion. Only when the Redemption Agreement was effected, and the peasants were on a payment schedule, were they legally "free."

Until they entered into the payment schedule, the one-time serfs were classified as "temporarily obligated." As temporarily obligated peasants, they had a number of obligations to their former masters, which the Statutory Charters defined. In general, these obligations were a combination of *barshchina* (*corvee*/labor), and/or *obrok* (*quit-rent*/money or in kind), and payments (usually in the form of silver rubles) for the privilege of using the former master's land until a Redemption Agreement had been worked out. To be clear, the village commune—not each individual male peasant—was the recipient of the land in toto. And the village commune, via its elders, was responsible for the actual distribution of the land earmarked to the community's individual males, as well as meeting the obligations to the former master. Thus, the commune cared very much whether adult males left the village, since their departure would almost certainly adversely impact the commune's ability to meet its obligations.

I have simplified the requirements itemized in both the Manifesto and the *Regulations*; they were authoritative, formulaic, and complicated. It is also clear that there were several stages involved in the protracted emancipation process. The tsar's authorities were correct when they anticipated that the peasants would object to the conditional terms of freedom. Therefore, toward the end of 1861, the tsar issued an edict that the noble landlords were to proceed with implementing their charters even if the peasants did not sign them. Thus the "contractual" element of the charter was a sham.[2]

While emancipation in Russia was a prolonged affair with numerous conditions, in America it was swift in the sense that it was enshrined in the forty-three-word Thirteenth Amendment to the United States Constitution, ratified in December 1865. Unlike the Russian former masters, former slave owners were neither commanded to earmark land for their former slaves nor compensated for the "loss" of their "property," which the freed people had been considered. Still, emancipation did appear to be prolonged insofar as it made its first appearance de facto, when news of the war's commencement in 1861 reached the slaves. Rumors of liberation were rampant. Indeed, former slave Dora Franks of Aberdeen, Mississippi, recalled that from the minute when her master came in the house announcing that a "bloody war" was about to commence, and he feared all the slaves would be taken away, "I started prayin' for freedom."[3]

While the war officially began as a conflict between those Southern states that seceded and the federal government, it set in motion a protracted emancipation process. With many white men leaving their plantations and homesteads to go and fight for the Confederacy, the traditional source of authority over the slaves was compromised. In addition, and especially as Union troops were rumored to be within the vicinity, many slaves left the plantations, seeking refuge in the armies' wakes. This, in turn, forced both the military and the federal government to develop policies to deal with them. Thus, while in Russia emancipation was an outcome of that country's defeat in the Crimean War, in the United States, it was contingent on Union victory.[4]

While it was during the extraordinary context of modern war that the emancipation process was managed from the top down, there was tension between this approach and the more traditional form of governing in the American federalist system. This tension was evident after the war's conclusion when the return to normality was contingent on reconciling centralized and federated governance. What played out was a series of competing and/or contradicting laws, rules, and regulations at the military, state, and federal levels with respect to the freed people. For example, the Preliminary Emancipation Proclamation of September 22, 1862, granted freedom to slaves in all states of the Confederacy that did not return to the Union by the new year. The final Emancipation Proclamation issued on January 1, 1863, named ten states to which emancipation applied. Unlike Russia's Manifesto, it made no mention of former owners' or freed people's responsibilities, other than enjoining the latter to "abstain from all violence, unless in necessary self-defence." Nor did it guarantee land to the freed people or provide any redemption payments. There were no conditional freedoms and no temporary statuses or obligations. Although the Proclamation implored the freed people to "labor faithfully for reasonable wages," it did not delve into the issue of labor contracts and requirements. Indeed, it encoded the purpose of liberation as a "necessary war measure for suppressing said rebellion." Similar to the tsar, who, "By the Grace of God," was "Called by Divine Providence" to bequeath to the serfs "full rights of free rural inhabitants," President Lincoln invoked the powers vested in him by the Constitution and "the gracious favor of Almighty God," declaring "the military ... will recognize and maintain the freedom" of the former slaves.

The Reconstruction Amendments followed. The Thirteenth (which prohibited slavery) was ratified on December 6, 1865. The Fourteenth (which, among many other things, both defined those born on American soil as U.S. citizens and applied the Bill of Rights to the states) was ratified on July 9, 1868. The Fifteenth (which gave African American men the right to vote) was ratified on February 3, 1870. When Mississippi passed the so-called "Black Codes" in late 1865, imposing numerous forms of social and labor controls, Congress replied with a Civil Rights Act in the spring of 1866.[5]

Although the post-emancipation era in Russia was marked by a period of reforms, Russians never had the task of "reconciling" interventionist and laissez-faire approaches to governing. Nor did Russia have to deal with often-competing pieces of legislation. In addition, whereas in Russia the terms of freedom were prescribed in advance of the event, in the American context they were mostly worked out afterward. The emancipation of American slaves was far less micromanaged by the central government than what happened in Russia. But the United States did have bureaucratic arms of government as well as private voluntary organizations to help with the emancipation process. In addition to the War and Treasury Departments, the Freedmen's Bureau was created in March 1865 to assist the freed slaves with food, housing, education, political rights, and labor contracts. In a way, the Bureau was similar to the Russian Department of Peasant Affairs. And although the Russian peace mediator was not an employee of the department, there were a number of parallels between this official and representatives of both the Freedmen's Bureau and the United States Army (such as superintendents and assistant and sub-assistant commissioners for the former and provost marshals for the latter). Although the peace mediator was not a rank member of the military, as were the American officials, both positions had sweeping authority during the emancipation era, and both served as mediators between the freed people and former masters.

One component that was shared by emancipation legislation in each country has to do with gender. While emancipation freed *all* who had been enserfed or enslaved, various legislative examples cited above (whether voting rights, contractual obligations, or land allotments) explicitly pertained to the freed *men*. Implicit in this were the notions that men were the heads of their households, the breadwinners, and the recipients of citizenship. Although abolition ended their unfree status, women were not included in many rights or privileges that each society assumed went hand in hand with freedom. Still, in both cases, women were citizens with some rights. For example, in Russia they could petition courts, and in the United States they were covered by the Civil Rights Act and the Fourteenth Amendment.[6]

Clearly, the emancipation of Yazykovo Selo's serfs and Palmyra Plantation's slaves occurred in contexts that generally featured similar components and issues but varied in degree and sequence. Some of these included modern war, the presence of armies sent in to enforce both liberation and order, the role of state edicts, shifting sources of authority, social beliefs and preconceptions about the subaltern groups, and economies that depended on their labor. The similarities in phenomena between the two lifeworlds are striking.

Emancipation Comes to Yazykovo Selo and Palmyra Plantation

The election of Abraham Lincoln as president on November 6, 1860, set the stage for the emancipation of the slaves at Palmyra Plantation. It represented the final straw in what many white Southerners perceived as a distant central power impinging on their local rights of self-determination and threatening the institution of slavery. One by one, most Southern states seceded from the Union. Mississippi's Secession Ordinance was issued on January 9, 1861. On February 10, Jefferson Davis, whose plantation (Brierfield) was adjacent to Palmyra on Davis Bend, learned that he had been elected provisional president of the Confederacy. The next day he left for the fledgling country's temporary capital in Montgomery, Alabama. Three months later, the bombardment at Fort Sumter, South Carolina, signaled the war's commencement.

Taking the Mississippi River was a crucial part of the Union's multi-pronged offensive strategy to retrieve the rebellious states. Securing the river would both divide the South and deprive it of its primary channel for the transportation of soldiers, supplies, and cotton. As early as the summer of 1862, Admiral David Farragut made his way up the river from New Orleans, which had fallen to the Union in April. At a number of points along the banks of the river (including Davis Bend), fugitive slaves, braving alligators, snakes, and the unknown, hid among the cypresses, cottonwoods, and willows, watching and waiting for one of "Massa Linkum's" boats to pass so they could signal for it to stop. A passenger on a Union sidewheel steamer, the *Maria Denning*, noted that, keeping pace with the boat, they would run along the shore and wave frantically, trying to convey "their eagerness to be taken aboard." Amid the fear that it was a trap, the boat did not stop. On another occasion, however, the *Maria Denning* did accept refugees. "When they were awake," recalled this same passenger, their solemn demeanor was occasionally punctuated by audible expressions of "relief and joy."[7] In this way and others (often through the confiscation of plantations by Union troops), African American escapees came under federal supervision. As Union troops made inroads into Mississippi, more and more refugees came under their authority. By 1863, estimates are that between thirty and forty thousand were in the armies' wakes. Comparing it to an exodus, a Union representative described one of these streams of refugees being ten miles long. As Noralee Frankel has observed, estimates are that "well over one hundred thousand Mississippi slaves, tasted freedom before the end of the war." As male runaways increasingly joined the Union armies, so, too, did women and children increasingly become the majority of "contraband," as the refugees were called by Union authorities.[8]

Both Frankel and Mary Farmer-Kaiser have documented the evolution of Union policy with respect to the conundrum of "what to do" with the women and children in the refugee camps and, owing to a variety of reasons, how it quickly devolved to the solution of putting them to work. But the freedwomen had their own conceptions of freedom and work in that context. In short, these included wanting to reunite with family members, solidify relationships, and make a home. Notwithstanding the fact that they had nowhere else to go and no money, it was their *decisions* that illustrated self-determination. For example, some chose to stay on their plantation of origin in exchange for room, board, and some kind of compensation. Aside from the obvious reason of their destitution, for them, it was about both the place and the lifeworld with which they were most familiar. As one Mississippi freedwoman explained, "[D]ere wusn't no difference in freedom cause I went right on working for Miss." But this scenario was far from universal, since many refused to live in any way that reminded them of the days of slavery.[9]

Meanwhile, the Quitman/Lovell family put its principles on the line. Remaining loyal to kin and region was one and the same. The Quitman daughters, including Tonie (William Storrow Lovell's wife) and Louisa (married to Storrow's brother, Joseph Lovell), celebrated the creation of the Confederacy. While Tonie fell into a "fighting pitch," Louisa condemned Northern abolitionists as "wretched fanatics," whom she "most thoroughly hated."[10] If relocating from the North and immersing themselves in the social, economic, and cultural milieu of the South did not demonstrate the ease with which the Lovell brothers made the transition from their Northern roots to being Southern nationalists, then certainly their actions during the war did. Along with another brother, Mansfield; a Quitman brother, Henry; and other extended family members, they actively participated in a variety of military efforts on the South's behalf. After the attack at Sumter, Joseph Lovell left Palmyra Plantation for the Virginia front. In September 1861, Storrow organized the Quitman Light Artillery in Natchez and then secured a major's commission in the 1st Georgia Battalion of the Provisional Army of the Confederacy. Stationed at Pensacola Harbor, Storrow patrolled the coastline for enemy troops and blockade cruisers. This position was completely in line with his career path. For example, in 1850 he had sailed as the second officer on the brig *Advance* in the first Grinnell Expedition to determine the fate of Sir John Franklin in the Arctic. This journey became a notorious story of epic proportions, since the ship was frozen in ice for 260 days and drifted over 1,100 miles. In 1853, Storrow sailed again for the Artic as the master of the search for Dr. Elisha Kent Kane. He received medals of honor from Queen Victoria for this act.[11]

Of significance, the Lovell brothers were in charge of defending New Orleans. When the city fell to Union forces on April 25, 1862, owing to their Northern roots, public opinion scapegoated them: "Yes, a Massachusetts man [Mansfield] ... was in command ... when ... the city surrendered without firing a gun. And this is one of the Northern generals who came over to our side *after* the battle of Manassas." Years after the war, Confederate general Daniel H. Hill went so far as to blame Mansfield (and a small handful of other Northern transplants) for the South's defeat.[12] From here, Storrow became an inspector general under Lieutenant General Pemberton, who was in charge of defending Vicksburg. After Vicksburg's surrender, Storrow went east and ran blockade runners from Wilmington, North Carolina, to both Bermuda and Halifax, Nova Scotia. He was in London negotiating supplies when the war ended. Thus, unlike his Russian counterpart, Vasili Yazykov, who, as a loyal subject of the tsar, followed the emancipation implementation instructions thoroughly, William Storrow Lovell, who was loyal to his kin and region, resisted emancipation by proxy. Also crucial to this comparison is understanding that, while the Quitman/Lovell properties were devoid of any adult white male presence for the war's duration (and therefore emancipation's unfolding), Vasili Yazykov not only was present at Yazykovo Selo but also played an integral part in the entire process, per the directives of the Russian Manifesto.[13]

When news of the Confederate routing of Union troops at the First Battle of Manassas reached them, the Quitman daughters' optimism was reinforced by the apparent joy expressed by their slaves. Clearly, Louisa believed that slavery would endure when she wrote to her husband Joseph:

> When I went out to the pantry and kitchen the servants all beset me with enquiries after "Master" and the good creatures ... all [sent their best regards to Master.] They have *all* behaved extremely well.... They are ... very sympathizing with us all. They often speak to me about the war and there was rejoicing ... at the news of our recent glorious victory in Virginia.[14]

But optimism soon faded. By September 1861, rumors were rampant that a widespread slave insurrection was imminent. In addition, Louisa wrote Joseph that slave "carelessness" had caused a fire at Palmyra that "destroyed the gin, all its appurtenances, all bagging, all unginned cotton, and 300 pressed bales," and that "quite a few of the blacks had 'run off.'"[15] Since the slaves were "pillaging stores and running off unafraid of repercussions," the overseer had "taken to drink." Next, due to the naval blockade, as early as Christmas 1861, the Quitman women experienced great difficulty coming up with money to purchase gifts, especially for their slaves who met them with the "ever recurring greeting of Christmas gif' miss!" By January 1862, they were experiencing shortages of the "most basic items."[16]

It was at this point that the Quitman women relocated to their city mansion, Monmouth, in Natchez. Because there was a large pro–Union contingent in Natchez, the city was largely left alone by Northern forces. Its mayor quietly surrendered to Farragut in May 1862. However, because of their father's notoriety as a fire-eater and proponent of secession, Monmouth was repeatedly targeted. Tonie's sister Rose documented Union "depredations." They "confiscated all of the horses and farm animals" and reduced the property to a "wilderness" by repeatedly "raiding the kitchen, the vegetable gardens, and the fruit orchards," as well as chopping down the oak forest for firewood.[17] Revenue from any of their plantation holdings was completely halted. With inflation setting in, the Quitman women proceeded to pawn items in order to purchase basic necessities. Furthermore, one by one, the servants began to leave. In complete despair, Louisa wrote to Joseph, "I have never ... been [so] alarmed before," adding, "It is ... dangerous to be so left alone as *we* are."[18] Thereafter, several Quitman/Lovell family members (including Tonie, her three young children, and a number of their enslaved servants) went east to Columbia, South Carolina, to be closer to Storrow. As Union armies burned the city to the ground in February 1865, they fled, with their nanny "Caroline shielding baby Annie and toddler John."[19]

As Farragut's fleet proceeded north, he sent out raiding parties. One of these moved in on Davis Bend in June 1862 and burned Joseph Davis' plantation, Hurricane, to the ground. As it went up in flames, Palmyra's overseer burned 413 bales of cotton rather than allow them to be seized by Union troops. By the end of the summer, Palmyra was visited by Confederate troops, who, with the intention of preventing its confiscation by Union authorities, destroyed cotton seed that could have produced 60 bales.[20]

Over the next several months it was relatively quiet on the Bend. In early spring,

Admiral David Porter took an interest in the freed people there, writing that "they prefer freedom," and he believed them to be "fully capable of supporting themselves," as they were "naturally astute at making money; and when they are not it is an exception to the rule." He also believed their character was related to that of their masters. Where they had not been treated like "brutes and kept in ignorance, they had profited." At the same time, Porter attributed their leaving to "the natural disposition of the Negro … to run away, and be idle." The juxtaposition of these two threads of analysis—one illustrating prescience while the other evidenced both prejudice and astonishing ignorance—is incredible. In addition, although he did not explain why, Porter noted that "those … at Davis Bend" offered "a strong contrast" to "many on the river."[21]

In May 1863, Farragut's fleet approached Palmyra and another punishing attack ensued. Although the *New York Herald* reported that "everything of value" on the peninsula had been either destroyed or carried away, Palmyra's main house had been spared.[22]

While liberation would be declared in the Emancipation Proclamation on January 1, 1863, the armies were clearly the harbingers of freedom well before that time. But the *meaning* of freedom remained to be seen, for it was inextricably linked to and contingent on the war's progress. It was also linked to how the freed people interpreted it. This, too, was susceptible to the vagaries of the war context. Freedom came in bits and pieces and was potentially pliable. While, on the one hand, the war presented an opportunity for slaves to escape from their condition, the turmoil and uncertainty put their freedom in limbo, on the other. And while they seized the moment to leave the plantation and seek refuge behind Union lines, "freedom" at this point on the spectrum was illustrated by Union policies associated with the occupation of plantations and supervision of the refugees. As will be explained in chapter 4, when Union forces occupied Davis Bend, they implemented an experiment in freedom well before de jure emancipation. Freedom for the former slaves during the Home Colony period was supervised in an authoritarian way. This situation continued through to the end of the war in April 1865. That same month the Freedmen's Bureau was established by Congress. In the summer of 1865, the Quitman/Lovell family began the process of recovering Palmyra Plantation. It is instructive to remember that, up to this point, all that had played out at Palmyra was *prior* to the Thirteenth Amendment's ratification. In the midst of the tumult of the Civil War, freedom made its first appearance there.

Meanwhile, liberation had also commenced in Simbirsk Province in the spring of 1861. Although the news of war and the sound of gunfire did not confirm to the serfs at Yazykovo Selo that emancipation was imminent, the presence of armies did. Like the Union armies, they were tools of both the implementation and the enforcement of liberation as well as social control. Indeed, as early as 1856, the tsar had preemptively ordered the military's readiness to quell any disturbances or rebellions should they develop after the Manifesto's release. One general and two infantry units were sent to Simbirsk. This was the first time since the Pugachev Rebellion nearly one hundred years earlier that military units were sent to the province.[23] Then, in 1858, Alexander II reminded the provincial governors of the Manifesto's imminence and that the armies were at their disposal for the purpose of maintaining order.

In the same way that Lincoln's Emancipation Proclamation was issued for strategic and symbolic reasons on January 1, 1863, so, too, was the tsar's Emancipation Manifesto carefully timed. Because the Russian authorities were most concerned about peasant unrest, the Manifesto was issued on the eve of Holy Lent, February 19, 1861 (O.S.). In the Russian Orthodox tradition, Forgiveness Sunday represented the most solemn, introspective, and abstemious of religious holidays. Presumably, this was the time of year when the serfs would be the most subdued, forgiving, and (literally) sober. Furthermore, it coincided with a pause in the work calendar. This temporal cushion was important for an adjustment period prior to the intense sowing season's commencement in the spring, when the integrity of labor was crucial. Across the Russian land, in churches, on the front steps of estate mansions, and at town and village squares, the Manifesto was read to the public by literate priests and marshals of the nobility.[24]

Although there does not appear to be any record of the Manifesto's reading on Emancipation Day at Yazykovo Selo, a number of inferences are possible. First, given that Vasili Yazykov had been a sitting member of Simbirsk District's Commission for the Preparation of Emancipation in 1857, as well as the fact that he was the marshal of the nobility for the district in which Yazykovo Selo was located, it is highly probable that he himself might have read the Manifesto on his estate. That Vasili received a "Distinguished Medal for the Successful Implementation of the tsar's Decree of Emancipation" on April 17, 1863, supports this theory.[25] It is equally plausible, however, that it was read by the village priest since the demesne was a parish.

There are a number of descriptions of the Manifesto's reading throughout Simbirsk Province that are instructive. Gendarme Officer A.A. Essen wrote to the tsar:

> Your imperial highness gave me a command to go to Simbirsk Province and assist with the implementation of the Manifesto Regulations. Upon my arrival I gave the Manifesto and the Regulations to the provincial governor to give to church leaders. Four thousand copies were printed and on March 9 they were distributed to bureaucrats in district capitals and churches across the province, for literate village priests to read to the people. Forty people from the police headquarters were also sent out to keep order as the Manifesto was being read. I am happy to report that the Manifesto was read and complete calm and order are in place, and your good will was accepted with gratitude. I had a chance to see this for myself at the market on March 10.

Officer Essen added that he had observed in the time since the "Manifesto's reading, the people, far from celebrating and going to the liquor stores, began to pray and reserved special prayers for your majesty's health and well being." This interpretation is remarkably similar to Louisa Lovell's reassurances to her husband that the slaves were fully engaged with and concerned about the South's performance early on in the war. Based on what we know would soon follow, it is clear that Essen's and Lovell's "reading" of the subalterns' behavior was either based on wishful thinking or evidence of the latter's double consciousness (or perhaps both). Just as the Quitman women's optimism soon faded as the reality of the situation set in, Essen added that it was impossible to define the exact impact of freedom on the peasants because they had not yet been introduced to the "complete rights and obligations." He also warned that "the Manifesto was smooth on paper," but "whoever wrote it forgot about the ravine and it's through it that you have to walk."[26] How prescient Essen was, for the peasants' solemn obedience was soon to take a sharp turn for the worse.

A manager at another Yazykov estate nearby documented the excitement associated with emancipation. N.A. Krylov observed that on "March 9, during the Spring fair in Simbirsk, the true news of the real freedom arrived." People gathered at the "church square" on the promenade and heard the news. Indeed, a rumor floated among the crowd that a merchant from a nearby town had a copy of the Manifesto and "wouldn't sell it for even 1,000 rubles! He was smart." Krylov added that rumor had it that the merchant "put the sheet on an icon in his home and showed it to the chief of police!"[27]

Another estate manager near Yazykovo Selo wrote, "On Saturday, March 11, during the first week of the Great Feast ... there took place a holy prayer at Usolie in which the local clergy, in the presence of a local sheriff, read the Manifesto from February 19."[28]

Finally, one reporter described the Manifesto's reception in the following way:

> Instead of noisy explosions of joy by listening to the Manifesto of liberation the people graciously crossed themselves and bowed low, and put candles to local icons and prayed for the Tsar. This event took place in villages and cities, according to the request of some people. [Indeed] they drank far less than [they normally do] as a result of the declaration.[29]

* * *

The contrasts and the similarities between the contextual circumstances in which freedom made its appearance at each location featured in this study are striking. In Russia, freedom was granted from the top down, with a stroke of the tsar's pen. Although cannon fire signaled freedom's ring in the American context, the president's Emancipation Proclamation on January 1, 1863, was similar to the tsar's edict. In essence, each act represented a bold, radical move with conservative objectives: to preserve the autocracy and the union. Both Tsar Alexander and President Lincoln invoked God's authority and blessings in the Manifesto and Proclamation, respectively. Even the respective emancipation dates held symbolic meaning, with the Russian one carrying religious weight, while the American one was significant in that it ushered in the new year. While emancipation happened at once across the Russian land, in the American setting liberation was protracted and could appear anywhere and everywhere, in both distant places and concentrated areas (as the Mississippi River corridor revealed).

In Russia, for both symbolic and pragmatic reasons, specific people and places were selected to deliver freedom's message. Village priests were harbingers of freedom, as they read the Manifesto in church settings. But this was also a matter of practicality, as the priests were literate and possessed both moral authority and imperial legitimacy. However, noble estates and market squares were also public spaces where freedom was announced. Conversely, the American slaves perceived any Union representative (especially soldiers) as a liberator. At once the armies were forces for order and of implementation. And freedom rang at any "location" when an individual chose to leave the plantation.

While the American context showcased a highly charged atmosphere of tumult and war, the Russian setting evidenced caution and carefully pre-planned, choreographed order. In the former, freedom was a weapon of war *and* something to be seized by the unfree. The American slaves were both objects and active agents of freedom. Indeed, the war presented a context in which the unfree had the freedom to *act*. Whereas in Russia all *appeared* to be pacific, and peasants reportedly met freedom with sobriety and appreciation, in America in general (and Mississippi in particular), evidence showed that the slaves understood the revolutionary moment in their midst. But there were armies present in the Russian context too. These were on standby, waiting to act in the event that any disturbances erupted. Indeed, it is a striking coincidence that the armies in each context had a role in the drama of the emancipation moment.

Another point of comparison can be found in the various elites' reading of the situation in each context. Russian authorities in the field no doubt had an interest in reassuring the tsar that all was calm. Similarly, the Quitman/Lovell sisters initially found their slaves loyal to family and region. This initial optimism was no doubt rooted in wishful thinking and/or naiveté about the subaltern groups' desires. In fact, the initial appearances of loyalty and appreciation were illusory, and warnings abounded that order and submission were no guarantees. As the next chapter will show, this reality was confirmed as the preparation period for the spring sowing season drew near.

The contrast between the behavior of the Russian serfs and American slaves is telling. The former came into contact with "freedom" in the abstract. That is, even though freedom was declared, there was no noticeable change in the status quo. The real meaning of freedom was yet to be seen. Therefore, the serfs' silence should not be confused with "compliance" or "satisfaction." In fact, it was a "wait and see" moment—one that was suspended between serfdom and "freedom." Meanwhile, the American slaves witnessed revolutionary change in many ways, especially in the fact of their mobility. Total war had broken out, and as males left the plantations in droves to go to the front, women and children remained to meet freedom in all its uncertainty. The slaves heard rumors of Union representatives in their midst and witnessed their friends and relatives making a break for freedom. The act of leaving the plantation is especially striking since it was a radical and desperate move into the unknown. However, with these dynamics in motion, freedom became a self-fulfilling prophecy. While there was no noticeable change in the status quo to comprehend in the Russian context, in the American example radical change was up close and personal. Still, in *both* contexts, freedom—and the myths, symbols, and rituals associated with it—had been unleashed. Now that the threshold of freedom had been crossed, all players would come to see that expectations, and freedom itself, meant different things to different people.

PART II

Planting and Plowing

3

Liberation

Conditions, Expectations, and Resistance

Following what appeared to be a peaceful reception of the tsar's Emancipation Manifesto in February 1861, Russia experienced a wave of peasant disturbances on the eve of the sowing season that spring. It was only then that reality set in for the peasants with respect to the terms of freedom. Now that the seeds of freedom had been planted, rumors about its meaning were rampant, and the peasants began to question the Manifesto's legitimacy. In reference to a disturbance on an estate not far from Yazykovo Selo, Simbirsk's governor reported, "When [the peasants] were called to the estate office by the manager for plowing instructions they showed their disobedience and responded to an order to be compliant by yelling 'not one of us will go to the barshchina and we'll not listen to the local sheriff, the manager, the elders, the boss, or anyone even if you cut off our heads!'" And they continued, "Now we are free and we don't have to work anymore!" The governor noted that "most of all they constantly repeated the first words of the Manifesto 'By God's Mercy,' arguing that their freedom came from God."[1] Such rhetoric demonstrated what freedom meant to them. It also provided insight into consciousness: the peasants, either with sincerity or as a rhetorical weapon—or both—located the source and dispenser of freedom in God. Drawing on the ultimate authority, and in the new contextual circumstances of de jure freedom, the peasants felt free to resist.

The American South also witnessed a wave of excitement following the climactic conclusion to what was arguably the most tumultuous episode in U.S. history. While the Confederacy's surrender in the spring of 1865 made freedom a reality, Congress' ratification of the Thirteenth Amendment in early December made it a fact. Freedom had been planted. Just as the former serfs asserted *their* interpretation of freedom in the immediate post-emancipation period—but on the eve of the crucial sowing season—so, too, did the freed slaves challenge freedom's meaning in the temporal gap between liberation and the commencement of a new planting period. As in Russia, the situation in the American South was one in which emancipation was juxtaposed against both the economic realities on the ground and conflicting expectations about the meaning of freedom. The state of Mississippi was not exempt from the turmoil. One Freedmen's Bureau officer reported in November 1865 that the freed people there had little interest in hiring themselves out for the next year since they fully expected by Christmas to be given land. "In this way," he continued, "they are going to begin to farm on their own account."[2] In a report to President Andrew Johnson, General Ulysses S. Grant observed the same phenomenon, noting that the freed people were utterly convinced that plantations were to be divided down and land distributed to the freed people.[3]

In this chapter, I examine what played out at Yazykovo Selo and Palmyra Planta-tion in relation to a specific contextual circumstance: the temporal moment immedi-ately following emancipation, but on the eve of the planting season—a crucial interval between the status quo ante and status quo futurus. This analysis balances what hap-pened at each demesne with the circumstances in the province of Simbirsk and the state of Mississippi, as well as the larger situational realities in Russia and the South. Since the economies of both regions were agrarian, both the *form* and the *performance* of labor on the demesne were crucial. Under the new circumstances, however, it remained to be seen what that would look like. Indeed, the nature of labor was crucial to the meaning of freedom for all involved. This temporal interval provided a moment when the freed people debated the meaning of freedom.

Herein lay one paradox of emancipation: On the one hand, it was about ending unfree labor. On the other, it neither solved the "problem" of the demand for cheap labor nor changed the elites' attitudes toward the freed people, which included beliefs about their role and station in society. While emancipation broke the relationship between the master and the bonded, the inertia of culture was great. Elitist and/or patriarchal attitudes toward the subaltern groups persisted. However, those who had been freed seized the moment of opportunity as emancipation compromised (if not broke) traditional sources of authority over them. The meaning of freedom was perceived differently by various groups. Con-testations ensued. A related issue was the phenomenon of rumor and the role it played in competing narratives. Discursive tactics and threats of force appeared. Notwithstanding the revolutionary break with past that emancipation represented, the outcomes in each sit-uation reveal much about the inertia of socio-cultural attitudes and the political-economic systems in which each demesne was located. What happened at Yazykovo Selo and Pal-myra Plantation speaks to both their distant and recent historical characteristics.

Conditions, Expectations, and Resistance in Russia and Simbirsk Province

As explained in chapter 2, in Russia the terms of freedom were built into the law and elaborated in detail in the 400-page *Regulations*. A blueprint for the nature of labor after emancipation was mapped out. Unfortunately, it appeared that the former serfs' objections to their "temporarily obligated status" were widespread. Ideally, this status was meant to last two years: within the first year a Statutory Charter was to be agreed to, and then, within the following year, a Redemption Agreement was to be finalized. While the former was intended to show the land that the former master would earmark for the estate's freed males in toto, the latter was the payment plan. When they agreed to the Redemption Agreement, their "temporarily obligated" status ended. Once the land was paid for, the peasants would be "redeemed." The Statutory Charter also item-ized the peasants' obligations to their former lord until the Redemption Agreement was finalized. Generally, these consisted of three days a week of labor obligations if they were on *barshchina* (a.k.a. *corvee*), as well as taxes and/or in kind (*obrok*, a.k.a. *quit-rent*). Indeed, the peasants would perceive both the "three days per week" of labor and the financial obligations as not only unfair but also illegal.

In the spring of 1861, Russia witnessed peasants' defiant outbursts. Incredulous, the peasants found it hard to believe that the tsar, whom they viewed as a distant, divine benefactor, would have subjected them to such terms. They suspected that the noble landlords had changed the Manifesto's terms, and even exploited their illiteracy, and then lied about it. Cries of "we have been robbed" and "the real freedom is hiding from us" were common. Calls to literally "look for the freedom" were typical, with one set of peasants arguing that the real freedom was hiding behind some papers in the estate office. Some said they would embark on a journey across Russia if they had to, even marching all the way to the capital, St. Petersburg, to get the freedom from the tsar.[4] Displaying profound suspicion, they came to label this emancipation as a "false freedom." Many peasants used gendered language, describing it as *Baba voli͡ a* (literally, old woman freedom), which, according to the socially prescribed role assigned to women in Russian society, relegated it to an inferior station. Instead, they demanded the "real freedom," or *Muzhchina voli͡ a* (male freedom). In Russian, the word *voli͡ a* means both freedom and "will." Specifically, the "will" has to do with being able to make one's own decisions, rather than following someone else's orders. It is the freedom to choose. Thus, the peasants were very specific in their understanding of freedom.[5]

Due to suspicion, or illiteracy, or cunning, or a combination of two or more of these factors, the peasants challenged the Manifesto's legitimacy when they interpreted the two-year "temporarily obligated" period as being retroactive, declaring that the genuine freedom had actually originated in 1858, which was the year of the last *Reviziia*, or census.[6] They came to this conclusion because of a section buried in the *Regulations* that discussed the methodology for determining how much land to allocate to each male peasant, instructing the master to refer to the most recent *Reviziia* count. Confusing this with the "two-year" interim period *after* emancipation was the "proof" that the local authorities had tricked them, since, presumably, their real freedom had been granted in 1858.

Equally galling was the fact that the one-time serfs were required to compensate their former master for the land that the Manifesto required the landowner to earmark for them. They believed that the land was rightfully theirs because they had tended it for generations. "Why monetary obligations?" and "The land was created by God for everyone" were typical comments expressed, thus illustrating both their *mentalité* and their rhetorical tactics.[7] One military official's report was sobering:

> There is trouble everywhere here in Simbirsk [Province].... On many, many estates the peasants refuse to do the three days barshchina and are insubordinate to the masters ... and ... consider themselves to be completely free ... and they stopped accepting any power of the landowners over them. Governor Izvekov [has] warned that uprisings [are] ... VERY CONTAGIOUS.[8]

The most notorious disturbance in Russia during this period occurred in the town of Bezdna, located just north of Yazykovo Selo, across the border in Kazan Province. The uprising there originated with one villager's esoteric interpretation of the *Regulations*, the language of which was described by the manager on another Yazykov estate as "so difficult that even the literate overseers couldn't understand it nor could they even explain it," and even if they tried, every individual would come up with "his own separate interpretation" as to its meaning.[9] Thus, the villager, Anton Petrov, a semi-literate Old Believer,[10] insisted that the true freedom stated that the peasants were no longer obligated to their former masters and that they were entitled to all the land on the estate because they had worked it for generations. Here was the proof that the noblemen were lying to them about the labor obligations. Indeed, rumors began to circulate that even the army officers were imposters. Above all, Petrov asserted that all local officials had betrayed the tsar! Maintaining that he alone had received the authentic, genuine charter from the tsar, Petrov prophesied emancipation's bloody atonement and called for the peasants to congregate at Bezdna to "spill" their blood for freedom.[11]

In this highly charged atmosphere, Petrov's revelations were transmitted via rumor, and Bezdna became a lightning rod throughout the Middle Volga River region. The rebellion's contagiousness was potent, in part, because it both articulated and reinforced what many peasants believed. Petrov attracted approximately 10,000 peasants from the region, and confrontations between them and the authorities rippled out from the epicenter. Bezdna's location held historic significance since this region was also the origin of both the Razin and the Pugachev rebellions.[12] On April 12, army units arrived, and thousands of peasants swore to defend Petrov. Acting preemptively in order to stave off a rebellion of epic proportions, the army snuffed out the commotion at Bezdna. After six volleys, approximately 90 peasants were killed, and casualties were estimated at 350. Petrov was arrested, tried, and shot on April 19, 1861. Countless peasants were reportedly flogged and sent to Siberia in the aftermath. Those who died at Bezdna became martyrs for freedom.

Not far from Bezdna and Yazykovo Selo, just to the west in Penza Province, another notorious uprising occurred in a cluster of villages, the epicenter of which was Kandievskoe, and which, remarkably, showcased characteristics similar to those of Bezdna, both real and symbolic. For example, a 65-year-old "Molokan," Leonty Yegortsev, posing as the late Grand Duke Konstantin, determined that the Manifesto declared that the "tsar gave all the land to us, and we should not work for the master." Cries for all peasants to obtain the "real freedom" and "exterminate all landowners" were common. Indeed, processions emerged, comprising thousands of people armed with scythes and stakes and carrying "red scarves attached to poles." On a number of estates, offices were broken into and clerks were assaulted. Over several days, the authorities tried to arrest certain ringleaders but were met by mobs, who yelled, "We will not obey!" and "We will die for God and the tsar!" This movement culminated in Kandievka, where the numbers were purportedly 10,000. After pleas to the peasants to "humble themselves," the army fired on the crowd. After three volleys and bayonet attacks, as well as numerous scuffles, the disturbance petered out, dissipating by the end of April. However, the record holds that 30 died (including 14 soldiers) and hundreds were injured; 174 people were convicted, with 114 of them sent to hard labor in Siberia, and scores forced to run the gauntlet.[13]

In general, Soviet and Western historians have held that, given the size of Russia and the number of people liberated, it is remarkable that there was relative calm and only one large-scale rebellion to speak of.[14] But this assessment is not quite accurate. The authorities were correct to fear disturbances and uprisings. Russians made a qualitative distinction between a rebellion and what they called a disturbance (*volnenie*).[15] A rebellion connoted something along the lines of the Razin or Pugachev uprisings, which included thousands or even hundreds of thousands of people, typically spanning a vast area and producing significant casualties. Although it connoted a local uprising or a confrontation, a disturbance was not something to underestimate. It involved an element of confrontation between the peasants and landlords and/or authorities. It could also include casualties. Usually, some form of corporal punishment was applied when all other persuasive measures failed. In fact, there was a specific set of protocols—indeed, ritual—that the authorities followed with respect to a disturbance. The estate manager would order, reason, and plead with the peasants to disperse and go back to their usual routine. If that did not produce compliance, then the noble landlord (or his steward or agent) stepped in. If his pleas were ignored, the district marshal of the nobility was summoned.[16] Then the sheriff was brought in. If these appeals were ignored, then perhaps the provincial marshal of the nobility and/or governor arrived, accompanied by several soldiers. Only in the end, after repeated warnings and as a last resort, was an army unit called to the estate. And even then, warnings, pleas, and reminders of the tsar's law and the like were applied. If and when it came to this point, a ringleader could be arrested, and likely flogged, which also served the purpose of setting an example to the others. Only if the peasants rushed the soldiers and/or the disturbance threatened to mutate into a full-blown rebellion did the army fire on the crowd. Thus, down through the ages Russia experienced countless disturbances, but only a few notorious rebellions.

However, disturbances were neither bloodless nor mild. If the disturbance became contagious, the soldiers on the ground in each province could have a difficult time containing the situation without major force (and perhaps even with it). Things became tricky once that line had been crossed, since the tsar could very well be blamed for the violence. Even though Russia was an autocracy, in a country where peasants were the majority, there was a fine line between maintaining order through force and triggering a full-blown mass uprising, thus undermining the tsar's authority. The goal was prevention and containment, rather than suppression. Also, even if a disturbance required a response, the logistical difficulties of, say, two army units covering an entire province meant that a military presence was intended more as a show of force rather than something that could be summoned at a moment's notice. As for the peasants, if they did not force concessions as a result of the ruckus, they nevertheless considered it a victory if troops were summoned to the estate.[17]

Historians have also attributed the prevailing calm in this period to the fact that it preceded the commencement of the sowing season in late spring. Initial reports from February that portrayed peacefulness, orderliness, and optimism, although accurate, were premature. Furthermore, even if reports coincided with disturbances, these accounts might not reach St. Petersburg until late summer. The lag time between the disturbance and/or knowledge of it, its documentation, and its receipt in the capital obviously affected the final numbers on which historians have drawn.[18]

The statistics can also be misleading.[19] Many disturbances escaped the attention of higher authorities. Perhaps the army was not called in, or could not be summoned, or was requested but not available, or simply could not reach the estate in time. This was often the case, since this period coincided with the spring thaw, and muddy roads were notorious for their impassibility. In fact, many Russian estates could only be accessed via waterways or cross country, thus making it virtually impossible for a unit to respond. Also, what was often described as one rebellion or disturbance could in fact have been a cluster of many.[20] One officer asserted that calling in the military could actually make things worse since "there is a real fear that there is such a profound sense of unity between the peasants and soldiers that ... you should keep the military away."[21] Thus, although using the military to suppress disturbances was the exception in Russian history, 1861 was an exceptional year.

Of the official tally of disturbances in Russia in 1861, there are only six listed for Simbirsk Province in which the military had to be summoned. On one of those estates, the sheriff punished the ringleader with a severe beating in the presence of the whole village.[22] On another, the peasants showed insubordination even after persuasions. An army battalion was brought in. Both the district marshal of the nobility and the sheriff explained to the rebels that they would be punished according to the law if they did not comply with their obligations. The peasants replied with "yells and screams." When the army attempted to assault the ringleaders, the peasants surrounded them, employing a kind of "all for one and one for all" defense, and so the marshal decided to let them go. The peasants responded with "Hoorah, we won! This is what it means to act together!" Clearly, the peasants' weapons were both their rhetoric and their solidarity.

But they also had another powerful weapon in the form of their labor. The authorities understood this fact. Incredulously, Governor Izvekov explained that the peasants "feel so free that they refused to do work." He also noted that he personally went to no fewer than fifteen estates in the neighborhood and reminded the peasants of their labor obligations.[23] At another estate, the governor reported that the peasants rhetorically asked their landlord, "If we're free, how is it that we have to do the barshchina?" When the authorities' pleas fell on deaf ears, two army units were brought in; once they surrounded the peasants, the latter handed over the ringleader, one Trukhlov, who was quickly arrested, brutally flogged, and sent to hard labor in Siberia. Only after all this, the governor concluded, did the peasants "understand their mistake of disobedience, and show their readiness to go to work."[24]

An estate owned by Yazykov relatives had more than 2,000 souls. Izvekov noted that when he and the sheriff responded to the landlord's summons, they were met with "wild yelling." The nobleman requested military assistance, and two companies of the army reserve were brought in. The ringleader of the disturbance was a soldier on leave named Dokukin. "I decided that leaving him with the peasants was like poison," Izvekov noted. He concluded his report with the following analysis:

> On the one hand the peasants themselves don't understand the law and want all their rights and privileges that are reserved for them in the future NOW. On the other hand, all use it for their own selfish interests. Some landowners have reorganized their households according to the new laws which make the life of their former serfs easier while others try to work them to their full capacity as in the days of serfdom as they know they have an interim period to squeeze out of them all that they can, thus triggering mistrust and agitation.[25]

Although not surprising, Izvekov's analysis is striking for its condescension. The governor attributed peasant defiance to their inability to understand the meaning of freedom. He was also patronizing in his criticism of the peasants' attitudes, implying that it was their immaturity and impatience that was stymying the whole process. Possibly he did not realize how prescient he was with respect to the peasants' definition of freedom—to *not* have any obligations to their former lord for *anything*. Still, Izvekov understood the complicated and nuanced situation on the ground as the reality of emancipation commenced. Not surprisingly, like most peasants, the landowners also acted in their own self-interest as best they could with what tools they had—namely, the *law* and the right to summon the army.

A summary of the disturbance at an estate next door to Yazykovo Selo, and owned by Vasili's uncle, is telling. It evidences deliberate labor disobedience, strategic passivity, the comprehension of a break from the past, and the belief in the right to land. A staff officer with the army, Gorsky, observed that, apropos of the estate manager's orders to use four plows, the peasants deliberately began using "six [plows].... [W]itnessing this break of routine [the manager] ordered them to go back to the usual way, and tried to reason with them. The peasants responded with 'now is not the past time! [and] we'll not work like that anymore ...we're free people and we have the right to share all of the master's land between us, leaving nothing to the master's use.'" With defiance, they added that no "sheriff, or boss, or manager has power over us anymore."[26] Staff Officer Gorsky explained that the cause of this disobedience was found in a "Kantonist"[27] released from the army, one Grigoriev. He was "literate" and had read the Manifesto to the peasants. He "put into their minds the idea that they are completely free, and they only have to work for their former owner one day a week." When the district marshal of the nobility explained to them that they were not interpreting the Manifesto correctly, the peasants still refused. As in the Bezdna case, the peasants invoked the "Good Tsar" myth.[28] "Grigoriev read to them that the Tsar's will was for them to be free," noted Gorsky, adding that what the peasants really wanted was "to get rid of all the managers on all the estates." As with the ringleader at Bezdna, Grigoriev was defined by the authorities as an outsider and a troublemaker, with literacy being a warning flag, and whose punishment and/or removal would remedy the situation. The marshal decided to arrest Grigoriev, but the peasants yelled that they would "not give him up," and even if he were arrested, "they'll follow Grigoriev to wherever they take him." In the end, Grigoriev was arrested and taken away. But the peasants had made their point.

Before examining the disturbance at Yazykovo Selo, an examination of the situational realities in the American South in general (and Mississippi in particular) will showcase striking similarities and significant dissimilarities.

Conditions, Expectations, and Resistance in the American South and Mississippi

The year 1865 was tumultuous. In April, General Lee surrendered to General Grant at Appomattox. One week later, President Lincoln was assassinated and his successor, Andrew Johnson, embarked on his own plan for the union's Reconstruction—that is, the plan for the Southern states' re-entry into the Union. Across the Southern land, many whites experienced an emotional shift from a siege mentality to a kind of collective post-traumatic stress disorder. For the freed people, however, although their plight seemed to be uncertain, this period held the promise of "Jubilee."[29] Indeed, there was much confusion and uncertainty with respect to how the former seceded states would be rehabilitated; what civil and legal status would be assigned to those who had supported the Confederacy; how the vast tracts of land confiscated by Union forces during the war would be handled; and what freedom would look like for the liberated.

Unlike the Russian emancipation legislation, the Thirteenth Amendment contained no stipulations with respect to land earmarks, labor obligations, and monetary compensation to former masters. Nevertheless, the American context exhibited similar characteristics to the Russian one in that there were powerful cultural characteristics and traditions that explain both the authorities' and the former masters' expectations for "good and faithful labor."[30] In need of labor, planters were anxious to proceed with contracting for the 1866 season, thereby securing some certainty in these uncertain times. In many ways, the Freedmen's Bureau was crucial to the shape that labor would take. In June 1865, indicating that it would not "pamper the freedmen," the Bureau mandated that the "Negroes must work." It also mapped out detailed regulations. For example, those who would not contract could be impressed into labor without compensation. The Bureau also suggested wage schedules. In all cases, food, clothing, houses, and medical attention should be provided by the planter. A payment of money or share of the crop was stipulated as a just compensation. Deductions would be made for idleness. And "all contracts for labor made with freedmen, free negroes, and mulattoes, for a period longer than one month, shall be in writing … and if the laborer shall quit the service of the employer, without good cause, he shall forfeit his wages for that year."[31] Although not formal, legal dictates like those in Russia, these were nevertheless clear expectations set by state authorities for the freed people and their obligations.

Similar to the Russian peace arbitrator, who was required to approve each Statutory Charter, provost marshals would "approve" each labor contract. Although Southern planters perceived Bureau representatives as sympathetic to the former slaves, Vernon Lane Wharton documented that in many cases, they privileged the former.[32] Thus, an institution that was designed for the purpose of assisting the freed people's transition to freedom, ironically, was also instrumental in establishing paternalistic and regulatory precedents for the control of labor.

As in Russia, the American freed people's struggles for land, autonomy, and self-determination were inextricably linked to what freedom meant to them. But these were also mainstream American tenets. In this regard, the former slaves were typical Americans. In addition, however, they believed that as a de facto component of liberation, they would have land allocated to them by Union authorities from territories that had been confiscated during the war. As noted by one Bureau officer for the Natchez District, "This was no slight error, no trifling idea, but a fixed and earnest conviction … among the negroes of this State."[33] Similar to the Russian freed people who believed that land went hand in hand with freedom, and who objected to paying for that which they considered rightfully theirs, the American freed people anticipated a land gift, not only because they believed that they had "earned" it as a result of their former condition but also because land and its cultivation were both a way of life and considered a cornerstone of freedom in America. As Peter Kolchin has explained, the control of land was crucial to autonomy and to independence from authority.[34] Here was a very close similarity to the Russian peasants' definition of freedom, as captured by the term *volĩ a*.

Expectations of land began with the "forty acres and a mule" rumor. This myth had its origins in a number of sources, some of which included the Confiscation Acts of August 1861 and July 1862, as well as the Home Colony settlements (especially Davis Bend), in which acreage and supplies, including mules, were allotted to the freed people.[35] Union officials also contributed to the rumors. Soldiers spread the idea, as they made their way across the South during the war, that the freed people would be awarded land.[36] Samuel Thomas, the Freedmen's Bureau assistant commissioner for Mississippi, held that "the Freedmen will never be thoroughly emancipated till they are allowed to own lands."[37] On January 16, 1865, the War Department's Field Order 15 earmarked for the freedmen confiscated lands along the South Carolina coast.[38] The Bureau's Act of March 1865, and in particular the notorious Circular 13 issued in July, authorized officials to set aside confiscated land. Also fueling the trope was the fact that the Confederate Congress and other Southern sources had frequently warned that failing to prevail in the war would result in the redistribution of confiscated land to the former slaves.

While they had not been allotted land by the year's end, the freed people still had great expectations. First, as was the tradition in the days of slavery during Christmas time, they anticipated that they would receive a gift, this time in the form of land. As Robert May has explained, Christmas had played a significant role in the master/slave relationship in the antebellum period. Insofar as normal routines were interrupted by feasting and presents, the holiday provided a psychological payoff for both master and slave in that it was a way for the former to allow the latter to "let off steam." It was also a time when discipline and authority were relaxed. Indeed, the holiday period allowed for a pause in the work calendar. This temporal cushion represented an adjustment period prior to the intense sowing season that would commence in the late winter/early spring, when the integrity of labor was crucial. It was also a way for the masters to assert power and confirm their benevolent paternalism to themselves and the unfree. Typically, a choreographed ritual played out: According to the socially prescribed rules, "white and slave residents of the mansion house were expected to shout 'Christmas Gif' [*sic*] upon first sighting each other on Christmas morning. The one who got the words out first was to receive a present from the other." But make no mistake: "masters rarely ... wanted or tried to win their Christmas Gif *competition with slaves.*" Rather, it was in their interests to let their servant "win."[39] The Christmas season doubly played a role in the freed people's expectations of land distribution since the Thirteenth Amendment's ratification coincided with the sacred holiday.

Another source for the freed people's hope for land had to do with their realization that they had a powerful chip with which to bargain in the form of their labor. If they were free, why should they "have to bind themselves to work for whites"? Toward the year's end, the freed people held out, at most, for a "gift" of land at Christmas and, at least, to leverage more favorable labor terms for the upcoming planting season, such as contracting for a monthly commitment rather than a yearly one. Indeed, refusing to sign a contract was the freed people's principal bargaining weapon.[40] In addition to articulating the equation of freedom with both mobility and liberation from the master's authority, an editor of the *New Orleans Tribune* indicated in December 1865 that the long-term labor contract was

> intended by the employer to renew a servitude or Bondage.... It is clear ... that the laborer must not alienate his freedom, for any term of months. The only means for him to escape the injustice and exactions of a bad master, is to remain free to leave the plantation and go elsewhere. This is the only way to teach the employers how they have to treat their employees.[41]

Implicit herein was the weapon of mobility, which, ironically, the Russian peasants did not need (or were unable) to leverage. Rather, their weapon was immobility. That is, the Russian emancipation legislation attached them to the land, and they could not be evicted.

Threats to the 1866 planting season worried planters and authorities alike. The slackening of authority meant that idleness and frolicking could easily degenerate into rebellion, or so they feared. Moreover, because Southern whites were fully aware of the Christmas tradition of gifting as well as the freed people's expectations of land, rumors circulated that an insurrection would materialize around the holiday.[42] Thus, the phenomena of vigilance and rumors, which had frequently accompanied the Christmas season's traditions in the old South, resurfaced in this new context of uncertainty. The Jackson *Mississippian* asserted that the reasons for white apprehensions "arise from the insolence, threats and general bearing of the negroes toward the whites."[43] In addition, that nearly 18,000 African American men who had been enslaved in Mississippi fought for the Union during the war was proof enough to fearful whites that their "former people" could and would use force for freedom.[44] Assuring the president that Mississippi was prepared to ratify the Thirteenth Amendment, acting governor William Sharkey was instrumental in forming the first militia in Mississippi as early as August 1865, explaining to Johnson that the "presence of negro troops was inflammatory to the people." The president ultimately backed Sharkey.[45]

In fact, the history of whites' atavistic fears of a slave insurrection, combined with the South's defeat and emancipation, provided fertile ground for paranoia. The most notorious example in Mississippi took place in April 1861, immediately after the war began, in Natchez. The plot reputedly consisted of the slaves planning to kill the white men and rape their wives and daughters after Union armies arrived in the South. There were also rumors that the white women who were spared would be taken as brides. Once the insurrection was over, the victors would march to meet President Lincoln. Also crucial to the story was the purported involvement of villainous white men, who would either instigate or abet these actions. Indeed, Louisa Quitman Lovell wrote to her husband Joseph in September that

> We have been kept in a great state of excitement for the last week with stories of insurrections etc.... It is indeed unsafe and dangerous to be so left alone as we are— ... They say, that a miserable, sneaking abolitionist has been at the bottom of this whole affair. I hope that he will be caught and burned alive for no torture is too good for the ... wretch.... It is indeed a tumultuous time—no one is safe.[46]

Several prominent local planters (including one "Mr. Lovell") formed an extralegal vigilance committee to investigate the situation. In early autumn the committee arrested, interrogated, and tortured scores with the lash. By November 1861, at least several dozen had been executed. Thus, while the rumored insurrection never materialized, the "plot" was brutally suppressed.[47]

In the more distant past, another infamous slave insurrectionary scare in Mississippi occurred in 1835, when the quintessential tropes were in full display: In the context of the immediate period following the notorious Nat Turner rebellion and a ramped-up abolitionist movement, rumors spread among the white population that poor, deviant white men—consisting of Northern abolitionists, peddlers, "steam doctors," gamblers, and even members of the John Murrell[48] gang—were conspiring with slaves to rebel on July 4. The plot reportedly consisted of the slaves planning to kill white men; the white women who were spared would be taken as brides. They would then proceed to march to New Orleans, where a greater insurrection would be triggered, thus ending slavery across the South. An extralegal vigilance committee was formed in this case as well, including William Sharkey's brother. After torturing many with the lash, the committee set free some "conspirators," while others were hanged in order to preemptively quell the purported insurrection. But this response did not put an end to the rumors. Indeed, alarm and hysteria grew, with many expecting the contagion to spread and culminate with the Christmas season. Mississippians turned each other, and terror reached a fever pitch. As one reporter observed, "The Mississippians are ruining their own State. By their own high-handed and violent measures, they are giving a magnitude and terror to the contemplated insurrection which it otherwise could never have attained."[49] Within months the panic dissipated, but not until twelve whites and numerous blacks had been hanged.

Now, in both the aftermath of the South's defeat and the midst of liberation, many Southern whites jumped to the conclusion of insurrection from any cue (real or imagined) that they perceived as evidence of such tendencies: from "changes" in the freed people's demeanor to an "odd" glance, to their whispers in an assembly, to their "ignorance of orders" or their use of muskets for hunting. The inertia of culture was great. Also, the freed people's newfound mobility caused much concern since whites, unaccustomed to this important outcome of emancipation, perceived it as threatening. Equally powerful as evidence was the fact that many former slaves, as part of the Union army, were now armed. The rumors also contained the "instigator" component. As was the case in previous scares, those targeted were poor whites and/or "outsiders."[50] An uprising in Jamaica in October 1865 also stoked the fears of an insurrection across the South. Although emancipation had occurred on the island nation in the 1830s, it struck a nerve that thirteen whites were killed in this uprising. (That it was in fact over taxation was irrelevant.)[51] Union armies themselves had a part in the narrative. On the one hand, they were perceived as outsiders, invaders, occupiers, and enablers of the freed people by those Southern whites who were sympathetic to the Confederate cause. On the other hand, their imminent departure meant that Southern whites took it on themselves to enforce order, maintain social control, and secure labor.

Because of the anticipated departure of Union armies, the fears of insurrection, anxiety about labor, and the widespread belief that the freed people required supervision, a variety of grassroots, ad hoc, vigilante posses made their appearance. But legal efforts also emerged. In addition to forming a militia in the late summer of 1865, the state of Mississippi enacted the notorious Black Codes in November and December of that year. As Michael Wayne has explained, the Codes "were an elaborate and extensive attempt to control labor, reimpose the paternalistic arrangement of the plantation, and reaffirm the inferior position of the black in Southern society."[52] While they allowed blacks to acquire and own property, marry, make contracts, sue and be sued, and testify in court cases involving persons of their own color, the Codes restricted their freedom of movement, rights to rent or purchase real estate, and ability to work in skilled, urban jobs. Significantly, these laws authorized the state to enforce labor agreements and plantation discipline, punish those who refused to contract, and prevent whites from competing with black workers. Moreover, all blacks were required to provide written evidence every January of employment for the following year; otherwise, they would be charged as vagrants. Those who left their jobs before the contract expired would forfeit wages. Any person offering work to a laborer already under contract could be imprisoned or fined a whopping $500. Above all, vagrants who were defined as "idle, disorderly, and who 'mis-spend what they earn' … could be punished by fines or involuntary plantation labor." Other criminal offenses included "'insulting' gestures or language, 'malicious mischief,' and preaching the Gospel without a license."[53]

As William C. Harris has explained, "one reason for the emergence of the Codes had to do with a much broader question about the place of blacks in Mississippi society."[54] For example, the governor of the state announced in late November 1865 that "the Negro is free, whether we like it or not; we must realize that fact now and forever." And he added with both paternalism and racism, "To be free, however, does not make him a citizen, or entitle him to political or social equality with the white race."[55] It is an interesting side note that precedent for these laws was found in the "codes" that governed the institution of slavery during the antebellum period.[56]

Unlike the Russian codification, which defined the features of freedom and was crafted by the state *before* the emancipation date, the legislation in Mississippi emerged *after* the South's defeat, when emancipation was certain, but *before* the Thirteenth Amendment was ratified. It is true that the Mississippi Codes had a racial component, and (especially a technicality) they applied not only to the newly liberated but to all African Americans in the state, including those who had not been enslaved. In this regard, the Codes were different from the Russian emancipation legislation. But it is also true that both the Russian legislation and a variety of codifications in America targeted the freed people, in addition to defining both the parameters and the meaning of freedom. And both sets of state legislation were designed to control the subaltern groups for the purposes of social order and the control of labor.

Not surprisingly, Union officials and entities objected to the Black Codes, with many taking steps to nullify them. On November 30, General Oliver Otis Howard instructed that no attention should be paid to laws that forbade the freedmen's ownership of land. On January 30, 1866, General Thomas J. Wood ordered that any legislation which did not apply equally to whites should be null and void. In addition, and in part to augment the Thirteenth Amendment, Congress passed a Civil Rights Act in April 1866. It also renewed the charter for the Freedmen's Bureau. President Johnson's vetoes of both bills were overridden by Congress. Thus, the state-federal tension was accompanied by the presidential-congressional political power struggle in Washington, D.C. But, like the latter's struggle (which culminated in impeachment proceedings in 1868), the center-periphery struggle between the federal and state entities also culminated in the shift from "Presidential Reconstruction" to "Congressional Reconstruction" (more correctly known as "Radical Reconstruction"), which was led by the most liberal wing of the Republican Party. In 1867, Congress divided the former Confederate states into five military districts, the goal of which was to enforce a uniformly peaceful, orderly reconstruction of the Union. Among a number of idealistic notions, Congressional Reconstruction envisioned a uniform national identity.[57] Congressional Reconstruction both antagonized and emboldened many Southern whites, in whose minds the South's defeat was still fresh, and who both objected to the concept of equality with blacks and were fixated on plantation labor. Although the emancipation process in the Russian context was never subjected to such a variety of political power struggles, to be sure, the triangulation between the tsar and his bureaucrats, the nobility and officials in the field, and the peasants was also kaleidoscopic and intense. Thus, in the midst of liberation, social interaction was not strictly a binary one, between former masters and the formerly unfree, but rather involved a host of groups, individuals, and officials of various ranks in numerous capacities.

Considering the revolutionary contextual circumstances, both the freed people's expectations of land and the whites' fears of insurrection are not surprising. In this regard, there were similarities to what played out in Russia. Indeed, some Union officials also perceived the potential for rebellion. One Bureau official for Mississippi came to believe there was some truth to the rumors, reporting that

> I found the Freedmen in the eastern portion of Noxubee, Co., Miss. holding [a] meeting of an insurrectionary character basing their reasons for so doing upon the plea that they did not believe they would receive justice at the hands of their late masters. I found them collecting arms and ammunition which I at once took possession of.

Another Bureau representative reported hearing the freed people discussing plans for a "grand ... fight." Still another noted "the illusion ... [of] a general division of property

... [was] very natural for their simple minds."[58] Newspapers in both the North and the South predicted insurrection, citing Christmas as the targeted date.[59]

But many Union officials were supportive of freed people's aspirations. And Colonel Samuel Thomas thoroughly rejected the idea of any insurrection, writing to General Howard that there was not a "sign of trouble anywhere in the South," nor was there any legion of "black insurrectionists." General Peter J. Osterhaus agreed, stating that there was "no trace of this great conspiracy." Added to the mix was the idea among some naysayers that the rumors of an insurrection were part of a plot by Southern whites to discredit emancipation. Still, as Dan Carter has documented, many Union officials who rejected the idea of an insurrection in the fall of 1865 had, by Christmas, succumbed to the paranoia.[60] Clearly, the situation was fluid and wrought with anxiety and apprehension.

Like their Russian counterparts who sought to disabuse the peasants of unrealistic expectations, Union officials launched a campaign to quell rumors of land distribution. Furthermore, many Union officials who, like many Southern whites, were concerned about securing plantation labor sought to remind the freed people of the responsibilities of being free. On November 11, General Howard issued a circular, stating that the rumors were "wrong. There [will] be no division of lands, that nothing is going to happen at Christmas, that ... [you] must go to work ... [and] make contracts for next year and ... insurrection will lead to nothing but ... [your] destruction." When he visited Mississippi, Howard advised the freed people that planters would not hire people who were "impudent, lazy, and fail to follow orders.... Indolence is not freedom."[61] Colonel Thomas wrote to his superior that his officers continued to disabuse the freedmen of such "false ideas" about land. Even on the last day of 1865, Thomas "ordered his subordinates" to instill "in the minds of the freedmen respect for the law and their obligations" to contract. He reported explaining to the freedmen that "The State cannot and ought not to let any man lie about idle, without property, doing mischief"; that freedom did not mean "freedom from toil"; and that emancipation did not free them from their "class responsibilities."[62] He repeatedly stressed the "sacredness" of the labor contract.[63] Another Bureau representative discussed the situation in the following way:

> Winter is coming ... go back to your former masters, work, be obedient, and show that you are worthy of freedom. You expect the Government to divide your late master's lands out to you, and about the first of January you will get buggies and carriages, but you are mistaken. You will not get a cent. It all belongs to the former owners, and you will not get anything unless you work for it.[64]

Still another in Mississippi wrote of the freed people with exasperation, "Their idea of freedom is that they are under no control; can work when they please, and go where they wish.... It is my desire to apply the Punishments used in the Army of the United States, for offences of the Negroes, and to make them do their duty."[65] If these rumors had some truth to them, it would be fair to see the similarity to the American freed people's Russian counterparts, who equated freedom with individual sovereignty.

The similarities to the Russian context are striking. For example, the tsar was compelled to address rumors about the "real freedom" in the months after the Manifesto's release. Circulars from the Ministry of Interior on May 2 and June 9, 1862, commanded provincial governors and other officials to travel throughout their constituencies to speed up the charter process. Moreover, Alexander II delivered a public relations speech of sorts on three separate occasions. First, on August 15, 1861, and then on September

9 and 25, 1862, he explained, "The rumors have come to me that you are expecting two years from now some new [freedom]. There is no new freedom.... Not any other freedom will be given to you besides that which has already been given." And he commanded them to comply with the local governments and "hurry to make a deal with your landowners."[66] Clearly, the subaltern groups were treated similarly by the authorities in Russia and the United States. Both sets of elites delineated freedom's parameters to the freed peoples, as well as their obligations. In true paternalistic fashion, in each country freedom had been both granted and defined from above, by the state.

In both the American South in general and the state of Mississippi in particular, the preceding pages have made it clear that, like the situation in Russia, there was much commotion and confusion, along with competing narratives over the meaning of freedom during this very fluid stage. A variety of rumors with respect to freedom's promises, parameters, and betrayals, as well as possible peasant disturbances and former slaves' insurrections, were rampant. What happened at Yazykovo Selo and Palmyra Plantation speaks to each demesne's unique characteristics.

Yazykovo Selo and Palmyra Plantation: Common Problems, Differences, and Unique Characteristics

As noted earlier, it was relatively rare for an army unit to be called to a Russian estate to address a disturbance. Therefore, the situation at Yazykovo Selo in the spring of 1861 was extraordinary. A report from Army Colonel Essen to Alexander II noted that at the estate of Vasili Yazykov, a disturbance was addressed by the district police and provincial marshal of the nobility, with no results. "So I decided myself to come to the place itself to investigate. The peasants of this village ... didn't respond to any persuasions" and "remained steadfast, standing like granite." Governor Izvekov accompanied Essen to the village, with a company from the 4th Reserve. "On May 18 we arrived and called a meeting." They also brought in representatives from the neighboring villages. "I tried to reason with the peasants," but to no avail, wrote Essen. Therefore, "I punished the main ringleaders which restored order and peace. The peasants now understand their guilt and show their complete submission."[67] In addition, he warned that what all the disturbances in the region seemed to share was the "idea that they have been cheated by the landlord."[68]

Yazykovo Selo's inhabitants' defiance had deep roots. During the Pugachev uprising in 1774, the army had to be called in after the peasants burned down the estate. Vasili's great-great-grandfather was trapped in the mansion as it went up in flames. Vasili's father, Petr, wrote an account of the event and noted that the uprising was put down by the army with such force that "to this day the peasants on the estate cannot recall it without shuddering."[69] If this is true, it is all the more remarkable that the peasants of Yazykovo Selo stood "like granite" in the spring of 1861.

By the fall of 1861, Vasili Yazykov's uncle, Alexander, summarized the situation in the following way:

> Here, there is really a bad situation with the peasants. Everywhere there are uprisings ... [for example,] at Bestuzhev's Repevka, Davydov's Maze, Gagarin's Zaborovke, Kindiakov's Golovine, and at brother Vasili's Yazykovo and [Kakhanov's] Linevke ... [but] all were handled and resolved by using the rod.[70]

By autumn 1865, so, too, was Palmyra Plantation experiencing tumult and uncertainty, but of a different kind. Emancipation was confirmed as a result of the South's defeat. Therefore, after having experienced a roughly two-year period of occupation by the Union army, thus insulating Palmyra from the ravages of war, the plantation found itself in yet another period of flux as Northern authorities began their departure and the Quitmans/Lovells proceeded to recover their property. This was far different from just the previous year, when the freed people at Davis Bend had experienced elements of stability and order relative to the rest of the war-torn South. In fact, the Home Colony experiment was such a "grand success" that

> No people had a better opportunity for making money than [the freed people there.] They paid no rent and no tax on their cotton. Free hospitals cared for their sick and their paupers were fed by the government. They were protected and encouraged and were given every opportunity to develop their capabilities.[71]

All this changed when, in June 1865, President Johnson ordered that all property (amounting to approximately 80,000 acres of farmland in Mississippi alone) be returned to its former owners after they submitted loyalty oaths and received presidential pardons.[72] Various members of the Quitman/Lovell family wasted no time. Moving quickly to recover Palmyra and other properties, they submitted their loyalty oaths in August.[73] Shortly after receiving amnesty, the family petitioned the Freedmen's Bureau for the return of their confiscated property on Davis Bend.[74]

As they prepared their loyalty oaths in July 1865, the Lovell brothers began what would become a protracted effort to rehabilitate Palmyra and the other Quitman properties. Oddly, there is only one labor contract in the Bureau records for Palmyra Plantation, which was dated July 12, 1865. The contract was between William Storrow Lovell and four individuals—Lewis, Britt, Vini, and Ranson, ages 45, 28, 25, and 5, respectively. (The five-year-old was hired as a "maintenance boy.") In the 1860 Slave List for Palmyra, a "Lewis" and a "Vini," both age eighteen, are cited. Because of the age disparity, it is unlikely that this could be the same Lewis hired in 1865. But it is possible that the Vini cited in each record is the same individual. The monthly wage agreed to was $5.00 per person, with room and board included. This amount seems paltry given that in March 1865 the Bureau recommended $15.00 per month (including supplies, rations, and Saturdays off). Indeed, in June 1866 some laborers at the Davis plantations were reportedly earning up to $15.00 per month.[75] However, a number of factors can explain this discrepancy, the main one being that this was a period of great flux and uncertainty, and uniformity was not the norm. To be sure, it does demonstrate that Lovell and this set of freed people were taking the first steps toward negotiation.

In addition, Lovell began preparing to diversify the plantation's economy in the early post-emancipation years, focusing on hay hauling, cattle, and corn, which are not labor-intensive tasks.[76] These are indications of deliberate adjustment to the new situation and planning for the future. Finally, these developments suggest that, unlike other areas in both Mississippi and the greater American South, Lovell was able to move quickly on the question of labor *because* the situation on the Bend during the war had been relatively stable and a comparably intact labor force remained.

Illustrating the bewildering fluidity of this period, as Lovell was recovering the property and preparing contracts in the summer of 1865, the Freedmen's Bureau was still trying to break down the plantations on the Bend and give land to the former slaves for three more years. One Bureau representative explained the way of life for the freed people there in the following way: "The Freedmen have built houses, and expended money on the land, with the expectation that the Government would sustain their claim to it in preference to that of the rebel owners."[77] And on October 14, 1865, Colonel Thomas reported that "the people are organized into a laboring community in which each family is provided with a small piece of ground. The head of the family has his house on his own land, and regulates his own domestic affairs, apart from others. At the beginning of the year he received a lease for the land and a permit to hold necessary stock."[78] Here it is plausible to infer that such moves reinforced the idea among the freed people that land allotments would be a de facto component of emancipation.

Simultaneous with this report, Union officials were setting in motion policies that contradicted such optimism. In October, Major General O.O. Howard, the Freedmen's Bureau commissioner, issued Order #117, which closed the post office on the Bend. On December 19, Thomas issued Property Order #43, which transferred ownership of Palmyra Plantation from the Home Colony to the Quitman/Lovell family. In early January 1866, Thomas again praised what had transpired on the Bend, noting that in all of 1865, the colony produced a profit of $159,200. The people there had "raised their own crops, made their own sales, and put the money in their own pockets."[79]

But rumors and expectations were still not put to rest. Expressing the idea that there was no inconsistency in the fact that the liberated worked *and* desired a "land gift," Lovell's neighbor and former Davis slave, Ben Montgomery (who, incredibly, acquired his former master's plantation for a number of years after the war), explained in early January 1866 that Thomas had been there "a few days ago and in his speech to an assembly at Palmyra informed them" that work would go on. Nevertheless, Montgomery continued, "It is still rumored that this land will be retained by the Government," presumably for redistribution.[80] Indeed, American freed people would cling to the hope for land distribution as part of a holiday gift for years. For example, a Bureau commissioner reported in December 1867, "There seems to be wide spread [*sic*] belief [among the freedmen] … that the land in this state is to be divided among them, and [therefore] … the freedmen refus[e] … to contract for the next year."[81]

* * *

From the above discussion, it is clear that the period under review was a crucial interval between the status quo ante and status quo futurus—that is, the brief moment between liberation and the commencement of the sowing season. It was marked by the raw, fresh, and uncertain nature of the new conditions ushered in by emancipation. It remained to be seen what freedom would look like, and its meaning was contested in the context of labor needs for the upcoming agricultural season. This was the first test of freedom. The freed people found themselves in a "temporary" condition, in which freedom was compromised, in limbo, and conditional. While elites and authorities in each country expected social order and the security of labor, the freed people in each place had their own ideas about labor. It is in this context of conflict that we can discern differences in *mentalité* and intention between the various groups.

Rumors and gossip about rebellion, insurrection, and the meaning and parameters of freedom were rampant. Indeed, rumors seemed to be particularly problematic because of the uncertain and revolutionary nature of the moment. Steeped in tradition and history, patterns of both formal and informal language and dialogue, symbolic and behavioral choreography, myths, and myth-rituals that contained atavistically pre-scribed codes of conduct were on full display. Both real and imagined rumors demon-strated categorical continuity with the past. Indeed, in some cases the near-identical content seemed to be of an artifactual nature, with turns of phrases and predictions pointing to their atavistic roots. For example, the difference between a Pugachev rebel-lion and the confrontation at Bezdna or disturbance at Yazykovo Selo was a matter of degree but not type. And rumors about a slave insurrection in the American South revealed familiar, recurring tropes. The specters of rebellion and insurrection were indelibly imprinted on the cultural memory of all involved.[82]

Tangentially related were the themes of fear about collaborators and instigators, as well as scapegoating. As both the Russian disturbances and purported slave insur-rections showed, authorities, who had their own atavistic fears and suspicions, believed both the peasants and African Americans were highly susceptible to being influenced by people considered "others" or outsiders. Literates were particularly suspect—explic-itly in the Russian example, and implicitly in the American one. (Many, if not all, Southern states, either legally or traditionally, eschewed educating slaves, since literacy could well arm the unfree with a crucial weapon in the struggle for freedom.) Thus, the "troublemakers" were singled out—indeed, made an example of and "scapegoated"—in order to make it clear that the authorities would not tolerate dissent. Torture and execution were not ruled out. As Abby Schrader has explained, corporal punishment "'makes an impression' ... and reinforces ... power by 'providing a universal exam-ple' of strength ... to local inhabitants."[83] Scapegoating can serve the social function of a sacrificial rite, which can lead to reconciliation or reunification. But it is by no means a permanent or even authentic resolution, for the "spectacle of punishment" can be counterproductive, garnering sympathy and support for the abused.[84] Indeed, those who died became martyrs for freedom. What the authorities interpreted as acquies-cence when the peasants "stood down" might be viewed more accurately as a kind of strategic retreat. And the fact that no insurrection materialized in Mississippi did not mean that the "coast was clear" as far as many were concerned. As history has taught, insurrectionary scares resurfaced time and again, typically in highly charged periods such as this one. Moreover, as Justin Behrend has explained, as Union forces continued to move across the Southern land, those enslaved can only have increased their talk of freedom, thus eliciting more paranoia from the Confederate population about an insur-rection. Rumors, fears, and suspicions persisted.

Like their Russian counterparts, the American freed people could not stage a mas-sive, successful disturbance. Even though Mississippi's one-time slaves represented roughly half of the state's population, like their Russian counterparts, they lacked the social capital to mount any meaningful challenge to the powers that be. They under-stood that an insurrection, real or perceived, could be suppressed violently. Further-more, each set of freed people, whether they knew it or not, was competing with the state's overarching preoccupation, which was the preservation of autocratic power (in the Russian case) and reconstructing the Union (in that of the United States). The for-mer slaves could not seize the land, they could not challenge the property rights of their former masters, and they could not rely entirely on Union authorities to defend them. By contrast, the Russian peasants, either subconsciously or in their collective, atavistic memory, were well aware of the history of uprisings and disturbances in their region, which meant they could draw on that possibility, for it had power. With just a few exceptions, the former slaves did not have a history of overt, collective confrontation on which to both draw and build momentum. Above all, survival's necessities meant that they were disadvantaged with respect to how much they could leverage with their labor in the bargaining process.[85] However, in the same way that the peasants took a stand at Bezdna (and, on a smaller scale, at Yazykovo Selo), many former slaves, including those from the Bend, asserted their firm position in the form of enlisting in Union armies. This demonstrates that, indeed, both sets of freed people had strong components of solidarity, and they were absolutely prepared to fight and die for freedom.

In addition, both sets of freed people did not have the money to purchase land. While the Russian government decreed that the peasants compensate their former masters for the land earmarked for them, they resisted this requirement because, they rationalized, the land was already theirs. In Mississippi, whites took steps to deny the freed people access to land ownership, as evidenced by the Black Codes. Like their Russian counterparts, the American freed people expected that land would be granted to them, *because* they had earned it with their toil.

Aside from the "technicality" of emancipation, clearly, elites and authorities expected the newly freed peoples to carry on the status quo and certainly to not be idle. They launched a public relations campaign of sorts, cajoling, lecturing, and warning them of their obligations. They also explained the conditions of freedom. They had patronizing (if not racist) attitudes about the freed peoples' station in society, schooling them in their civic duties and obligations. In addition to pronouncements and dialogic persuasion, those in positions power turned to state edicts, laws, and codes as sources of legitimacy. Anticipating that the freed people might be disappointed in the terms of freedom "granted" to them, and fearing the potential violence they believed the former serfs and slaves were capable of, the elites and authorities took steps, both formal and informal (and backed by state as well as community power), to prevent and/or quell disturbances or insurrections, real or imagined. Thus, armies and other sources of policing power were used. Indeed, the military presence at each demesne was very real. However, whereas the Russian army was pitted against the "defiant" former serfs at Yazykovo Selo, at Palmyra it was *both* a force for order and a shield of protection against the greater Confederate society. Conversely, while Russian authorities were suspicious of the potential for collaboration between peasant soldiers and their brothers and sisters on the estate, pro–Southern actors worried about armed blacks, as exemplified by those in the blue uniform.

The freed people did not need lofty, philosophical treatises on freedom's meaning—they knew instinctively what it looked and felt like, and what *they* expected, especially when it came to obligations, conditions, labor, land, and the "will" (or "right") to self-determination. Like others in their region, and *because* of the emancipation moment, both sets of freed people were emboldened, confident in their expectations. The peasants of Yazykovo Selo used symbolic language with rhetorical power to assert what freedom meant to them. Even "yells and screams" had dialogic meaning. They wanted to be free from all ties to their former condition, as well as all monetary and labor obligations. This included having the freedom to be free from their former lord's yoke. On the eve of the sowing season, the Russian peasants knew they had a powerful chip in their labor with which to bargain. African Americans also anticipated land gifts and understood that, while they were dependent on Union authorities for their immediate sustenance, they, too, had a powerful bargaining chip on the eve of the sowing season. Like their Russian counterparts who tapped into both the "Good Tsar" myth and religious authority to invoke the law and delegitimize their opponents' position, former slaves drew on the prospect of a "Jubilee" as well as the traditional norm of gifting at Christmas to legitimize theirs. Both utilized myths as rhetorical weapons as well as leverage.[86]

Another theme that appeared was that of mobility. While the Russian Manifesto attached the peasants to the land, because they could not be evicted, the freed people stood firmly against any toil for their former masters. Conversely, the American freed people could use their mobility as a bargaining chip, withholding their labor during the "contracting" period.

Each demesne showcased extraordinary characteristics with respect to what was typical in each country. Just as freedom's rollout was not seamless at Yazykovo Selo, neither was it at Palmyra Plantation. The former serfs staged a disturbance that elicited a visit by the army. So, too, did the former slaves at Palmyra experience a series of extraordinary events. After enduring the war, occupation, and the exceptional Home Colony period, the incremental nature of freedom continued after the war's conclusion, with the commencement of the Union's Reconstruction program and Palmyra's former owners' recovery of the property. William Storrow Lovell contracted with a number of former slaves well before both the Thirteenth Amendment's ratification and the planting season's preparation period. It is significant that he made arrangements for labor as he and the family were preparing their allegiance oaths. As we shall see in the next chapter, Vasili Yazykov was not unlike his American counterpart. He proceeded to move quickly into the next stage of the emancipation process. Both were getting on with adjusting to the new contextual circumstances.

4

Regulating Freedom

Contracts and Agreements

Following the tumultuous twin events of the Civil War's conclusion and the assassination of Abraham Lincoln in April 1865, members of the Quitman/Lovell family moved swiftly to apply for amnesty pardons from Lincoln's successor, Andrew Johnson. Receiving a pardon would both restore their U.S. citizenship and put them on track to recover their property. The logistics of land restoration was placed in the hands of the Freedmen's Bureau. Anticipating that Palmyra would soon be returned to its original owners and that the state would no longer be operating the Bend according to its notorious "Rules and Regulations," a Bureau commissioner gave instructions in late August 1865 to his subordinate, Provost Marshal Gaylord Norton, to move swiftly with respect to cotton production:

> [I] expects [*sic*] [you] to control the colony at Davis Bend until the present crops are harvested. Not a pound of cotton must be shipped from the Bend till it is ginned and then only on permit [from your superior].... Be kind and conciliatory to the Freedmen generally but firm in all points in which it is necessary to secure the interests of the whole colony and the Government. You know the necessity of crowding the work forward with all possible haste. Reduce rations used to the lowest figure possibly [*sic*].

Two weeks later, that commissioner's superior instructed Norton to report "the number of [labor] contracts made," which should include "the number of hands and dependents" per "contract."[1] Clearly, the officials knew that time was running out. The Home Colony experiment appeared to be reaching its conclusion. It was critical that the crops be harvested and retained for sale and profit by the state.

A sense of urgency was also present amid the sweeping changes underway in the weeks and months after emancipation in Russia. In his report to the tsar about the disturbance at the Yazykov estate in May 1861, Colonel Essen warned, "It is of the utmost importance that the positions of the peace arbitrators be filled as the peasant complaints from the estates are increasing and increasing.... I have heard that many have been elected." But, he complained, the source of the delay was St. Petersburg's bureaucratic red tape connected with the approval process.[2] Created by the emancipation legislation, the peace arbitrator (a.k.a. peace mediator) was at once an arbitrator and a mediator, whose job included seeing that the negotiations for land settlements between former serfs and former masters proceed smoothly. Every district in every province across Russia was assigned two arbitrators. Members of the nobility elected them, but the tsar's approval made their positions official. Not surprisingly, the peasants viewed these individuals with great skepticism. However, arbitrators could also be viewed as potential turncoats by the nobility. Like the Freedmen's Bureau, their job was temporary in nature. The position of the peace arbitrator was officially phased out by 1874.

Similar to their American counterparts, Russian officials instructed their subordinates to proceed to the next stage of the emancipation process as quickly as possible, so that the agricultural season would not be disrupted. This task involved working out the terms of a mandated document—a Statutory Charter—for every estate across Russia.[3] Among a number of issues, the charter both prescribed for the freed people and preserved for the noble landlords a certain amount of land. It also included a variety of obligations that the former serfs owed their former masters until they worked out a payment schedule (the Redemption Agreement) for the land they would receive. One of those obligations had to do with compulsory labor. It is significant that the noble landowners and their associates were charged with drafting the charters. Vasili Yazykov wasted no time. On the eve of the spring sowing season in March 1862, he secured the charter for Yazykovo Selo.

The Statutory Charter at Yazykovo Selo and the "Rules and Regulations" at Davis Bend were the legal arrangements that regulated freedom during one phase of the protracted emancipation process. These were official documents utilized by each set of authorities for managing the demesne, controlling labor, and maintaining social order. Both had the backing of state power. Both contained labor obligations premised on a contractual agreement with the freed people. In varying degrees, this was a matter of both overarching state economic policy and the priorities of the local authorities with jurisdiction over each demesne. But implementation and enforcement of these legal parameters was just one side of the coin. The freed people at Yazykovo Selo and Palmyra Plantation responded to, or complied with, these mandates in different ways. As was seen in the previous chapter, there was a discernible element of tension in the government officials' humanitarian goal of emancipating the unfree, protecting the economic integrity of the demesne, and contending with what the freed people wanted.

A Brief Overview of the Russian and American Contractual Arrangements

Contractual arrangements shaped the contours of freedom at each demesne in this phase of the emancipation era. As explained in chapter 2, the Russian emancipation legislation made provisions for labor obligations. While the Thirteenth Amendment to the United States Constitution did not, subsequent federal and state policies did.

The Statutory Charter was a critical tool for implementing emancipation in Russia. Indeed, Allan Wildman has described the charters as its "defining moment."[4] The legislation required that every estate across Russia have one. The charter was supposed to have the appearance of contractual agreement, in that the former master and his/her former serfs were meant to negotiate the terms of land distribution and obligations, albeit within a range prescribed by the government. The contractual agreement was intended to be between the estate's former master and the individual male peasants in toto, with a few selected representatives signing the document on behalf of the collective. In fact, the charter's contents were filled in by the former master and the peace mediator. Moreover, it could go into effect without the peasants' consent. Compliance was mandatory. The charter was to be drafted within one year of the emancipation date, February 19, 1861 (O.S.), and put into effect within two.

At Palmyra Plantation, a set of commands known as the "Rules and Regulations" governed the freed people during the Home Colony period. One of those rules mandated that all freed persons must enter into a labor contract. In general, the business or labor contract was a cornerstone of economic practice in the United States at the time. Therefore, government officials turned to the "labor contract" as the vehicle for labor relations on the cotton plantations after emancipation. As this policy was set in motion, mainstream society soon followed suit. Ideally, the contract was envisioned to be between the former master and/or plantation manager and an individual or set of freed people being hired. The latter would sign the contract collectively, all putting their "X" on the document if they could not write, or, often, a "leader" of the group would sign on behalf of the entire group. During the Home Colony period, all the former slaves were required to sign labor contracts with the Union officials who were in charge. However, typically, there was one labor contract for every group of laborers on each plantation at Davis Bend. Although no contracts survive for Palmyra during the period of Union occupation, there is plenty of documentation that informs us about levels of compliance and productivity.

There was only one charter contract per Russian estate, and it was issued one time only.[5] In the American case, there could be as many contracts as there were laborers on any given plantation, but usually they were collective, and they were typically for one year only, with a new contract needed for every subsequent season. However, an American contract could also be verbal. Although each landlord (and, in principle, the peasants) on each Russian estate did have a little wiggle room with which to bargain in terms of what was prescribed by the state, the charter was based on a template provided by the government. Thus, the template created thousands of duplicated charters for a uniform outcome. There was an element of uniformity with American contracts in that both market forces and Union authorities' prescriptions governed contract terms. Indeed, the Freedmen's Bureau recommended contract terms, such as labor obligations and compensation. It also provided contract templates. Therefore, as in Russia, while allowances for a little maneuvering were made with respect to those terms, there were elements of structure and formulae in the American contracts. One glaring difference is that while agreeing to the charter was part of the emancipation process in Russia, in America, former slaves were free regardless of whether they signed a labor contract. Still, both the Russian charter and the American labor contract enshrined into law expectations for and compliance with the demand for labor.

In a sense, the Statutory Charter represented *both* a labor contract and a legal document that governed the estate during the temporarily obligated phase. In addition to the labor contracts, Union authorities utilized a governing document during the Home Colony period. These "Rules and Regulations" had such far-reaching implications for social control and labor management that they even exceeded the authoritarian parameters of the Russian Statutory Charter. Major points of comparison and contrast between the two include (1) the terms of the contracts; (2) the subaltern groups' reception of the contracts; and (3) the extent to which they were complied with, as exemplified in their labor patterns and productivity.

The Statutory Charter at Yazykovo Selo

Within one year of the emancipation date, Russian nobleman and landowner Vasili Yazykov composed the Statutory Charter that implemented the terms of freedom for his former serfs. Both the Manifesto and the *Regulations* set forth the Statutory Charter as the legal, contractual settlement that codified a predetermined amount of land allotted by the former master to the peasants on his or her estate. It also codified the peasants' obligations levied to compensate the former master until a Redemption Agreement was worked out between the two parties. Obligations included *barshchina* and/or *obrok*, as well as a variety of rents, taxes, and payments for other privileges, such as the use of the former master's land.

The edict also mandated that the charter be signed "within two years" of the February 19, 1961, emancipation date. Until the peasants entered into the Redemption Agreement with their former master, they remained in a "temporarily obligated" state. In this condition, their obligations remained intact. To the extent that they were no longer under the yoke of their former master, they were "free." But their full freedom was on hold until they signed the Redemption Agreement and therefore entered into the payment plan. Because the peasants did not have any money, the government advanced most of the price of the land up front to the former noble landowner, about 80 percent, in the form of bonds—not cash. From this amount, the noble landlord's debts to the state were subtracted. The peasants were to repay the money to the state with 6 percent interest in installments spread out over 49 years.[6] They were also responsible for paying the remaining 20 percent directly to the noble landlord. The legal unit responsible for these payments was not the individual peasant. Rather, the village community, or "commune"[7] (also known as "rural society"), made the payments collectively. Instead of being tied to their former master, the peasants were now tied to the commune's authority. Once the peasants had paid for the land, they were "redeemed" and therefore completely free.

The significance of the Russian emancipation legislation transferring governing power—and, indeed, social control—from the landed nobleman to the commune elders cannot be exaggerated. In fact, the individual peasants at each estate were simply re-subordinated, from their former master and noble landowner to the village elders, who now had the power to collect taxes, distribute the land allotted to the commune, and issue travel passes to leave the village (the latter of which they were rarely prepared to do, since they needed every "hand" available to help with the agricultural production levels for which they were responsible). Obviously, the emancipation legislation inadvertently built into the new system corruption, favoritism, and cronyism.

Both the Manifesto and *Regulations* mandated that a kind of ombudsman should oversee and verify the negotiation process and legitimize the charter by adding his signature to the final draft. Embodying the "political spirit of the age," the peace mediator was a "potential generative agent of civil society in the post-emancipation countryside." While those who became peace mediators were noblemen, their mission was to be a kind of broker, a crucial link between state and society as well as between the nobility and the peasants. Under the mediator's tutelage, rural peasants ideally had the potential to experience freedom and become political actors by communicating and negotiating for their individual and group interests with their former master. However, the tsar mandated that if the noble landlord and peasants failed to draw up a charter, the peace mediator could draft and implement one independently.[8]

A comparison between the position of the peace mediator and various representatives of the Freedmen's Bureau can be made since, like the former, the latter served as intermediaries between the planters and the freed people. These officials also sought to cushion the freed people's transition to freedom in a number of ways, some of which included organizing rations, medical attention, clothing, shelter, and education on their behalf. Furthermore, it is a striking similarity that the Statutory Charter was not valid without the peace mediator's signature and the labor contract between a former slave and a planter needed a Bureau official's validation. (As Union officials left the South, this required signature was phased out.)

Each district in Russia was to have two peace mediators, and each was selected by the marshal of the nobility of that district. Vasili Yazykov was the marshal of the nobility for Simbirsk District, and he promoted his own first cousin Mikhail Bestuzhev as one of its two mediators. To be sure, all of the approximately 1,700 men who became peace mediators in Russia were noblemen, and most had owned serfs. But Simbirsk Province was notorious in Russia for being saturated with an intricately related web of noble families, and the Bestuzhevs and Yazykovs were close.[9] Thus, while it was not surprising that Vasili was closely related to the peace mediator for his estate, it was unique for Russia.[10]

As Bestuzhev was the signatory of Yazykovo Selo's charter, he undoubtedly assisted Vasili with its terms. As it happened, Vasili was generous in that he earmarked for his former serfs the highest amount that fell within the range recommended by the *Regulations* for Simbirsk Province. More important were the obligations delegated to the peasants.

Yazykovo Selo's charter was significant for several reasons. That it was signed on March 30, 1862, meant that Vasili had complied with the tsar's time restriction for its completion. This is rather unusual because most estate owners in both Simbirsk Province and Russia in general had not completed their charters by this time.[11] In this respect, Yazykov was a dutiful subject. Moreover, by effecting the charter in a timely manner, Yazykov leveraged himself into a position of power vis-à-vis his former serfs. Swift implementation of the charter was a way for him to get ahead of the historical moment, and in this sense he was pragmatic. Further, in autocratic Russia, the tsar's edict was irrevocable, so why drag one's feet? Besides, the emancipation legislation was favorable to the nobility in that it inflated the price of land for which they would be compensated.[12] Therefore, the larger the parcel, the greater the compensation. So why not move quickly, especially if (as in Yazykov's case) the landlord stood to gain financially at a time when his estate had been mortgaged serially prior to 1861? Equally important, because he effected the charter on the eve of the spring sowing season, he was able to preemptively secure a legal claim to his former serfs' labor. Significantly, not only was the charter *not* signed by Yazykovo Selo's freed people, but, in an act of great defiance, legend has is that they even refused a copy of the document.[13] These acts compromised the charter's legitimacy, especially in the minds of the former serfs at Yazykovo Selo.

In order to understand Yazykovo Selo's charter, it will be instructive to briefly explain what was prescribed by the emancipation legislation. First, the nobleman/woman was required to earmark land for the freed people. The charters standardized the land obligations by law for every region across Russia according to exact maximum and minimum amounts, which took into consideration the soil quality and fertility. Therefore, land allotments were not proportional across any given region. In general, every soul[14] was entitled to anywhere between 6 and 2.75 *desiatiny* (1 *desiatina* = 2.7 acres). In Simbirsk Province, the maximum and minimum earmarks were 4.5 and 2 *desiatiny*, respectively.[15] Although typically minimum amounts were set at one-third of the maximum, the estate owner was entitled to at least one-third of his pre–1861 estate, even if it reduced the soul's allotment to less than the minimum.

The former master was obliged to ensure that the peasants had a garden plot, usually adjacent to their household. This requirement was crucial, in that (in addition to having their homes intact) the garden plots provided security for sustenance. The *obrok* dues for the maximum amount of land were set at 8–10 silver rubles, or the equivalent thereof in kind, per soul per year. (This fee was essentially applied for the use of the former master's land during the temporarily obligated period.) *Barshchina* obligations could be retained if the estate owner was entitled to at least one-third of his former lands. Vasili Yazykov retained far more than one-third of his former lands, and therefore he could legally impose *barshchina*. Like those for *obrok*, the charter's regulations standardized *barshchina* payments. That is, the typical amount for the maximum land allotment was 40 labor days per year per able-bodied man (age 18–55 years old) and 30 labor days per year per able-bodied woman (age 17–50). This was a sharp reduction from what had been common before emancipation, when typically each soul was obligated to work three days a week for his master, totaling roughly 156 days a year.[16] Obviously, a noble landlord looking to legally squeeze the maximum labor obligations allowed would be incentivized to allot the largest parcel of land prescribed.

Other, even more complex rules governed estates that had had mixed obligations prior to emancipation, the point being that a combination of prescribed obligations was relative to the region's traditions and quality of soil. That *obrok* was never used at Yazykovo Selo before emancipation is significant, since the emancipation legislation also allowed for the salience of tradition at each estate. Two years after the February 1861 date, the peasants had the right to request that *barshchina* be converted to *obrok*. However, the noble landowner had the privilege of renewing *barshchina* every three years indefinitely. The experience at Yazykovo Selo illustrates this latter point, as Vasili renewed *barshchina* (40/30 days per year) every three years until he sold the estate in 1881.[17] In addition, the so-called "beggar's allotment" (*bednyatskiy nadel'*) was allowed, whereby a peasant could opt out of the entire deal, thereby forgoing both labor (*barshchina*) and financial (*obrok*) obligations, in exchange for a sliver of a plot, one-quarter of the prescribed maximum, typically 1 *desiatina*.

Following Tsar Alexander II's assassination in March 1881, a Redemption Law ended the hated *barshchina* once and for all. It also forcibly ended the "temporary obligated" phase by mandating that a Redemption Agreement be entered into immediately, thus ideally converting the landlord/peasant relationship into something that resembled more of a business labor contract with wages as compensation. Above all, it required the former serfs to begin paying for the land, thus making them "property owners." These examples are just a smattering of those itemized in the 400-page *Regulations*. But it is clear that they were authoritarian and formulaic. Above all, it is staggering to understand that they imposed an overall uniformity on the vast geographic space across Russia, impacting millions upon millions of individuals.

Indeed, this uniformity consisted of a number of required entries in the Statutory Charter, including a list or inventory of property and a set of demographic statistics for the estate. Statutory Charters contained the information prescribed by the *Regulations* in orderly paragraphs, citing the estate owner; the commune that was party to the document; the soul count from the most recent census (*Reviziia*), which was 1858; a breakdown of field serfs, household serfs (who were not entitled to any land allotments), and

those serfs who chose the "beggar's allotment"; the number of souls entitled to allotments; the exact size of the estate prior to emancipation; the peasant obligations prior
to emancipation; the allotments calculated; the amount of land remaining for the landlord; the types of holdings with or without access rights such as plow land, pasture, forest, woodlands, gardens, ponds, fishing privileges, mills, bazaars, and the like; whether
there was any disconnected or "splintered" land (cherespolositsa); whether the landlord planned to relocate any former serfs because, say, their dwellings were too close or
blocked his/her access to land or property that was exclusively "his"/"hers"; the landlord's property privileges over peasant holdings (such as the right to open a tavern or
distill vodka); and, in addition to many more details, the exact amount of barshchina
and/or obrok obligations per soul.

The charter for Yazykovo Selo was regally official: "Charter: By Decree of Simbirsk Province, Simbirsk District for the village of Bogorodskovo, known as Yazykovo
Selo, the estate of 2nd Lieutenant Vasili P. Yazykov, 1862." It indicated that the 1858
census recorded 23 male household souls out of a total of 101, as well as 422 male field/
worker peasants. (The latter number included 160 who worked in the wool factory.) The
charter noted that 28 field/worker peasants refused the land allotment and obligations,
thus accepting the "beggar's allotment," amounting to 1 desiatina each. Next, it registered that the total land amount at Yazykovo Selo in 1860 was 6,807 desiatiny, and from
this number the total amount of land the peasants used and had access to at that time
was 2,162 desiatiny.[18] Next, Vasili earmarked 4 desiatiny—the maximum amount prescribed for Simbirsk Province—for those former male serfs who were eligible, which
was 394. Given this number, Yazykov was obligated to allot 1,576 desiatiny, leaving
him with 5,231 desiatiny. As these numbers show, even though he was "generous," in
that he earmarked the maximum amount of land to those eligible, Vasili gained 586
desiatiny relative to his holdings prior to 1861. Beyond this point, the charter reflected
that wherever there was a discontinuous plot of land, Yazykov exchanged his own land
with peasant plots in order to make their plots contiguous. This amounted to 294 desiatiny.[19] Further, at the end of the charter, an addendum paragraph indicated that Vasili
pledged a total of nearly 223 desiatiny of wooded area dispersed around the estate for
the peasants to have access to at no additional or obligatory cost. It also noted that the
river and two ponds on the estate could be used freely by the peasants. Finally, no peasants were to be relocated on the estate (see table 4.1).

Regarding obligations, it is important to remember that until the Redemption
Agreement was made, the liberated peasants remained in a "temporarily obligated"
state. Therefore, because the charter registered that in 1860 the estate used barshchina
only, this meant that it remained as part of the obligations. The peasants were also obligated to pay obrok dues for the use of land, for which Vasili charged 9 silver rubles per
soul. Since the prescribed obrok was between 8 and 10 silver rubles for the maximum
amount of land earmarked, Vasili's charge fell in the middle of that range. Therefore,
the village commune was responsible for a total of 3,546 silver rubles ($9 \times 394 = 3,546$),
to be paid in two installments of 1,773 rubles each. The first of these was slated for April
1, 1862, with the second to be paid six months later. However, it is presumed that the
peasants never made payments to Yazykov since (1) no records exist indicating such
was the case, and (2) they did not have access to any financial aid. It is worth noting that
the first payment was expected just two days after the charter was signed by Yazykov
and Bestuzhev.[20]

The charter went into effect on March 30, 1862.[21] Following the mandated protocols in the *Regulations*, Bestuzhev submitted the charter to the district conference of peace mediators, which was composed of nobles. The conference forwarded it, with other charters from Simbirsk District, to the Senate in St. Petersburg. All this was accomplished before the spring sowing season's commencement in 1862.

Table 4.1 Summary of Statutory Charter, Yazykovo Selo

The charter for Yazykovo Selo indicates the maximum and minimum allowances for Simbirsk Province were 4 and 1.3, respectively.

101 household serfs not entitled to land allotments (of whom 23 were male)

422 (male) field serfs (including 160 male serfs who worked in the factory)
- 28 refuse land allotment & obligations, accepting "beggar's allotment"

394 male field serfs entitled to land allotments

Vasili Yazykov allotted 4 *desiatiny* to each of the 394 souls

Prior to 1861: 6,807 *desiatiny* total land at Y.S.
    2,162 *desiatiny* total land serfs entitled to (422 × 5.1 *desiatiny* per male)
    4,645 *desiatiny* total land at Y.S. in V. Yazykov's personal possession

After 1861: 6,807 *desiatiny* total land at Y.S.
    1,576 desiatiny total land earmarked for former serfs (394 × 4)
    5,231 *desiatiny* total land at Y.S. left in V. Yazykov's personal possession

The Differences	Before 1861	After 1861	
Vasili Yazykov	4,645	5,231	gained 586 *desiatiny*
394 eligible peasants	2,162	1,576	lost 586 *desiatiny*
	(or 5.1 *des.* per individual)	(or 4 *des.* per individual)	

By way of comparison, the charter for Undory (the estate of Vasili Yazykov's brother, Alexander) showed that before 1861 there were 696 souls, (surprisingly) no household serfs, and a total of 2,784 *desiatiny* for the serfs' use, which amounted to 4 *desiatiny* per soul. The charter reflected that Alexander earmarked 3.4 *desiatiny* per soul (well below the maximum requirement in Simbirsk Province), or roughly 2,366 *desiatiny* for the lot. This total amounts to a 418 *desiatiny* negative discrepancy. Interestingly, the charter indicated neither the total amount of *desiatiny* that made up the estate before 1861 nor what Alexander was left with after the apportionment. However, we can extrapolate from the following numbers that after emancipation, Alexander Yazykov had approximately 7,663 *desiatiny* since a document from 1853 indicated that Undory estate comprised 10,029 *desiatiny*. Subtracting the 2,366 *desiatiny* that were earmarked in the charter from that number leaves 7,663. Given that the math would indicate that Alexander possessed 7,245 *desiatiny* before 1861, he therefore gained 418 *desiatiny* afterward.[22] It is interesting to note that while Alexander possessed more land and more serfs than his brother, he earmarked less for them both before and after emancipation. One crucial variable could be the soil quality: whereas Yazykovo Selo was approximately thirty miles west of Simbirsk and contained a mixture of black earth, sandy dirt, and rocks, Undory was on the banks of the fertile Volga River.

Why did the freed people of Yazykovo Selo neither sign the charter nor accept a copy? In both the Manifesto and the *Regulations*, the prescription for a commonsense, agreeable approach for all parties involved was made clear. Peasants' deputies were to give their "consent" to the "agreement" with their signatures. Implicit herein was the modern notion of a contractual arrangement regarding property made between two equal, civil parties, procured by the broker (in this case, the peace mediator). But we know this was not the case. In fact, it was a coercive, state-engineered consent that bore no resemblance to the idea of a freely entered agreement. Instead, the arrangement privileged the noble landowners: *they* were compensated for the loss of their property (land) in the form of bonds (not cash); *their* rights to their former serfs' labor and other forms of obligation were preserved; and the peasants lost in terms of both the amount of land that was earmarked for them relative to that before 1861 and their compensatory obligations for it. The peasants may have been illiterate, but they knew this "contract" was not freedom. Although they had little social capital, the peasants acted in a sovereign way, as best they could.

In fact, peasant refusal to sign the charters was common not only in Simbirsk Province but also across Russia.[23] For example, on an estate just to the south of Yazykovo Selo, the peasants refused to sign the document even when pressured by the peace arbitrator. They were "very rude" to him, "disrespectful, impudent, and … yelled at him 'no way, we'll not sign it'" until "we see the real *Regulations* from the Tsar!" Eventually the 4th Reserve Battalion was sent to punish the two ringleaders.[24] At another estate nearby, villagers refused to sign the charter even after the landlord tried for "seven months" to get them to sign it by offering (like Vasili Yazykov) an addendum with pledges of more land. Despite the landlord's promise to reduce *barshchina* obligations and *obrok* fees, and his offer of an additional 144 *desiatiny*, they still declared that they "didn't want any of it," adding that "what you ask of us is illegal."[25] The governor of Simbirsk even noted, "The peasants are actively refusing to sign the charter, [for they expect] that the signature will [reimpress] … them again."[26]

One topic of contention common to peasants on many estates in Simbirsk Province had to do with the fact that, frequently, terms in the charters had to do with the *type* of work being mandated: task work rather than field work. This requirement was associated with the large presence of woolen factories in the region. Unlike field work, task work in this setting was typically more difficult since it was more regimented, required specific production quotas, and was far less collegial.[27] Thus, at one estate where, like Yazykovo Selo, a wool factory was in operation, after refusing to sign the charter, the peasants literally stole the peace arbitrator's stamp so as to undercut its legality. The confrontation here descended into violence, and among the 81 arrested was the village priest. Just a year earlier in May 1861, after a battalion was called in to arrest the ringleaders of the disturbance at this particular estate, the peasants there had yelled, "We'll not let anybody punish them, even YOU!"[28]

Numerous discursive tactics were employed by peasants in these examples that demonstrate opposition to the charters. Variations on the themes of both the "Good Tsar" myth and the two-year obligation period emerged. It will be recalled that in the spring of 1861, the peasants invoked the former, either because they genuinely believed the distant ruler was their benefactor (and, like them, had been betrayed by the greedy, conniving noblemen) or because they could use this claim as a discursive tool for leverage against the noblemen—or possibly both. They argued the tsar had been tricked by the noblemen and, acting on behalf of his wishes, asserted that the two-year obligated term contained in the Manifesto was really retroactive, and the *real freedom* had actually commenced in 1858. Now, in the spring of 1862, the peasants, utilizing the same discursive tactic, insisted the *real freedom* would commence two years *after* the Manifesto, making the spring of 1863 the startup date. Confusion about or manipulation of the February 1863 deadline to effect a charter may well have played a role in producing this rumor. Nevertheless, why play into the hands of the enemy and sign a document that was designed to trick them out of their land, labor, and freedom? And why sign it if their freedom did not commence until the spring of 1863? Cries that the tsar "will declare a new *Regulations*" and "the Tsar will be angry if we accept any land before 1863" were common. Therefore, the peasants argued that they should ignore the authorities' demands.[29]

Furthermore, they did not even want copies of the document.[30] Accepting a copy implied their explicit participation in the process. Of course, rejecting a copy precluded the possibility of defending their rights to the land in a court of law should that necessity arise at a later date. But in that scenario "rights" may well have been moot since the terms were stacked against the peasants.

Other grievances expressed by the peasants included objections to paying for land that they perceived as already theirs, refusing allotments assigned to them in the charter when they were smaller than their holdings prior to 1861, and flat out rejecting payment requirements: "Why monetary obligations? ... The land was created by God for everyone."[31]

The state was correct when it anticipated peasant obstruction. In an effort to accelerate the negotiation process before the spring sowing season in 1862, the Ministry of Internal Affairs issued a circular as early as August 29, 1861, ordering that peasant signatures were not mandatory for the charters' legitimacy.[32]

Historians have debated why the peasants did not sign the charters. Roxanne Easley has argued that above all their refusal was rooted in the mediator's inability to promise peasant subsistence, which required at least 8.5 *desiatiny* per soul.[33] Although Soviet historiography continues to be valuable in that it provides crucial primary source and statistical information, it focused on the "revolutionary nature" of the peasants' responses, promoting the themes of "the crisis of the feudal order" and (similar to Easley's conclusion) claiming that "the peasants were robbed of the land."[34] But Wildman has concluded that although the peasants were concerned about land and subsistence, they were far more worried about obligations. Since the obligations (*barshchina*, *obrok*, and redemption payments for the land) were tied to the size of the plots, the greater the land allotment, the greater the obligations.[35] He holds that although it was meager, 4 *desiatiny* did not threaten subsistence, especially when the peasants had their garden plots. And as for Soviet historiography, Wildman explains that it was only with the population explosion in the late 19th and early 20th centuries that the land-to-subsistence ratio became an issue, and, therefore, Soviet scholars projected this situation back when analyzing the 1860s.[36]

In addition, Wildman has argued that the nobility's structurally severe debt explains the "generous" terms set forward in charters, as exemplified by Yazykovo Selo's. Indeed, 60 percent of landed estates across Russia were mortgaged in 1860, and more than 65 percent of estates (or 897 of 1,380) in Simbirsk Province were heavily in debt. Over the years the nobility put up estates, serfs, and town mansions as collateral in order to receive government credit. At 81 percent, Simbirsk Province had the highest number of mortgaged serfs in 1860.[37] Indeed, upon inheriting the estate when his father died in 1851, Vasili Yazykov mortgaged the entire property.[38] Even Seymour Becker, who has argued against the "declension of the nobility after emancipation" thesis, has conceded that in the Middle Volga region, the debt actually rose in the post-emancipation period.[39] All this background helps us understand both the peasants' and Yazykov's motivations when it came to the charter. As a side note, it is inadvisable to conflate indebtedness with poverty. As the next two chapters will make clear, Yazykov (and Lovell) lived well during their stewardships.

Official numbers on charters the peasants signed (and therefore "consented" to) are also problematic. Less than half of the total number of charters across Russia that were effected by the January 1, 1863, deadline (42 percent, or 36,413 of a total of 50,284) contained peasant signatures. Obviously, Yazykovo Selo's charter was in the category that did not show peasant consent. Once again Wildman has warned that even these numbers can be misleading, since there are 854 documented cases in which the military was deployed during the charter implementation period to force the peasants to sign.[40]

All this said, it is not difficult to understand Vasili Yazykov's motivations for a swift execution of the charter. While Yazykovo Selo's inhabitants had demonstrated resistance the previous year when they created a "disturbance" on the eve of the sowing season, and Yazykov countered by summoning the army, this was a new year and a new plowing and planting season. Like the year before, Yazykov wasted no time and moved quickly to stay ahead of developments. As for the "generous" land allotments Yazykov offered to his former people, it is obvious that he acted in his own self-interest, since they were at the high end that the *Regulations* mandated for Simbirsk Province. In this way, he could garner a higher amount of financial compensation in the form of government bonds and peasant obligations.

But the peasants, too, were worried about financial indebtedness. Typical cries of "We don't want the redemption [the code word for the monetary requirement to pay for the land] even if you kill us" are anecdotally attributed to the peasants at Yazykovo Selo.[41] In addition, Wildman insists that because so many peasants across the Russian land did not request conversion from *barshchina* to *obrok* up through the release of the 1881 Redemption Law, they (like their former masters who sought to maximize monetary benefits) were probably motivated by *their* realities, preferring to minimize their financial obligations. Clearly, the "arrangement" reached was based on the facts that everyone knew the peasants had no money, and therefore work could be extracted. That the peasants could have preferred *barshchina* under these circumstances and yet refused to sign the charter are not mutually exclusive, for while it minimized their monetary obligations, they had the option of simply withholding their labor.[42] For the time being, however, they did not participate in the charter stage of the emancipation moment. For the former slaves at Palmyra Plantation, the existential realities and outcomes were very different when it came to the contractual arrangements imposed on them by Union authorities.

The Rules and Regulations at Palmyra Plantation

The Quitman/Lovell family's recovery of Palmyra Plantation began with the Civil War's conclusion and the commencement of Reconstruction in April 1865. Its completion coincided with the ratification of the Thirteenth Amendment in December 1865, which made freedom a fact. But de facto emancipation was set in motion much earlier, with the eruption of hostilities between the North and South in 1861. As has been discussed, when the Russian serfs were emancipated in February 1861, they were not free just yet, as the Manifesto had a number of qualifying provisions built into it. Although the conditions and historical sequences were not identical, the American emancipation experience was similar to the Russian one in that freedom was also evolutionary and provisional.[43]

As a member plantation on Davis Bend, Palmyra was on the war's front line since Union strategy in this region included securing the Mississippi River. The idea was to line the riverbanks with a loyal population that could give aid in securing navigation on the river. Resettling liberated slaves on confiscated plantations in the region also kept them away from the armies' wakes. Still another reason for concentrating them in this area had to do with trying to salvage what was left of cotton crops for sale in this lucrative region: ten Mississippi counties and Louisiana parishes within a one-hundred-mile radius of Vicksburg produced more than one-seventh of the entire South's cotton for the 1860–1861 growing season. This fact also explains why Union policy relocated scores of refugee slaves to augment the labor force for cotton crops in this region.[44] During General Grant's Vicksburg campaign in the summer of 1863, he decided to seize the entire 12,000-acre peninsula of Davis Bend and make it a "paradise" for former slaves. By December 20, 1863, all the plantations on the Bend were occupied. "[T]he Yankees came and set the Negros [*sic*] All Free and the Work All Stoped [*sic*]," noted an overseer from a plantation opposite the Bend in his record book.[45]

Over the course of the next two years, what played out on the Bend was a mixture of positives and negatives for the liberated people. At once the war presented an opportunity for and a constraint on their freedom. First, freedom's fate was contingent on both Union victory and policy. Second, while the former slaves were liberated from their former masters' authority, they were now subordinated to that of Union authorities. (This transference of supervision paralleled the transition from the nobleman to the village commune in the Russian context.) Third, the former slaves lived in a "free zone" of sorts, protected by both geographic isolation and the Union overseers. And fourth, they were caught in the crosshairs between their liberators' expectations of freedom and their own.

Both the exigencies of war and the nascent stage of providing for the freed people on the Bend meant that the situation there was ad hoc and fluid. In fact, a bewildering series of Union representatives, both official and voluntary, and both military and civilian, jockeyed for institutional power and management there. This revolving door of custodians was disruptive, and often their sets of rules and regulations competed with each other. Further, while the kaleidoscopic sets of authorities posed a problem for consistency and order, like the charter for Yazykovo Selo, the final "Rules and Regulations" that were put into place were authoritative and doctrinal.

Because of their close supervision and protection, the freed people on the Bend arguably fared better than most across the war-torn South. These facts explain the wide range of historiographical evaluations about the "success" of the Home Colony experiment. For example, Clifton Ganus insisted that it was a "grand success." James Currie concluded that, for a place "so grandly conceived," it was not a "failure" since (quoting General John Eaton) it proved "the capacity of the Negro to take care of himself." Others have not been as celebratory. Vernon Wharton concluded that because the confiscated properties were returned to their original owners, "Davis Bend was doomed at the end of its first year." Thavolia Glymph's detailed study stressed the freed people's "disappointment" and "discouragement" with Union overseers, as well as their lack of autonomy and the coercive nature of the rules and regulations. Janet Sharp Hermann's opus remains the most thorough, balanced, and consistently solid analysis of what played out. She focused on the Davis brothers' plantations from the early antebellum period when Joseph Davis hoped to create a model slave community based on the principles of his idol, Robert Owen, through to the Home Colony experiment, and finally to the relocation of its black community to Mound Bayou ten years after Reconstruction's conclusion. Hermann concluded that Union policies and attitudes "permanently embittered" the freed people toward the "Yankee officers." However, all these historians agree that, due to its history of benevolent paternalism and geographic isolation, the Bend's laborers possessed a unique sense of enterprise and work ethic.[46] Also, accounts of the Davis Bend experiment rightly focus on Joseph Davis' former slave Ben Montgomery, as he represents an extraordinary case study. Implicit in any study of the slaves' liberation is the task of weighing the liberators' directives against the actions of the liberated. Therefore, I am concerned with the nameless, but real, liberated people on Davis Bend and with the extent and meaning of their compliance with their liberators' directives.

At first glance, the former slaves' condition on the Bend appeared to be relatively good after liberation, since their quarters were still intact and the former owners were no longer there.[47] One Northern missionary on the Bend described Palmyra as follows:

> [Palmyra] has been saved from depradations [*sic*] of soldiers, etc. it looks very well.... The Negro quarters are good and comfortable, and being arranged in rows each house separate [*sic*], all whitewashed had a very neat appearance forming a street with houses uniform on either side. I ...found them cleanly and ... comfortably supplied with needful clothing.[48]

This situation changed when the army ordered the eviction of many freed people from their homes so that Union soldiers could live in them. Then, over the next two years, a total of eight companies of African American troops were stationed there.[49] Soon a canal was dug across the neck of the peninsula, thereby completing the moat that wrapped around the Bend. A gunboat was strategically positioned to guard the island's entrance at the canal. Designed to secure the Bend and protect the freed people from Confederate guerrilla raids, a military order was issued that forbade whites to cross over without a pass.

At first the Bend was managed by the Freedmen's Department, an adjunct to the War Department and headed by General John Eaton, who, with respect to those freedmen under his care, advised his subordinates to "adopt a rule to require utmost deference and obedience on the part of the Negroes and whenever anyone gets up to any disturbance or insubordination turn him out of our lines." Still, with respect to the fate of the freed people, he expressed a blend of Jeffersonian Republicanism and free labor ideology that was typical of Northern sentiment:

> Our aim was ... to bring labor and its rewards ... to the [freed] people ... their present skill at labor on this rich soil ... yields fabulous profits. Freedom will increase the productiveness of that skill by rendering the laborer more intelligent and earnest, under its clearer light and new motives.... [T]he facts indicate ... [in] five years ... [we] will see this country cut up into small farms, and glorying ... productiveness it never before attained.

Thus, freedom and labor were inseparable. Indeed, labor was the key to freedom. Labor created virtue, and the latter was the key to being a civilian in a free republic.[50] Still, white officials frequently found it difficult to "be kind" to the former slaves since "the feeling against serving [him] in any capacity still prevailed."[51] One white overseer even concluded that the freed people "worked one-third less time per day than had the slaves; hence cotton could never be produced as cheaply again."[52] Clearly, old attitudes persisted in the new era. But if the freed people were truly working far less than in the days of slavery, perhaps this change was evidence of strategic resistance.

In the spring of 1863, Congress made the Treasury Department responsible for supervising all abandoned and confiscated property in the South. This decision meant that the Treasury Department and the Freedmen's Department had joint authority on the Bend. The former created a set of "rules and regulations," some of which included the creation of "Home Farms" supervised by "white lessees." Here refugees would obtain all provisions that were contingent on their labor. They were divided into companies of approximately 20 laborers and allotted small tracts of land to farm on their own account. At $25 per month for men and $10 for women, the wages recommended were more than what the War Department would soon set. Palmyra Plantation's white lessee was one A.W. Hunt, a Louisiana planter with "Union sympathies" who had fled to the North when the war began. The department agreed to pay him $75 a month to "exercise complete supervision" over all the "colonists." This included labor contracts. Hunt and the other lessees were instructed to see to it that each company planted all the land allotted to each group, with at least two-thirds of that land reserved for cotton. Like the other white lessees on the Bend, Hunt was expected to supervise the allocation of mules and equipment that had been confiscated from both near and far. Further, the lessees were expected to require that the freed people keep their houses and grounds "swept every morning and the filth removed." Rations were regulated. Given that this activity was all playing out in the midst of a total war, such close scrutiny and quality-control measures are understandable. Still, the fact that the freed people were not left free to manage their own affairs was a direct contradiction of what the mission statement for the Home Colony professed.[53]

By September 1863, the War Department drew up its own set of rules and regulations. The Freedmen's Department was assigned the duties of registering all freed people on the Bend, issuing all labor contracts, and ensuring that all persons were occupied with some kind of work. Companies of freedmen were to be organized to pick, gin, and bale all cotton. A 10 percent tax was levied on the wages, which were set at $7 per month for men over the age of 15 and $5 per month for women. All horses, mules, oxen, wagons, carts, and farming equipment that the armies had confiscated in the area (as well as from the Bend's inhabitants) were inventoried for the purposes of redistribution.[54]

Seeing that its authority was compromised by the Treasury Department's rules and regulations, the Freedmen's Department petitioned the War Department for a change in policy that, coincidentally, was more in line with white lessees' complaints: namely, that the colonists' wages were too high. By March 1864, the War Department persuaded the Treasury Department to reduce wages to a pay scale ranging from $10 to $3.50 per month, plus rations. Thus, freed people previously employed by the War Department saw their wages increase while those hired by the Treasury Department saw theirs fall.[55]

In March 1864, General Eaton's assistant, Colonel Samuel Thomas, endorsed a management plan put forward by the provost marshal for Davis Bend, Colonel Gaylord Norton. This became the final, official, and notorious "Rules and Regulations," which remained the working blueprint for the Bend's management until Union representatives left at the end of 1865. Historically, the provost marshal was an institutional figure who operated in the capacity of military police. During the war and Reconstruction, however, the marshal's position and responsibilities were expanded. To be sure, the provost marshal was responsible for maintaining order and social control. To the extent that he (in either a formal or an informal capacity) served as a liaison between the freed people and various Union representatives, the provost marshal was similar to Russia's peace mediator. Especially with respect to labor, the provost marshal's powers were almost unlimited.[56] In the same way that the Russian Statutory Charters had to be signed by the peace mediators, all labor contracts with the freed slaves during the first few years after liberation had to be signed by the provost marshal. Although I did not find one labor contract with any laborer at Palmyra Plantation for the Home Colony period, this does not mean that no one contracted for work there, as the final numbers below indicate.

Consisting of thirteen numbered paragraphs, the "Rules and Regulations" had sweeping mandates for both social order and labor control. As detailed below, former slaves had to organize themselves into "companies" composed of up to "twenty-five hands" and were required to "do their share of the labor." The laborers would be registered in a "book," which also included their children. Similar to the village elders' responsibilities in the Russian context, each company's "head" would transact all business on behalf of the group. Once the company had been formed, there could be no changes in its makeup. No company could hire hands out to work for someone else. If any laborer refused to work, he/she would receive no rations. Land would be allotted to the laborers, with white superintendents as their managers. Supplies and equipment, housing, and rations were provided—all closely inventoried in account books, and all to be settled when the cotton crop was marketed. All crimes and disobedience would be punished "according to the nature of the offense." Thieves would be banished to "Big Black Island."[57] In closing, Norton explained that

> Great efforts must be made by all good men ... to change the present disgraceful and bad conduct of a large number of the negroes now living here who are stealing, plundering, killing stock, and living in idleness.... Extensive measures for punishment will be adopted and vigorously carried out. All those interested in the welfare of the people, and who wish to see the Bend improve will assist ... in the efforts to bring about good order.

Clearly, the rules were uniform and doctrinal in that they laid out the military's expectations for labor and production on the Bend. Equally clear, the military had the power and authority to dictate the terms of freedom, maintain order, and coerce labor.[58]

Meanwhile, Tonie Quitman Lovell and several of her sisters were oddly successful in temporarily retrieving Palmyra in the spring of 1864 when they made statements of allegiance to Union authorities in Vicksburg. This incident is curious since it was in the middle of the raging war, and the Home Colony was still in its organizational inception. It is not known why Union authorities returned a third of the Bend to its original owners when they needed that earmarked territory for former slaves. The sisters quickly hired a Northern man, one Alexander Warwick, to manage the plantation. Because of this development, the Home Colony experiment at Palmyra and under Hunt's management never got beyond the planning stage. Those freed people who had received allotments from the government now saw them returned to the Quitman/Lovell family. (This, in part, explains the absence of labor contracts for Palmyra.) But the existential realities of the war's tumult and fluid circumstances, combined with Palmyra's proximity to Union authorities, meant that Warwick (an individual manager competing with and surrounded by the Union's grand experiment) had great trouble getting the plantation up and running. Furthermore, the fact that Warwick was hired *after* the season preparation time meant that production at Palmyra for the 1864 season was compromised.

Table 4.2 Rules and Regulations, Davis Bend

(Notice the glaring salients between the Statutory Charter and the Rules and Regulations included provisions for labor obligations, earmarked land allotments, and individual leaders or representatives to act on behalf of the collective.)

The following *Rules and Regulations* will for the present be adopted for the *Government* of the *Freedmen* at *Davis Bend, Miss.*

I. The *Bend* with the exception of the *Jeff Plantation* will be leant to those who seem willing and able to work lands upon their own accounts.

II. Those wishing to work lands upon their own account will be required to form themselves into companies of from three to twenty-five hands that are able to do their share of the labor. Before the land will be allotted, the companies will be registered (in a book kept for that purpose) together with the parents and children belonging to each member of the company. At this time each company will be required to select one from their numbers who will be known as the head of the company and who will transact the business for the entire company and no account will be kept with any other partner.

III. After the companies are formed and registered no changes will be allowed except by the consent of two thirds of the members and the approval of the *Post Superintendent.*

IV. No company will be allowed to hire hands to work for them except by the consent of the Post Superintendent. Each hand that is registered with the company and remains with it through the season will pay their portion of the expenses and receive their share of the profit.

V. Each company will be required to pay for all the rations they receive and for the use of horses, mules, and farming utensils they receive from [the] Government. Rations will be issued to the companies only for the number registered.

VI. In dividing land the quantity will be regulated according to the number of hands in the company—the number of acres to a hand will be regulated by the Post Superintendent.

VII. The companies will be divided into colonies for which Superintendents will be provided and whose duty will be to see that every company in his colony work their ground in the proper manner. He will have a general supervision over all the people in his colony and all companies and people living within his colony will be subject to his orders.

VIII. Any member of a company who shall refuse or neglect to perform his share of the labor (except in cases of actual sickness) or shall absent himself from the company without their consent can be reported to the colony Superintendent and if he think it proper will be turned over to work without pay until he is willing to work for himself.

IX. *The Jeff Plantation* will be reserved and worked as a *Government Farm* where all hands that are not registered with companies can find employment with pay and rations.

X. No rations will be issued on the Bend except to companies and those employed on the Government Farm. All those not able to work will be required to show a certificate to this effect from the surgeon in charge or furnish their own rations.

XI. All those having certificates of disability from the surgeon will be placed in a camp by themselves at some suitable place where they will be fed and properly cared for.

XII. All crimes and disobedience of orders will be punished according to the nature of the offense. Thieves and robbers will when proved guilty be banished from the bend and sent to Big Black Island.

XIII. *Heads of companies* who allow any of their numbers to steal from one another or from the Government will be dispossessed and sent from the Bend.

All this changed again for Palmyra when the War Department issued an order on November 5, 1864, that reserved the entire Davis Bend peninsula to the military for the 1865 planting season. Thus, Palmyra was reconfiscated and reincorporated into the Davis Bend Home Colony and, therefore, again fell under Union authorities' management.

Identifying specific numbers for the 1864 season is problematic. Janet Hermann used General Eaton's numbers to identify 76 companies, with at least 70 freedmen as heads, who closed out the year producing a combined total of 150 bales of cotton. This total is not impressive given that in the antebellum period a typical crop in a good year amounted to 1,500 bales. Indeed, Eaton had expected at least 1,000 bales to be produced in 1864. After their debts and rentals had been cleared, these workers were left with between $500 and $2,500 in profit for the year.[59]

Looking ahead to the 1865 season, Provost Marshal Norton issued an addendum to his "Rules and Regulations," in the form of twelve strict orders. One of these prioritized planting operations above all else, telling superintendents to "exercise a complete supervision over all the people in your charge ... [but listen] to their complaints and do all in your power to get along peaceably with them."[60]

The 1865 planting season coincided with the war's conclusion, the assassination of President Lincoln, and Congress' creation of the Freedmen's Bureau. Now this institution was put into the mix of managers and administrators on the Bend. It seems that no sooner had the Bureau's takeoff begun than the realization set in that the Bend's property would soon be returned to its original owners, yet again. Still, by the year's end, the Bend's plantations, including Palmyra, produced a staggering profit of nearly $160,000 (see table 6.1). As in the previous year, the freed people had worked solidly for Union officials. But 1865 showed a more disciplined and stable production, with 181 companies (comprising roughly 7 adults each) producing 1,736 bales of cotton and 12,000 bushels of corn and vegetables, which produced a total crop value of $397,700. After deducting expenses, the Union realized a profit of $159,200, for an average of almost $880 per company, or $125.65 per adult. However, the superintendents and Union received the majority of this money, with the laborers (or "colonists") receiving little or no cash at year's end because of the deductions for rations and supplies.

On the one hand, these numbers point to a great success, considering the economies of both Mississippi and the greater American South experienced devastation and dislocation. On the other hand, behind these numbers were hundreds (if not thousands) of individuals who were, first and foremost, trying to survive in the midst of the war's turmoil. The census numbers for the Bend were in constant flux. From January to February 1864, refugee numbers alone swelled from 950 to 3000, and by summer the total reached 4,000. While in April 1864, missionary Henry Rowntree counted "about 2,000 freedmen" at Palmyra alone, the Freedmen's Department's census for August listed a total of 318 freed people there. Of those, 110 were women and 208 were children, with no men accounted for at all. Indeed, as early as December 1863, the vast majority of freed people remaining on the Bend were women and children.[61] This result is not surprising, since most of the men had enlisted in the Union army—a bold expression of freedom.[62] These demographics for Palmyra stand in stark contrast to those listed on the eve of the war in 1860, which recorded 91 men, 93 women, and 109 children under the age of 15.[63] But the larger point here has to do with the numbers of laborers cited above with respect to the Bend's profit for 1865: if the records show that 181 companies with 7 adults each labored in the fields, this number falls far short of the population swells at the Bend that were also documented. This discrepancy is curious.

Noralee Frankel, Mary Farmer-Kaiser, and others have addressed the supervision of women and children by Union representatives, especially the Freedmen's Bureau. As African American men enlisted in the army, Union officials looked to African

American women and children as a source of labor. In fact, Frankel has pointed out that Davis Bend was essentially a kind of clearinghouse for freedwomen and children, in that scores of refugees would be placed there, only to be relocated soon thereafter to other confiscated plantations across the region in order to be put to work. In this one example, we see the intersection of many issues in the context of emancipation: For Union officials, work was at the heart of freedom. It was unthinkable to let the plantations lie fallow. With the freedmen off at war, it made sense to put the women and children to work. This approach would also reduce the number of refugees in their care, so that they could prepare for more. Thus, as one official explained to the freedwomen:

> I know that it is quite natural that you should associate work with slavery, and freedom with idleness.... After all ... you have seen slaves working all their lives, and free people doing little or nothing. And I should not blame you if you should ask, "What have we gained by freedom, if we are to work, work, work!" ... There is nothing degrading in free labor,—nay it is most honorable.[64]

It appears that, in its conception, there was a structural contradiction in Union policy at Davis Bend. On the one hand, Grant envisioned it as a "paradise," where the liberated slaves could demonstrate the virtues of freedom and have self-determination. On the other hand, the Bend was earmarked as a place to relocate thousands of former slaves because of its isolation and its production capacity. And the turnover was great.

As Union officials continued to relocate refugees to the Bend, and as numbers swelled, tension emerged between the Bend's original inhabitants and the newcomers, and the differences in their standards of living were striking. For example, the same missionary who reported that the former slaves' homes at Palmyra were neat and tidy simultaneously observed a ghastly sight, one that captured the other half of the story on the Bend:

> There huddled together were 35 poor wretched helpless negros, one man who had lost one eye ... and the sight of the other fast going.... Five women all Mothers, and the residue of 29 children, all small and under 12 years of age. One of the Women had the small pox, her face a perfect mass of Scabs, her children were left uncared for except for what they accidentally rec[eive]d. Another woman was nursing a little boy about 7 whose early life was fast ebbing.... Another was scarcely able to crawl about. They had no bedding ... being literally ... destitute.... They were filthy and will all ... have the small pox.... Their fare was hard biscuit and smoked bacon which I saw some of the children eating uncooked ... they had no cooking utensils, nor any furniture.

In addition,

> About 150 poor, miserable hovels or sheds each filled to overflowing, in one I found 17 in a place I should not think over 12 ft. square[. M]any had a dozen and so on, these cabins are simply sticks reared up, brush put on & around and some sods put on the top ... residences [which are] ... not fit to shelter cattle in during a storm, yet therein are our fellow creatures in all weather subjected to disease, degradation and immorality.[65]

This dire situation at Davis Bend was not unique. Indeed, reports emerged of "thousands of people dying" and "the most frightful misery and sickness" at neighboring contraband camps, such as Young's Point, Louisiana, and Natchez and Paw Paw Island, Mississippi.[66]

Other problems also adversely impacted the final production numbers at Davis Bend in 1864 and 1865. These included pestilence, agricultural pests, and raids. As the above quotes illustrated, disease was prevalent. Waves of smallpox, cholera, and yellow fever swept through the area cyclically for the war's duration.[67] Hunger and starvation were also serious problems. The notorious army worm devastated the crops in the spring and fall of 1864, with a summer of heavy rains sandwiched between them. The quality of equipment left much to be desired, and supply shortages were rampant. Indeed, livestock was often unhealthy and diseased. Lastly, notwithstanding the Bend's relatively secluded location, it was not completely immune to guerrilla raids. Frequently, mules and supplies were stolen by "roving bands of soldiers." There were even reports of freed people being kidnapped.[68]

As discussed in the previous chapter, the freed people had great expectations for land gifts by the end of 1865. But another great debate emerged about contracting versus wage labor in the context of freedom. Reminiscent of former serfs' fears about being tricked into another form of servitude, freed slaves argued, "What [do] you want me to sign [a contract] for? I is free…. If I is already free, I don't need to sign no paper." As Leon Litwack explained, the freed people lacked "confidence 'in the white man's *integrity.*'" Many freed people feared the binding nature of the contract, as well as its potential to annul both their newfound freedom and the possibility for land distribution. An opinion piece in a local African American newspaper best summarized the freed people's sentiments about these issues:

> "insist upon regular weekly … wages." … The contract … is intended by the employer to renew a servitude or bondage … [it is] … the means of coercion…. It is clear … that the laborer must not alienate his freedom, for any term of months … remain free to leave the plantation and go elsewhere … laborers are always found on hand, under a regime of liberty…. Compulsion is nothing short of disguised slavery…. The laborer has nothing to lose by making … no written contract at all, but working by the week or by the day … [only in this way] he preserves his freedom.

A Bureau official dismissed these concerns as "absurd."[69] However, here we see the debate about the meaning of freedom in which the role of wages as an incentive, the fear of coercion, and the meaning of labor contracts intersected. Clearly, labor was identified as the crucial tool of leverage, and refusing to sign a contract represented real power. Embedded in this quote was a discussion about the authenticity of freedom. Like the freed serfs, the former slaves were concerned for their future.

* * *

Although nuanced, a number of similarities and differences can be identified between the two demesnes in this study with respect to the theme of contractual agreements during the emancipation era. At Yazykovo Selo the serfs had been liberated, but their freedom was contingent on moving into the next phase—namely, the implementation of the Statutory Charter. Contrasted with what played out on the Bend, where all seemed to be in motion and in flux, there was a sense of an impasse at Yazykovo, where the peasants wanted nothing to do with this "agreement." Against the backdrop of epic military maneuvers and efforts to organize the liberated people, Davis Bend witnessed the ebb and flow of refugees. In annual cycles, the former slaves were expected to agree to labor contracts and work. Although many complied, compliance does not necessarily indicate consent.

What explains these differences between the Russian peasants' outright rejection of the Statutory Charter and American freed people's evident cooperation with the "Rules and Regulations?" One answer has to do with the "nature" of their freedom at this point in time. The peasants were presented with a document masquerading as a contract that etched into stone something that did not comport with what freedom meant to them. It attached them to the land and assigned labor and financial obligations in perpetuity (or at least until negotiations for a Redemption Agreement commenced). In the American South, although the freed people on the Bend were "liberated," "freedom" was not yet a fact. They were at the mercy of their liberators, and their "liberated" status was contingent on compliance with the "Rules and Regulations"—for the time being, that is. At this juncture, and like their Russian counterparts, the freed people at Davis Bend were attached to the land and assigned labor obligations, albeit with the promise of compensation. But compensation was subject to accrued expenses. In addition, the "Rules" assigned strict codes of conduct. Moreover, in the long term, the war was not yet over, and freedom was not yet certain. In each scenario, there may have been a settlement, but there was no resolution.

Still another variable has to do with the nature of the "contracts" themselves. These were issued and backed by the power of the state (and military). And they were authoritarian. While the Statutory Charter was a one-time-only arrangement, the labor contracts imposed at Palmyra were both short-term and long-term agreements. That is, while the Statutory Charter froze an arrangement in place, each labor contract in the American context was for one season only, with the expectation that with each year it would be renewed. The Russian peasants did not have the option of looking ahead to a new year, to anticipate that another opportunity could emerge for new negotiations. In this sense, the permanent nature of the charter hindered cooperation. Although the "Rules and Regulations" did not allow for any negotiation, there was an element of impermanence, as the entire situation was part of the fluid war context. Both implicitly and explicitly, the situation on the Bend was a temporary one. Freedom hung in the balance at both Yazykovo Selo and Palmyra Plantation.

While freedom was front and center in these scenarios, as far as the authorities were concerned, nothing was to change with respect to labor. Both sets of authorities demonstrated that social control and the integrity of labor were paramount. Both were concerned about getting labor and productivity set in motion; idleness would not be tolerated. Both placed conditionalities and expectations on the freed people. Crucial players in the process of enforcing emancipation in both countries were the peace mediator and provost marshal—figures charged with ameliorating the plight of the liberated, in addition to acting as intermediaries between former masters and the liberated. In each locale there were overtones of paternalism, the idea being that the authorities knew what was "best" for the freed people and that the latter required supervision. Indeed, both sets of authorities believed that the freed people needed to "grow into" their freedom, with labor being the vehicle for that transition. Above all, the priority was compliance. The essential message was "You will work so that you can be free."

Both the Statutory Charter and the "Rules and Regulations" were lawful and determined the parameters of both station and choice. Each form of legal documentation imposed formulaic uniformity, especially with respect to labor obligations and land earmarks. Considering that both sets of liberated people were almost certainly illiterate, the authorities used the tool of a written, legal document as both a norm and a pretense to coerce labor obligations from people because of their identity. Each document was legally valid irrespective of the freed peoples' consent. Just as labor contracts divided the former slaves on the Bend into groups with designated leaders as signatories to the agreement, so, too, were their Russian counterparts required to have specific representatives—namely, the village elders—as cosigners of the charter. All this speaks to a duplication of organizational and logistical methodologies.

How did the freed people respond? In each context the formerly unfree were suspicious of the authorities. While the nature and implementation of the Statutory Charter disincentivized Yazykovo Selo's inhabitants, Palmyra's had both practical and tangible incentives—food for survival, as well as wages—that elicited compliance. What explains this difference in terms of compliance? Because the freed people at Yazykovo Selo could not be evicted and had their homes, garden plots, and community intact, why would they comply with the authorities if there were no adverse repercussions? Above all, emancipation made it possible for them to be certain in their position. These were not the old days. By contrast, the nature and implementation of the "Rules and Regulations" incentivized the American freed people to remain and work since they faced banishment and almost certain destitution if they did not comply. As a side note, it is significant that the incentive of wages was offered to people who, in their former condition, had not been compensated in this manner. These, too, were not the old days.

Were the liberated people in each context free? Were they authors of their own determination at this point? No. But neither were they as they had been before. In a sense, this stage was an intermediary one, in which there was no "resolution" per se. However, although a "settlement" had been reached, it was for the time being only. The next two chapters will address the wider and longer-term implications of both the Statutory Charter and the cyclic nature of the American contracting experience in conjunction with land, labor, compensation, and rates of compliance.

PART III

Tending and Reaping Freedom

5

Understanding Contextual Realities

*Background to the Post-Emancipation Story
at Yazykovo Selo and Palmyra Plantation*

In March 1881, Russian nobleman Vasili Yazykov sold his estate, Yazykovo Selo, to a merchant named Feodor Stepanov. This sale included a wool factory that Yazykov's father had built at the estate in 1851 in anticipation of government requisitions for military uniforms, which the Crimean War (1854–1856) confirmed. Ever since the emancipation of his serfs in 1861, Yazykov had attempted to balance his responsibility of service to the state with managing the demesne. When Stepanov bought the estate, however, it was in complete disrepair, and the atmosphere there was one of idleness and ambivalence. The fields lay fallow, and the factory's condition was deplorable. The building's doors and window frames had vanished, the wheel for producing steam was out of commission, and the spinning machines were broken and missing parts. The estate was producing less than half of its capacity with less than half of the total number of laborers working in 1861.[1] Neighbor and poet D.P. Oznobishin reported that across Simbirsk Province, the terms of freedom led to the peasants' "deliberate sabotage" regarding work. As historian Zhores Trofimov has explained, in the first year alone after emancipation, the use of land in Simbirsk Province "declined by half."[2]

Stepanov initiated repairs, investments, and a system of wage labor. Incredibly, within two years the factory's production was recognized by the All Russian National Industrial Exhibition in Moscow.[3] But much effort and adversity were involved in reaching this result, especially when it came to the freed people living there. In 1895, the factory's laborers staged a strike so disruptive that it forced the merchant to increase their wages.[4]

Meanwhile, in the American South, William Storrow Lovell had by 1877 become a "planting magnate," reportedly operating Palmyra Plantation on Davis Bend as a "closed island community under his control."[5] Since the end of the war Lovell had pursued his dream of becoming a planter—one that had commenced when he married General John A. Quitman's daughter Tonie in 1858. Although of "noble, high toned and intelligent" character, Lovell "lacked estate." Still, this Northern transplant had earned $1,500 a year on his naval salary.[6] When Tonie's father died one month after their marriage, Lovell, by proxy, inherited Palmyra Plantation. Therefore, he rationalized, "there was no need [for him] to continue a military career … houses will burn down, stocks will break and fly to the winds, but a plantation is a solid thing, it is always there."[7] But the Civil War put Lovell's ambition on hold when he left to serve on behalf of the Confederacy. Only in late 1865 did he return to the Bend and pick up where he had left off.

By submitting his oath of allegiance along with the rest of the Quitmans, Lovell simultaneously pledged his loyalty to the Union and re-acquired Palmyra, which he would manage for the next thirty years. Although the plantation was worth far less than what it had been on the war's eve, by 1880 the Agricultural Census valued the plantation at $114,150.[8] However, this prosperity did not come easily. In late 1879, when agitation associated with the first migration from the delta to Kansas was reaching its peak, Lovell faced collective action in the form of threats to stage a walkout over the meager wages he paid his laborers, which amounted to $10 a month with board (or 50 cents per day without).[9]

While the situation at Yazykovo Selo during Vasili's tenure appears to have been one of decline, with its recovery coinciding with Stepanov's purchase of the estate, Palmyra Plantation became a profitable enterprise during the period under study, only to meet its demise by 1900. This outcome is extraordinary for a number of reasons. First, unlike Palmyra, Yazykovo Selo did not experience the confiscation and occupation associated with a total war. Even though the Home Colony episode displayed similarities to the authoritarian nature of emancipation at Yazykovo Selo, after the Thirteenth Amendment's ratification in December 1865, there were no de jure "stages" of freedom in America. Therefore, unlike what happened at Yazykovo Selo, William Storrow Lovell did not have to navigate a process of freedom dictated by governmental decrees as the plantation recovered from the war and occupation. Still, in order to make production at the plantation feasible, he did have to adapt to radical changes that emancipation set in motion with respect to labor. In this regard, the series of adaptations did constitute a de facto counterpart to the de jure "stages" of emancipation in Russia.

Second, unlike his Russian counterpart, Lovell was new to the way of life at his demesne and to its management. Born and raised in the North, Lovell's upbringing did not include the expectation that he would become a member of the elite planter class. As the oldest son of a noble landowner, Vasili Yazykov knew full well what to expect (and what was expected of him). While Yazykov did share with his American counterpart a military profession in his formative years, as a Russian nobleman, he was imbued with a profound service ethic associated with his estate (*soslovie*). And because his orientation was toward service, "managing" the estate after emancipation represented a challenge. Other than being a military man, Lovell possessed no "service" ethic, and yet he demonstrated that he had no qualms about transitioning into the American South's planter class.

Third, while Yazykov was heavily in debt before emancipation, the Quitmans/ Lovells were not. However, even though cotton was still "king" after the Civil War, Palmyra's "recovery" was by no means certain. All this said, the trail of family and business correspondence indicates that various members of the extended Quitman/Lovell family traveled frequently and lived well for the time. Similarly, despite being plagued by indebtedness in the post-emancipation period, Yazykov was hardly poverty stricken. Indeed, he continued to indulge in extravagance.

Finally, both circumstantial and contextual evidence suggests that the former serfs at Yazykovo Selo seemed to be, at best, ambivalent with respect to working per the labor obligations required by the *Regulations*. At worst, they seem to have actively resisted it. However, records show that the freed people at Palmyra Plantation worked solidly and consistently.

In order to understand the post-emancipation developments at each demesne, an appreciation of the contextual realities at each locale is critical. For example, understanding the prevailing economic systems in each country, as well as how each demesne was integrated into its respective regional economy, is important. Delineating a number of unique traits associated with each demesne further helps us understand what played out in the post-emancipation period with respect to labor, productivity, and production, which are addressed in the next chapter. In a word, this chapter lays the groundwork for the next by addressing the "lifeworld" of each demesne.

Also relevant to understanding the post-emancipation realities at each demesne are the effects, both direct and indirect, of the emancipation mandates in each country. Here it will be clear that the terms of freedom played a role in determining labor's features at Yazykovo Selo and Palmyra Plantation. The Russian emancipation settlement was premeditated and prescriptive, and it charted a course for what labor would look like. Although in the United States labor was crucial to the viability of the lucrative cash crops, what that labor would "look like" remained to be seen. Therefore, labor (both in general and at Palmyra Plantation) went through a series of fine-tunings. While the Russian Manifesto technically broke the master's authority over his or her former serfs, it was replaced by the village commune authority. Because the legislation required that the peasants' obligations, taxes, and compensation for land to both their former master and the government be collective, a communal response with respect to labor was predictable. In the American case, the freed people became "bird free" at freedom's gate. They were essentially homeless. Although the liberated slaves' ideas about freedom included land ownership, as it became evident to many (if not most) freed people that this expectation would not materialize, either because they wanted to or because they had no choice, they evidently subscribed to the prevailing American tenets of individualism, free labor, and the idea of a "fair wage" for a day's work. To be clear, the fact that the freed people appear to have subscribed to these tenets does not mean that they were content with the arrangement or that they were free participants in an economic system of equal players. It does mean, however, that they did what they could with what options they had under the circumstances, at that point in time. Thus, whereas the Russian commune's authority was inserted between the freed people and the former masters, the American marketplace of supply, demand, and compensation stood between the former slaves and the plantation owners/managers.[10] In both instances, albeit for different reasons, the freed people were compelled to work.

Herein lay a similarity between the two subaltern groups: Under each set of circumstances, the freed people acted in their self-interest in the ways in which they could. Each set responded to or worked within the constraints of the institutional and traditional structures in which they found themselves, as well as the new revolutionary context that emancipation ushered in. As the previous chapter made clear, the freed serfs of Yazykovo Selo repudiated the Statutory Charter. Now they were entering a phase in which they were expected to agree to a Redemption Agreement with their former master. The latter was the "payment plan," whereby the landowners were to receive their compensation in government bonds and the peasants were to purchase their lands through a government loan of up to four-fifths of the value, which would be paid off in 49 yearly installments. How could the former serfs enter into an agreement to financially compensate their former master as well as the government for land when they had neither cash nor (technically) freedom of movement, especially since, for example, the Peasant's Land Bank, which was designed to assist them regarding these financial issues, was not established until 1883? Moreover, they questioned the principle of paying for land that they considered already theirs. On the one hand, they faced a variety of obligations. But, on the other, they could not be evicted. Therefore, they were highly disincentivized to work for their former master. And under the new terms, their former master could not *force* them to work. Resistance, either passive or overt, was a form of agency.

Conversely, while the freed people at Palmyra Plantation did not have land tenure, they did have freedom of movement. This had both salutary and negative effects. In a place and time in which plantation owners needed laborers, the freed people's mobility was an advantage during the crucial negotiating period on the eve of the planting season. However, without the guarantee of land tenure, the freed people had to find work in order to survive. They could not hold out forever. Therefore, they displayed what could be called pragmatic agency. They negotiated as best they could for a fair wage with Lovell, and they worked hard. Unlike Yazykov, who did not have to think about labor compensation as long as the freed peasants were obligated to him, Lovell compensated his hired hands. Unlike their Russian counterparts, who faced what was in fact an obligatory status in perpetuity, the freed people at Palmyra Plantation were prepared to commit to short work stints, as epitomized by seasonal work contracts. Thus, each set of freed people took advantage of the favorable aspects of their particular situation where the means of survival and the realities of emancipation intersected. Choices were made out of the need to act, as well as the ability to act.

At the heart of this story is a consideration of how emancipation affected each demesne's raison d'être. Because Yazykovo Selo and Palmyra Plantation were exceptional in a number of ways in relation to the typical profile of demesnes in each region, their respective stories complicate standard narratives. This comparison illustrates that labor, both as a sought commodity and in its performance, is an important theme in the emancipation context, irrespective of place and time. And it brings into sharper focus the process of liberation and the meaning of freedom in each society at the time.

Contextual Realities at Yazykovo Selo

The land on which Yazykovo Selo stood was gifted to a family ancestor in the 17th century as part of an expansionist policy by the tsar. Yazykovo's serfs could trace their family roots back to this time. Continuity and tradition were fully entrenched by 1861. Seasonal crops and agricultural production ran their typical course. But the inhabitants could not rely solely on an agricultural economy. The landscape was dotted with forests, craggy hills, and bluffs overlooking the Volga River, and it was marked by river estuaries. Its soil was sandy and primarily composed of clay. The climate produced seasonally extreme temperatures, and droughts were frequent since rainfall was irregular. Deposition of topsoil was an outcome of the frequent wind that blew west from Central Asia. Thus, the demesne's inhabitants traded supplies and produce with other estates in the region. The peasants augmented their subsistence by selling produce and crafted products at local markets. One example of the latter was a lucrative trade in cat pelts.[11] Thus, the demesne was at once the Yazykov family nest and a peasant village community.

Beginning in the mid–19th century, a number of changes ensued at Yazykovo Selo. In 1851, Vasili Yazykov retired from the military when he inherited the estate upon his father's death. That same year he married his wife, Praskovia. At this point the demesne was registered with 430 souls and 5,379 *desiatiny*. Yazykov immediately mortgaged it, in order to draw more credit from the State Loan Bank.[12] Founded in 1786, the bank was set up primarily for serf owners. Loans were secured not by the value of the land but by the number of serfs a landlord claimed, and the loan was typically for terms of 28 or 33 years. In the post-emancipation period, however, the state policy of providing long-term credit to noblemen was eclipsed when the decision was made to redirect state funds toward the financing of railroads and steam navigation.[13] Thirty years later, the expiration of Vasili Yazykov's loan in the late 1870s or early 1880s must have played a role in his decision to sell the factory to Stepanov in 1877 and the remainder of the estate to him in 1881.

On the one hand, although vibrant market economies existed throughout Imperial Russia, it would be incorrect to describe its economic system as similar to the liberal, free market economy that developed in the United States. On the other hand, similar to the United States when, for example, the federal and state governments spearheaded public works projects such as highways, canals, and railroads in the early 19th century, the Russian autocracy initiated economic development and strategies, and specialization was often regional. In anticipation of requisitions for military uniforms, the government initiated a development in which a number of wool factories were built on estates in Simbirsk Province. In 1852, a wool factory was built at Yazykovo Selo, and Vasili Yazykov signed a lucrative agreement with the Treasury to produce uniforms for the military.[14] On the eve of the Crimean War, production had spiked across Simbirsk Province. Now wool production represented 55 percent of the province's industry.[15]

By the end of the Crimean War in 1856, the factory at Yazykovo Selo must have been in relatively good shape, since government requisitions had been certain and serf labor guaranteed production. It was profitable only to the extent that it was part of the economic system's structure. Vasili Yazykov neither paid wages nor had a large overhead expense associated with operations. He certainly did not have to negotiate any terms in labor contracting. The factory buildings were quickly constructed and minimally outfitted. Because of the serf labor, low overhead, and the factory's raison d'être, there was no need to retain capital for further investment.

It can be argued that the emergence of wool factories in the Middle Volga region was an example of a tsar-vassal relationship, in which the former commanded and rewarded service and the latter complied. In fact, it was not part of the typical provincial noble landlord's *mentalité* in the mid–19th century to imagine investing in and profiting from an industrial enterprise. To be sure, there were exceptions. But the economic system in place with respect to the wool factories in the province consisted of requisitions emanating from the Treasury, with the latter paying the landlord up front. Indeed, John LeDonne has described the relationship between the noblemen and the government as

> less a public commitment to private individuals to pay a definite sum for the delivery of goods than a mutual agreement between members of the apparatus and the political infrastructure and even an internal arrangement among members of the apparatus.[16]

Although there is currently a body of scholarship on Imperial Russia that emphasizes greater upward mobility, more limited political and economic control and direction on the part of the state, and the presence of far more individualistic commercial and entrepreneurial drive, local sources with respect to the regional characteristics in

Simbirsk Province indicate that merchants could not compete with estate landlords who were privileged by government policy.[17] Merchants had to pay wages and did not receive government contracts. As a result, over time merchants devised strategies to not only insert themselves into the system but also constitute vital parts of it. The most common of these tactics was in the trader profession, with the merchant being the point person between camel and/or sheep herders to the south and southeast and the nobles and/or their estate/factory managers in the province. In fact, it was at this point in the system that real profits could be made. Thus, merchants in the Middle Volga region were Asiatic in their geographic orientation and trade practices, and, while they used goods as collateral, they also had cash.[18]

After the Crimean War, many factories closed in Simbirsk Province because of the decline in government requisitions. Among those that remained, a trend emerged whereby landlords rented them out to those very merchants who had been excluded from the formal system. This is what Vasili Yazykov's brother, Alexander, did at his estate, Undory.[19] It was not uncommon for merchants to graft the system and/or "fail" to right an enterprise whose sole purpose was to comply with central command requisitions. They were more comfortable operating in their economic niche. The factories that merchants had been hired to manage were not *their* investments, and the noblemen frequently failed to pay them due to (1) the unavailability of hard currency; (2) a lack of money altogether; (3) ambivalence; or (4) any combination of these factors. In addition, even in managerial positions, the merchants had no clout to force serfs to work.[20]

On the eve of emancipation, Vasili Yazykov produced a detailed inventory of his wool factory. He noted that it was fully outfitted and in good working order, with 300 workers registered there. Although he made no note of their gender or ages, this number is significant because in 1862, 160 factory laborers were listed in the Statutory Charter.[21] Also, Yazykov now contracted with a merchant by the name of Mangushev to manage the wool factory for a two-year period, from September 1860 to September 1862. On the one hand, he was doing what many noblemen had already begun to do. On the other, it is plausible to infer that this was a preemptive move since Yazykov, as both a district marshal of the nobility and a member of one of the provincial committees on emancipation, had received a heads-up about what was to come. That is, he would no longer have direct control over his former serfs and therefore acted to "get ahead" of history.[22]

Mangushev's pedigree made him the perfect managerial candidate. He was a member of the third guild, he was from the province's southern port district of Sengilei, and he was a Tatar.[23] In the Middle Volga area, while first and second guilds were mostly composed of noblemen, the third was dominated by that region's subset of minorities—Tatars (Muslim) and Mordvins and Chuvashi (Russian Orthodox, but often a syncretization of Christianity and traditional ethnic religions). While it would be fair to say that members of the first and second guilds were neither structurally integrated in nor traditionally linked to a fully functioning economic market separate from the political system, the third guild's membership could be fluid and vulnerable to the vagaries of both the economy and autocratic power. However, it was distinguished for its integration into a fully thriving, informal economy, both horizontally and vertically. Many third guild merchants were enterprising, versatile, experienced, and well connected. They frequently managed more than one enterprise and most often were point people in a chain of trade (for example, as retail buyers and sellers in the markets). They had a number of sources of income, and they were notorious for their shrewd business sense. Because Russia's industrial development was marked by regional specialization, the merchants of the Middle Volga area, like their counterparts in other regions, were both insular and tied by alliance networks.[24] Tatars were urban and literate, and, because they were not Russian, they had never been enserfed.[25] As it would play out, Yazykov would expect maximum results from Mangushev, who had minimum authority. As long as the factory workers had land tenure and, after emancipation, the commune's authority, they were not bound to be obedient to Mangushev.

As for Yazykovo Selo's factory workers, before 1861 they were generally like those on most other estate factories in Simbirsk Province: they were on *barshchina* labor, with three days per week of seigneurial labor. Typically, the estate factory labor pool was endogenous and hereditary, and it was devoid of an institutional artisanal/apprenticeship profile. By the Crimean War, a new system had evolved, whereby the laborer worked full time and came to live in barracks attached to the factory. They were no longer field workers.[26] It is reasonable to infer that this system developed at Yazykovo Selo, since a workers' barracks was itemized in the bill of sale when Stepanov bought the factory in 1877.

Historians have grappled with understanding the consciousness of these rural laborers. Lenin and subsequent Soviet analysts asserted that they were rural proletarians who, although still residing in the countryside, shed their peasant *mentalité* and village roots, acquiring instead an industrial working-class consciousness whose lifestyle and expectations were shaped by the factory. Many Western scholars have held that they were "mere peasants in the factory," who were far less concerned with labor organization than with subsistence, and whose work stoppages and idleness were just variations of peasant disturbances (*volneniia*).[27] In fact, it was not an "either/or" profile, since factory and field work were *integrated* on an estate. Therefore, whether the village peasant worked in the estate factory or field, it was the village commune that was the most significant determinant of individual behavior and consciousness. The fact that the emancipation legislation relocated the noble landlord's authority to the commune is significant, since the individual peasant was not emancipated from authority per se. Indeed, Boris Mironov has argued that the emancipation legislation actually strengthened both the commune and the peasant *mentalité*.[28] This background helps us understand both their refusal to sign the Statutory Charter and their outright resistance masquerading as ambivalence with respect to labor in the post-emancipation period.

Contextual Realities at Palmyra Plantation

John Quitman acquired his claim to Palmyra Plantation in 1824, when he married his wife, Eliza Turner, a daughter of one of Mississippi's most prestigious families. With hopes of fully owning one of the "finest estates" on the Mississippi River, he bought out Eliza's siblings' shares of the plantation in 1842 for $200,000, which included "230 slaves and ... 60 head of cattle."[29] In addition to its lucrative cash crops, Palmyra was abundant in wooded areas, and Quitman sold processed timber to river steamers from the plantation's own river landing. Palmyra was also an integral part of the Quitman web of plantations, whereby products, tools, supplies, and slaves were exchanged, swapped, and moved around according to need.[30] Tables 6.1 and 6.2 contain a number of categories illustrating that Palmyra was a significant economic player before the war.

Between his military, political, and business interests, John Quitman was in constant motion. A number of overseers managed the demesne over the years. It seems most of these were "semiliterates," to whom Quitman "accorded little respect." His letters indicate that they were a constant source of stress and disappointment. By contrast, his son-in-law William Storrow Lovell would hire an overseer of sorts after the war with whom he was well pleased, and who was with him for the duration of the period under study.

With respect to his slaves, Quitman was a paternalistic master. As an absentee planter, his letters included frequent pleas to Eliza to be patient, permissive, and kind to the slaves. He fired an overseer in 1853 for being too "severe" with them. The slaves' quarters consisted of a main path behind the big house, which was "neatly lined" with "whitewashed" homes. Evidently, they had gardens and chicken coops, since Quitman frequently purchased fowl and other products from them. A number of individuals were with the Quitman/Lovell family for many years, including long before emancipation and afterward as free people. A few Quitman descendants left provisions for the former slaves in their wills. This is an important distinction from Vasili Yazykov, who not only did no such thing but also did not even mention his own children in his will. (This is not surprising since he died penniless, with his marriage in shambles.)

Quitman's paternalism was a quintessential characteristic of the planter class during the antebellum period. Its defining attributes included an emotional attachment to and concern for the well-being of one's slaves. It meant responsibilities and duties toward dependents, both biological family members and slaves. Paternalism was a way of perceiving relationships, as well as a particular outlook or worldview. Thus, the master sought and maintained order, possessed a sense of purpose, and would exercise an understated as well as stated authority.

Likewise, paternalism was found in the master-serf relationship in Russia. Sources on the Yazykov family and other noble families in Simbirsk Province cite and describe numerous examples of paternalistic behavior, the cornerstones of which can be summarized as a combination of an emotional connection between the master and serfs; a concern on the part of the master about the management of the estate and the well-being of his/her serfs; participation in a variety of charitable organizations; and humanitarian benevolence. For example, Vasili Yazykov's father and uncles (one of whom was the famed poet and close confidant of Alexander Pushkin, Nikolai Yazykov) shared a beloved nanny, Domna Kushnikova. She was like a nurturing mother to them, instilling in the boys a love of and appreciation for the pantheistic and animistic qualities found in nature. In addition, an account from an inhabitant at Undory indicates that after a devastating fire in the village in 1851, the master, Alexander, and mistress, Alexandra, had the homes rebuilt at their own expense. After another fire burned down the entire wool factory located there in 1855, Alexander rebuilt it with a loan from the nobility of Simbirsk. And when yet another fire devastated a number of homes in 1865, Alexandra nursed those who had suffered severe burns around the clock for days.[31] Here, and in the earlier reference to Quitman's request that his wife be kind to their slaves, we see small but significant signposts with respect to the role of the mistress on the demesne, the signature characteristics of which included the "household manageress" (*pomeshchitsa* or *khoziaika*) and "cult of domesticity" paradigms.[32]

Of course, the paternalism found among the American planter class and the noble serf owners in Russia did not mitigate the unequal relationship between the master and the slave or serf. Coercion, the threat of violence, obligations, and fear were always beneath the surface.[33] Eugene Genovese informs us that, rooted in European medieval chivalry, the paternalism of the planter class was a self-assigned code of Christian conduct that included duties, responsibilities, and humane treatment, but it also evinced a "prickly" kind of violence stemming from honor, which could instantly mutate into a feeling of "self-martyrdom." Unpacking this idea even more, James C. Scott has explained that paternalism is a form of "social climbing" and functions, ritually, as a kind of auto-ennoblement since it establishes power and prestige, in addition to eliciting loyalty from those in the "sponsor's debt" in the form of obligations and "labor (manpower)."[34] Although subalterns participated in the unspoken rules of paternalism, it does not mean that they wanted to be subordinated or agreed to the social inequality and power structures in play. It does mean, however, that they were navigating an entrenched cultural milieu in their lifeworld. It can also mean that, given the opportunity, they could and did exploit the arrangement to their benefit. For every encounter between the philanthropist and the recipient, there were potentially numerous intentions and machinations in play.

Although the freed Americans could well have had fondness for their former masters, the ease with which they fled once the traditional sources of authority were weakened when the war broke out both shocked the planter class and demonstrated that the ties that bound them together were weak.[35] The Quitman/Lovell family's slaves frequently ran away, and, when the war broke out, many fled from both Palmyra and the mansion in Natchez, Monmouth. Eventually some returned and became wage laborers, hired for a specific task or as help on a weekly or monthly basis. By the turn of the century, some even purchased a few plots of land at Monmouth from Quitman descendants. This fluidity contrasts sharply with the experience of the peasants of Yazykovo Selo, the majority of whom remained at the estate for the duration of the period under study and beyond.[36]

Although various members of the Quitman family may have had fond feelings for their slaves, they also exhibited stereotypical attitudes based on both their race and their condition.[37] On the one hand, this situation was no different from how the elites viewed the serfs on estates like Yazykovo Selo. Shared beliefs in each society viewed the subaltern groups as simple, naturally lazy, childlike, and careless.[38] On the other hand, the racial component as well as their ancestral origin meant that the slaves at Palmyra had an experience distinct from that of their Russian counterparts. Based on tradition, as well as the fact that there was an idea embedded in the emancipation legislation that former serfs were entitled to land allotments on site, the peasants could lay claim to the land at Yazykovo Selo. True, the freed people in the American South did argue that because they had tilled the soil, they were entitled to land earmarks. But both the specter and the reality of being sold away from the plantation during the days of slavery meant that feelings of attachment to the actual land where they had lived and worked as slaves were more nuanced. They may well have had feelings of attachment to the demesne, but the former slaves appear to have shared with their American countrymen the values of freedom of movement, owning land, and earning a living based on one's labor. In fact, if having one's homestead, determining one's own labor and production, and being independent from any authority was the ultimate statement of

American freedom, then this was not very different from the Russian peasants' idea of freedom. It is true that while peasants could and did have feelings of attachment to land and place, running away (whether off to Siberia or down the Volga) was the ultimate statement of freedom.[39]

During the Home Colony period on Davis Bend, the groundwork was laid for what free labor would look like in this region after the war. Ronald L.F. Davis has informed us that the U.S. Army played a key role in setting in motion the transition from slavery to sharecropping, therefore creating the guidelines for the freed people's treatment during and after the war. The Union forces put liberated/refugee slaves to work in gangs in the cotton fields for subsistence wages and rations. In addition, this was a way to raise money to offset overall war spending. They also sought to "educate" the freed people about the binding nature of the "contract," as well as "good and faithful" labor. Officials viewed wages as the perfect incentive, as they could be garnished for disobedience, insolence, and time lost to illness or foot dragging. Furthermore, they could be paid in set portions, on a monthly basis, thereby enabling employers to withhold the incentive until the job was complete. And, it was believed, wages built into a labor contract had the salutary effect of "instructing" the freed people on how to negotiate. Independence, not charity, was the goal.

Due to the lack of cash in the agrarian, war-torn South, the need to secure labor for the entire season, and widespread exploitation of the freed people (by both Northern lessees and Southern planters), Union officials came to embrace and promote annual/seasonal contracting, which evolved into a variety of forms. These included (both verbal and, ideally, written) contracting for monthly wages, wages plus board, tenancy (or rent) in exchange for work (with the laborer keeping all or part of his/her produce), and full sharecropping—with the "cropper's" share (rather than income) being the form of payment, or the cropper's profit being that which remained after he/she handed over the crop amount to the landowner for tenancy and land rent. Falling cotton prices meant that both planters/managers and the freed people came to prefer one form of sharecropping over wages (as the drop in cotton prices depressed wages).[40] Thus, the adjustments to the emancipation mandates with respect to work meant that, generally, whereas the freed serfs ignored these directives because they were able to, the former slaves complied with them because they needed to.

Economic Realities in the Post-Emancipation Era

Appreciating the contextual economic realities where each demesne was located is crucial for understanding what played out after emancipation in each place. First a note about sources and their interpretation: Unlike the American case, where tax and census documentation and diaries and plantation records exist that provide crucial information, gauging the relationship of Yazykovo Selo to the Russian national economy is tricky. As Carol Leonard has explained, because the first Agricultural Census in Russia occurred in 1881, it is difficult to ascertain and measure with precision the economic situation anywhere in Russia between 1861 and 1881. Quoting a Russian bureaucrat writing in 1869, Leonard noted, "The amount of land under crops is unknown; exacting and well defined household surveys do not exist ... therefore, the evidence collected by committees for the public supply of food can be accepted only with extreme caution."

Furthermore, one of a number of historians who have addressed the lack of thorough records on agricultural and industrial production and trade during this period, Arcadius Kahan, has stressed that up to the revolution in 1905, whatever political or economic decisions the Russian government made, it went without saying that the agricultural sector was the source of all funding. Beyond this, it is impossible to discern a consistent pattern associated with government agricultural policies.[41]

However, there are some things that we do know. For example, the end of the Crimean War in 1856 signaled a drop in wool requisitions. Because wool factories like the one at Yazykovo Selo depended on government requisitions, this decline obviously impacted production. Requisitions did not begin to rise again until the eve of the Russo-Turkish War (1877–1878). This event coincided with Vasili's sale of the factory to Stepanov.[42]

Another reality that impacted the economic outlook after 1861 was the fact that emancipation signaled an end to unfree labor. Historiography has stressed that the inability of landowners to continue to rely on unfree labor after emancipation explains the "declension" of the Russian estate in the post-emancipation period.[43] However, while ten factories in Simbirsk Province closed in 1861, the one at Yazykovo Selo remained open. Many estates had *barshchina* labor built into the mandatory obligations itemized in the Statutory Charter.[44] Moreover, because the *Regulations* mandated that *barshchina* obligations be no more than 40 days per year, this may further explain the apparent stagnation of production and productivity at Yazykovo Selo relative to the period before emancipation. In addition, although the peasants had the right after 1863 to request that *barshchina* be converted to *obrok*, the landlord also had the right to renew the former every three years, indefinitely. This point helps us understand why Vasili Yazykov's former serfs remained severely limited on *barshchina* until 1881, the year he sold the estate to Stepanov.[45] It also demonstrates the technicality that Vasili had a legal right to his former serfs' labor, which amounted to between 30 and 40 days per year, and that he was never required to even consider wages or any other form of incentives. His "former people" were obligated to *him*. Despite this situation, many historians have explained that Russian peasants, both *before* emancipation and as "temporarily obligated" people *afterward*, were far more "productive" under *obrok*.[46] Moreover, if they were "temporarily obligated," peasants could not "seek" employment, as the freed Americans could (at least in theory), since they were attached to the demesne, bound by their obligations there, and, especially, had to get permission from the commune if they wanted to leave. Their condition made it difficult (without securing a pass) to seek work outside of that to which they were assigned.[47]

On the one hand, all this background helps us understand the "stagnation at the estate" theory. On the other hand, because the former serfs were no longer bound to their former master's authority, emancipation provided the means with which they *could* resist working, in the form of either work stoppages or even noncompliance. These are not mutually exclusive explanations. Moreover, and as the next chapter will show, emancipation triggered a marked rise in economic activities other than agricultural production.

Conversely, despite the controls that the Black Codes in Mississippi attempted to place on the freed people, although William Storrow Lovell was determined to resuscitate Palmyra Plantation and may well have *felt* entitled to the freed people's labor and/or could not conceive of looking to any group of people to work the plantation other than former slaves, the American emancipation legislation neither enshrined nor implied the plantation managers' claim to this labor. In fact, Lovell initially turned to the norms set forth after March 1865 by the Freedmen's Bureau—namely, contract wage labor.

Furthermore, even though the Black Codes were quickly countermanded by federal authorities, policymakers in Washington, D.C., never intended for the lucrative plantation system in the American South to be disrupted. Indeed, a de facto policy of "containment" was employed. For example, Adjutant General Lorenzo Thomas, who had been stationed in the Mississippi River valley region since 1863 and was in charge of the freed people there, explained, "You cannot send them North. You all know the prejudices of the Northern people against receiving large numbers of the colored race … [the plantations in the Mississippi River valley] are the places for those freedmen where they can be self-sustaining and self-supporting." And, obviously concerned about the international cotton market and the impact an interruption in production would have on the textile industry, the British minister to the United States, Sir Frederick Bruce, conveyed the hope to officials in Washington, D.C., that "measures are being taken to force the Negroes to work."[48]

Other realities, both national and international, proved that there was uncertainty about Russia's general economic picture in the 1860s. It is reasonable to assume that because of its expansive agricultural economy, Russia had the potential in the post-emancipation period to become a powerhouse in terms of grain exports to Europe and beyond. But this did not happen because of the nearly total absence of infrastructure such as a streamlined financial system and efficient transportation, which are hallmarks of economic modernization. In fact, the United States came to enjoy a boom in agricultural exports to Europe, filling the void that Russia left open. Russia's decline in agricultural exports was proportional to America's increase.[49]

Grappling with the impact of emancipation on economic productivity, Peter Gatrell has asserted that the first several years after 1861 present a "disturbed picture," especially when compared with the real "take-off" period (roughly 1880–1910). "Industry was thrown into confusion by the emancipation of unfree labor…. Capital investment and exports also behaved disappointingly," all "reflecting uncertainties." Above all, Daniel Field has made a critical contribution to understanding Russia and its economy in the immediate post-emancipation experience. It is worth quoting him at length:

> The abolition of serfdom regulated and systematized more than it changed…. Because the reform deliberately perpetuated so many of the social and economic characteristics of serfdom, it may be that the regime was indulging in wishful thinking or placing hopes in the power of words, supposing that great benefits must accrue simply because it had found the courage to declare that serfdom … was abolished…. The [emancipation legislation] could not and did not provide a great, immediate stimulus to economic development. The tsar and his advisers feared chaos more than they wanted progress. So the reform produced an imposed stability.[50]

The absence of credit and cash in the economy adversely impacted production on Russian estates in the post-emancipation period. The Treasury relocated funds to railroad and steamer development and away from credit available to the nobility. Ironically, one of the purposes of this shift in policy was to aid both industrial and agricultural production on rural estates, since railroads would greatly assist the delivery of products to markets.[51] In addition, there was a general lack of cash in circulation.[52] These problems with capital availability made it difficult for an estate manager to maintain (let alone modernize) a demesne in the post-emancipation period.

Dmitri Murashov has detailed the logistical complications associated with operating a demesne *after* emancipation but *before* the real "take-off" period of economic modernization in Russia, after 1881. Already in debt before emancipation, noble landowners were hamstrung by the unavailability of credit afterward. The lack of circulating cash was problematic for those former serfs such as house servants, cooks, doormen, butlers, gardeners, and the like. As part of the category of non-field workers, they were not entitled to land. Therefore, many disappeared from estate operation since noblemen could not, or would not, pay them wages. In addition, noblemen did not adjust their extravagant lifestyles, but rather continued to look for ways to borrow both money and time. In 1864, 75 percent of Simbirsk Province's estates had been remortgaged, a 25 percent increase over 1855.[53] On the estates where there were factories, all were in decline—with the exception of vodka plants. Landowners were not accustomed to entrepreneurialism (in the Western meaning of the word). They were risk averse and relied on bureaucratic measures. Nor could they imagine challenging the peasants' age-old methods of tilling the land. It appears that in the post-emancipation period the nobility was caught between its lack of concern for costs and expenses and the nascent economic system, which could not accommodate formal economic initiative.

As for the peasants, in February 1861, they first faced the Statutory Charter, which imposed land allotments. Until a redemption payment schedule was established, the peasants were temporarily obligated. But the peasants were not inclined to reach an agreement for a number of reasons: They considered the arrangement fundamentally unjust, if not a devious trick to cheat them out of their land, which they considered rightfully theirs. On top of that, they knew they could not possibly pay for it. In addition, now that they had to supply and use their own materials, the peasants prioritized their own garden plots over work for their former masters on the land allotments. Furthermore, there was not just one sowing season per year. In Russia, the agricultural year consisted of several sowing and harvesting seasons depending on the crop being planted, such as barley (spring), wheat (summer), or beets and cabbage (fall). All this said, it is hardly surprising that they were, at best, ambivalent with respect to their obligations (and outright hostile at worst). Indeed, the passive tactic of work slowdown was a classic form of everyday resistance for peasants.[54]

Murashov explains that many Russians believed that the old order was over, but a new economic era in which money would be a formal, common denominator in an impersonal cash and credit system had not yet arrived. In the meantime, the 1860s was a period of agricultural barrenness. Even where the soil was good and a harvest was produced, getting it to market was difficult and uncertain. Mechanized threshers and fanners had made their appearance but were not always available, and the technical expertise to operate and repair them was lacking. Railroad improvements were anticipated, but they only became a reality by the late 1870s. Thus, rather than doing nothing, noble landowners began renting and selling estates to merchants, as Vasili did.[55] In addition, and as the next chapter will show, peasants in Simbirsk Province increasingly participated in a shadow economy of sorts, with diversification in terms of cottage industries, trade, and marketing.

In general, a comparison can be made between the economies of the American South and Russia. Both were largely rural and, at best, just on the cusp of modernization. Like the Middle Volga River region, the Mississippi River delta area seemed to be locked in time, trapped in the inertia of its past, and devoid of access to modern methods such as mechanization, scientific techniques, and fertilizers, all of which are geared toward maximizing efficiency and returns. Similar to Murashov's study, which details the nuances and particularities associated with the logistical difficulties of modernization in the Middle Volga region, Stephen Cresswell has explained the economic realities in Mississippi in the second half of the 19th century. On the eve of the Civil War, when Mississippi plantations were essentially self-supporting, intricately connected to the economic infrastructure assisting cotton, benefiting from slave labor, and practicing some diversification (such as corn crops, cattle, and the like), the state, as a producer of 1.2 million bales of cotton, was first in the nation in 1860. Notwithstanding the marked drop in the price of cotton over the course of the post-emancipation period (see table 6.3), Mississippi remained stalwart, producing 960,000 bales in 1880.[56]

The economic "adjustment" period in the Mississippi River delta region involved a number of dynamics. Cash and credit were in short supply.[57] When the war ended, the region was almost devoid of liquid assets. The paper currency used locally during the war was worthless. "Railroad notes" and "cotton money," which Mississippi had issued during the war, were also useless. While merchants and planters in river counties had access to Union greenbacks, these were not reliably available everywhere. Gold and silver specie had been driven out by the war. Those people who hoarded money during the war continued to cling to it amid the economic uncertainties. While both new railroad and cotton notes were authorized for redemption by the legislature throughout the period of Reconstruction, the problem was a matter of establishing a reliable, accessible, and stable currency, which the notes were not. While the nation's banking system had been overhauled during the war, it was not integrated into the yet-to-be-reconstructed states, such as Mississippi.

Similar to the Russian government's policy of prioritizing the railroads, the United States not only moved to rebuild what had been started before and damaged by the war but also expanded track laying for the purposes of aiding trade. Indeed, while the federal government financed much of the construction of new lines, private firms (including factors in New Orleans, New York, and abroad) also invested in railroad development. Still, there was a gap between enthusiasm and results. With only 120 miles of new railroad track opened in Mississippi by 1875, the river and its tributaries continued to be the main mode of transportation, especially for cotton.[58]

In addition, by 1880 there was little (if any) mechanization. For example, while planters may well have been drawn to the idea of a mechanized cotton harvester, which was developed as early as 1850, it remained a rarity until the 1940s. But even if it had been readily available, cash and credit were difficult to come by. And even if a planter could secure a loan to purchase a harvester, taking this step would have been a gamble he would have been hard pressed to make given the realities of planting: in this region, floods and the army worm could turn a good crop into an unmitigated disaster overnight. Furthermore, even if a planter had purchased one of the earliest models, the harvester would still have needed to have been pulled by draft animals since tractors were in short supply. These examples illustrate the many loose links in the chain of modernization. "[F]rom Appomattox to the Great Depression, cotton culture" remained "fixed in time."[59] All this said, the purpose here is not to characterize both the Mississippi River delta and the Middle Volga River regions as "backward." Rather, it is to explain the realities of their respective, historical-economic contexts.

The Personality of Each Demesne

Discussing each demesne's raison d'être—its purpose, function, and orientation—is instructive for understanding outcomes. As has been explained, most (if not all) Russian estates, and certainly the Yazykov properties in Simbirsk Province, originated as "gifts" made to the nobility by the tsar. In the Yazykov family's case in the 17th century, this gift was bestowed for the purposes of rewarding service and ensuring it for the future, as well as expanding Russia's territory via anchoring populations of loyal subjects to the land. While it is true that in the first half of the 19th century, during the early American Republic, waves of migrants (often poor) traveled to the southwest frontier, thus effectively settling territory that either had already been earmarked by the U.S. government or would soon be, they were clearly claiming land for the purposes of creating identity, securing socio-economic upward mobility, and participating in and expressing their interpretation of individual freedom that the revolution set in motion.[60] Insofar as he was a man who came from nothing, migrated to Natchez, married into "nabob" culture, and blended the management of extensive properties with local and national political participation, Palmyra Plantation's patriarch, John Quitman, was a perfect example of the phenomenon of migrating westward in order to self-improve, both socially and financially.

Regardless of the fact that demesnes in Russia and the United States were rural, small communities, with similar modes of social organization, Yazykovo Selo and Palmyra Plantation were fundamentally different, and certainly so after emancipation. The latter was, in and of itself, a unit specializing in cotton production and intricately connected to the regional and larger market grid supporting that lucrative cash crop. Before emancipation, Yazykovo Selo was a self-contained, semi-closed community, largely determined by and dependent on both a distant tsarist policy and the whims of its landlord. Moreover, while Yazykovo Selo comprised peasant households that were the units of production, the agricultural way of life was not a business geared toward profit, but rather subsistence and tradition.[61] This is not to suggest, however, that the estate's inhabitants did not venture beyond its perimeter. They regularly participated in local and regional trade, fairs, markets, and celebrations. Especially after emancipation, the latter phenomena intensified, with peasants increasingly participating in an even greater degree of economic diversification in cottage industries and market activities.

Even though Yazykovo Selo had a wool factory and Palmyra had its own cotton gin, the economic arrangement at the former was generally typical of the norm in Russia: an integrated industrial/agricultural complex in a rural context that, by design, was oriented toward the maintenance of the status quo rather than profit, where the labor could be used interchangeably. This situation is contrasted with a plantation like Palmyra, which was an agricultural enterprise in a rural context. To the extent that there were a variety of jobs within the entire process of cotton production, the labor was diversified. But the plantation was profit oriented toward (and integrated within) a regional and national cotton economy. Finally, whereas Palmyra was essentially self-supporting, with a variety of crops, livestock, and gardens, Yazykovo Selo's inhabitants depended on other Yazykov properties for sustenance.[62] The key correspondences here are *diversification* for the Russian example and *specialization* for the American one.[63] In the post-emancipation period, both Russian and American legislation pertaining to the freed people appears to have *reinforced* those distinctions between Yazykovo

Selo and Palmyra Plantation. After emancipation, while Palmyra continued as a capitalist enterprise with a community composed of a labor force, Yazykovo Selo's characteristic feature continued to be the peasant village community, which was bound together by history, tradition, habits, mores, beliefs, and work.

Mentalities, Consciousness, Agency

The interpretive tool of *mentalité* can be tricky. In making generalizations about one group or another, the historian can do violence to history by implying that they exist in a timeless, homogeneous state with rigid outlooks, beliefs, and thought. However, culture matters. If the historian carefully delineates common beliefs and perspectives rooted in historical experiences and cultural traditions, understanding can be gleaned. Indeed, shared experiences foster shared perspectives, interpretations, and worldviews.[64]

Regarding the patriarchs at each demesne in this study, during the pre-emancipation period Yazykov and Quitman exhibited paternalistic characteristics and habits with respect to their "people." In the post-emancipation period, however, while the impulses of formal political participation and paternalism at Palmyra may well have disappeared, these traditions persisted in some ways at Yazykovo Selo. Although after emancipation there was an element of fluidity and greater possibility for upward mobility in Russian society, one's station in life could also be relatively rigid. Patron-client practices (if not paternalism) and service were part and parcel of the nobility's profile.[65] Whereas William Storrow Lovell's ambition was to manage a plantation, Vasili Yazykov was neither "programmed" for nor interested in "developing" or "modernizing" Yazykovo Selo. Indeed, Seymour Becker has explained that state service, and not land, was the supreme orientation of the Russian nobility.[66]

In addition, it is worth considering that the "mobility versus immobility" theme in this comparative study played a role in perpetuating rather than suppressing paternalism. That is, whereas the peasant village community and Yazykov's presence there remained, at Palmyra, the constant turnover of laborers weakened, if not broke, a paternalistic impulse on the part of the landlord. (Lovell's Northern roots may also have played a part in this development.) Despite the earlier observation about Lovell family members remembering some of their former "people" in their wills while Yazykov did not, embedded in this analysis is a consideration of the potential conflict between paternalism and "modernization," for paternalism appears to be more entrenched in societies where the social, class, or estate system is more rigid and where there is less in- and out-migration.[67]

A contrast between the Russian peasants and their American counterparts is also instructive. On the one hand, it can be useful to discuss Russian society in terms of its estate structure, which can be loosely compared to the social stratification in the antebellum South. On the other hand, while Imperial Russia can be described roughly as one great demesne with the tsar as its landlord, at the local level Russia comprised villages that were essentially semi-autonomous, self-contained entities, where each individual peasant was subordinated to the power and peer pressure of the community.[68] Historians continue to debate whether the Russian emancipation legislation reinforced this arrangement, which, the argument goes, repressed or arrested individual initiative.

As has been pointed out several times in this study, the relocation of the nobleman's authority over his/her former "people" to the village commune (as well as the fact that the emancipation legislation mandated the collective nature of peasant obligations, allotments, and taxes) implies that individualism and initiative would have been suppressed by these bodies. After all, if all are responsible, no single individual is; if one does not work, why would the others, especially when they could be neither evicted from their homes nor dispossessed of their garden plots?[69] While these points may well be true, the Russian peasant, given the opportunity, was the ultimate individualist. Indeed, the Russian peasant was an anarchist—not in the theoretical sense, but rather in the practical one (that is, someone who rejects any form of coercion and authority, instead desiring complete autonomy). In fact, if we consider the long arc of the history of the Russian peasant, the "communal" aspects of his/her existence were grafted onto the society either through edicts or by force (or both). In this regard, we need look no further to find what freedom meant to the Russian peasant: to be free from all authority and constraints. It was not that the peasant objected to work. The issue was working for another.[70]

While the slave system on American plantations may well have included both formal and informal hierarchies of authority (such as gang leaders or drivers in the field for the former category, and a rank or a pecking order because of age, occupation, gender, or association with the master class for the latter), as well as tightly knit communities, the freed people had limited or no experience with a formal, structural, institutional, authoritarian construct of intra-social organization such as that grafted onto the Russian demesne in the post-emancipation period, nor with one that was so closely contained. Although the American freed people had strong ties of kinship and solidarity to their brethren, historians have stressed that two of the most significant ways they expressed their freedom after emancipation were their mobility (when, for example, they searched for lost relatives and/or sought to establish nuclear families) and their desire to set up living arrangements that were dissimilar to those during the days of slavery. (Often the physical and social cohesiveness of the slave community disappeared as the houses in the "quarters" were dismantled and relocated as dispersed, individual tenant homes.) Indeed, there was great mobility to and from Palmyra Plantation during and after the war. After the Quitman/Lovell recovery, the demesne witnessed a steady injection of hired hands every year, for years.

Emancipation also led to a strong "separatist" impulse among the American freed people in that they preferred to live in communities set well apart from the plantation, composed of their own churches, schools, stores, and the like.[71] On the one hand, insofar as the American freed people sought mobility in search of both loved ones and work, emancipation weakened community cohesiveness. On the other hand, to the extent that, in their desire to seek distance from the authorities and whites in general, the freed people sought to craft their own communities on their own terms, emancipation strengthened community cohesiveness. Above all, the freed people possessed a consciousness in which they identified with each other on a fundamental level because of their shared race, history of being enslaved, and African heritage.[72] The town of Mound Bayou, Mississippi, offers a perfect illustration. It was founded in 1887 by many former slaves who had been permanent residents on Davis Bend during both the pre- and the post-emancipation periods. To this day Mound Bayou has approximately 1,500 inhabitants who are direct descendants.[73]

As for Palmyra in the post-emancipation period, a small subgroup of freed people who had lived there as slaves continued to do so after the war. But it also witnessed an annual turnover of laborers who were hired by Lovell from labor factors (or agents) in New Orleans on the eve of each planting season's commencement. Although it is true that, like all Russian peasants, the freed people at Yazykovo Selo left the village to go to the local markets, bazaars, festivals, and the like, Palmyra had a far more fluid and mobile community of former slaves. And while it is correct that the seasonal hands at Palmyra were "attached" to the demesne for the term of their service, they did not necessarily consider the plantation their permanent home, as the annual turnover rate suggests. Of course, these characteristics impacted the nature of the "community" on each demesne—it being far more immutable at Yazykovo Selo than at Palmyra. This situation also helps explain the more uniform and consistent "neglect" of work for the former master at Yazykovo Selo.

* * *

This chapter has laid the groundwork for understanding what happened in the more protracted post-emancipation period at Yazykovo Selo and Palmyra Plantation regarding labor, management, production, and productivity, which is the focus of the next chapter. I comparatively analyzed the contextual realities in Russia and the American South and tracked them over time. I discussed the historical development and characteristics of the economic systems in each country and each region, as well as how these shaped the "personality" of each demesne. I also identified a number of precedents that took place regarding labor patterns and productivity, which influenced what would come after emancipation. And I pinpointed several shared characteristics and beliefs, clusters of themes, and connections that show important similarities.

Over time, each demesne's "founding" family had migrated to Simbirsk Province and Mississippi, respectively, and they integrated themselves in those regions' political/ economic systems and elite social echelon. They developed each demesne and acquired forms of unfree labor that were typical in each region. It is true that the raisons d'être of Yazykovo Selo and Palmyra Plantation differed in that the former was amalgamated in and depended on the command economy, while the latter was a cash crop, profit-driven enterprise integrated in a greater national cotton economy. In spite of each region's/demesne's distinctive characteristics (and the extent to which they were typically "Russian" or "Southern"), there were similarities between the two. Each was situated in a rural, agrarian context that, due to a variety of logistical and infrastructural issues and traditional realities, seemed "fixed in time" with respect to the coterminous modernization trends. "Place" in each region shaped each demesne's lifeworld. However, the overall "rural character" does not change one fundamental difference between the two: whereas economic development in Simbirsk Province fostered the integration of the wool factory and agricultural work, with integrated labor, at estates, in Mississippi plantations specialized in the production of cotton cash crops, albeit with a labor force that specialized in the diversified aspects of that industry.

I also comparatively identified aspects of *mentalités* and consciousness for each set of players in this story. Doing so helps us understand both Yazykov's and Lovell's motivations and actions, which will be scrutinized in the next chapter. And even though we understand that groups of people are made up of individuals, delineating the experiences and consciousness of the serfs and slaves (especially as they crossed the threshold of freedom) helps us understand both their interpretations of freedom and the actions that were to come. In short, all—both individuals and groups—acted in their own self-interest.

Before emancipation, each demesne's patriarch demonstrated elements of paternalism. As I suggested, the fact of emancipation in each country seemed to weaken the paternalist impulse, especially in the American South. With respect to this view, C. Vann Woodward once observed that emancipation triggered "a ... withdrawal of master and slave from obligations of the old allegiance: duties on the one side, responsibilities on the other," moving toward a more formal and impersonal relationship between employers and employees in a free market system. This was easier said than done, as Michael Wayne has explained, since both planter and freedman brought "attitudes to the marketplace that inhibit[ed] immediate ... change."[74] Indeed, this new relationship was a tenuous one, based on mutual dependency: the new planter counted on laborers to make the plantation viable, and the freed people depended on labor for sustenance. Vasili Yazykov did not have to think about and plan for the seasonal labor cycle every year as William Storrow Lovell did. Nor was he fixated on the problem of how to modernize his estate. However, as will be made clear, both patriarchs sought managers, the success of whom was mixed. And, as we will see, if Yazykov evidenced any vestiges of paternalism, it was in the context of his service ethic, compliance with tsarist edicts, and philanthropic activities.

With respect to the freed people, I touched on what was most important to them in terms of freedom. Suspicion of and distance from the authorities was important. And the dichotomy of mobility versus immobility had both salutary and adverse effects in the midst of liberation.

With respect to labor, elites in each country mapped out what labor should look like after emancipation, in either de jure or de facto manners. In fact, this vision proved to be difficult to implement, and it manifested as a series of fine-tunings and adjustments. It is this subject, as well as the tension between labor expectations and prescriptions, on the one hand, and the nature of compliance with them, on the other, that will be addressed in the next chapter.

6

Reaping Freedom

Management, Labor, and Productivity
in the Midst of Liberation

The overarching theme in the more protracted post-emancipation period has to do with labor. Who would work and who would not? Who would work for whom, and why or why not? How did Vasili Yazykov and William Storrow Lovell shape up as managers in the new conditions set in motion by emancipation? What happened to production and productivity at each demesne after emancipation, and why?

These specific questions have been addressed in generalized ways by many historians, typically as separate histories—some relating to the history of Russian emancipation of the serfs, and others to that of American emancipation of the slaves. One significant and recurring debate among historians within each of these separate histories takes place between those who emphasize "top-down" or state (or greater, more distant) power as the determinant of change and those who point to numerous examples of individual agency and contingency, nuance, fluidity, and exceptions to norms—in short, historians who focus on developments from the "bottom up." For example, utilizing a top-down but meticulously detailed analysis that presents the political economy as commanding, Nicolas Spulber persuasively makes the case in *Russia's Economic Transitions: From Late Tsarism to the New Millennium* (2003) that after 1861, in spite of the state's efforts to modernize, due to a multitude of complications, interconnected problems, entrenched formal and informal practices, and uneven development, Russia remained overwhelmingly backward in 1917.[1]

Whereas Spulber gauges Russia's development over time against other global regions (especially the West), in his opus *Empire of Cotton: A Global History* (2014), Sven Beckert's conceptual framework is explicitly global—the category of analysis being cotton capitalism—and it is a top-down analysis over a *longue durée*. He argues that slave labor originated in (and was violently established by) a global capitalism—or "war capitalism," as he calls it—before industrial capitalism arrived, the latter of which replaced the former after the American Civil War. Asserting that American emancipation actually sharpened and accelerated capitalism's insatiable drive for cotton, he explains:

> Just as slaves had revolutionized the cotton empire, emancipation forced cotton capitalists towards their own revolution—a frantic search for new ways to organize the cotton-growing labor of the world…. Throughout Europe and the United States, economic and political elites agreed that former slaves must continue to grow cotton…. Many "experts" feared that the freedpeople, as they had in the West Indies a generation earlier, would engage in subsistence agriculture.

Any other source of labor was unthinkable. Implicit in Beckert's analysis is that, although the American slaves were liberated, a new form of servitude replaced the old one.[2] Certainly, what has been discussed thus far in this study regarding developments and labor adjustments initiated at Palmyra Plantation appears to fit with the Beckert thesis.

Years ago, Charles E. Orser, Jr., surveyed what has become known as the squad system—that form of labor organization that evolved in the American South immediately after emancipation. Neither the gang labor that was one of the defining characteristics of cotton slavery nor that which would become fully entrenched by the turn of the century (namely, sharecropping), squad labor was indeed a "link between slavery and sharecropping." Orser defined its quintessential features: closely supervised laborers receiving a share of the crop; each squad being typically a small kinship group; and its members living not in the slave quarters of the old days, but rather in individual, dispersed tenant farm settlements on and around the plantation. It was a form of agricultural tenure. On the one hand, Orser's explanation of this significant reorganization of labor speaks to the Beckert thesis of cotton capitalism's stages, and adaptations and adjustments, so that the lucrative cotton industry would remain viable notwithstanding emancipation. On the other hand, Orser's rather textbook definition of its features was based, as he states, on a number of labor contracts and the archaeological remnants of dwellings that existed both before and after emancipation at one plantation (Millwood, in South Carolina).[3] In fact, William Storrow Lovell utilized such a variety of sources and forms of labor over the years at Palmyra Plantation that a strict definition of "squad labor" presents limitations in terms of understanding what actually played out in the more protracted post-emancipation period. In addition, such a specific definition does not allow for the plasticity and accommodating range of labor adjustments and compensationary methods that the squad system entailed. The period was one of nuanced adjustments and tinkerings in the system, as the former institutionalized source of labor was no longer available.

The work of Alessandro Stanziani is important because, in general, he is concerned with the institutions of serfdom and slavery, reforms and abolitions, and what happens with respect to labor after emancipation. He challenges the reader to move beyond traditional conceptualizations of abolitions, which, in short, examine legal reforms (established from above) that set emancipation in motion, as well as the socio-economic relations (on the ground) as demonstrated by statistics, the latter of which, he argues, were compiled by elites. He puts forward a number of analytical and conceptual theses: First, he maintains that it is incorrect to compare Russia's development with that of Western Europe or the United States just because it has long stood as a "negative counter-example of historical developments in the West." Not only has each country or region had its own rate, path, and characteristics of development, but even countries that are "developed" and/or "modernized," such as those in the West, have had their own degrees or stages of developmental progression. (Here, we can see a dovetail with the Beckert thesis with respect to his "stages" framework as exemplified by "war capitalism" and the progression to industrial capitalism.) Progress, development, and/or modernization, Stanziani argues, should be considered as a course along a continuum, the opposite ends of which consist of entirely unfree labor and completely free labor. Therefore, "[r]ather than looking for missing factors to explain Russia's backwardness, we want to reevaluate the rules and the practices of labor in some Western countries on the basis of the Russian case." In addition, Stanziani argues that Russian peasants were much less bound and freer than is usually held, and, in most Western countries, rural labor was not so much free but more akin to service. Rural laborers were not "'independent producers' making a free choice. On the contrary," they were "intermediate forms" along a continuum, their condition being similar to that of an indentured servant. Stanziani's framework accommodates gradations, nuance, and adaptations with respect to labor in the context of emancipation.

Inspired by both Beckert's and Stanziani's work is a global framework in which we can see elements of convergence. That is, in the context of the emancipation era, the economic behavior (including forms of labor and labor performance) of the formerly unfree shifts, mutates, and adapts, according to the political, economic, social, and cultural characteristics associated with each region. In both Russia and the United States, these adaptations ushered in a new stage of development—an intermediary period of sorts, in which serfdom and slavery were no more, but the liberated were not completely free. Here we can see a conceptualization that considers nuance, local traditions, agency, and dynamics rather than a framework of the binaries of "backward" and "developed" and/or "unfree" versus "free."[4]

The work of Andrei Markevich and Ekaterina Zhuravskaya is significant. First, unlike landmark studies of American slavery, such as *Time on the Cross* (1974) by Robert Fogel and Stanley Engerman, and *Without Consent or Contract* (1989) by Robert Fogel, which posited that the institution was profitable because of, among other things, economies of scale and the fact that plantations were managed rationally in order to maximize profits, utilizing an empirical analysis of a dataset of variables that include provincial agricultural productivity, industrial output, and peasant nutrition, Markevich and Zhuravskaya argue that Russian serfdom was not profitable because of the ratchet effect, especially in regions where the majority of the serf population were private serfs and worked as agricultural laborers. (In their study, Simbirsk Province fell into the category with the highest percentage of the latter group, that being 73.8–83.3 percent.) That is, as serfs produced according to labor obligation requirements (the surplus of which they could retain), the landlord would increase those obligations, which would disincentivize the laborers. (Even if landlords simply neglected to revise obligations, these acted as significant disincentives to work productively on the part of the serfs.) Emancipation ended the ratchet effect by *fixing* obligations and assigning them to the commune, not to individual peasants. Therefore, a huge attitudinal shift took place on the part of the former serfs. Emancipation set in motion an element of ambitiousness that was absent in the days of serfdom. However, Markevich and Zhuravskaya also find that once land reform (land distribution set in motion by the Statutory Charters) kicked in, productivity again diminished. They conclude that serfdom was a determining factor in causing a slowdown of economic development. Had emancipation occurred much earlier—say, in 1820—Russia would have been "twice as rich by 1913, compared to what it actually was."[5]

In chapter 4, I pointed out that, per the terms of the Statutory Charter at Yazykovo Selo, Vasili Yazykov retained *barshchina* obligations for the freed people there. Markevich and Zhuravskaya's analysis is at the (macro) provincial level; therefore, it does not address labor performance at the (micro) village level. Nor do they analyze the impact of the *terms* of Statutory Charters on productivity, such as *barshchina* obligations versus those of *obrok.* Thus, notwithstanding the fact that the majority of Simbirsk

Province's freed people had been private serfs in the agricultural sector before 1861, and therefore, presumably, emancipation would have triggered an increase in productivity, the fact that the hated *barshchina* was fixed at Yazykovo Selo (both before emancipation and afterward, until a Redemption Agreement would be established) may well explain, at least in part, the fields lying fallow and the factory's deplorable condition, as described on the eve of Yazykov selling the estate to Feodor Stepanov in 1881. But there were additional factors in play, which will be addressed in this chapter.

While it is important to demonstrate the ways in which my accounts of the developments at each demesne square with and depart from these and other historians' findings, this study is a comparison, and it is Stanziani's paradigm that provides the framework for my concluding remarks.

Management at Yazykovo Selo

Figure 6.1. The wool factory at Yazykovo Selo around 1910 (during Stepanov's management) (copyright © 2021 Literaturnyĭ muzeĭ "Dom Yazykovykh" [Literature Museum "The House of Yazykovs," Ulyanovsk, Russia]).

The Wool Factory and Recovery Efforts

During the twenty-year period that followed emancipation, Vasili Yazykov grappled with managing Yazykovo Selo. This included the wool factory's operation at a time when there was a drop in government requisitions. But requisitioning did not disappear entirely. To the extent that he sought to comply with government directives,

Yazykov attempted to improve production at the factory—this, at a time when he no longer had supreme control over his former serfs. Thus, he launched a series of business and financial maneuverings designed to assist production, delay (if not avoid) financial ruin, and sustain the lifestyle to which he had been accustomed. Managing the estate also entailed complying with tsarist directives associated with the emancipation legislation. As a member of the nobility, and thoroughly imbued with a service consciousness, he complied with directives from above—to an extent, that is, for Yazykov also acted in his own self-interest.

As explained in the previous chapter, Yazykov hired a Tatar merchant to manage the factory prior to emancipation, most likely in anticipation of the decree that severed the landed nobleman's authority over his former serfs. I also explained that, in spite of the fact that merchants were notorious for their shrewd business acumen, Mangushev's hands were essentially tied since (1) although the peasants were temporarily obligated (in the form of *barshchina* labor), they could neither be forced to work nor be evicted, and (2) the real source of authority on Russian estates after emancipation was the village commune.

In fact, in May 1862 Mangushev produced a handwritten, dismal report that he submitted to Yazykov, defending his inability to manage the factory. Just two years after Yazykov documented that everything was fully intact and in good working order, the merchant noted that the factory was in appalling disrepair. The building had no frames, the doors as well as steps leading up to the buildings were missing, the water pump transmission was broken, and all the wadding, combing, and rolling machines (as well as a speeder and a spinner) either were broken or had missing parts. Mangushev further indicated that since each of the seven wadding machines' parts were presumably interchangeable, he had attempted to reconfigure them, but they still would not operate. The shearing machines were also inoperable. In a blatant criticism of his noble employer, Mangushev noted that ideally the factory was capable of producing more than one million *arshina* a year, but his failure to meet the Treasury's requisition had to do with "Lord Yazykov's poor management." The factory was utterly "hamshackled" and could not even produce half of the requisition. He concluded that the factory was a complete "burden." What a striking contrast between Yazykov's inventory report in 1856 and Mangushev's in 1862.[6] What had happened in the interim? In 1856, the wool factory had just concluded a boom in requisitions associated with the Crimean War. Then emancipation occurred. Had the factory been cannibalized as a result of the commotion that took place following emancipation? Clearly, Mangushev shifted blame to Yazykov for the situation.

Remarkably, on January 1, 1863, Yazykov renewed the contract for another two years, the only difference being that it was now extended to include the "Mangushev brothers." The new agreement made the brothers responsible to the Treasury for the production and delivery of 37,770 *arshina* of dark green and grey cloth by November 15, 1863. In fact, the Mangushev brothers delivered only 9,622 *arshina* to the Treasury by that deadline. Because Yazykov owned the factory, he was responsible for the debt. Pointing the finger at the Mangushevs, he petitioned the Treasury for an extension, arguing that the brothers had taken a portion of the produce and sold it in the private market, making a profit of 2,660 silver rubles. The Treasury granted the extension, with the new due date being March 15, 1864. Crucial to the extension was Yazykov's posting of his city mansion in Simbirsk as collateral. Clearly, Yazykov was seeking to salvage the factory, and the Treasury accommodated him.

The new rent timetable began on February 1, 1863. Yazykov pledged to come through with the requisitioned amount of cloth within the two-year period ending February 1, 1865. Achieving this goal would have required substantial repairs and investments in the factory. He closed the factory from June 29 to August 16, 1863, as he was waiting for a new "transmission." Since it was during the summer months that production was supposed to be at its highest, this delay further exacerbated the situation.

Chapter 5 noted that on the eve of emancipation there were about 100 wool factories operating in Simbirsk Province. By 1864, only 25 wool factories remained in operation. This decrease represents a marked shift in the status quo.[7] Furthermore, reports indicated that noblemen across the province had begun renting out their factories to traders who they believed possessed managerial traits. Then, as early as 1870, a trend emerged of noblemen selling their factories to the merchant traders. This constituted an end to the monopoly that the noblemen had with respect to the wool factories and signaled the beginning of a far more diverse system in terms of ownership, management style, and combined (or vertical and/or horizontal) production.[8]

It was at this point that nature delivered a blow to the region in the form of the Great Simbirsk Fire in August 1864.[9] Owing to a rumor that Vasili Yazykov had somehow had a hand in starting the fire, the tsar's notorious Third Department initiated a secret investigation of him three years after the event in 1867. This probe is not surprising, given that fire had often been used as a form of subversion. Indeed, arson was used especially by Russian revolutionaries in 1862 to express their dissatisfaction with what they considered the conservative nature of the emancipation statutes. But the Russian nobility was also suspected of using fire to express its opposition to what it considered the liberal terms of emancipation.[10] No one was exempt from suspicion. In the end, the department found Yazykov innocent of the charge of arson. Local spies reported that while he was often seen at the local "whorehouse," he was nevertheless a "man of good character, very well educated, and a loyal and reliable patriot."[11] Clearly, the dire state of his finances did not prevent Yazykov from indulging in his appetites.

The fire spared the Yazykov family's city mansion. Now Yazykov took steps to sell it to his wife. In the bill of sale, he wrote, "I … sell out to my wife my home which I inherited from my father…. I was paid 3,000 rubles by Praskovia." Interpreting the purpose of this move is not difficult. Yazykov "sold" his wife their city mansion either to remove his responsibility for the presumed multiple mortgaged debt incurred on it (especially as it was collateral for the recent extension granted by the Treasury) or to make it possible for Praskovia to re-mortgage the property thereafter, or both. This said, Praskovia owned the mansion in name only. By the late 1860s, the Yazykovs began renting it to a local Tatar merchant by the name of Kartashov, who opened it as a hotel called "Yazykov Suites." By 1875, they sold the mansion to the merchant, who changed the hotel's name to "Kartashov Suites," with Yazykov retaining a room for his use when he was in the city.[12]

In 1865, Vasili Yazykov took out a mortgage on the land at Yazykovo Selo. This should not be confused with his mortgage of the estate in 1851 when he inherited it. In that deal, he had mortgaged his serfs. In light of the fact that after 1861 the Treasury redirected funds from credit lines for the nobility to those for developing the railroads and river steamers, it may seem odd that Yazykov was able to mortgage the land. However, he was well connected. Indeed, he was a council member of the Provincial Committee of Simbirsk for the State Land Bank. He would also work on the Provincial Committee of the Nobles' Land Bank, which was founded in 1885.[13]

Aside from trying to manage both the demesne and his finances, Yazykov was involved in an array of philanthropic endeavors and responsibilities associated with service.[14] Arguably the most significant were his roles as marshal of the nobility for Simbirsk District from March 1862 to December 1873 and district deputy of the Department of Peasant Affairs from 1863 to 1868. In these capacities, he was directly involved in both the politics and the peasant affairs of Simbirsk District.[15]

The year 1865 was also significant in that Yazykov severed his ties with the Mangushev brothers and proceeded to rent the factory out to another Simbirsk merchant, Repev. By the end of the decade, his son was renting the factory. The younger Repev registered the employment of 70 men, 4 women, and 70 teenagers, which was much lower than the pre-emancipation number. It is curious that the record indicates that Repev paid the laborers 600 rubles per month (which amounted to an even distribution of a little over 4 rubles a person) since the Statutory Charter of 1862 indicated that 160 of the 394 souls (adult men) who were entitled to land allotments and who had *barshchina* obligations worked in the factory. Without evidence of what the breakdown was between the men, women, and children, or what wages might have been paid on any other comparable estate, it is difficult to estimate the significance of this figure. However, that a record exists of an earmark for wages is significant, for it suggests that work *was* taking place. It is also unclear whether these paid laborers (at least the men) were new hires or those in the "temporarily obligated" category as indicated by the Statutory Charter. Furthermore, while Peter Zaionchkovskiy has explained that the *Regulations* abolished *barshchina* obligations in manorial factories and automatically transferred them to *obrok*, the bill of sale to Stepanov in 1881 indicated that all the male peasants, including the factory laborers, remained on *barshchina*.[16] However, this situation clearly demonstrates one merchant's approach to labor management in the post-emancipation period. Under Repev's tutelage, the contract with the Treasury was 50,000 rubles for an unspecified number of military uniforms, as well as 2,000 carpets. Reminiscent of the Mangushev story, Yazykov complained that, although production at the factory seemed to be underway, Repev was taking produce that was earmarked for the Treasury and selling it at the city market for profit.[17]

By 1870, a fragment statistic indicates that the factory averaged 288 *arshina* a day. While this number was close to the average for 1853,[18] it was much lower than what was being produced at Vasili Yazykov's brother's factory on his estate, Undory. Also managed by a Tatar merchant, the Undory factory reportedly averaged 465 *arshina* per day.[19]

Yazykov switched managers again in 1871; another Tatar merchant, one Kozlov, was hired. By 1872, he found Feodor Stepanov to manage the factory. In 1876, Stepanov placed an ad in a local newspaper for "teenage children" to come to work at the factory "for wages."[20] This was significant, as Stepanov's move to offer wages for labor preceded the tsar's command to do so in the Redemption Law of 1881 by nearly five years.

Field Work and Shadow Economic Behavior

As for agricultural labor and productivity at Yazykovo Selo, evidence regarding conditions both in the demesne's neighborhood and elsewhere in the province is instructive. First, Simbirsk native, friend of Vasili Yazykov, Slavophile philosopher, and Emancipation Manifesto coauthor Yuri Samarin wrote that peasant refusal to work in the fields was widespread in the immediate post-emancipation period. He noted that many peasants in one village even refused to work on their own garden plots. As usual, a number of authorities were called to that estate. When the local peace mediator tried to persuade them to work, clearly speaking to the issue of the relationship between labor obligations and freedom, they replied, "We're prepared to go to the military, Siberia, and even to the death, but we'll not work."[21]

Second, an article in the weekly *Simbirsk Provincial Gazette* (*Vedomosti Simbirskoy Gubernii*) in November 1863 was devoted to the life of the peasants since emancipation. Making the point that the overwhelming trend in the province was that the fields lay fallow, it noted that, in general, both the landowners and the peasants in the province had stopped producing grain because of the high cost of preparing the land for sowing—they did not have cash available for the venture. In addition, while most landowners may well have understood the "fad" of "rational" agricultural practices, they considered it more of a "pipedream" than a realistic endeavor since (1) there was a shortage of both cash and credit to purchase machinery, and (2) even if the landowner could upgrade and purchase machinery, what was the landlord then to do with all those "idle" peasants who were attached to the demesne, per the terms of the emancipation legislation?[22] Plus, even where the peasants were on *barshchina*, the question remained as to whether they would fulfill their obligations. A related issue even had to do with the fact that in cases where the Statutory Charter's terms had reduced land earmarked for the peasants in relation to what they had been entitled to prior to 1861, and therefore had similarly increased it for the landlord, this meant that now, under the new conditions, the latter had more land that needed to be worked, but with more restrictions in the form of those on *barshchina* obligations. (As was made clear in chapter 4, the Statutory Charter at Yazykovo Selo did just that.) On top of all this, there was the perennial issue of dealing with the uncertainty of land arability. Finally, the editorial noted that, concomitantly, landlords began renting various facilities out to merchants, including factories, fields, and even city mansions.[23]

The larger point is about coming to grips with the "idle peasant" myth. It is not that the Russian peasant was averse to "work," per se. Indeed, Russian peasants worked exhaustively for "Mother Russia"[24] for hundreds of years. It is more accurate to frame the issue in terms of understanding the peasant *mentalité* and the attitude toward work (and for whom). In a subsistence *and* service-oriented society, the Russian peasant's attitude toward work had to do with notions that working and saving money for the future were outlandish. The reasons for these beliefs were many. One had to do with the religious idea that it was a sin to covet money, while another reasoned that if one did have any extra money, one would not save it, but rather spend it. Why save money? To reinvest? Invest in what? Or, if you didn't spend the money immediately, you might save it only as a way to self-furlough from work later. When the money ran out, then you would go back to work. In addition, in principle, the peasant respected neither hard work nor someone who worked hard—for the purposes of "getting ahead," that is. To "get ahead" for what? Moreover, Russian peasants viewed the land (and the air, and the water, and the trees) as gifts from God, to everyone. So the concept of private ownership of these elements was alien—indeed, blasphemy—and certainly theft. But the wealth of and property owned by either the state or rich noblemen, and even well-off merchants and peasants such as *kulaks*, meant that those entities not only "had more than enough" to get by but also, peasants rationalized, had acquired it at *their* expense. Therefore, to "steal" from any of those entities was not theft, but more akin to a correction, a redemption, or a reparation. And anyway, they reasoned, "stealing" from this or that entity was not harming them since they had plenty left over. All this is not to suggest that *all* peasants felt this way, especially since it was not unheard of to find an "entrepreneurial" peasant with ambition. Nor is it to suggest that peasants in general were averse to work. It is to suggest, however, that the peasants were averse to being dominated. It is also not to suggest that peasants were *naturally* communal, for they deeply resented the fact that they had to pay taxes communally and that they shared a collective responsibility for the village's obligations. Nor is this all meant to suggest that the Russian peasant was incapable of abstract, rational thinking. Indeed, it was very rational and self-interested to think in these ways in a society whose orientation was service focused with entrenched social stratification.[25]

A number of Russian sources state that even though most peasants continued to adhere to traditional farming after 1861, there was increasing economic diversification and participation in non-agricultural trades in the second half of the 19th century because of the dual effects of the emancipation legislation: a decrease in land available to them and more free time pushing the peasant population further into these sinews of market behavior, especially what could be called "out-of-pocket" trade. For example, increasing numbers of peasants came to supplement their income by migrating away from their villages and working according to a seasonal or semi-permanent contractual arrangement in either agriculture or non-agricultural work, such as a kind of sharecropping (*otkhodniki*) for the former and the building of railroads and jobs in industry and urban areas for the latter.[26]

Specifically, Simbirsk Province's peasants participated in a wide range of productive work in a variety of cottage industries, both in terms of specialization and diversification and in terms of skilled, artisanal (*kustari*) and unskilled labor. Some examples of these include the very labor-intensive sowing and processing of flax and hemp (where the soil quality made it possible); the cutting and sewing of shoes and clothes; fishing (especially sturgeon, ruffe, pike, catfish, and carp) on the Volga and its tributaries; tanning and leather making; metal making; blacksmithing; coopering; carving (furniture, utensils, tools, toys, and the like); felting; embroidery; weaving; rope braiding; holstering; handcrafts; and animal husbandry[27] such as horses, cattle, pigs, and sheep. Horticultural activities were also prevalent, especially hops; in addition, a number of estates showcased arboretums. Victualling (especially potatoes) and peddling seeds and fertilizers such as manure and ash, as well as beekeeping, were widespread in the region. A lucrative trade in cat pelts also existed, especially in and around the district capital of Karsun, which was just ten miles from Yazykovo Selo. Plus, peasants from Simbirsk province also worked in more distant places that utilized migrant labor on a seasonal basis. Given Simbirsk's geographic proximity via the Volga River to locations to the south, early in each spring hundreds of locals were hired by agents at the port and sailed to places like Astrakhan for fishing and Baku for the oil factories, returning home by winter with earnings that farming could not provide. Thus, a vibrant market activity took place both formally (or officially) and informally (or unofficially), the latter of which could be typified as a shadow economy, in which the practices of bartering and haggling were the norm. These trading activities not only provided sustenance but also made it possible for peasants to market their surplus at local bazaars, fairs, and markets, the most famous in the region being the National Team (*Sbornaya*) in Simbirsk and the Trinity (*Troitskaya*) in Karsun. There were many urban and rural fairs, the latter of which were on estates. In general, whereas fairs differed in size and specialization (and were primarily wholesale or trade exhibitions), bazaars were more akin to a market, where vendors of all kinds sold their goods to consumers. Each district had its own regular fairs and bazaars.[28] All this said, one local source has concluded that, between the remnants of serfdom and the adverse conditions imposed by emancipation, Simbirsk "was the most backward in socio-economic terms among the black earth provinces of European Russia."[29]

The marked uptick in peasant participation in a shadow market may well explain the "fields lying fallow" meme.[30] This view speaks to both the Beckert and the Stanziani theses. That is, we see a shift, an adjustment, an adaptation to the new realities set in motion by emancipation with respect to both the supply side and the demand sphere of economic activities. A new stage of economic behavior emerged.[31] Regarding the Stanziani conceptualizations, we discern this stage of development as being one unique to the circumstantial realities in Russia (and certainly Simbirsk Province) at the time. Further, a consideration of this post-emancipation development in the province speaks to another component of Stanziani's paradigm—namely, that the Russian peasants were much less bound and exhibited much greater freedom. Understanding that the peasants at Yazykovo Selo were, on the one hand, bound to the estate and assigned labor obligations to their former master, per the terms of the emancipation legislation, and yet participating in this vibrant trade activity, on the other hand, is not a contradiction. Rather, it demonstrates the simultaneity of top-down/bottom-up phenomena. Yes, the terms of emancipation attached inhabitants to the village and subordinated them to the commune elders, but they also participated in a host of cottage industries and trade in local markets, fairs, and bazaars. Finally, when we consider the findings of Markevich and Zhuravskaya, which were that agricultural productivity increased overall after 1861 but then slowed dramatically after the land reform was set in motion by the Statutory Charters, the accounts of an uptick in market activity in Simbirsk Province on the part of the peasants would both confirm and explain the evidentiary drop in agricultural participation. That is, while the terms of emancipation *initially* liberated the peasants from the "ratchet effect" of serfdom, the Statutory Charters introduced another disincentive to work on the land for the lord in order to fulfill their mandated obligations. This situation, then, pushed them into other forms and arenas of commercial activity. Perhaps, however, it was emancipation itself that was the greatest incentive, for now they were free to pursue such activities on a much greater scale.

In the 1870s, a series of events unfolded that must have played a role in Vasili Yazykov's decision to sell the estate in piecemeal fashion to Stepanov. First, triggered by a severe drought, the Volga Famine of 1873 has been cited as worse than even the more notorious ones of 1891 and 1921–1922.[32] Second, a severe economic downturn began in 1873 and continued through to the end of the decade. Indeed, an overall economic decline of twenty years followed thereafter.[33] This decline notwithstanding, because it coincided with the Russo-Turkish War (1877–1878), Stepanov's purchase of the factory in 1877 was salutary, since the conflict triggered an increase in government requisitions for wool. In 1878, the merchant renewed the advertisement for teen laborers he had placed two years earlier. Then, in 1880, a local newspaper advertised "the grand reopening of the clothes factory at Yazykovo Selo."[34] On March 13, 1881, Tsar Alexander II was assassinated in St. Petersburg. At the very least, this tragedy signaled an element of uncertainty with respect to his successor's policies and directives. At worst, it marked an end to the reformist impulse associated with Alexander's reign.[35] Next, on September 26, 1881, and evidencing the breakdown of his marriage, Vasili Yazykov's wife voluntarily entered the women's monastery located across the street from their city mansion.[36] Two months later, on December 16, 1881, Stepanov purchased the estate mansion.[37] Most significant, on December 28, 1881, a new Redemption Law went into effect. It decreed an end to both *barshchina* labor and the peasants' "temporarily obligated" status. It also standardized a legal concept of property. Most significant, it made redemption payments and wage labor obligatory. Stepanov had already begun paying wages prior to this time. The merchant also initiated repairs and investments at the demesne. Remarkably, in 1882 the factory's products were praised by the All Russian National Industrial Exhibition in Moscow.[38]

No Redemption Agreement

When Stepanov completed the purchase in 1881, records show that there were 394 souls at Yazykovo Selo who were still on *barshchina* obligations. They also show that the estate did not have a Redemption Agreement. Therefore, the peasants had remained in a temporarily obligated status throughout the period under review.[39] It is also significant because the number of souls cited on the bill of sale is identical to the number entitled to allotted land listed in the Statutory Charter of 1862. Clearly, this was done out of expediency, or else the sale was effected hurriedly without attention to accuracy (or both). Nevertheless, the official record shows that the population at Yazykovo Selo between 1861 and 1881 was stagnant.[40]

Given that Vasili Yazykov effected the Statutory Charter in 1862, for which he received imperial recognition, it is significant that he did not impose a Redemption Agreement. To be clear, unlike the Statutory Charter, the terms of emancipation did not require that landlords initiate a Redemption Agreement. In fact, they had the choice of doing nothing at all with respect to a redemption plan.[41] By contrast, Vasili's brother, Alexander, implemented a payment schedule in 1864 at Undory.[42]

Why did Vasili fail to carry out this step? To this day, many historians in Ulyanovsk argue that he was incompetent and frivolous, and his personal life was in shambles.[43] But this view is not entirely correct. Vasili Yazykov was neither idle nor incompetent, nor was he ambivalent. To be sure, he was not a "planting magnate," nor a farmer, nor an entrepreneur. In fact, members of the nobility often considered agricultural work a low-class occupation.[44] He may well have led a life of frivolity, but in addition to living up to his commitments and obligations associated with service and philanthropy and working within the realities and constraints of the political economic system in which he lived, Vasili was fully engaged with managing both the logistics of production at the estate and his financial problems. As for a comparison with his brother's tenure at his estate, in spite of Alexander's implementation of a Redemption Agreement, Undory's fate was practically identical to Yazykovo Selo's, as Alexander auctioned it off to Tatar merchants in 1881.[45]

In fact, Vasili Yazykov's "failure" to impose an agreement is understandable. First, when considering the contrast between Yazykov's completion of a Statutory Charter and his failure to secure a payment schedule, it should be remembered that he had a number of incentives to implement the former in March 1862. First, it was mandatory, and it had to be implemented within two years of the Manifesto's release in the spring of 1861. Second, he wanted to put the peasant "disturbances" behind him. Third, he wanted to preemptively effect the charter before the sowing season commenced. Finally, he was assisted by the peace mediator for his district—his cousin, Mikhail Bestuzhev. Moreover, as discussed in chapters 4 and 5, indebted noble landowners were incentivized to effect Statutory Charters, since a larger allotted plot size to a soul guaranteed a greater amount of financial compensation for it.

Conversely, there were issues that discouraged the implementation of Redemption Agreements. Although the government was responsible for compensating the landowner up front with 80 percent of that which he/she would gain on securing a Redemption Agreement, the amount was in bonds, or, more correctly "redemption certificates"—not cash. These redemption certificates could not be transferred or converted into other government bonds or cash. In addition, since the landowners' debts were to be subtracted from that which the government would pay, and this, in theory, seemed like a convenient way to alleviate oneself of one's debts, doing so meant that an indebted nobleman could very well remain indebted even if the Redemption Agreement went into effect, since he/she could end up with nothing. In this sense a noble's financial extravagances could well have caught up with him/her in the Redemption Agreement.

Historians have sought to explain the discrepancy between swiftly executed Statutory Charters and tardy Redemption Agreements. First, there was a legal caveat. Tracy Dennison has explained that, in order to avoid a stampede, the government mandated sequential Redemption Agreements, privileging estates on *obrok*, and then those on *barshchina*, of which Yazykovo was one. Next, delaying an agreement as long as possible deferred the payment process required of the peasants. Holding out was a form of resistance. It was a tactic to negotiate for reduced payments. But landlords also had an incentive not to reach an agreement, since the longer they held out and did not impose redemption, the greater their chances of receiving full payment. While Avenir Korelin has explained that during the two decades following emancipation land prices steadily rose, Boris Mironov has added that the allotted land for which the peasants had to compensate their former owners was priced above market. And Leonid Ivanov has argued that landowners who did not have cash, but who were indebted, and whose freed people were on *barshchina*, had no incentive to switch to a Redemption Agreement. Thus, in an era of rising land prices (either natural or deliberate), selling as late as possible on the part of the aristocrats seemed to offer the maximum price. It was only when rumors began swirling about the tsar's Redemption Law of 1881 being imminent that landowners either moved to create a payment schedule or proceeded to sell off their estates.[46]

A Redemption Agreement could take effect either through a mutual agreement or through a noble landlord's unilateral act. However, while it was one thing for Vasili Yazykov to push through the Statutory Charter irrespective of the peasants' participation, it was another thing altogether to fashion out of thin air a Redemption Agreement that both documented and enforced a payment schedule. Herein was a crucial juncture in the trajectory of freedom after emancipation: the liberated serfs would never be free until they agreed to pay up front to their former owner one-fifth the amount of land earmarked for them, and the remaining 80 percent to the government over the next 49 years. We know that the peasants of Yazykovo Selo utterly rejected the Statutory Charter in 1862, reportedly refused to accept a copy of it, and never made any payments in silver rubles for the land rent stipulation. Therefore, it is not only plausible but also probable that they were not interested in entering into any agreement that extracted payment for land they considered already theirs.

Contextual evidence and national sources support this theory. For example, the minister of internal affairs reported to the tsar in 1871 that in twelve provinces (including Simbirsk), there was widespread peasant rejection of Redemption Agreements and even the allotted land plots. Sources are saturated with quotes of peasants' vehement rejection of payments for land. For example, statements like "we don't want the redemption ... [and] we'll not pay [it] ... even if you'll kill us and bury us in the ground" were typical. Embedded in this quote was the sentiment of the old Russian peasant proverb that stated, "Die, but do not leave your father's land."[47]

Statistics suggest that, although it was not an overwhelming phenomenon, the absence of a Redemption Agreement was not uncommon. By the end of 1862, Russia had 7,082 agreements (or 7.5 percent) completed. By the end of 1865, only 16,800 (18 percent) were made. By 1870, roughly 55 percent of Russian estates were on a redemption schedule. By 1877, there were 61,784 agreements. Of those, about 35 percent were "mutual" and roughly 65 percent were forced through by the landowners. In January 1881, there were still 1.5 million peasants, or approximately 15 percent of the total number, who remained classified as "temporarily obligated." Yazykovo Selo was among this 15 percent.[48]

Things only changed at Yazykovo Selo after both the Redemption Law went into effect and Stepanov purchased the estate in 1881. Significant variables in this situation included both wage labor and the official end to the temporary obligated status that the law set in motion. Stepanov's management experience, motivational direction, and financial capabilities also played a role. It is worth suggesting that all this coincided with a quirk of history: the groundwork of modernization that had been laid during the twenty years after 1861 had, by the early 1880s, begun to make a difference.[49]

Management at Palmyra Plantation

When the Quitman/Lovell family recovered Palmyra Plantation in late 1865, the nature of labor patterns and related issues changed. The departure of Union officials from the Bend meant that the freed people there were no longer anchored to the demesne. The policy of mandatory work in exchange for rations and (some) compensation ended. While it is true that many American freed people were not keen on signing labor contracts with planters because (similar to their Russian counterparts who wanted nothing to do with Statutory Charters and Redemption Agreements) they saw these as tricks to reimpress them into servitude, they were also destitute.[50] But the American freed people had a card to play in their mobility, and, given the demand for labor in the region, they could and did negotiate with planters, such as Lovell, who now had the task of finding and maintaining a labor force. As pointed out in chapter 3, Lovell did make an official contract for the 1866 season with four freed people in the summer of 1865.[51] This is significant, for it demonstrated that during this transitional period Lovell preemptively adjusted to the new contextual realities.

Lovell's plantation journals document his complete attention to Palmyra.[52] He was a driven, entrepreneurial planter who, like all serious planters, obsessed about weather patterns, water levels, insect scourges, the health and well-being of livestock, the quality of the gin and equipment, labor recruitment and efficiency (including plant-ing, picking, and ginning as well as production levels in relation to previous years), and Palmyra's overall management. Furthermore, the journals show that, similar to Vasili Yazykov, Lovell was in engaged in a real-life game of financial cat and mouse, shifting, borrowing, and paying monies to this or that entity and/or person (including many fam-ily members) in order to stay afloat.[53]

Although Vasili Yazykov was not idle during his tenure at Yazykovo Selo, Lovell was far more *effective* than his Russian counterpart, if by this term we mean success-ful at making the demesne operate according to its raison d'être. First, Lovell was man-aging a plantation that not only was viable and had a proven track record but also had an exceptional capacity to produce. Second, even though Lovell was working in a new, post-war context (which had witnessed a complete disruption of the cotton industry and an end to the form of labor that made it run), reminiscent of the Beckert thesis, he was also operating within an economic context that demonstrated resilience, pliabil-ity, and adaptability. In addition, Lovell found a foreman to supervise the plantation who, like Mangushev and other Russian merchants, was competent but, unlike these counterparts, was given incentives, tacit guidelines, and authority with respect to the demesne's mission. Above all, while the freed people at Palmyra were not on an Amer-ican equivalent of *barshchina*, they certainly had terms of labor obligations to which they contractually agreed (albeit temporarily) on a seasonal basis. Significantly, Lovell was able to secure every year, for years, seasonal, migrant labor to make the plantation work. Finally, notwithstanding the war-torn South, the fractured nation, and the drop in prices, cotton remained king.[54]

In a sense, Lovell exemplified what historians have identified as the "new mas-ter" prototype, displaying a "time is money" industriousness and an ethic of overcom-ing "obstacles."[55] Like his father-in-law John Quitman, Lovell was a man in constant motion. But unlike Quitman, Lovell was far more directly involved with Palmyra's management. Attributable either to his personality or to his experience as a navy man (or both), temperamentally he expected everything to run smoothly and according to schedule. Years later, his own daughter compared being around him like "living on a volcano. You never knew what moment it would blow up!"[56] Lovell's plantation journals demonstrate his rigorous schedule for over thirty years. For the purposes of securing labor, managing credit, purchasing supplies, and conducting field work for the inspec-tion of crops and productivity, Lovell traveled at a dizzying pace, by boat, train, horse, and/or carriage, from Palmyra to the family's city mansion in Natchez, to New Orleans, to Vicksburg, to Jackson, to Cairo, and to other Quitman/Lovell properties, and often a combination of many of these all within the same week.

The Cotton Gin and Recovery Efforts

The year 1866 was a difficult one for the Mississippi Delta region's plantations. Heavy rains in the spring prevented cotton cultivation, and the summer produced a severe drought. In September, the dreaded army worm appeared and devoured any crops that had been planted. Signaling what would become a trend until the turn of the century, a drop in the price of cotton further reduced profits.[57] In spite of all this turmoil, Lovell closed out the year with a staggering 188 bales of ginned cotton—not from Pal-myra, but rather Belen.[58] Although this amount was paltry compared to the property's

Figure 6.2. *Cotton Gin*, **by William Aiken Walker (The New Orleans Museum of Art: Gift of Paul J. Leaman, Jr., 94.267).**

yields in the antebellum period, Lovell noted that one of those bales weighed about 570 pounds, which, according to the price of cotton in New Orleans at the time, accrued about $171. However, hay production at Palmyra supplemented cotton. Although it was far less labor intensive and less vulnerable to pests, hay did not have the lucrative potential of cotton. Typically paying a laborer $15 (or even as little as $2) to cut hay in the meadows, Lovell recorded one bale in June weighing 840 pounds, which brought in $101. Glancing at his entries for 1866 alone, one discovers a rough tally of 173 "loads," with one earning a paltry $8.73 and another $5.[59]

The following year was one of "wreck." The bottom fell out of the market when the price of cotton dipped to 14 cents a pound. Creditors called in loans, setting in motion a chain reaction of recalls. These developments not only adversely affected planters but also brought home to the freed slaves the full force of their destitution and made clear their only option for survival—turning to plantation work. In addition, the 1867 flood was one of the worst in the region's history. The Bend was almost completely submerged, although the plantation house, outbuildings, and former slave quarters were spared. Indeed, the narrow isthmus that connected the pear-shaped peninsula to the mainland was washed away. Now the Bend became an island, permanently.[60] Because Palmyra was situated on the east side of the Bend, it had direct access to the traffic on the river's new route. However, this benefit would prove to be offset by the burden of maintaining the levees needed to protect the Bend from the river. Many of the Bend's inhabitants fled, throwing an already fragile labor pool into further disarray. Those who remained worked around the clock all spring to rebuild levees and repair buildings, including the gin and sawmill. The flood-soaked fields drew insect pests like a magnet. Cutworms appeared at night and disappeared into the ground at dawn. Army worms arrived by mid–July. A local planter noted that the worms worked so swiftly that, whereas one day the fields looked green, by the next they were "blackened like fire had swept over them." Of the cotton that was produced, the drop in prices for that year made things worse. Still, although it was far less when compared to Palmyra's production in the past, Lovell closed out the year with about 310 bales.

With little to no crop to put up as collateral against loans from cotton factors in New Orleans and elsewhere, combined with the fact that many (if not most) laborers had fled, the preparation time for 1868 was also devastated. But these were learning opportunities. Innovation and adaptation emerged. One development involved renting the fields out for so many dollars per acre or season. Contracting (both written and verbal) was also used. The important questions are how and from where the planter attracted laborers. Lovell's example is instructive. Rather than attract labor *to* the plantation, he *left* it to seek out and hire laborers for the season.[61]

On the one hand, 1868 shared some similarities to the previous year. Lovell hired eight "teams" (typically two or four hands each) of laborers for several weeks in the spring to reinforce the levees. This effort was a success: they held when the river peaked again in late spring.[62] That summer a drought adversely affected both crops and livestock. Afterward, the arrival of fall rains ushered in another blight of worms. On the other hand, 1868 proved to be a pivotal year in a number of ways. During the next five years the region was free from floods, droughts, and pests. The cash that was laid out for investments immediately after the war, which purchased draft animals and farm equipment, was by now in an economy of scale mode. The year was also a watershed in that it witnessed the departure of most of the Northerners who had come to the region immediately after the war's conclusion to try their luck at planting. The cotton rush had begun as early as 1863. But these "new masters" left in droves as they conceded defeat in the face of droughts, floods, army worms, and falling cotton prices.[63]

Above all, adjustments in labor's shape and arrangement began appearing as 1868 ushered in an element of confidence. A variety of sharecropping arrangements began to accompany wage labor. This modality was desirable for a number of reasons: it was a way to get around the problems of scarce cash and credit; planters saw it as a means of securing a labor force for the duration of the planting season; and it was more appealing than paying cash, which had meant that, irrespective of the crop produced, one would have to pay a laborer for his or her work. In good years, and if the planter had cash, this arrangement was fine. But in bad years, such as the seasons of 1866 and 1867, it was a further loss to have to pay cash salaries. Vernon Lane Wharton attributed the adoption of sharecropping modalities to the planters' realization that there was no turning back: slavery was dead, the freed people's mobility was a fact, and their status as free laborers had to be reckoned with. In addition, Wharton continued, short of owning land, the freed people preferred a variety of forms of rent since this option allowed the "maximum of freedom for themselves and in the supervision of the land ... and offered the possibility" of profits.[64] Thus, the freed people saw it as a way to have greater control over their earnings and as a stepping-stone to land tenure.[65] Indeed, Sven Beckert has stressed that the emergence of sharecropping, in all its varieties,

testified to the collective strength of freedpeople, allowing them to escape a far worse system of gang labor for wages on plantations. [It] gave freedmen and -women a modicum of control over their own labor, allowed them to evade day-to-day supervision so reminiscent of slavery, and permitted families—instead of individuals—to contract with landowners and to decide on the allocation of the labor of men, women, and children.[66]

In a sense, sharecropping was a great compromise.

Gerald David Jaynes has disagreed sharply with this interpretation, arguing that *both* the planters and the freed people much preferred wage labor (the former because it was more efficient than sharecropping, and the latter because it gave them greater mobility and independence from the lien system). He also argued that sharecropping was not "chosen," but rather the only "option" the South had given the shortage of cash. Jaynes asserted that, had the United States government provided planters with credit lines so that they could pay wages, and had it distributed land to the freed people so that they could settle "bourgeois" family farms, a "capitalist" system would have been established and sharecropping would not have emerged. Instead, once it became fully entrenched after 1880, and reminiscent of the Stanziani theory of an intermediate stage between the polar opposites of completely free and totally unfree labor, sharecropping—a "debt peonage"—represented a new stage.[67]

Lovell's plantation records show that after 1867, he began utilizing both share and wage contracting for the planting season as well as specific, self-contained jobs, such as reinforcing levees, planting corn, cutting hay and wood, and ginning. For example, in January 1868, Lovell made the following agreement:

> I now have about twenty men hired and some four or five women. I am going to put in a strong man force and a small woman force. I think about 30 men and 10 women will work the place ... with the arrangement I have made with the women who do not contract, that is to hire them when we require them and for only such days. Most of the men do not want to put their wives in regularly. I like the plan very much, for they are on hand when we want them and at no expenses to us when we do not. I am giving first class men $7 women $5. I get some men for $6, half grown for $4 and $5.[68]

Here was evidence of verbal contractual negotiations, with both sides asserting their self-interest, demonstrating elastic and ad hoc methodologies for labor agreements.

Lovell closed out the year 1868 with 554 bales of ginned cotton. Since the average cotton price in 1868 was 16 cents, and if we assume the average weight per bale was 400 pounds, this means that Lovell would have grossed a whopping $35,456.[69] However, this figure was before expenses and interest, which could be very dear. For example, in 1876 Lovell himself was featured in an article in the *New Orleans Times*, which was meant to personalize what was evidently a widespread phenomenon in the region—namely, that the planter was squeezed between low cotton prices and the costs of production to such an extent that the article questioned how any planter under these conditions (especially the smaller producers) could "go on." In the article, Lovell provided a summary of the costs over the calendar year of 1875, which showed him essentially breaking even and, implicitly, before seed and mules were purchased and commission agents paid.[70]

What did it mean to gin cotton in this new era? In general, emancipation constituted a break in the evolution of cotton ginning in the United States. Before, the slave work force was closely supervised and participated relatively uniformly in a regimen that was integrated into all the phases of the plantation's production of cotton, from plowing and planting in the spring to ginning in the fall. After emancipation, however, and as the phenomenon and varieties of sharecropping slowly emerged, the whole crop no longer belonged entirely to the planter/owner. Now the laborer, depending on the terms of his/her contract, was entitled to a share of the crop. Results of this shift could affect the overall uniformity of a crop since, at least in theory, each share group or family would gin their cotton on their own time schedule; alternatively, tenants would not necessarily come together at once to operate the gin. Thus, and over a period of time that lasted well into the 20th century, "public" gins emerged—along the lines of a co-op.[71]

But this is not what happened at Palmyra. Like the other plantations on the Bend, Palmyra had a fully operating gin to itself during the antebellum period. Although all the gins on the Bend were utilized during the Home Colony period, the war nevertheless took a toll. Early in 1866, Lovell set out to replace broken and/or worn-out parts, ordering three Eagle brand gin stands, with seventy saws each, to be outfitted in the building.[72] Within a month, he had collected them from Vicksburg and was able to deliver to New Orleans shortly thereafter one bale of cotton weighing 570 pounds.[73] More to the point, however, over the period in this study (and well beyond) all ginning of the cotton produced at Palmyra was done on site. Given that over the next forty years the plantation's population consisted of a minority of inhabitants who had been enslaved there before the war, alongside a majority of contractual laborers whom Lovell brought in to work on a seasonal basis, this meant that there was a mixture of ginning practices. That is, while those who worked for Lovell on one or another sharecropping arrangement undoubtedly ginned and pressed their own bales of cotton, those who worked in the squad modality most certainly produced and prepared the crop according to Lovell's specifications. Thus, over the entire period under study, Palmyra's population was a mixture of veteran inhabitants, tenant sharecropping families, and seasonal laborers, the latter of whom were men. They all had one form or another of contractual arrangements with Lovell, who in turn utilized a variety of compensation modalities, such as wages, shares of crop, room and board, or a combination of these. And Palmyra's gin was operating at full capacity—when the elements permitted.

Field Work and Shadow Economic Behavior

It was not until roughly 1870 that something resembling a standardized system of labor emerged in the delta region, and that was what one historian has classified as "slavery's stepchild"—namely, squad labor. Growing out of the planters' paramount need for labor and the freed people's destitution and rejection of anything that resembled gang labor, the squad modality was described in *De Bow's Review* in the summer of 1869 as a system in which "from two to eight hands only work together, in many instances a single family."[74]

The *De Bow's* definition aside (and unlike Orser's strict identifying criteria as introduced at the beginning of this chapter), Michael Wayne rightly explained that squad labor was almost as varied and nuanced as the phenomenon of sharecropping. Indeed, squad members were often sharecroppers. While some planters could and did lease their land and/or crops to small, nuclear families of freed people (which could include tenancy and victuals), others, such as Lovell, had squads comprising twenty-plus "hands" each, and they were mostly men. Still others utilized a combination of these approaches, as did Lovell. Wayne has suggested that the difference between a planter's squads (like Lovell's) and the slave gangs of yesteryear was in name only. However, this view is not accurate for a number of reasons.

First, the numbers of squads and hands per squad at Palmyra over the entire period of Lovell's tenure was not fixed, although, according to his records, by the 1880s and 1890s he typically had three that were composed of approximately 20 hands each. I stress the latter because the *New Orleans Times* article cited earlier noted that Lovell had in his employ "1,400 hands." This figure could be plausible if what Lovell recorded in his records was grossly understated or, alternatively, if the article meant the entire population at Davis Bend. The latter seems correct since Lovell's daughter-in-law, Caroline Couper Lovell, estimated in 1884 that "seventeen hundred" African Americans lived on the entire Bend, which included the Davis plantations.[75] That said, not all of the Bend's African American population was in Lovell's employ.

Second, in relation to other plantations in both the region and in the South in general, the squads at Palmyra were in proportion to its size and scope. That is, Palmyra was exceptional both before and after emancipation in both its acreage and its capacity to produce. Often eight or even twelve plows were in operation on the plantation, and, later, in 1885, Lovell noted that twenty-four were running.[76] Planters of smaller holdings could not afford to pay for this migrant labor in the form of wages (at least not consistently), nor did they have the acreage to earmark for shares, much less the connections with both creditors and labor factors or agencies to acquire them. Lovell not only had the means and connections with which to achieve these ends but also did the groundwork. He traveled to New Orleans, points in Alabama, and elsewhere to procure hands. For example, he repeatedly made trips to nearby plantations, such as the famous Perkins Place adjacent to the Bend on the Louisiana side.[77] In addition, the fact that Palmyra (like other large holdings such as the Davis plantations and Perkins Place) was situated on the Mississippi meant that Lovell had the advantage in attracting laborers. As Wayne has explained, the planter who lived far from the river found that he had to make substantial financial concessions to overcome the disadvantage of his unfavorable location. Former slaves expected far more compensation for going to work at a remote demesne. This situation had the effect of pushing the labor pool even further into the realm of the already more lucrative and exceptional holdings such as Palmyra.[78]

Large squad groups typically had leaders who were responsible for motivation and productivity. John C. Willis has observed that often it was these leaders who were charged with traveling to hubs such as New Orleans or Selma to hire migrant laborers and secure the form of compensation. In Lovell's case, although his squads did have leaders, *he* was the one who traveled to engage the laborers and personally negotiated labor agreements. Willis has also explained that while some freedmen contracted individually, others did so collectively. In the early years after 1865, it appears that Lovell contracted with individuals. But after 1880 he regularly engaged large numbers of laborers comprising many squads.[79] Thus, the squad system became a feature adjustment at this point in time: planters of large holdings could hire seasonal (temporary) laborers to work solidly through the planting cycle and pay them in either wages or crop shares at the season's end.[80] Reminiscent of the Beckert thesis, it is clear that the period during Lovell's tenure, between 1865 (the year of his recovery of Palmyra) and 1879 (the era of labor unrest associated with the exodus to Kansas), was one in which adjustments and calibrations were made, with sharecropping becoming the entrenched norm later on.[81]

What were the terms of Lovell's contracts? These represent a moving target in terms of form, composition, and documentation. On the one hand, it is astonishing that nowhere in Lovell's journals did he present a detailed, orderly pay scale. On the other hand, why would he? This nascent stage in the aftermath of emancipation was raw. The financial fine-tunings and adjustments illustrate an informal, improvisational, shadow economy of sorts and/or the residue of an oral, barter-oriented economic culture. It was also an approach that elites have utilized down through the ages—namely, using their connections and clout to procure agreements, both formal and informal. Thus, references in Lovell's records are circumstantial, cursory, occasional, and embedded in the overall general numbers he cited when he paid this or that lump sum to this or that individual or factor and/or creditor (the latter of which are amply referenced in the records).[82] While the exact arrangement Lovell had with all of those whom he employed in their totality over time is lost to history, the numbers of bales ginned and earnings inform us that the freed people worked hard for Lovell (see table 6.5).

In order to engage seasonal labor, when Lovell negotiated with individuals or factors (or, as they were increasingly known after the war, furnishing merchants), he could pay the agents a lump sum or borrow on a credit line, the balance of which would ideally be paid once the season's cotton had been sold. (If it was a bad crop, then obviously the planter had a debt that rolled over into the next year.) Inferential and vague entries in his records, in notation form, far outweigh specifics. For example, "some of the hands have cotton crops," or "I have made arrangements with Mr. Adams [a squad leader] to manage ... Palmyra for next year ... for $1,500.00," or "employed Mr. Lane as overseer at Palmyra @ $75.00 per month," or "contracted with Mr. Dillard to oversee for one year," were typical. Or, for example, in 1871 an entry noted that "hands $472.63" were "paid." Much later, in 1886, Lovell wrote that he had returned from Natchez with "a large family," including "11 hands. They [sic] have 2 mules." And he would occasionally refer to "tenants" by name. In a number of places, especially after 1880, there are citations of families, including children, working for him.[83] A noteworthy figure is one cited in table 6.4, which shows that Lovell entered wages for the year 1879 as an even $12,000. We also know that his neighbor and former Davis slave, Ben Montgomery, charged his hands $4 to $6 per acre tenancy share in the early years and that Lovell "charged more."[84]

In terms of the logistics of hiring temporary or seasonal hands, the story runs in two directions, following Lovell's experience of going to factors or labor agents and securing migrant hands and that of the laborers securing work and going to the plantation for that stint. With respect to the former, Lovell documented this process only in short notes, such as those indicating he had gone to "N.O." or Selma (Alabama), or the Perkins Place, and elsewhere, and returned with the number of hands. Caroline Couper Lovell explained that hiring laborers was part and parcel of the whole cotton industry at this time. Like other planters of large holdings on the river, her father-in-law would obtain an advance from cotton factors, or agents (or commission merchants, as she called them), and presumably use part of that money to hire hands. By the end of the season, he owed the amount he had been advanced. Indirectly supporting the message in the *New Orleans Times* article cited earlier, Caroline insisted that Colonel Lovell (as she called her father-in-law) never understood that these agents were "draining his very life's blood ... [for] exorbitant commissions kept [the planter] ... strapped." Indeed, citing Steven Hahn, Sven Beckert has explained:

> Ironically, at the same time that the landlords consolidated their regional power, they themselves experienced ... a "rather dramatic irreversible decline in power" within the national economy. Bound to worsening cotton prices, faced with protectionist tariffs for products they consumed, and plagued by the scarcity and high cost of capital, they became junior partners in the political economy of domestic industrialization.

Prior to the Civil War, planters exhibited regional political control and significant political influence nationally. The war and emancipation shifted that power away from them and to a cabal of global merchants.[85]

Regarding the supply side of the labor nexus, the freed people's scattering (set in motion by the war) continued. This movement is exemplified by the phenomenon of migrant labor. While little is known about the labor factorage system, it is not difficult to connect the dots. Like sharecropping, labor factors, or agents, or brokers, as they were variously called, adapted to the post-emancipation realities in a context where the demand for labor was great and when the freed people had mobility and needed sustenance.[86]

Before the factor system was completely eclipsed by the local plantation or community stores, merchants, agencies, and cotton factors in New Orleans, Selma, and elsewhere continued to operate essentially as clearinghouses. They attracted people looking for work and paired them up with planters. In one sense, this operation functioned as a shadow economy. In another, however, it was a formal enterprise functioning in an entrenched cotton economy. For example, newspapers and/or directories from the time contained oblique advertisements for migrant laborers.[87] (For one example, see figure 6.3.)

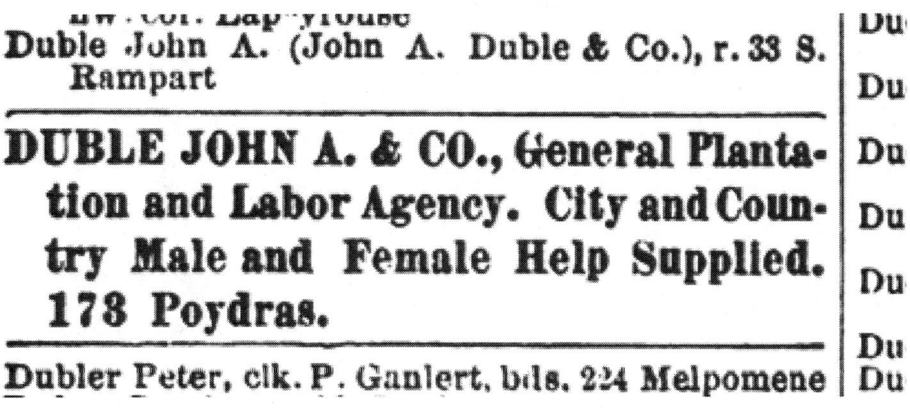
Duble John A. (John A. Duble & Co.), r. 33 S. Rampart

DUBLE JOHN A. & CO., General Plantation and Labor Agency. City and Country Male and Female Help Supplied. 178 Poydras.

Dubler Peter, clk. P. Ganlert, bds. 224 Melpomene

Figure 6.3. Labor ad, *Soards' New Orleans City Directory* (1875), p. 256.

Many laborers hired for the season were part of a much larger migration phenomenon that originated in the Upper South even before the end of the war. In a recent study, William G. Thomas III, Richard G. Healey, and Ian Cottingham found that, acting as a kind of labor broker, and beginning in mid–1865, the Freedmen's Bureau had a policy of issuing travel passports (or "transportation vouchers") to liberated people from Virginia, with Alexandria being a major hub of departure, and later, by 1867, from Memphis. The purpose of this policy was to relocate individuals, families, and groups to points in Maryland, Ohio, Arkansas, and the Deep South so that they could both find work and respond to submitted employment requests, some of which included plantation placement.[88] Later, another migration wave emerged out of both the Upper and the Lower South headed toward the Deep South. There were legitimate and pragmatic realities for this shift. One of these had to do with the fact that the economies in the region had deteriorated greatly as a result of both the war and the elements, with years of wind and rain destroying the topsoil. Another was related to the abuse and terror that white inhabitants inflicted on the freed people. While the Freedmen's Bureau ended its presence in Georgia as early as 1870, it officially remained in Mississippi until 1872. Moreover, by the mid–1870s, Mississippi was still under a Reconstruction Republican government. Thus, all these aspects offered the hope of better protections and security. There was also a greater demand for labor in the delta region, as well as the promise of higher wages. Hence, people left in search of a better situation.

Entrepreneurial opportunists seized the moment and led the charge. Agents— including former slaves and African American pastors and activists, such as Georgia state senator and minister Isaac Anderson; teacher and Republican activist George Ormond; former U.S. congressman Jefferson Long; politician, activist, and editor William A. Pledger; newspaper founder, editor, educator, and activist Sheriff Merrimon (alt. Merryman and Merriman) Howard; and others—went into business as head hunters of sorts, enticing the freed people with ads in newspapers and statements such as "It is the will of God that negroes should move to Mississippi.... Your failure in [Georgia] is proof that God [wants you to] go to Mississippi," the "Promised Land," and if people were "determined to emigrate," they would find "equal rights and fertile lands" in Mississippi. These labor agents escorted freed people as consignees westward across the American South to Selma, New Orleans, and beyond, to Arkansas. Indeed, by 1873–1874 a "flood of migration resembling the movement of troops at wartime" came in "railroad cars to Vicksburg and Meridian," and "fleets of covered wagons shuttled between Alabama and the Delta," while hundreds simply walked. Indeed, William Pledger settled a "colony" of migrant laborers in Jefferson County, Mississippi, not far to the south of Palmyra Plantation. Mississippi state senator, railroad promoter, and minister Henry P. Jacobs placed ads in Natchez's newspapers offering his services as an agent.[89]

Who were the migrants who made the trek? Countless freed African American men and many families. To be sure, in addition to those veteran inhabitants at Palmyra and intact families employed in sharecropping modalities, Lovell contracted with scores of migrant freedmen during his tenure.[90]

Although Lovell employed many people, one individual stands out. O. Kelly was the foreman at Palmyra for over ten years, as well as a business associate of Lovell's well up into the 1890s. While Lovell made no mention of him until September 1871, Kelly was at Palmyra well beforehand since (1) he is listed in the Freedmen's Bureau records regarding the Home Colony period at the Bend, and (2) his particulars are listed in the 1870 Agricultural Census (see table 6.4). With respect to the former, the Bureau records note that Kelly had owned three slaves there: Betsy, Thomas, and Lucinda Murray. Significantly, in the Quitman slave inventory from 1859, Betsy, Thomas, and Lucinda are registered (but no surnames are mentioned). Whether these were the same individuals is difficult to say for certain. With respect to the 1870 Census, clearly, Lovell provided Kelly with the incentives of both land and sharecropping.

As a resident sharecropper and foreman, Kelly performed the nuts-and-bolts tasks of the planting season. He regularly wrote notes to Lovell that could be likened to reports, keeping him informed of both productivity and the quality of produce. He also evaluated chattel and farming equipment and ensured that they were working properly. Lovell would go on to hire other foremen, or "overseers" (as he came to refer to them after 1880), but the records are laced with references to Kelly, including one note in

1886 indicating that Lovell had contracted with him for a specific job of levee augmentation for $224.63 for a week's work.[91]

Over the years Lovell routinely commented on the quality of Kelly's performance, as well as that of the squads. For example, he praised "everything running smoothly," "everything looking well," "Mr. O. Kelly commenced planting cotton," and "Mr. Kelly hard at work," elsewhere noting that Kelly had "Palmyra in [a] better fix than anywhere else on the island." He even admitted that "Kelly's cotton is better than mine."[92] Other positive evaluatory comments were "Found everything working well," "I think I never saw a better cotton stalk on 365 acres than there is in the Palmyra Squad," "I have never seen finer farming than was done in R. Squad this year," and "there is not as fine [a squad] a[s] Rosedale Squad."[93]

However, Lovell did not hold back when he was disappointed with those he employed, occasionally even discharging them. "Things have not been working as well as they should ... [the foreman's replacement] does not work well," "discharged Mr. Rhea as Overseer of Rosedale Squad," "Ichler [sp.?] is a poor manager ... and I am fearful," and the like were typical notes on this subject.[94] In these comments we see a similarity to Lovell's father-in-law's dissatisfaction with his overseers in the antebellum days.

The Precarious Nature of Recovery

During the 1870s, a series of events unfolded that, on the one hand, pointed to unprecedented production in the postbellum period and yet, on the other, produced one disaster after another. Long-term recovery was never certain. The decade opened with a bumper crop, the proof of which came on October 9 when the Davis plantations earned a prize of $500 for the best single bale of long-staple cotton at the St. Louis Fair.[95] Then the Panic of 1873 hit, causing widespread distress and triggering an economic depression that lasted until 1879—the year, coincidentally, when the Exoduster movement began. Reminiscent of the early post-war years, 1874 was disastrous for planters of the river counties. Spring brought several floods, which delayed planting, and the summer brought a drought. In addition to the dire economic situation, the mules at Palmyra were besieged by buffalo gnats, with 10 dying in the space of one week in April. And the river swelled again to record proportions in the early fall, with Lovell indicating that he had informed the hands that they all should expect to rebuild the levies, noting somberly, "hope better times are coming."[96] Cotton prices continued to drop, which squeezed earnings. While Lovell would comment regarding the dreadful developments of 1874 that "our prospects are truly gloomy," he would also report by the year's end that 1,440 bales of cotton had been produced.[97]

Lovell was consistently emotive and anxious about the water levels. His exasperation with both the weather and the battle to reinforce the levies was shown as flood after flood came. For example, during the flood of 1882 he had a total of 300 laborers working at a fever pitch to augment the banks. He feared the whole Bend would "go under." Then, when the levees did break, he documented that water had completely surrounded the main house. He also noted that the "people at Ursino" (which was Kelly's place on the Bend) were "truly in a deplorable condition," and "many hands are leaving daily. The future is anything but bright. Hard times ahead." Two years later, during another onslaught, he despaired, "I have given up all hope ... nothing can save us but a miracle," "it is a hard [battle] for a man to fight," and "having a devil of a time." He also expressed complete exasperation with Jefferson Davis, who "will not keep up" his end of the bargain in maintaining the integrity of the Bend's levees, adding that "if I had control of the island I would make it the finest place in the South."[98]

The economic situation, floods, and droughts of the mid–1870s were not the only menaces with which the inhabitants of Davis Bend had to contend. The Mississippi Delta region was also a breeding ground for diseases such as malaria and yellow fever, and despite the development of a vaccine as early as 1798, smallpox was common. A combination of drought, low cotton prices, and a deadly outbreak of yellow fever in 1878 irreparably damaged the delta's economy. Estimates were that roughly 3,000 laborers in the river counties would be laid off. All this said, Lovell's reports for the year portrayed an entirely different scenario, with "everything looking well," "good farming weather," and "Mr. Kelly thinks we shall make ... more than last year."[99]

Like his Russian counterpart, Lovell had his own set of problems associated with finances and family issues. With respect to the former, Lovell's fiscal gymnastics were exhaustive. His financial responsibilities were most often one and the same as those of his extended family. He was constantly extending, exchanging, and collecting notes of credit, loans, and cash with multiple factors, agents, brokers, insurance companies, employees, family members, and other individuals, both named and unnamed. He was also the point person who spearheaded and managed the family's thirty-five-year effort to receive compensation from the federal government for its confiscation of Palmyra during the war. Lovell's practice of transferring titles to property and IOUs from one family member to another was not dissimilar to the types of financial machinations Vasili Yazykov engaged in. For example, on January 1, 1875, Lovell documented that, as a result of General Quitman's estate being compensated to the tune of $22,550 by the federal government for its confiscation of Palmyra in 1864 and 1865, Tonie, as the rightful heir, "loaned" it to her husband, Lovell, at 8 percent interest. Lovell put Palmyra up as collateral to secure the loan. This was no small amount.[100]

Notwithstanding the financial cat-and-mouse games, like the Yazykovs, William Storrow Lovell's family lived well. For example, the "Family Account" list for 1873–1874 alone included payments for income (state) taxes; food; coffee; ale; markets; drinks; chickens; eggs; rents; factors; insurance; church; medicine; doctor; dentist; children; school; books; pants; shoes; hats; tailor; "things for Tonie"; cigars; theater; opera; races; trips to Toronto, Sewanee, and elsewhere; the Hancock Club; the Gator Club; "things for Christmas"; and a "dog chain and collar" (to name just a few).[101]

As for the freed people at Palmyra, unlike their counterparts at Yazykovo Selo, it appears that in general they worked solidly for the plantation's landlord over the entire course of the period under study. To be clear, they fulfilled their obligations or provided the services for which they contracted. It is here that a nuanced but striking set of differences between the two groups is discerned. Whereas the peasants of Yazykovo Selo did not participate in the terms of the Statutory Charter that Vasili Yazykov imposed, the freed people at Palmyra did engage in the contracting process, even if it was by proxy, in the form of labor agents who arranged the agreements on their behalf. The variety of compensationary modalities at the American demesne also seems to have made a difference. In addition, the labor obligations for the American freed people were seasonal and, in theory, for one season only. The labor for which they were obligated was within a contained time frame, whereas, for the Russian freed people, the obligations were in perpetuity (at least until a Redemption Agreement was arranged). Further, the fact that Yazykov was the "former master" meant that after emancipation, working for the landlord was perhaps too personal—too reminiscent of the former days. At Palmyra, with the exception of the veteran inhabitants, there was an impersonal relationship between Lovell and his employees.

The exception to this rule, however, was the commotion associated with the 1879 Kansas Exoduster movement cited at the beginning of chapter 5. In January, Lovell confided that "six familys [*sic*] ... left ... for Kansas," adding that he didn't "like the look of things." He also noted that he could not pay his double sister-in-law, Louisa Quitman Lovell, the $2,250 he owed her because "the Hands had struck for a reduction in work & gin[ning] which I will have to grant." Although by March he wrote with relief that the "Kansas ... strikes appear to be over and every thing [*sic*] [seems to be] working smoothly," Lovell added, "I truly hope it will keep ... for I have had a hard time of it getting anymore hands." Soon, however, he observed that things appeared "to be over and everything" was working "better than I had expected," adding cryptically, "Kansas fears [are now] quiet[.] Peace not suffers much by it." By September, Lovell optimistically noted that, with respect to the cotton crop, "[we] ... have shipped over double [the] amount up to this time last year." But yet again, with another lurch back to pessimism, he expressed that his fear that "1880 will I think prove the hardest year since the war," as there was so much "dissatisfaction among the hands." At 1879's end he concluded that the year would prove to be "a heavy loss."[102]

That being said, the 1880 Agricultural Census indicated that the plantation was worth $114,150.[103] The information in tables 6.1 and 6.4 indicates that Palmyra's cotton production in 1860, 1867, 1868, 1870, and 1880 was 325 bales of cotton, 310 b/c, 554 b/c, 1,228 b/c, and 1,600 b/c, respectively. This success did not happen by accident or without effort. That each bale of cotton weighed 400 pounds before 1870 and 450 pounds afterward makes these figures even more significant. Such an increase in output could lead us to infer that squad labor was more productive than the slave labor of earlier days. Whether the increase was related to the seasonal commitments, the forms of compensation, the mobility of freed people (which would imply a steady turnover rate), the fact that squad labor was "freer" than slave labor, or a combination of these factors, is difficult to say. But certainly, just as freedom made the difference, negatively, with respect to Yazykovo Selo's inhabitants' labor performance and productivity, so, too, does it appear that it had a positive effect at Palmyra. Interestingly, although the categories are not available in the censes before 1870, the "land under cultivation" afterward increased at Palmyra, with 4,400 acres worked in 1870 and 5,670 in 1880. This change also must be considered when explaining the increase in production. In addition, the stewardship of William Storrow Lovell must be taken into account, as he was a hands-on manager who was fully engaged with the demesne's operation for decades. Advantageous though Palmyra's location and productive capacity were, it did not operate on autopilot.

Equally important is interpreting the 1880 value of the plantation at $114,150, which, clearly, had diminished when compared with the valuations of $129,490 in 1870 and $200,000 in 1860. Obviously, it decreased over time. (In 1850, the plantation was valued at $90,000.) One factor that may well explain the difference is that before emancipation the value of slaves would have been part of the equation. Another glaring issue is the steep decline in cotton prices over the years, with one pound garnering $1.90 in 1860 versus 10 cents in 1879.

In these respects, what happened at Palmyra in the post-emancipation period is in line with what Michael Wayne has argued—namely, that the wealth and number of plantations in the Mississippi River delta region contracted after 1865, and, by 1880, there were fewer large plantations. But those that remained were very productive and wealthy. Indeed, notwithstanding the great challenges that Lovell faced over the years, the Quitmans/Lovells lived well. They traveled to spas, sent their children to private schools, and had class and station. In this respect, this analysis is in line with the Seymour Becker thesis, which is that while the Russian nobility's holdings contracted after emancipation, those that remained prospered.[104] For the reasons explained in the first half of this chapter, the Yazykovs' fate did not comport with the Lovells'—at least not at this stage. As the epilogue will explain, years later, whereas Palmyra would become an abandoned wilderness, left with no trace of the vibrant economic activity of its former days, Yazykovo would be a thriving community, showcasing great economic and cultural production, albeit with a completely new steward at the helm and a modernized economic infrastructure.

An Important consideration is what the American freed people believed about freedom in its relation to the labor question. Robert Follette has pointed out that a starting point for understanding is to acknowledge that their direct, firsthand experience of slavery influenced their postbellum outlook. Acculturation and assimilation were neither assured nor linear. For those who experienced liberation, their path to freedom revealed an aspect of double consciousness: looking back to "their" culture, as well as forging ahead into the unknown, crafting an identity that did not have a blueprint. Citing Thomas Holt, Follette has also explained that the freed people's task was to reconcile their new, de jure political, economic, and social status as free agents with the sobering, physical realities of sustenance and survival.[105] To be liberated in the instant that emancipation ushered their new status in was not the same as "becoming" free. The former is an event. The latter is a process. At the time, both the implicit and the explicit prevailing definitions of freedom were related in one way or another to labor. Thus, concepts like owning land and/or property; being an entrepreneur or a farmer; and, in particular, having the self-determination with respect to one's labor—that is, being free to choose where to work and with whom to negotiate a fair wage for an honest day's work—were the norms.[106] While the freed people may well have been unable to actualize freedom immediately according to those definitional principles, as Frederick Douglass pointed out at the time, emancipation did open the door to a different future.[107]

This idea of a future orientation helps us find meaning in what the freed people at Palmyra Plantation did with respect to labor. For example, phenomena such as migrant and seasonal labor patterns, the migrations, the agitation relating to a variety of adverse work conditions that emerged in 1879, and, especially, the *turnover rate* all illustrate how "freedom" was expressed in their mobility and their understanding of time. That is, their lives were no longer frozen in a static, presentist mode. This was a radical shift when compared to the days of slavery. It evidences efficacy, autonomy, self-determination, and an orientation toward the future. As freer agents, they had the freedom to act because of the contingency of their mobility. In this regard, there was a commonality with their Russian counterparts, where the peasants in Simbirsk Province were mobile in their commercial pursuits.

* * *

In this chapter, I have comparatively examined issues associated with labor, management, production, and productivity during the more protracted post-emancipation period. As other categories of analysis in previous chapters have indicated, I identified a number of similarities that, although they did not manifest in identical chronological trajectories, suggest that specific phenomena go hand in hand with an emancipation process engineered by the state, irrespective of the differences between the national cultures, geographic distance, and political-economic systems of Russia and the United States.

First, as the landlords and managers of their demesnes, both Vasili Yazykov and William Storrow Lovell grappled with a variety of problems over several decades. On the one hand, they repeatedly (and at times preemptively) acted on behalf of their own self-interest, in order to get ahead of developments. On the other hand, each struggled with finances, as well as finding both competent managers and reliable labor. They also wrestled with personal family issues as well as natural disasters, such as fires, famine, floods, and pests. The general economic conditions in each region likewise presented problematic scenarios. While both Yazykov and Lovell were military men in their early years, they later became stewards of demesnes, acquiring them either through inheritance or by proxy via marriage. Ironically, both men even shared the experience of having their loyalties to tsar and region questioned.[108] However, the fact that Yazykov continued to live and act according to his estate and that Lovell seemed to epitomize the "new master" prototype demonstrate continuity with the trends and typicalities in their respective countries. Notwithstanding the difficulties, both lived well.

Yazykov and Lovell each sought a particular "type" in a manager. At Yazykovo Selo, Yazykov, like many noble landlords in Simbirsk Province, hired Tatars because of their merchant status and business acumen. Even though Tatars had traditionally been excluded from the formal economic grid in the province, they were still highly successful in navigating it for a variety of reasons. Conversely, O. Kelly was not an "outsider" (someone who was marginalized in the larger mainstream society because of his religious/ethnic characteristics). He had an association with Palmyra Plantation going back before emancipation, and, although Lovell was fully engaged in overseeing management at the demesne, it appears that Kelly was indispensable and had Lovell's confidence. But similar to Yazykov, who had a rather acrimonious relationship with some of the managers he hired, Lovell also grappled with a number of bad hires. It is interesting to note that Lovell, like Stepanov, utilized child labor. And both Stepanov and Lovell promoted the incentive of wage labor, though at opposite ends of their tenure. That is, whereas the American planter utilized this approach immediately after his recovery of the demesne and more infrequently as years went by, wage labor emerged with Stepanov's proprietorship, which happened to coincide with the Redemption Law of 1881.[109]

But what of the labor needs at Yazykovo Selo and Palmyra Plantation after liberation? Each demesne's raison d'être was not changed by emancipation. Yazykovo Selo continued to be a community composed of both a village society and a noble nest, and it featured an agricultural mode of production as well as a wool factory, the latter of which continued to depend on requisitions from the Treasury. Palmyra's purpose was also unaltered. Its capacity as a powerhouse of cotton production continued. What *had* changed was the *form* of labor that each manager sought, *to whom* they looked to supply that labor, and *on whom* they could rely. Irrespective of the de jure prescriptions for that labor in the Russian case, and the de facto ones in the American instance, both contexts showed that the elites looked to the former serfs and slaves as the source of that labor, because of their traditional identities. However, whereas Lovell could rely on those freed people with whom he contracted, it appears that Yazykov could not count on his "former people" to work, even if they were legally obligated to do so. The former serfs at Yazykovo Selo may well have been deliberately ambivalent with respect to the labor obligations imposed by the state, but they were neither passive nor marginalized. They participated in a variety of cottage industries and diverse trade practices for both sustenance and support. They may well have been attached to the land, but they were not rendered immobile. These variables were also present at Palmyra, but obligations, mobility, and restraints manifested in a configuration unique to the plantation's contextual circumstances. That is, because of their mobility, the American freed people could negotiate a fixed time frame in which they did have labor obligations. And in that "fixed time frame" they were "attached to the land." But this arrangement was not permanent. They were neither passive nor marginalized. Squad labor proved to be the pliable and versatile answer to the labor question during this intermediary stage. In a sense, mobility was the "escape hatch" for both sets of freed people.

In the spirit of both the Beckert and the Stanziani theses, the time frame in this study represents an intermediary stage during which great adjustments occurred with respect to labor. This period witnessed an acceleration of market activity and cottage industriousness in the Russian case, as well as the appearance of the pliable, adaptable institution of "squad labor" in the American one. This stage was situated between one of unfree labor (serfdom and slavery) and one that ushered in still more new adjustments—namely, the institutionalization of wage labor after 1881 by the Redemption Law in Russia and fully entrenched sharecropping modality after 1880 in the American South.[110] In addition, in this intermediary stage, although the freed people were no longer enserfed and enslaved, neither were they completely free. It is in these discoveries that an element of convergence, or a parallel progression, is identified between the two examples in this study.

Table 6.1:[111] Produce at Davis Bend

1850

	Cotton Bales (400 lbs. per bale)	Indian Corn (bushels)	Butter (lbs.)	Implements & Machinery	Value of Stock	Value of Farm	No. of Slaves
Davis Plantations	251	20,000	600	$4,000	$21,500	**$125,000**	314
Palmyra Plantation	369	16,000	2,300	$20,500	$23,000	**$90,000**	423

1860

	Cotton Bales (400 lbs. per bale)	Indian Corn (bushels)	Butter (lbs.)	Implements & Machinery	Value of Stock	Value of Farm	No. of Slaves/ Houses
Davis Plantations	232	1,000	500	$900	$20,000	**$175,000**	467/104
Palmyra Plantation	325	1,000	2,000	$1,000	$10,000	**$200,000**	308/80

Produce at Davis Bend during the Home Colony Period and Mid- to Late 1860s

	Cotton Bales (400 lbs. per bale)	Year	Profit	Cotton Bales (400 lbs. per bale)	Year	Profit
Home Colony	150	1864	n/a			
Home Colony	1,736	1865	$159,200			
Davis Plantations	620	1866	n/a	790	1868	n/a
Palmyra Plantation	310	1867	$2,000	554	1868	n/a

1. The contrasts between 1850 and 1860 for both the Davis plantations and Palmyra Plantation are striking: Although the value of the farm was considerably less for both properties in 1850, the Davis properties had more slaves in the later decade and Palmyra had fewer, the difference being that the former gained 153 and the latter lost 115. Also, the number of cotton bales remained essentially the same. Variables such as weather, pestilence, and insect damage might help explain these differences.

2. The contrast between 1860 and the mid- to late 1860s for the number of cotton bales for both properties is great, with the Davis plantations gaining 558 and Palmyra Plantation gaining 229.

3. While the produce for 1860 indicates that Palmyra Plantation listed 308 slaves, table 6.2 shows that in 1859 it had 359, the difference being that the demesne lost 51 in one year.

4. Table 6.2 shows that, although the Davis plantations had twice as much acreage under cotton cultivation as Palmyra in 1879, the latter produced twice as many bales. Using the New Orleans market rate ($ .10; see table 6.3), Palmyra would have made twice as much money as the Davis plantations.

Table 6.2:[112] Personal Tax Rolls

Davis Plantations

Year	Cattle (over 20 head)	Slaves (under 60 yrs.)	Amount of State Tax ($)	Cotton Bales (400 lbs. per b/c)
1848	350	289	194.00	
1854	45	300	118.00	
1856	115	336	132.00	1,265
1857	200	384	167.00	
1858	200	410	176.00	
1859	169	402	173.00	
1860	—	429	332.65	

	Acres Tilled for Cotton	Total Farm Production ($)	Bushels (corn)	Bushels (sweet potatoes)	Cotton Bales (400 lbs. per b/c)
1869	3,700	192,000	2,000	100	1,900
1879	**1,000**	50,000	6,000	1,000	**800 (worth $32,000)**

Palmyra Plantation

Year	Cattle (over 20 head)	Slaves (under 60 yrs.)	Amount of State Tax ($)	Cotton Bales (400 lbs. per b/c)
1848	110	311	189.00	
1854	50	291	110.00	
1856	50	310	117.00	2,200
1857	60	338	136.00	
1858	134	348	140.00	
1859	108	359	145.00	
1860	—	—	—	
1871	22	—	2,326.00	

	Acres Tilled for Cotton	Total Farm Production ($)	Bushels (corn)	Bushels (sweet potatoes)	Cotton Bales (400 lbs. per b/c)
1869	3,700 (approximate)				1,228
1879*	**500**				**1,600 (worth $64,000)**

*Property in 1879 valued at $7,720.00

Table 6.3:[113] Cotton Prices in U.S. Dollars

New York Market (per pound)		New Orleans Market (per pound)	
1860	$1.90	May 1865	$.045
1861	$0.31	November 1865	$0.50
1862	$0.67	December 1866	$0.30
1863	$1.01	December 1867	$0.15
1864	$0.83	December 1878	$0.12
1865	$0.45		$1879.10
1866	$0.25		
1867	$0.19		
1868	$0.16		
1869	$0.19		
1870	$0.18		
1871	$0.13		
1872	$0.15		
1873	$0.14		
1874	$0.13		
1875	$0.13		
1876	$0.12		
1877	$0.11		
1900	$0.05		

Table 6.4:[114] Produce at Palmyra Plantation

	1870 Agricultural Census		1880 Agricultural Census
	WSL	Kelly	WSL
Total Acres of Land	4,400		5,670
Value of Farm	**$85,000**	**$800**	**$103,650**
Value of Farming Implements	$5,500	$40	$3,500
Horses	10		7
Mules	36		100
Cows	7	2	10
Butter (lbs)			104
Oxen	8		8
Cattle	11		20
Sheep			45*
Lambs			**10**
Swine	8		20
Value of Livestock	$6,800		$7,000
Oats (bushels)		20	
Indian Corn (bushels)	2,600		
Cotton (Bales 1=450 lbs.)[†]	**1,228**	**18**	**1,600[‡]**
Improved Land	**400 acres**	**40 acres**	
Estimated value of plantation	**$129,490[§]**	**$1,860**	**$114,150**
Estimated value of all Farm Production			$83,200
Amount paid for wages for Farm labor during 1879 Including Value of Board			$12,000

*Does not include 10 killed by dogs.
[†]Note: In the 1870 Census, cotton bales were 450 pounds, whereas in 1860 they were 400 pounds.
[‡]See Hermann, *Pursuit*, pp. 208–209.
[§]Clearly, these total figures are more than the sum of their parts, which is $97,300 and $840, respectively. However, these were the entries on the 1870 Census.

**Table 6.5:[115] Bales of Cotton (year end)
at Palmyra Plantation Over Time**

Year	Bales
1866	188*
1867	310[†]
1868	554
1869	100[‡]
1870	N/A
1871	N/A
1872	N/A
1873	1,640
1874	1,440[†]
1875	2,018[†]
1876	1,093[†]
1877	1,674
1878	1,129
1879	1,634[‡]
1880	1,174
1881	1,713
1882	685[†]
1883	1,084
1884	678[†]
1885	981
1886	704[†]

*This was from Belen.

[†]Year of severe flood. The river's course at the Bend's site was changed in 1867. The flood of 1875 was the notorious anomaly "August flood." However, even though 1875 was a flood year, Palmyra produced a postbellum record crop.

[‡]The contrast of these years with the bales of cotton produced at the Davis plantations is striking: in 1869 they produced 1,900, and in 1879 they produced 800. (See table 6.2.)

PART IV

Gleaning and Taking Stock

7

The Meaning of Freedom
in Daily Life

Thus far, this study has comparatively examined emancipation's rollout and the terms of freedom in Russia and the United States in general (and at each demesne specifically). Aside from issues of land, labor, obligations, expectations, laws and regulations, suspicions, rumors, and resistance, the historian still craves answers to the following questions: What about the freed people? What did freedom mean to them? How were their lives changed after emancipation? Here we are met with answers that are insufficient primarily because firsthand accounts are rare (if they exist at all). That said, there are ways to address this lacuna by posing different questions: For example, in what *ways* were the freed people free? In what ways did they live that were different from their pre-emancipation experiences? In what ways did a sense of community and identity change? The evidence I uncovered can be categorized into subheadings under the broad topic of daily life. Some of these categories include education, festivities, and sources of sustenance. What today is quotidian was on the eve of emancipation unimaginable. Still, although changes in circumstances represented great strides after emancipation, many old attitudes and habits persisted.

Education and the Freed People

Before emancipation, it was extremely rare in the American South for a slave to receive a formal education. To be sure, there were exceptions. The experience of Frederick Douglass demonstrated that a slave could both self-teach and receive informal reading and writing instruction. However, that example was extraordinary, and it demonstrated the surreptitious nature of (and danger involved in) educating slaves. Still, a scouring of the famous *Slave Narratives* from the Federal Writers' Project of the 1930s reveals that, at best, "stolen ejucation" could well have happened, but it was piecemeal; at worst, it was atypical.[1] In general, while many Americans in the Northeast had access to formal education in the antebellum period, for a variety of reasons, most in the South did not. But to be sure, in one way or another, all slave states outlawed the education of slaves. As one former slave, Mr. Jim Allen, explained, "Dey didn' want us to learn how to go to de free country." Although there are no tabulations of slave literacy from the antebellum period, illiteracy among the population was widespread, though not universal. For example, in the cities educated slaves could be found. Therefore, it would be fair to say that roughly 5–10 percent of slaves were literate.[2]

In Russia, education also reached a small portion of the country's overall population before emancipation. However, unlike America, which saw the initiative for public education emerge in the 1830s and 1840s in New England, most Russian schools were set up by state initiatives and were reserved for male members of the nobility, specifically in the forms of *gymnasia*, *lycées*, and cadet corps. In addition, various government departments sponsored schools.

Like their American counterparts, the overwhelming majority of serfs were illiterate. However, unlike the slave states, it was not illegal for serfs to be educated. Indeed, Russian peasants could set up and run their own schools—*if*, of course, they were approved by their master. For a variety of reasons, however, these efforts were often short lived. Some problems included cash and supply shortages, attrition, and the peasants' privileging of seasonal work over studies. Already overtaxed and burdened with obligations, peasants did not like chipping in money for schools, especially when they perceived education as a bad thing for their children. In a rural society where children were needed by the family for both their labor and their youth, education was often eschewed because parents saw it as pulling the young away from the field and family. And anyway, they rationalized, the merchants were a perfect example that education was not needed to "get ahead." Furthermore (and as has been pointed out in a number of ways throughout this study), because they were suspicious of authorities' motives,[3] Russian peasants could also be wary of formal education. While they may very well have sent their children to school to learn to read or write, often, after perhaps one or two years, they had no use for the cultural baggage of educated Russia. Peasants could also consider that education spoiled their children, even teaching them to be disobedient.

During the pre-emancipation era, peasant children often attended parish schools run by Russian Orthodox priests. These were the closest approximations to the parish school system in America. Many pupils at the Russian parish schools lived on the premises. Moreover, in addition to their studies, they participated in—or, more correctly, were impressed into—service in the form of helping with the maintenance and operation of the church and/or monastery. In fact, often "education" was merely a smokescreen for attracting boys for the sole purpose of being assistants (or more accurately servants) to the clergy. Peasants were frequently suspicious of the clergy because of the history of abuse and exploitation of children at their hands. Conversely, and similar to how the Russian army was often a "dumping ground" for villages that wished to cull their population of, say, wayward and/or difficult young men, poverty-stricken parents might send their offspring to parish schools if given the opportunity. This was a way for parents to unload an unruly or unwanted child. Or it could be a way to guarantee a reliable and structured standard of living for a child whom they could not support.[4]

Emancipation appears to have not only reinforced these attitudes toward education but possibly contributed to even more negative ones. As Ben Eklof has explained, many came to see education as another attempt by elites to re-enserf them. Indeed, some historians even say that after emancipation two-thirds of all peasants opposed schools. Conversely, because of the state's historic distrust of private initiatives, peasant schools were often suppressed.[5]

Following emancipation, Russian elites proceeded to initiate both formal and informal educational efforts. Conceived of and established by the government, the rationale for education in the context of emancipation was to uplift the newly liberated children (both girls and boys), instill proper religious beliefs, and make them reliable politically. Furthermore, in conjunction with the decision to modernize the country, the vision for public schools also made allowances for schools in factories, the idea being that it would aid productivity. In 1863 and 1864, statutes pertaining to education were issued. The latter established public literacy schools that primarily targeted the peasant population. The most common school after emancipation became that run by the local government (*zemstvo*) councils.[6] Also per the 1864 law, women were allowed to teach.[7] Ideally, the subjects earmarked for instruction included reading, writing, arithmetic, science, geography, history, and Bible studies. Three years of education were guaranteed for each pupil.[8]

The Russian government estimated that by 1864, 1 in 117 Russians was enrolled in a school of one kind or another. This number was up from 1 in 170 in 1854 and 1 in 208 in 1838. But, to borrow an expression of Ben Eklof's, the accuracy of these statistics was a "comic unreality." They did not consider important qualifiers such as the fact that "enrollment" did not necessarily mean attendance or that both the cities and the western provinces (especially in the Baltic region) had far more schools than those in rural and eastern Russia. In fact, one could make the case that the farther east from Moscow one went, the fewer formal, functioning schools were found. Also, those statistics did not include informal schools such as those established by the peasants.[9]

Besides official efforts set in motion by government edicts, a more informal approach was initiated by upper- and middle-class elites who sought to "go to the people" and educate them. Originating as an agrarian, socialist, and populist movement, the "Narodniks" (*narodniki*), from the word *narod*, or people, debated among themselves about the place of capitalism in Russia. Indeed, some of them were the forebears of the kaleidoscopic and multifaceted collection of revolutionaries and terrorists that would be a significant feature in Russian society for the next sixty years. While Avrahm Yarmolinsky criticized the movement as a "children's crusade," Daniel Field has explained that in its nascent form, the movement comprised many professionals and members of the intelligentsia, mostly students and academics, who sought to "bring light" to the liberated peasants. To be sure, in addition to an activist agenda, many were motivated by paternalism and benevolence.[10]

The first wave of activists appeared as early as 1861, when a small number of propagandists set out to tutor the peasants. Speaking and writing in peasant *patois*, these populist reformers used colloquialisms and invoked biblical law. They seized on and exploited the peasants' suspicions of the authorities' intentions and fed into the rumors that the "real freedom" had been thwarted by the greedy nobility.[11]

Many education "inspectors" were also *narodniki*. A combination of facilitator and critic, the inspector had broad powers to effect state educational policies. Some inspectors were passive, paper-pushing bureaucrats, while others were socialist opponents of the government. Still others were enthusiastic reformers, such as the "extraordinary" father of Vladimir Lenin, Ilya Ulyanov. Of Chuvashi heritage, Ulyanov was an educator by profession, had great organizational talent, and, with a "missionary zeal," had high expectations for modernizing the education system in Simbirsk Province. Appointed inspector of the province's schools in 1869, he served in this capacity until his death in 1886. Indeed, Ulyanov was a man in constant motion over the course of his career, traveling throughout the province, working to open schools across the rural landscape, and then repeatedly following up with inspections.[12] One of these was the school at Yazykovo Selo.

In the spring of 1869, under Ulyanov's supervision, schools were opened at both Yazykovo Selo and Undory. In fact, he attended the inauguration event at the latter. This was a historic moment for both demesnes. Although, like many Russian estates, the peasants at Yazykovo Selo and Undory may well have had some kind of tutoring affiliated with the village church, this was a first in that these were official, government-sanctioned schools.[13] While records indicate that after 1861 Vasili Yazykov stopped funding both the church and the hospital,[14] they do show that he paid for the renovation of a house that became the school, in addition to purchasing materials and supplies. In 1875, Yazykov funded the building of a new school specifically designed for education, which included proper windows and a blackboard at one end of the room. Although records do not indicate how many of Yazykovo Selo's inhabitants were enrolled, in 1876 the school at Undory registered 30 students ages 9–14. This number is astonishingly low given the fact that the village's population in 1881 had 321 households and 1,856 people.[15] Thereafter, records make no mention of the fate of education at Yazykovo Selo until the turn of the century. In the same way that Vasili Yazykov carried out his duty when he swiftly effected the Statutory Charter, and yet did not act on implementing a Redemption Agreement, it is plausible to infer that his efforts regarding education followed a similar pattern. Moreover, the school and hospital were not included in Feodor Stepanov's rehabilitation of the estate after he purchased it in 1881. To the extent that Stepanov seems to have been devoid of paternalistic proclivities, here was a similarity to William Storrow Lovell. However, things changed when he died in 1898 and his son inherited the demesne.

Mikhail F. Stepanov's upbringing was exceptional for a member of a Russian merchant family in that he was educated in Western Europe and steeped in its culture. Clearly, he considered the historical value of Yazykovo Selo since, after building a smaller but charming two-story home for himself on the estate grounds, he preserved the mansion and its contents, freezing it in time, including the Pushkin room where the famous poet had spent several nights and left a personalized example of graffiti when he etched his initials in the pane glass of one of the windows. The younger Stepanov expanded the estate's gardens, paid for the village church's restoration, and organized a salaried church choir as well as an orchestra comprising the factory workers' children. He modernized the factory by implementing mechanized processes, including electricity. Next to the factory Stepanov modernized a barracks for its workers. In 1903, he was instrumental in opening a school near the factory for 60 of the workers' children. In all, he spent an estimated 15,000 rubles to buy books for the school's library and the children's education. He also built a small maternity hospital for the village and donated thousands of rubles for its maintenance.

But it was in the arts that Mikhail Stepanov took his boldest steps when he funded the construction of an 800-seat theater/cinema at the estate, where operas, concerts, and dances were performed by the village's former serfs. Additionally, Stepanov was instrumental in opening the opera house in the city of Kazan, north of Simbirsk on the Volga, where, in the first month alone of its opening season, the box office made 40,000 rubles.[16] All this and more was the result of the younger Stepanov's makeup, which was a combination of merchant-entrepreneur, paternalist, and aesthete. His power as the new lord of Yazykovo Selo meant that he had the authority to effect and implement his goals. Most of all, and in the tradition of estate culture, the Peasant Orchestra of Yazykovo Selo demonstrated a merchant landlord's creative way to simultaneously attach the factory workers to the demesne, "uplift" the peasants, display "folk" culture, and provide entertainment both at the estate and beyond via touring events. Fifteen years later, when a Yazykov relative visited the estate, he observed that the village had one hospital and two schools that were "fully functioning."[17]

Sources cite the establishment of schools at Yazykovo Selo and Undory, but they tell little else about the education that followed and the peasants' experiences with it. Just as the previous chapter demonstrated that after emancipation, production both at the factory and in the fields stagnated, does it follow that the school at Yazykovo Selo languished in the period between its founding in 1869 and its rehabilitation by Stepanov in 1903? Indeed, opening a school is one thing; sustaining it is an altogether different matter.

One way of trying to understand what happened is to consider an account left by Valerian N. Nazar'ev, a Simbirsk native, close friend and colleague of Ilya Ulyanov, and neighbor of Vasili Yazykov. Like Ulyanov, Nazar'ev was an educator and an inspector. He was also instrumental in opening the schools at both Yazykovo Selo and Undory. Nazar'ev documented the grim realities associated with educating the peasants after emancipation. Writing approximately seven years after the first wave of post-emancipation schools had opened, he addressed the logistical difficulties associated with founding and especially maintaining schools. It was one thing to open a school and another to maintain it by collecting money from the peasants every year, for years, and retaining both students and teachers. In addition, the facilities were ghastly, including roach and other insect infestations, poor ventilation, and no heat. The "school" would often be a dark, damp, and filthy room in a basement, or in an old shack behind the church, or even in a former jail. No thought was given to whether its location was beside a noisy factory or tavern. Moreover, there was no oversight or organizational professionalism (that is, no lists of teachers and their assignments), no uniform curricula had been implemented, and no inventories existed. For example, 10,000 books had been collected for distribution across the province. They were discovered years later, still in a warehouse, many devoured by mice.

Another theme addressed by Nazar'ev is the *mentalité* of various groups. For example, he maintained that the peasants' lives were "devoured by isolation and boredom." He was "astonished" by their "apathy" and "manners," and he noted that they could not understand that being educated required months (if not years) of work. Rather, they expected an "instant result." When that did not happen, they lost all interest, which only reinforced their preconceived notions about education. They completely distrusted education and were suspicious of the authorities' motives. They were not receptive to the teachers, associating them with both the history of abuse and the distant, modern city—indeed, modernity. They certainly resented the petition drives for financial contribution to maintain the schools, including teachers' salaries and even candles for the icons.

In fact, Nazar'ev concluded that what was on the peasants' minds was that which had been seared into their memory: the desire for land. For them, freedom did not mean education and work. Rather, it meant having land and being free from authority, domination, and obligations. Down through the ages, peasant societies across the globe have had an attachment to the land, the kind that has an almost spiritual dimension, and Russian peasants were no exception. Their relationship to the land, *their* land, was indissoluble. Indeed, it was so deep that it was a cornerstone of their identity. But Nazar'ev rationalized that for the peasants, being free meant being "idle." However, we know this cannot be true since at regular local markets, fairs, and festivals, and even impromptu gatherings, traveling salesmen and -women peddled crafts and products. Actually, showing *his* lack of understanding of peasant culture, Nazar'ev supported his conclusions by citing the peasants' superstitions, *patois*, and cultural style of communicating, such as the use of archaic, quaint, or esoteric sayings and homespun advice and parables. All these, he argued, inhibited education, insisting that dialogic conversation and reflection was alien to them. Nazar'ev noted that when peasants did attend school, the village pecking order was transferred over to the new environment, and therefore the concept of equal treatment was absent. If they were taught and learned anything at all, it was to memorize this or that, but not to understand why.

Nazar'ev was even more critical of the bureaucrats and teachers who had been in the education system. Not only were they "lazy" and "incompetent," but they also grafted the system at every opportunity. In a scathing portrait, Nazar'ev noted they were all "talk" and no "do," making "endless pronouncements" (a frequent one being "Hope and Change") and voluminous reports. They could participate in all kinds of organizational meetings, which simulated productivity, but when the time came to make a decision or implement one, nothing came of it. Everything reverted to the status quo. And if anyone tried to right the ship and make corrections—indeed, expose incompetence— s/he was frozen out by her/his colleagues. Education was a "sham," with no instruction or studying going on. Instead, games, pranks, brawls, boozing, idleness, and even beatings and orgies were the norm. Those who were competent and had a conscience got themselves out and escaped to the cities.

He was far more conciliatory toward and supportive of the new crop of activists who had set out to help the peasants. Driven by a "sincere desire to serve society," these teachers, especially the women, were a new breed who demonstrated and believed in Christian morals, cleanliness, self-discipline, and self-control. Nazar'ev reserved his highest praise for his friend and colleague, Ulyanov, whom he described as someone who saved the schools in Simbirsk from complete destruction with his energy, persistence, and genuine dedication. He concluded his account with the opinion that, although serfdom had ended, emancipation did not liberate the people from their culture. (In this comment we are confronted, once again, with a theme that reappears throughout this book—namely, the gap between what the authorities established, and the goals they desired, and what the freed people wanted.) As was so typical of Russia, Nazar'ev argued, "education" had gotten off to a great start with an enthusiastic burst of energy, but thereafter it plunged into "ambivalence."[18]

On the one hand, it is important to put Nazar'ev's stereotypical views of the peasants into context. These ideas were typical of an educated bureaucrat in the post-emancipation period. With a mixture of condescension and paternalism, he considered the peasants uneducated, simple, and essentially incapable of adjusting to the norms set by cultural elites.[19] On the other hand, imbued with a genuinely deep sense of responsibility, Nazar'ev was critical of all social groups in Russia who either would not or could not come together to work for the overall betterment of Russian society. The problems he described help us understand the difficulties associated with education in the reform period.[20]

While the decade or two following emancipation witnessed an initial flurry of enthusiasm and participation on the part of authorities and elites, what followed was a "withering" of initiative and idealism. The official account claims that the initial period of "ferment" was followed by a languishing of schools. However, Ben Eklof has explained that an informal and remarkable expansion of peasant schools took place in the thirty years after 1861. While there are no official records of these informal, grassroots schools, literacy statistics bear out the impact of schooling on the populace, the main ones being military/conscription and factory records. For example, whereas in 1897 21 percent of the Russian population was literate, that figure had almost doubled by 1913, with 40 percent of Russian men and 68 percent of military recruits being literate. Indeed, after 1874, if a conscript was literate, his service was reduced from six to four years. And the literacy rate of the rural population increased from approximately 5 percent in 1869 to 24 percent by 1913.

What explains this marked increase after the period of languishing education? Peasants were the driving force behind unofficial, "un-schooled," or "wild" (as they were called) literacy schools. Even in villages where there were no schools, due to lack of funds or an inability to sustain those funds, the peasants could privately hire a tutor on a temporary basis, especially in the winter months—a local who might be literate, or a village "newcomer" (*prikhodimtsami*), as they were called—to educate the children.[21] Of course, increased literacy does not mean that schools were universally available and widespread or that enrollment was 100 percent and sustained. There is also a difference between learning to read and learning from reading. But it does mean that, given the dismal record of official school and education records following the initial flurry of enthusiasm, something must explain the widespread literacy rates observed by Russian authorities after 1900. It was the peasants themselves. As Jeffrey Brooks has explained, peasants came to see that education would greatly assist them in a modernizing, market economy, especially in the areas of borrowing and lending, buying and selling, and contracting. And Jeffrey Burds has noted that, aware of their lack of social status and political sophistication, peasants were motivated to learn to read, and they were especially drawn to newspapers. Indeed, after 1900, Russia was awash in publications of popular literature, such as folk stories, travel tales, mysteries, adventures, romances, and even translations of popular stories and novels from Europe.[22] The publication of the first complete Russian Bible in 1876 meant that Christian peasants could increasingly participate more directly in their religion.

These developments showcase efficacy and self-determination, and they may well explain the apparent ease with which the younger Stepanov was able to establish a school at Yazykovo Selo during his tenure. During this period, official, formal schools frequently (if not always) built on and incorporated that which had already been set up by the peasants themselves.[23]

Coincidentally, education in the American South also emerged with a burst of energy and an optimistic spirit of reform. Although schooling for the freed people was built into each state's Reconstruction legislation, unlike in Russia, it was not part of the central government's reform mandates. Nevertheless, as in the Russian case, education was at the forefront of ideas about the meaning of freedom in the midst of liberation. And just as both central government directives and local public leaders established schools in Simbirsk Province, to the extent that organizations such as the Freedmen's Bureau were created by federal authorities to set education efforts in motion, this also happened in Mississippi. Plus, similar to the Russian "go to the people" movement of the 1870s, officials and volunteers flooded into the American South from the North. With them they brought their ideas about education. As was true for the Russian activists, these beliefs included the conviction that servitude had degraded the unfree and kept them in the dark. Whereas both emancipation and education were part of the Russian government's modernization policies, the American activists believed that literacy was not only crucial for both moral and Christian religious purposes (specifically for reading the Bible) but equally key to American beliefs in "upward mobility," "self-improvement," and the work ethic. In addition, they considered education conducive to civil society and the republic's survival. In short, the education agenda was about integrating the former slaves into the mainstream American body social. As in the Russian case, a marriage of sincere benevolence and paternalism motivated Northerners to set up schools in the South. A passage in a report from one activist to another is instructive:

> I often say to our teachers … that the great results of emancipation are not by any means yet developed. What these results shall be will depend greatly upon the character of the instructions given by the teachers and missionaries now on the ground laboring among them. I cannot think it right to refer very often to the past and I think it is especially unwise & [sic] dangerous to inculcate the feeling among the ignorant peoples that they are now to be elevated to all the rights of the citizens here. The time may come when they should be entitled to all the privileges of white citizens but that time is not yet…. Privileges guaranteed to citizens will be theirs when they are qualified to use them wisely.[24]

Here is clear evidence of a sentiment similar to that which was enshrined in the Russian legislation—namely, that freedom was conditional.

Also similar to both the sentiment and the evaluation contained in the Nazar'ev article, especially touching on the theme of "wildness" and specifically alluding to "idleness," a federal circular from February 1865 noted that

> [due to t]heir time in idleness, and vagrancy … [the freed people] must be taught, and encouraged to provide better homes, to labor, and to understand and conform to the domestic, and civil laws which should govern them…. The educational interests of this people should be more general … than mere book education … greater efforts [should be] made to instruct them in the more practical lessons of life. Much good can be done in visiting their houses and assisting them in organizing and conducting their homes by many suggestions, which are much needed…. Their social and family relations should be fully explained to them, and they should be urged to faithfully observe them. They should be taught a greater regard for truth, and the right of property, and to more faithfully observe and fulfil [sic] all contracts … [live with] less caprice and spend less money for trifles.[25]

Here is yet another example of the quintessential mixture of condescension, paternalistic benevolence, and didacticism for which many authorities in each context were notorious.

When the Freedmen's Bureau was established in March 1865, part of its mandate was to cooperate with private benevolent organizations that were spearheading and funding schools for the freed people.[26] Scouring their records, one notices the overarching theme that educating the freed people was a high priority. In addition, unlike sources that portray the Russian peasants as suspicious of not only the authorities but also education in particular, the history of this period is saturated with records of the American freed people themselves considering education one of the most important things they associated with freedom. Indeed, Michael Wayne has noted that education was *the* symbol of freedom.[27] Although it is true that the majority of those liberated from slavery were never served by the schools set up by the Freedmen's Bureau and other aid societies, many, both adults and children, male and female, for the first time participated in a process that would improve their lives. Here was another dissimilarity between the two subaltern groups in this study. Whereas in Russia education efforts targeted children, in the American South it was for both adults and children.

Even before the Freedmen's Bureau was mandated, schools were established at Davis Bend as part of the Home Colony. As in the Russian case, the schools were under the government's supervision:

> All the schools in this Department are brought under Military rule. No Schools are allowed, except such as the "Powers that Be" chose to favor, & as in all government operations, there must be an infinite amount of Red Tape.... No One can teach a private School, or any other without permission.[28]

In February 1864, the Bend boasted 3 schools, 10 teachers, 7 schools, and a staggering total of 699 pupils, which included some men but mostly women and children. They were instructed in reading, writing, arithmetic, and religion. In April, Quaker missionary Henry Rowntree reported that "it is gratifying to witness how eager they are to obtain it [learning]. These schools ... furnish good opportunities of giving religious and moral influences with their scholastic requirements." By February 1, 1865, the schools were run by the United Presbyterian Mission, and Palmyra Plantation had four one-room schools with 6 teachers and 493 pupils. It is not surprising that the former slaves at Davis Bend utilized their freedom to obtain education. Again, Rowntree observed that they seemed "universally eager to learn to read and write."[29] Furthermore, and like their Russian counterparts, the freed people soon understood that the practical value of education was that they could prevent any employer from taking advantage of them due to illiteracy.

Similar to those singled out for praise by Nazar'ev, the majority of the teachers on the Bend were young women from middle-class families who came to the South with a sincere desire to help the former slaves. The conditions they lived and worked in were far from ideal: the only housing available was in the main houses and outbuildings on the Bend, which had already been cannibalized as a result of both the owners' abandonment and the war's ravages. But even these paragons of civic virtue were not above criticism from the freed people. Recalling the days when the Union was operating the Home Colony, Palmyra inhabitant "Uncle Washington" recalled the following encounter with one of the female teachers in order to illustrate how some people "hates to see you git erlong on de yearth":

> De fust I experienced uv it, was wen we was countyband. I was walkin' erlong in dese vay quarters ... an' I seed a new lady standin [there]. An' she says, "Go, git me a pail er water." Da ooman astonishe me. I des stan' still. "Go git me a pail er water, and git hit quick," she says. "Is you 'flicted, Madam?" I ast. "No, I ain't," she says. "Is yo damaged no way? Cos, if you is, den I'll fotch you a pail." ... At dat she was so mad she upped and says, "You'll not live to see yo' days out here. I'll see to dat." ... She sho' was a sassy ooman.[30]

He closed out the story by pointing out that, contrary to the teacher's prediction, he *was* still there.

The context of war, occupation, and Reconstruction in which schools for the liberated made their appearance meant that things were not seamless, and a variety of problems plagued the efforts. First, even though Union authorities controlled movement to and from the Bend, the population of freed people there fluctuated greatly, which had an adverse effect on any kind of academic salience. Often, a pupil who had left weeks before would reappear, ready to pick up the lessons where they had left off. And not all freed people saw education as a priority. Similar to their Russian counterparts, many parents could not afford the luxury of losing their children to schooling when they needed them to help out. Plus, both the benevolent societies and the Freedmen's Bureau consistently urged a policy of taxation and tuition for the freed people's education. Typically, this might be around $1.25 per month. The tuition could be a tall order for the former slaves to fill, and it triggered defections.[31]

In addition, and in contrast to Nazar'ev's descriptions of the grim realities associated with education (such as the absence of standardization, recordkeeping, and quality control), as more teachers arrived in Mississippi, their superiors required that paperwork and reports be submitted with increasing regularity, the goal being improved standards and accountability. This task took time away from teaching. Friction and even competition between teachers and the organizations they were affiliated with ensued. For example, one activist explained that teachers from different groups all seemed to scramble to "get the best" students and locations. He also accused a teacher from another affiliation of having motives that had "something besides the glory of God in view." A government official observed that the agents' "zeal produces ill-will and recrimination." Moreover, the competition had the potential to "diminish the confidence of the" freed people in them and in "the Government."[32] Plus, while many of the teachers were well-intentioned, sincere people, others were depicted in a most disparaging way. For example, with condescension and racism, one report described some teachers as "unchaste miscegenationists, promoters of social equality between whites and blacks, and of discord between employers and laborers, and encouragers of idleness."[33]

Both volunteers and students succumbed to the delta's hot, humid, mosquito-filled summers and damp, chilly winters, with the roads during the latter seasons constituting knee-deep mud. Because much of Mississippi was rural, most people—teachers and students alike—were frequently isolated. Illness and death were commonplace. Since mules and horses were earmarked for production in the field, walking was the primary method of transportation.[34]

As Union soldiers and representatives receded from the South after the war, so, too, did their educational efforts. To be sure, the local white population was opposed to educating the freed people, and they rejected the idea of contributing to the efforts financially. However, as it became clear that there was no turning back and that the former slaves' identity as free people was a certainty, many plantation owners came to see that it was in their interests to allow a school on the premises.[35] Like the younger Stepanov, they recognized schools' salutary benefit of anchoring the freed people to that location for their labor. Regardless, Justin Behrend has explained that even if this happened, sustaining the schools was a challenge since itinerant teachers were difficult to engage; often the climate (including the summer heat, the winter cold, and the spring floods) was enough to make anyone flee. Furthermore, the planting and harvesting seasons hindered attendance even if a school was established.[36]

But not for William Storrow Lovell. While the former slaves on the Davis plantations (which were approximately seven miles from Palmyra) operated their own schools, there is no record of one existing at Palmyra after the family's recovery of the plantation in 1865. Indeed, thereafter the Bend's freed people were forced to get "most of their education on their own." One account stated bluntly that the Palmyra freed people "were uneducated."[37] Why? First, as has been explained, for the next thirty years there was a steady turnover of laborers at the plantation. On the one hand, we can speculate that this fact alone worked against establishing a permanent school, since a high turnover rate would have inhibited cohesiveness and sustained financial and material support. On the other hand, it should be remembered that even though the population at Yazykovo Selo was stable over the time period in question, it, too, struggled with sustaining (formal) education. Second, Davis Bend was remote. Maintaining a school on what was essentially a closed island in the middle of the Mississippi, with the old riverbed abutting up to Louisiana, meant that securing a public school would have been very difficult. In fact, by 1872, due to lack of funds, the county closed the one public school that had been established at the Davis plantations. Third, Lovell may have been financially well off relative to the majority of Mississippians, but it is clear that he did not make any paternalistic or benevolent efforts with respect to his employees. In this regard, there is similarity to what played out at Yazykovo Selo. That is, in the same way that Vasili Yazykov *implemented* the educational mandates but appears to have not sustained schooling, so, too, did Lovell not continue the educational efforts put in place by Union representatives during the Home Colony period. Arguably, because he was neither born nor raised on a plantation, nor steeped in its culture, Lovell was not imbued with paternalistic tendencies. Perhaps this is a clear example of emancipation breaking the ties between paternalism and the plantation culture of the planter class as well as the estate culture of the nobility.

Similar to their Russian counterparts, while the freed people may well have appreciated the idea of education, they also had their suspicions. There is evidence that they were fiercely autonomous, desiring full independence from all authorities. This wish was illustrated in a number of reports discussing the situation at the Bend. For example, one African American teacher, who did appreciate the Bureau's assistance, was a nationalist, asserting that

> I trust that at no distant day we shall not need assistance from a Government we have labored to enrich without remuneration, and fought to preserve without citizenship, or a share in her glory if she has gained a victory.

Another account explained that

> There is a colored young Lady, well educated, who has for a long time been teaching a Sort of Select School & has some thirty scholars. She rents a room at $6.00 per month, & her scholars pay her $2.00 per month, but under the Military rule, her school must be broken up, because the Authorities will recognize no teacher that is not in connection with some regular organization.... I have visited no school room that was kept in better order & no school that appeared to be under better discipline. She is a pious young Lady, & ... Her name is Miss Josephine C. Nicks.... There is another colored woman here, not as well qualified ... but who has taught among her fellow slaves for many years, & that too, when she had to do it in the night & by stealth. She is a pious woman.[38]

More condescending was the following observation by another official:

> I have come to the conclusion that [the freed people] are truly an ungrateful people, buried in the idea that to be free is to be ungrateful and to do what they are entirely unfit for.... One case to illustrate what I have stated [is] I asked permission to open a school in the gallery of ... [their] Bapt. Church. I was refused upon the plea that the ... church was not the proper place to have a school. Since [then] ... they have opened a school there.... There are other schools opened here under "black colors," in small rooms crowded to their utmost extent. It is

the prevailing opinion among those laboring for the "Freedmen" that they are determined to have the rule in regard to teachers and preachers and their favorite is Black.

Quoting a colleague of his, this official added, "The greatest hinderance to the elevation of this people was their ingratitude and ... unappreciation of what was being done for them. It will be impossible for us to do anything here after the Military is removed." Still another official warned in November 1865 that there was "no safety for teachers where there are no troops ... the feelings of the white citizens throughout the state, they are generally opposed to Schools for the education of Freedmen & will do all they dare to break them up."[39] Tangential to this idea, speaking of the "extreme prejudice" the freed people had regarding formal institutions, a surgeon stationed at the Bend's hospital observed that they would "rather die or linger than go to a hospital," adding that "some planters keep a 'granny' or doctor [traditional healer using homeopathic or traditional remedies] on the premises of the plantation because they are preferred" by the freed people.[40]

By January 1866, there were 68 schools in Mississippi, with 5,271 pupils enrolled.[41] These were mostly either in urban areas or on plantations where the population of freed people was relatively dense. Vernon Wharton showed that even though the state's constitution mandated education in 1868, thereafter the number of enrolled students declined steadily. Indeed, he pointed out that by 1870 the state had gained only four schools, bringing the total number to 72. However, the tide quickly turned again; by 1872, 230 schools had been established across the state, with nearly 42,000 new African American students enrolled. This change is due to a number of developments, such as the decline of the KKK and the emergence of a public sentiment that saw education for the freed people as a good thing. In addition, the quality of both teachers (in terms of their qualifications and experience) and lessons improved as the years passed.[42]

Both Ronald Butchart and Christopher Span have stressed that black literacy rates in the entire American South surged from 20.1 percent in 1870 to 69.5 percent by 1910. Like those of Eklof and others in the Russian context, these observations inform us that the American freed people not only took charge of their education but also sustained it for decades.[43]

A minority of former slaves did remain at Palmyra after emancipation. One was "old Nicey" (short for Bernice), a former slave of Lovell's wife, Tonie. In her account of life at Palmyra, Lovell's daughter-in-law, Caroline Couper Lovell, noted that other than when she had been "refugeed to Alabam" during the war, Nicey had never left Palmyra. In fact, she had never even been to the other side of the Bend, where the Davis plantations were located. Nicey explained to Caroline, who tried to document her *patois*, that she "'didn't had no edycation.—Pity? Education don't tek you no furder'n de grave.'"[44] This sentiment is not surprising since, perhaps, it is not so much about education, but rather profound disappointment, or dashed hopes and dreams with respect to freedom's promise. For example, Mr. Pet Franks, after citing examples of how more than one teacher in the school (which he attended only twice) was run out of her profession by the locals, told how he decided it was better not to know how to read or write, "less'n I might git in some kinda trouble, too." Or Ms. Nettie Henry, who recounted how the

> Yankees ... promise [*sic*] to give ever'body forty acres o' lan' an' a mule. A lot of 'em didn' have no better sense dan to believe 'em. Dey'd go 'head an' do what de Yankees 'ud tell 'em. Well, dey didn' give 'em nothin', not even a rooster. Didn' give 'em <u>nothin'</u> but trouble.[45]

Education emerged in the midst of liberation as central to freedom. On the one hand, the authorities in both Russia and the American South believed it was their moral duty and crucial to their respective country's future to uplift the former serfs and slaves. Here was a tenuous mixture of sincere benevolence and condescending paternalism. The governments were either directly or indirectly responsible for setting up schools for the freed people. Their good intentions aside, clearly there was a gap between the authorities' and elites' expectations and those of the freed people. While the Russian peasants did not see education as central to freedom, the liberated Americans did. And yet both subaltern groups understood that literacy would aid them as they increasingly participated in the modernizing economy. Furthermore, it appears that because of their experiences with education before emancipation as well as their atavistic memories of past exploitation and abuse, the liberated peoples were highly suspicious of the authorities' motives and supervision. Therefore, both groups wanted self-determination and autonomy with respect to education.

In addition, it would seem that after the initial burst of energy and enthusiasm, a structural educational system at each demesne could not be sustained for a variety of reasons. Beyond the initial founding of schools at each place, they either languished or disappeared altogether. Only with Stepanov's custodianship of Yazykovo Selo was reform, sustained commitment, and logistical and financial support evident. This shift coincided with the overall "surge in energy" and commitment to public school education that emerged in Russia in the late 1890s. Conversely, while the previous chapter demonstrated that William Storrow Lovell was a competent plantation manager, clearly, at a profit-driven cotton enterprise like Palmyra, the planter did not include education as part of his agenda. Above all, these stories and statistics demonstrate that in the midst of liberation, it is one thing to establish schools, and another to sustain them. But they also show that, despite their limited resources, the freed people effectively took responsibility for their own education.

Festivities, and Other Sources of Sustenance

Festivities are a way for people to come together, to communicate, and to commemorate something. They provide a format for a community to memorialize something lost, or that which has passed, as well as celebrate something gained. Festivities are also a way for people to acknowledge that they have a shared history as well as an identity. They provide a sense of belonging and a source of sustenance, especially in hard times. In times of change, they can provide continuity and cohesiveness, in addition to signaling hope for the future. In times of boredom or routine, they are a source of entertainment and pleasure. In the days before emancipation, both serfs and slaves had their festive traditions.[46] But these were sometimes surreptitious. Freedom allowed them to come out of the shadows. Freedom gave them the chance to be openly festive.

On July 4, 1863, an event took place at Davis Bend to celebrate the fall of Vicksburg. The conflation of the country's independence and the fall of the strategically important city on the bluff overlooking the Mississippi River was a cause for celebration. A photograph was taken of the liberated people that day (see figure 7.1). The group in the photo consists of a number of women, men, and children, both standing and sitting. The backdrop is significant because it is the recognizable "Library" at Joseph

Davis' plantation, Hurricane. That they are dressed well is extraordinary, given that their condition on the Bend was dire (see chapters 4 and 5).

Although no photographs exist of Yazykovo Selo's liberated people, it is possible to glean information by extrapolating from an image of the former serfs at Undory. The "Emancipation Day Commemoration" photo was taken on March 3, 1862, to mark the first anniversary of emancipation[47] (see figure 7.2). This photograph is significant for a number of reasons. First, because the Undory mansion was torched in 1921 (along with the fact that there are no other photographs of the estate), it is a valuable primary source. Also, like the Davis Bend photo, this image is significant because it documents real people, in real time, in a recognizable context.

These were the freed people at Davis Bend and a Yazykov estate. This was their lifeworld. The photos represent a "visual anthropology," in that they give us a sense of both the people and the place. They humanize the subjects of emancipation, therefore creating a connection between the subject and the viewer. With respect to "place," each photo, at once, presents a "generic" rural demesne and landscape, as well as a specific, particular location, with its own unique characteristics. Each place was a home. Each set of people represented a community and a new identity. What is our experience, our perception, when we scrutinize these photos? It is true that we do not know whether the freed people in each photo sought their own documentation or whether it was designed by an authority intending to self-congratulate. To be sure, the freed people knew these were historic times. But the photos are also a kind of sacred iconography, in that, at once, the subjects are frozen in time as the personification of freedom, and yet they are transcendent. That is, years after the day that each photo was taken, the subjects "are." It has been written that photographs promise to reproduce "truth" and "reality."[48] While the subjects are clearly staged and all are dressed for the occasion, the photos are meant to be both a portrait and a historical documentation of significant dates.

Figure 7.1. Liberated slaves at Hurricane Plantation Cottage, Davis Bend, July 4, 1863 (from the photograph collection of the Old Court House Museum, Vicksburg, MS).

Figure 7.2. Emancipation anniversary of the liberated serfs at Undory Estate, Simbirsk Province, March 3, 1862 (copyright © 2021 Literaturny? muze? "Dom Yazykovykh" [Literature Museum "The House of Yazykovs," Ulyanovsk, Russia]).

All this suggests festivity, celebration, and commemoration. Therefore, the significance of these photos is that they are simultaneously historical artifacts *and* documentation of the identity of freedom's recipients.

One year later, on July 4, 1864, a gala event was organized by the white authorities at Davis Bend to celebrate and commemorate both Independence Day and the anniversary of the fall of Vicksburg one year earlier. An army officer who wrote an account of the event, which was published in a local newspaper, noted that a number of speeches were delivered, and patriotic songs were sung. Although the Civil War was still raging across the American South and supplies and victuals were scarce, tables were spread with assorted food. A sign reading "The House that Jeff Built" was mounted over the front door of the home of the Confederacy's president (see figure 7.3). However, although the location was described as a "Freedmen's Paradise," the account specified that other than those who were present in the capacity as servants, no freed people participated in this festival. This absence is significant, since it was at the height of the Home Colony period, when all whites were banned from the premises. Whether it was because the freed people chose not to participate or because they were excluded is difficult to say. However, if the former was the case, this would suggest an act of independence. By contrast, the latter explanation would indicate that old patterns and beliefs remained entrenched in Union officials' beliefs and practices after liberation. Given that, over thirty years later, Caroline Couper Lovell documented that the former slaves at Palmyra had celebrated the "fath" day every year since emancipation, it is likely that the freed people fashioned their own celebration that day.[49]

Sunday, January 1, 1865, was the second anniversary of emancipation. A celebration/commemoration took place at Davis Bend. "It was of course a day of uncommon

Figure 7.3. "House that Jeff Built" at Davis Bend (from the photograph collection of the Old Court House Museum, Vicksburg, MS).

interest," wrote a Union representative. The day opened with a "Sunday school celebration," which consisted of the pupils singing and reciting prayers, culminating in a reading of the Emancipation Proclamation. This was followed in the afternoon by a series of short speeches, declarations, and orations. Although the records indicate that about 400 children attended, the number of adults present was not recorded. Speaking of the children's efforts, the representative noted:

> They did remarkably well, & ... repeated their verses with great accuracy. Occassionally, ... an amusing mistake would be made, but ... of such a nature as to show that the children think as well as memorise, & if they can't recall the exact word, they will substitute another, expressing the idea they got from reading the verse. For instance, one boy ... [said] "Little children let no man fool you."[50]

Despite Union oversight, this account documents the freed people's participation in a festive, commemorative event. Like the photographs discussed earlier, although the events may well have been organized by the authorities, the freed people were not passive but, significantly, participants.

Commemoration took on a far more somber tone when, in April 1865, President Lincoln was assassinated. Now a military authority observed that all the freed people, "men, women, and children have" black crepe string attached to their lapels.[51]

Meanwhile, in Simbirsk Province, the inhabitants of Undory received a significant guest of honor on May 20, 1868, when they hosted the Tsar Liberator's son, Grand Duke Alexei Alexandrovich, who at the time was traveling down the Volga on a tour of the region. Indeed, it was a day of celebration since it was the grand duke's "angel day." Dressed in "festive outfits," Undory's inhabitants met Alexei at the pier, and the day's events included a mass and prayer service, with the village priest hosting the grand duke for a luncheon. Alexei presented a gift of 100 rubles for the clergy and another 100 for the poor. Next, Alexander, Vasili Yazykov's brother, gave the grand duke a tour of the manor house and the wool factory. "His Highness" also presented the village's inhabitants with oranges and treats, which he had purchased at local shops. The grand duke even rode a horse through the village and stopped at several peasant homes for a visit. The day ended with a musical presentation, including singing and dancing. On his departure, the grand duke presented Alexander with a gold pin as a keepsake.[52] No doubt, as the son of the Tsar Liberator, Grand Duke Alexei's visit must have given meaning to and reinforced the freed people's identity as emancipation's first recipients.

Whether they were photographs or accounts of commemorative festivals honoring national events and distinguished dignitaries, in these examples it seems as though the freed people were auxiliary to that which was being honored. But this in no way suggests they were bereft of their own excitement and joy. Furthermore, as David Blight has made clear, emancipation was the benchmark of African American history, and it was commemorated openly in a variety of ways after 1865, including parades, feasts, magazine and newspaper articles, exhibitions, and all sorts of retrospectives.[53] So, too, did the Russian peasants have their own events, in which celebration, procession, and the extraordinary were honored. These gatherings were symbolic gestures that confirmed identity, gave meaning to experience, and fostered cohesiveness in this fluid time period.

Of significance, and as part of the long wave of revivalism that had begun prior to and was interrupted by the American Civil War, a religious impulse swept the Bend during the summer of 1872. Although the Lovells were vacationing in Niagara Falls and the planter's journals are devoid of any references to the event, records indicate that emotional worship occurred for two weeks during July and August:

> Women go into a frenzy of excitement and roll on the floor for two or three hours together, screaming and crying, "lord, take me," "Jesus save me," till, utterly exhausted, they fall asleep, or experience … "coming through," when they jump up in ecstasy of joy … shouting "Glory, glory, hallelujah."[54]

This description speaks to the quintessential emotive nature of African American worship at the time. Indeed, as Lawrence W. Levine made clear in his anthropological study of African American culture during the emancipation era, they were profoundly religious. Over the *longue durée* of their history, the slaves blended vestiges of their "old world" religious characteristics with those of Christianity, so that there was a complete syncretization by 1861—neither African nor Euro American, but uniquely African American. Indeed, each civilization, African and European American, had its own characteristics of "magic, diviniation, witchcraft, astrology, and ghostlore," which facilitated syncretization. As both anthropology and the history of religion have taught, syncretism is an aspect of the human lived experience. Levine also explained what happened before (as compared with after) emancipation. Before, their reality was a "sacred universe," where those enslaved constructed an internal world that "transcended the narrow confines" of their physical lifeworld realities. Quoting anthropologist Paul Radin, Levine agreed that the antebellum African American "was not converted to God. [Rather] He converted God to himself." After emancipation, although a kind of creeping "modernization" and secularism diluted aspects of "old beliefs," these were not entirely purged, but rather persisted.[55]

To be sure, as was the case in Russia in general, life at Yazykovo Selo was determined by a calendar year governed by an agrarian work routine that coincided with a syncretized pagan/Orthodox Christian holiday schedule. Thus, peasants recognized Yuletide, Christmas, the New Year, Epiphany (Blessing of the Waters), Shrovetide/Carnival (Maslenitsa), Lent, Easter, Trinity Day (Pentecost), the Feast of All Saints Day, and the name days of numerous saints, as well as pagan holidays such as Krasnai͡a Gorka (spring), Rusal'nai͡a and (Ivan) Kupala (June), Koli͡ada (winter solstice), and a host of others. These important celebratory events contained rituals and traditions that were deeply entrenched in Russian peasant culture. As Christine Worobec has made clear, "The rituals that post-emancipation Russian peasants observed, and the mores and behavioral norms they set were remarkably resilient."[56] The salience of these important mores must have continued to provide stability and sustenance to Simbirsk's rural inhabitants in the midst of the sweeping changes resulting from emancipation.

Taking one final example, each group celebrated a holiday time at the end of the spring sowing season, both before and long after emancipation. Known in Russia as I͡Arilo Mokryĭ Troĭan, and in America as "laid-by" or "laying-by crop jubilee," these events celebrated the end of the sowing season as well as, in the former case, deceased ancestors and, in the latter case, July 4. Indeed, camp meetings could accompany the "laying-by crop jubilee." Like many celebrations, their characteristics included food, singing accompanied with musical instruments, storytelling, and processionals.[57] A number of similarities between each set of freed people in this context can be discerned. What many of these celebrations appear to have shared is that significant dates or events of national and/or symbolic significance were incorporated into the community. In doing so, the local community and its identity were affirmed. In turn, this affirmation provided sustenance.

Daily Life

What was the daily rhythm of life like after emancipation at each demesne? While emancipation irrevocably altered life for the freed people in each context, the drag of culture and contextual realities were major determinants. As in any rural, agricultural setting, life at Palmyra Plantation was set by the routine of the cotton crop season. Winter clearing and plowing were followed by spring planting. Cultivation with plow and hoe was completed by midsummer. Now the cotton bolls began to open. From August through November cotton was picked. Before Christmas, the harvest pace slowed to a near halt, with the winter months consumed with ginning. Sometimes the autumn months "brought the excitement of competition between individuals and farms to see who could pick the most in a day, and which planter ... produced the largest quantity ... of cotton that year." Indeed, as Nicey boasted to Caroline Couper Lovell in 1913, "I was jes de same as er mule wen I was young ... I was a fiel' han'. I could pick my two hundred poun' a day—and den some. Ole Marster rid by de fiel' one day, and seed me pickin'. Say 'Dat she is a dandy gal!' Dat wot he *say* [sic]." Lovell noted that Nicey was seldom emotive, but during this story "she could not ... suppress a smile of pride." Similarly, another inhabitant of Palmyra, Kitty, interviewed at age 88, explained to Lovell how her husband, Washington, had been the "steward" of Palmyra since the days of "Master Henry," John Quitman's father-in-law. For decades he "toted the sto' [and] ...

house keys. An' everything on dat plantation pass thu his hans. He helt dem keys smak ontel Freedom … [and] [w]e all rejoice an' sing, an' pray wen we was sot free." Kitty concluded the conversation with two observations. The first was "Wotever you try to do to others will be done to you," and the second was her belief that she and Washington were the Bend's oldest inhabitants and longest-term residents. "Yes, us de old foundataions uv de place." Indeed.[58]

Still, there were some changes that were marked breaks with the past. For example, notwithstanding Nicey's experience, as well as William Storrow Lovell's occasional note that he had hired a family who pooled their labor, it was reported that in general women and children had all but disappeared from the fields on the Bend.[59] As the previous chapter made clear, most of the laborers at Palmyra Plantation were migrant and male. But certainly, when formerly unfree women and children worked in the fields after emancipation, they did so to augment the family income.[60] Because American slavery had "fostered a family structure among blacks that was often radically different from the dominant white pattern and at odds with the social ideals upon which white family relations were based," in the post-emancipation period liberated people sought to both recover family ties and establish legal marriages.[61] The love for and legal right to family was arguably the most important aspect of freedom to the former slaves. This phenomenon followed the nuclear family model, with the patriarch as the family head. Noralee Frankel has explained that a number of things, such as the fact that leadership roles on plantations were assigned to male freed people, as well as the Fourteenth and Fifteenth Amendments, privileged men in black communities. But, she continues, it is not accurate to describe the families as completely "patriarchal," since, although black men now held more power over black women and children than in the days of slavery, "they held much less power than white men did over white women, African American males, and African American female laborers." Moreover, now it was easier for African American women "to quit relationships" because "of the economic marginality of African American men." Tangential to this claim, Frankel points out that, as in the days of slavery, women continued to be a great source of support to each other after emancipation.[62]

All this said, because their children were not legally theirs in the days of slavery, after emancipation taking on the guardianship of one's children was deeply important, with men assuming the responsibility for their children. For example, ex-slave Mr. Wayne Holliday recalled how, not long after emancipation, his

> pa started getting' a li'l work here an' dar an' purty soon he got all his chullun started out…. We all went to … school … an' dat was whar I l'arned to read an' write … [later] I went to work on de I.C. Railroad…. I was faithful to my job an' made good money an' soon built me a house of my own whar I raised by family. I sent all my chullun to school an' day is doin' well.[63]

In the post-emancipation era, marriages were a time for great celebration. Weddings fostered community, linked neighborhoods, and established new, legal identities. In addition to their natural desire to marry, federal policy mandated marriages. As one Union official observed, "There is a great time of marrying among this people now, in accordance with directions from the War Department. No matter how long they have lived as Husband & Wife, they are required to be married. One boy in reciting a verse [he has been taught] says, 'I am the true vine & my Father is a married man.'"[64] Irrespective of the mandate, on their path to freedom, making marriages official was both a formal and a festive rite of the passage.

Because it had not been denied them, marriage was not a cornerstone of freedom in the Russian context. Certainly, after emancipation, marriage continued to be celebrated with feasts and ritualized festivities. In Russia, it was common for weddings to coincide with important religious events, such as Lent, as well as pauses in the agricultural calendar, particularly the year's end.[65] However, as Christine Worobec has explained, "The patriarchal ... family was but a microcosm of a [centuries-old] hierarchical social order ... which depended upon an elaborate misogynist ideology that could successfully subjugate just over 50 percent of the peasant population." Via cultural norms, which included forms of "power, rewards, and safeguards," Russian peasant women "accommodated themselves to the patriarchy." In this regard, the patriarchy that Worobec documents worked much in the way that the paternalism discussed in chapter 5 did. That is, it was an arrangement that gave women (or, in the case of paternalism, subalterns) certain privileges and protections, so that they would thus be participants in their domination, and, in exchange, those who dominated had responsibilities (and privileges—the greatest being dominance). Therefore, while the marked break of the noble landlord's authority over his/her former people was revolutionary, the peasant family was an entrenched component of the overarching Russian culture, which was hierarchical, service and obligation oriented, and (at least in the rural/peasant sphere) subsistence oriented. Acknowledging structural patriarchalism, Svetlana Kruikova has explained that over the *longue durée*, extended patriarchal families evolved (1) from the top down, with laws being passed so as to ensure order, social stability, and tax optimization, and (2) from the bottom up, out of the utilitarian need for the survival of the community. She also has observed that after emancipation, with the increased scattering and migration that unfolded, socially prescribed roles along gender lines were progressively broken down, thus giving women more choices and freedoms.[66]

Of course, another significant fact of Russian emancipation is that both land earmarks and the responsibilities for all obligations were assigned to men in toto, which reinforced their privileged position in the commune. Still, some flexibility emerged, albeit slowly. For example, as early as the 1870s court records show that occasionally peasant women went to court to challenge extraordinarily abusive treatment from their husbands or in-laws. However, following the informal "law of non-interference," the village commune typically handled domestic disputes.[67] Arguably more significant, recent scholarship has pointed out that before emancipation, for a variety of reasons, people married within their community. Afterward, this constraint progressively disappeared, and people became freer to find a spouse beyond the boundaries of their village of origin.[68] All this said, it is true that after emancipation, both the commune and the family remained powerful examples of communitarianism, interdependence, and mutual support.

Like life at Palmyra Plantation, that at Yazykovo Selo was similarly determined by tradition and annual routines. Valerian Nazar'ev explained that, before emancipation, the typical village in Simbirsk witnessed deadly boredom in the winters, spring and fall sowings, late fall weddings and orgies, and frequent fires. Above all, he stressed that after emancipation, there was an overwhelming feeling on all estates of "incompleteness." That is, the former serfs knew that they would not be free until they received their land. And so they waited. Writing almost one hundred years later, M. Naĭdenov confirmed Nazar'ev's analysis: the freed peasants overwhelmingly did nothing but "hold out for the land."[69] However, it would be incorrect to infer that "the long wait" translated to an absence of vibrant activities that sustained communities and identity, as these ideas are not mutually exclusive.[70]

It is striking that the sentiments cited by both Naĭdenov and Nazar'ev are similar to ones often expressed by former slaves. For example, an ex-slave of Jefferson Davis explained in the 1930s that

> Slaves didn' know what to 'spec from freedom, but a lot of 'em ... all had diffe'nt ways o' thinkin' 'bout it. Mos'ly though day was jus' lak me, day didn' know jus' zackly what it meant. It was jus' somp'n dat de white folks an' slaves all de time talk 'bout. Dat's all. Folks dat ain' never been free don' rightly know [how] de <u>feel</u> of bein' free.... When de sojers come dey turnt us loose lak animals wid nothin'. Dey had no business to set us free lak dat.

Here we can discern a level of incompleteness, along with an anticipation of what freedom had to offer, but beyond one's reach—beyond the horizon. Another ex-slave from Mississippi also expressed disappointment as well as the crux of freedom when he asked rhetorically, "What's de use of being free ... if you don't own land enough to be buried in? Might just as well stay [a] slave all yo' days." Still another blamed the carpetbaggers for turning "us loose, jus' lak a passel o' cattle, an' didn' show us nothin' or giv' us nothin'." And yet another explained, "De slaves spected a heap from freedom dey didn' git. Dey was led to b'lieve dey would have a easy time—go places widout passes—an have plenty o' spendin' money. But dey sho' got fooled. Mos' of 'em didn' fin' deyse'ves no better off. Personally, I had a harder time after de war dan I did endurin' slav'ry." Last but not least was Nicey's evaluation of freedom. She estimated that "dese times ent wot dee uster be.... Wen you was ole ... you was well token keer of.... Gawd knows I war'nt glad when I was sot free. [But you] Call dis freedom! I calls hit bondage!"[71]

In these passages we discern disappointment, incredulity, and dismay. However, this does not mean that slavery was preferred over freedom. Rather, in and of themselves, these evaluations are profound in that those who expressed them had the freedom to speak their truths. Moreover, they were speaking to an innate understanding of the meaning of freedom and, abstractly, those things that would have made the *real* freedom possible. Here is a central point of comparison between the terms of emancipation in Russia and the United States. Each country emancipated the unfree, but they could not logistically equip (or would not conceive of equipping) each set of liberated people with the tools that were crucial to securing freedom, as it was understood at the time. The reasons for this failure are manifold. Boiled down to their essence, they include (1) the fact that the state, in each country, was in an epic balancing act of countervailing forces, and (2) the logistics of such an undertaking—to effect the "real freedom"—were too great, even for the autocratic Russian government and the victorious one of the Union. Indeed, each country's "vision" for what freedom would "look like" was explicit. In Russia, a de jure "plan" for freedom was mapped out, while in the United States, the assumption seemed to be that an "invisible hand" of sorts, would naturally usher the freed people across its threshold.

How are we to make sense of the gulf separating the liberated from freedom? In the spirit of Alessandro Stanziani's work, a different conception might be helpful. Rather than perceiving what played out in both Russia and the American South as "falling far short" of freedom's promise, perhaps a "new stage" conception is more accurate. This new stage was further from the "completely unfree" end point of the continuum and less distant from the "completely free" opposite end. Jeffrey Burds has put forward the framework of a "third culture" that emerged in Russia after emancipation. As a result of the "sheer magnitude of the migration phenomenon" (and, I would add, the undeniable fact of a conceptual freedom that emancipation injected into the culture's bloodstream), a "neither fully traditional nor fully urbanized" peasant society emerged. It could not be called exclusively rural or completely urban. And it was neither completely unfree nor totally free. Similarly, Lawrence W. Levine discussed the mutation of the African American community after emancipation, in which their folk culture—indeed, consciousness—changed. Freedom weakened their "cultural self-containment" and pushed them into a sphere of "cultural marginality."

> The former refers to a group whose cultural standards and world view are determined ... by the values of the group itself and are held with a relative lack of self-consciousness. [Cultural marginality] refers to a more obviously bi-cultural or multi-cultural situation in which a group, poised to some extent between two worlds, finds its desire to absorb and emulate the culture of a dominant group, in an attempt to attain and enjoy the latter's privileges and status, [but also] in tension with its urge to continue to identify with many of its own central cultural traditions.[72]

Emancipation released the former serfs and slaves from a far more rigid condition into a new identity, which was more fluid and set in motion greater mobility, both physically and socially. And in this new stage, freedom's first stage, both possibilities and limitations coexisted.

* * *

In this chapter, I have discussed some of the ways in which the freed people at Palmyra Plantation and Yazykovo Selo experienced freedom in their daily lives. Although it is impossible to capture the "polyphony," and multiple and overlapping spheres and spaces of demesne life, I touched on some ordinary and extraordinary aspects of the lifeworld at each place, where freedom made its appearance and could be experienced.[73] To the extent that it aided our understanding of what happened after emancipation, I contextualized each demesne within some trends in each region (and in each country). Emancipation represented such a marked break with the past that nothing was ever the same again. Yet, in other areas, the inertia of culture was great, and old beliefs and practices persisted. Change and continuity with the past materialized in a number of ways.

First, clearly, the authorities believed education was a crucial component of freedom. However, both sets of freed people had old as well as new ideas about education. On the one hand, they were deeply suspicious of the authorities and their motivations. Would the authorities use education as a vehicle for reimpressment? Because the American freed people had been deprived of education in their former condition, it was one of the cornerstones of freedom for them, which was not the case for Russian peasants. Yet both sets of freed people saw it as a way to improve their ability to navigate a modernizing economy. Alternatively, the authorities held both benevolent and paternalistic, condescending, and even racist attitudes toward the freed people regarding education. One overarching trend was the initial burst of energy and enthusiasm associated with education, subsequently followed by an ebb. Education was only resuscitated at Yazykovo Selo at the turn of the century, arguably because it was an intact community and because of the new patriarch's commitment. This was not the case at Palmyra, where there was a high turnover rate of inhabitants every year, for years; in addition, the proprietor, Lovell, evidently was not interested in such an endeavor. At the same time, the evidence suggests that there were parallels with respect to the freed people in both contexts taking charge of their own literacy. Here, the emancipation context made all the difference for that to happen.

The routine of daily life, seasonal cycles, and annual turnover in each context was punctuated by festivals, commemorations, and celebrations, both old and new. These and other sources of sustenance, such as family and religion, proved to be important for contributing to community cohesiveness and charting a course for the future. These were revolutionary times, and there was no going back. What stands out in this new emancipation context is that *now* the freed people had the freedom to come out of the shadows and live with elements of efficacy and a future orientation.

8

The Meaning of Freedom in a Global Context

In the preceding pages, I have comparatively examined the process of emancipation of the serfs and slaves on a Russian estate and a Southern plantation. I identified the distinguishing characteristics of emancipation in each country and described its "roll-out" and the ways it impacted each demesne, as well as the various players involved. This review included looking at ways in which the various players responded to emancipation. To the extent that it helped engender an understanding of what happened at each demesne, I touched on developments at estates and plantations that were in the respective neighborhoods and/or regions, as well as the general trends in each country. What specifically played out was a result of each demesne's distinguishing characteristics in relation to the terms of emancipation, the various traditions and practices in each country and region, and the personalities and *mentalités* of specific players and groups in the story. Clearly, history, context, culture, and intention mattered.

What has been gleaned? This comparative micro case study has put the spotlight on the richness of these local stories. Getting down into the "weeds" allowed me to effectively illustrate broader themes associated with emancipation. It also allowed me to point to the ways in which each place did and did not square with a number of overarching narratives, as well as recent historiographical trends. For example, it is striking that Yazykovo Selo was still on *barshchina* labor obligations until 1881. Also, although it was not unheard of for a Russian estate to not have a Redemption Agreement by the time the Redemption Law was put into effect in 1881, I explained why both Vasili Yazykov and the estate's former serfs were likely incentivized *not* to agree to one. On the American side, although the phenomenon of squad labor has been touched on in other studies, I teased out the mechanics associated with it—the links in the chain of this post-emancipation development. The freed people's mobility and annual contractual negotiation were not insignificant, as these factors afforded them elements of autonomy and self-determination. The squad-labor/mobility nexus is as central to understanding the expression, experience, and meaning of freedom in the American context as the attachment-to-place/immobility nexus in the Russian one. Yet, although the fields were fallow and the freed people evidenced ambivalence with respect to their obligations, sources demonstrate that the inhabitants in Yazykovo Selo's vicinity were in fact very mobile, participating in a burgeoning shadow economy of sorts, comprising cottage industries and vibrant market and trade activities.

Even though both demesnes were located in rural, traditional contexts, I delineated both significant similarities and distinctions between the two. For example, it would be fair to say that, before emancipation, the estate of Yazykovo Selo was an entrepôt in a command economy, essentially "closed" to itself and dependent on government requisitions. Afterward, however, the village's inhabitants increasingly participated in a diversified range of craftsmanship and local trade, in part because the terms of freedom pushed them to do so, and in part because of the general, overall trend of modernization in the country. Palmyra was a capitalist powerhouse of cotton production and fully integrated in the regional and national economic grid that supported it, both before and after emancipation. However, during the Home Colony period, Palmyra was unique relative to what played out across the American South. The authoritarian economic and social controls in place at this time were similar to those mandated by the Russian emancipation edict at Yazykovo Selo. In addition, notwithstanding the appearance of stagnation at Yazykovo Selo and evidence of economic activity at Palmyra Plantation, it was clear that (1) although Vasili Yazykov worked to manage the demesne within the political, economic, and social context in which he lived, his primary function in Imperial Russia continued to be in the capacity of service and philanthropy, and (2) although William Storrow Lovell was an engaged, hands-on manager, he was not the sort of paternalistic plantation patriarch that was a hallmark of the antebellum period. Both men repeatedly acted in their own self-interest (and often preemptively).

With respect to the various groups involved, each set of players acted according to norms that culture had historically shaped, which evolved in the new context. The master's authority was broken and the former serfs of Yazykovo Selo showed noncompliance routinely, especially with respect to labor obligations. Conversely, the population of freed people at Palmyra was fluid and fulfilled its labor obligations under the restricted conditions of seasonal contractual commitments. It was a watershed moment that emancipation placed constraints on the former masters' power. While in the immediate post-emancipation period authorities in each case feared real or imagined disturbances and/or insurrections, and acted in cases when they saw fit, in the aftermath of such turmoil they still demonstrated a great desire to "get on with production."

A number of recurrent themes showcased important distinctions between the societies, as well as emancipation's parameters. These included the themes of immobility versus mobility; a communal versus an individual ethos; a service ethic versus an entrepreneurial ethos; wage labor; and the levels of obligations and compliance between former masters and their "former people." To a large degree, these factors explain the differences in behavior and outcomes, especially when it comes to accounting for rates of ambivalence at Yazykovo Selo versus compliance at Palmyra.

A number of similarities emerged that have implications for the understanding of emancipation as a category of analysis in global history. First, emancipation came about as a result of *defeat*—for the Russians in the Crimean War, and for the South in the Civil War. These defeats exposed a number of things. Occurring on the periphery of the rapid political, economic, and social transformations that had taken place in the first half of the 19th century in both Europe and the American North, each war put the spotlight on real disadvantages faced by Russia and the South in terms of their opponents' far superior industrialized capacities of war materiel and manpower. Second, liberation was granted from above, by the state, but for conservative reasons—the preservation of the nation and the structures of its political governing system. Both sets of authorities were concerned about social order and the security of labor. In terms of implementing and/or enforcing emancipation, armies were significant players in each case. Authorities in both countries used the strong arm of the law to enforce the terms of freedom. And in each of these examples, agreements or contracts were the state-backed, legal tools of enforcement.

The contrast between the intentions of both sets of authorities and those of both groups of freed people was great in terms of their respective expectations for freedom. The former held patronizing attitudes about the latter and on numerous occasions explained, cajoled, and lectured them about their obligations and responsibilities. By contrast, the desire for distance from anything that had the trappings of their former condition (especially their former masters) was a shared goal of the freed people. In fact, the sets of binary groups in each context were shaped by a long history of cultural distance from (but close physical proximity to) each other. That is, in each context, the other was the "other," and yet each was who they were, in part, because of the other. Each played a historic role in shaping and reinforcing the other's *mentalité* and experience of each other. Emancipation broke that "relationship."

Although emancipation charted a new course for interaction, the authorities often (if not always) sought to control the freed people, and the latter sought freedom from the former. Just for example, whereas the Russian emancipation anchored the freed people to the land, indeed, the Black Codes in Mississippi made this effort too. In addition, whereas the "elders" in the Russian commune had the authority to issue "passes" for an individual to leave the community, Union authorities also retained sole authority over who could leave the Bend during the Home Colony period.

In a number of places, the power of myth, rumor, symbolism, atavism, and suspicion surfaced. Here the drag of culture persisted. On the part of the authorities, this tendency was made clear regarding disturbances and insurrectionary scares. It was also made clear in the fact that they could not conceive of looking to any other group of people as the source for labor. On the part of the freed people, this trend emerged with respect to land gifts, autonomy, and fears about reimpressment into servitude. What was playing out were great dialogues between the various players about freedom, but transmitted via myth, ritual, rumor, symbolism, and suspicion.

The concept of continuity and change was addressed. As this study has highlighted, emancipation was a revolutionary moment in each country's history. The unfree were liberated, and there was no going back. However, because I focused on the nascent stage of freedom in each country, it became clear that even where there appeared to be little change, the freed people's outlook and expectations for the future were transformed by emancipation. A "future orientation" was made possible. And many contingencies that they had were available to them *because* of emancipation.

In spite of the new day that emancipation ushered in, the freed people were living in the moment, and my approach looked at their world as they encountered it. They did not have precedents or blueprints to follow. However, they did have a sense of what freedom looked like, as they saw how those who were free in their respective societies lived. Moreover, their respective histories informed them about what they wanted and did not want. This explains, in part, why the freed serfs and slaves often used the tools and mechanisms with which they were familiar and seized on both the metaphysical fact (the idea) of freedom and practical facts of life to promote what was in their self-interest. The ways in which the freed people experienced freedom had to do with their immediate needs. Definitions of freedom were not articulated as abstract concepts or lofty principles of political philosophies. Rather, freedom was defined in terms of how it had a direct impact on their everyday lives. This perspective was made clear in their contestations or negotiations with respect to labor, contracts, and expectations of land, as well as fears about reimpressment. Increased mobility as well as access to education for both sets of freed people expanded their horizons. In many ways, it appears that aspects of both paternalism and deference were greatly compromised, if not eliminated. In this new context, new identities were forged.

Like the former slaves who looked to Union authorities to take action against their Southern oppressors, yet eschewed paternalism and deference, the Russian peasants could look to a distant beneficent tsar to invoke against the noble estate. The irony is that, as the peasants resisted the nobility, and other state authorities, they were in essence resisting the tsar, since the emancipation command filtered down from him. Here we see the scapegoating theme, in which the peasants projected their anger about the terms of freedom onto the landlords, former masters, and local authorities. Meanwhile, in the American case, Southern whites targeted both Union representatives and the freed people. Tangential to this trend, another triangulation phenomenon appeared in the context of disturbances and insurrectionary scares, with the scapegoating of the so-called "ringleaders" or instigators. In the midst of the fluid circumstances associated with liberation, social interaction was not strictly a binary one, between former masters and the formerly unfree. Political and social machinations of many kinds were simultaneous, kaleidoscopic, and multidirectional.

Another theme has to do with the difference between establishing something and sustaining it, whether it had to do with forms of labor or establishing schools for the freed people, and the like. In both Russia and the American South, the period following emancipation and roughly concluding with the respective years of 1881 and 1877 was one of anticipation, adjustments, and varieties of contingency and resistance. This occurred because of the raw, or uncooked, nature of the emancipation moment. Only after the cutoff dates of 1881 and 1877 did new norms take hold, such as wage labor in the Russian case and sharecropping in the American one, as well as developments associated with economic modernization and education. The period between emancipation and the cutoff dates in this study represents a kind of incubation stage, and thereafter one of maturation. It also represents an intermediary stage, in which both sets of freed people were no longer unfree, but neither were they completely free. Indeed, this "stage" itself contained a number of incremental phases, where kinks in the system were worked out, especially with respect to the terms of freedom and labor obligations. Freedom was being defined as it unfolded.

The phenomena replications identified in the preceding pages is compelling. Implicit in this analysis has been the search for understanding and explaining *why* such duplications occurred, especially in a study like this one in which there is no geographic proximity or political, civic, and cultural commonality between the two case studies under review. Although the similarities may not have followed an identical sequential trajectory in each case, they confirm that the struggle for freedom contains a number of salient hallmarks, especially when it is state engineered. The phenomena replications identified here provide foundational knowledge for future comparative studies within a global framework using emancipation as the category of analysis. Notwithstanding the existence of nuance, agency, contingency, diversity, and difference, patterns and replications exist in pockets of history in specific contextual circumstances, the meaning of which points to a commonality of the human endeavor and experience.

Epilogue

On a cold January day in 1894, the big house at Palmyra went up in flames. Whether this misfortune was due to an unkept fire in the hearth or arson is unknown. However, the "plantation bell was rung in the Lower Quarters," and the hands "came rushing from every direction to the Big House, and made heroic efforts" to save the place. William Storrow Lovell's daughter-in-law wrote that she was "perfectly shocked" that the "dear old house" had burned down. Injecting elements of what would later be labeled Southern Gothic, Caroline Couper Lovell expressed the following:

> To think of its being no longer in existence. To me it was consecrated by the happiness of my life there & I will always hold a peculiar place in my heart & memory [for it].... I cannot bear to think of it a heap of charred ruins—how desolate—melancholic.... I don't think I could bear to see it—How terribly sad for the old man [William Storrow Lovell] to lose his house.... It is a real sorrow to think the dear old place is no more. I loved it almost as though it had a being.[1]

Herein is an example of how Southern elites attached to the plantation house strong feelings of family history and identity, as well as tinges of animism. Equally significant is the symbolism of the house's demise and Lovell's emotions about it. In her comments we see elements of nostalgia, the history of Palmyra reduced to a Ruskinesque remnant, and the old social order's demise.

A few years later, during the Great Flood of 1897, Todd Lovell, Caroline's husband and William Storrow's son, wrote that a staggering "164 negroes" were rescued at the place's levee. When Todd and his family left Palmyra and moved to Birmingham, Alabama, to go into the coal business, Palmyra's demise was complete. None of the family ever returned, and soon thereafter Palmyra was bereft of those freed people who had remained.[2]

But the story of Palmyra's freed people did not end there. Early in 1888, a number of Davis Bend's freed people left the peninsula and established a community, Mound Bayou, in the northwestern corner of Mississippi. By 1907, Mound Bayou, the "Jewel of the Delta," had become the center of a "thriving agricultural community of some 800 families, with a total population of about 4,000" people. Of the 30,000 acres in the municipality, approximately 6,000 were under cotton cultivation, producing about 3,000 bales annually for a number of years. There were 13 stores and a number of shops "doing a combined annual business of about $600,000." The train station was a "hub of activity, handling $40,000 in freight and $6,000 in passenger traffic each year." The town could also boast one sawmill and three cotton gins, as well as a telephone exchange, a weekly newspaper (*The Demonstrator*), a bank, ten churches, and two schools. Although it remains in a rural corner of Mississippi, to be sure, the community

179

Figure E.1. Mound Bayou, about 1910 (New York Public Library, https://digitalcollections. nypl.org/items/510d47dd-e64b-a3d9-e040-e00a18064a99).

Figure E.2. Annual Pushkin and Yazykov Festival, Yazykovo Selo (copyright © 2021 Sergey Anatolyevich Oikin, photographer).

Figure E.3. The House of Yazykov "Pushkin Literary" Museum, Ulyanovsk, Russia (copyright © 2021 Literaturnyĭ muzeĭ "Dom Yazykovykh" [Literature Museum "The House of Yazykovs," Ulyanovsk, Russia]).

Figure E.4. Monmouth Mansion, Natchez, Mississippi (copyright © 2020 Monmouth Historic Inn and Gardens).

of Mound Bayou is historically significant for its continuity with its rich past. It is also significant as an example of the freed people's self-determination[3] (see figure E.1).

After the Russian Revolution in 1917, the Bolsheviks confiscated Yazykovo Selo. By the early 1930s, Mikhail Stepanov and his young adult son were purged. No record exists of what ultimately happened to them. In 1921, as one of War Communism's requisition gangs approached the village in order to confiscate produce, the estate mansion went up in flames when a *Sovkhoz* farm official set fire to it in an attempt to hide evidence of the grain the community had been hoarding in its rooms.[4] Nevertheless, the village of Yazykovo Selo and its inhabitants (many of whom are direct descendants of the freed serfs) remain as the estate's legacy. Every June the inhabitants organize a festival showcasing songs, dances, food, poetry, and drama, all of which are designed to honor and commemorate the Yazykov family and its impact on the region. Their recent decision to rebuild the mansion is the latest installment of their efforts to recover the purged culture of the Russian noble family[5] (see figure E.2).

It is ironic that the demesne in this study that was marked by apparent stagnation in the post-emancipation period endured, while not a trace is left of the one that evidently thrived as an economic enterprise. All that remains of Davis Bend is a nearly inaccessible swamp, infested with alligators and snakes. In this sense, Yazykovo Selo was what David Moon has asserted—namely, that "most noble estates were peasant villages far more than they were 'nests of gentry' portrayed in some nineteenth-century Russian literature." Conversely, Palmyra Plantation and its environs became a gothicized landscape, marked by swampy ruins and decay, bereft of the lively productive activity that once defined it.[6]

Meanwhile, the Yazykov and Quitman/Lovell mansions in Simbirsk and Natchez survived and today are historic landmarks in their respective cities. The former is a literary museum and houses the Yazykov family archives (see figure E.3). The latter's fate is one shared by many antebellum mansions: it is a high-end bed and breakfast where patrons can be exposed to the grace and charm of the Natchez nabobs' way of life, as well as the life experience of the servants who lived and worked there (see figure E.4).

As for the freed people of Yazykovo Selo and Palmyra Plantation, liberation from serfdom and slavery opened a fresh chapter in their lives in which a new identity was forged. They were among freedom's first recipients. As has been made clear in the preceding pages, they did not have the social capital to completely overcome the hurdles that were in front of them. Despite their struggles and the "reimposition of 'hegemony' by the dominant elites," the freed people were active agents.[7] They were the trailblazers for future generations, who would press on for equality and full citizenship.

Glossary

Russian Terms

Arshin: (other forms: *arshiny, arshina, arshinov*) a unit of length amounting to 28 inches.

Barshchina: (*corvee*) labor obligations owed by a peasant to his/her lord.

Desiatina: (other forms: *desiatiny, desiatin*) 2.7 acres.

Kazna: The Treasury in Imperial Russia.

Kontora: From the French word *comptoir* (counter), the administrative office located on most large Russian estates.

Krepostnoe pravo: Serfdom.

Kulak: A Rich peasant.

Nadel: Land allotment (for the peasants in conjunction with emancipation).

Narodniki: From the word *narod* (or people), a populist, intellectual, and political and social conscious movement created by the Russian intelligentsia and middle class beginning in the 1860s; initially focusing on reforming Russia, it soon morphed into a revolutionary movement.

Obrok: (quitrent) fee obligations owed by a peasant to his/her lord in the form of money or in kind; in a sense, it was a kind of tribute.

Obshchestvo: Village commune or society.

Osvobozhdenie: Emancipation; liberation.

Pomest'e: Land allotment (an estate earmarked for a member of the nobility).

Reviziia: Literally "Revision list," the method of counting the population in Imperial Russia for the purposes of taxation and the draft (sometimes referred to as a fiscal census).

Svoboda: Freedom.

Selo: Russian village that has a church.

Soslovie: The estate system in Russia.

Usad'ba: The estate where the noble manor house was located; also, often the garden plot that surrounded a peasant house.

Volnenie: Peasant disturbance, resistance, and/or uprising.

Zemstvo: An elected council at the local and provincial levels set up by a decree in 1864, for the purpose of establishing a kind of representative government to administer local affairs.

English Terms

Beggar's allotment: (*bednyatskiy nadel'*) if the emancipated (male) serf could not afford to pay for the allotted land, he could opt to receive a quarter of the maximum earmark for the region for free, with no obligations.

Peace arbitrator/peace mediator: (*mirovoy posrednik*) an intermediary created by the emancipation legislation in 1861 whose job was to see that the negotiations for land settlements between former serfs and their former masters proceeded smoothly; legislation on June 27, 1874, ended the tenure of all mediators.

Redemption Agreement: (*vykupnoy dogovor* or *sdelka*) essentially, the mortgage payment agreement/schedule whereby the peasants would thereafter make annual payments until the land allotted to them was paid for.

Regulations: (*Polozheniīa*) the 400-plus-page manual that accompanied the Russian Manifesto emancipating the serfs and that detailed the complicated terms of emancipation.

Slavophilism: A Russian manifestation of a pan-European, counter-Enlightenment phenomenon that eschewed rationalism, reason, and universalism, instead embracing and promoting the Romantic Era's ideals of feeling, empathy, individual experience, and particularism; drawing on both a real and an imagined past, the Slavophiles believed that the Russian peasant was both the personification and the carrier of an authentic, pristine Russian culture uncontaminated by Western modernization.

Soul: (*dusha*) male serf/peasant.

Statutory Charter: (*Ustavnaya Gramota*) official document that established the amount of land that would be allotted to the peasants; the document also detailed a variety of particulars about each estate, including demographics.

Temporarily obligated: (*vremenno obyazanniy*) the status held by the emancipated serfs until they entered into a Redemption Agreement with their former master.

Chapter Notes

Preface

1. The Great Reforms were a series of political, educational, social, military, and judicial reforms introduced in the 1860s and 1870s, of which emancipation was one.

2. I refer here to the title and subject of Peter Kolchin's book *First Freedom: The Responses of Alabama's Blacks to Emancipation and Reconstruction* (Westport, CT: Greenwood Press, 1972).

3. A radical advocate of slavery.

4. I use this term deliberately. Central to the philosophy of phenomenology, lifeworld is the "world we live in ... that we take for granted in daily life ... [which] has its own criteria of validity and truth." See Dan Zahavi, *Phenomenology: The Basics* (New York: Routledge, 2019), pp. 51–52.

5. For solid discussions about the global history paradigm, see Diego Olstein, *Thinking History Globally* (New York: Palgrave Macmillan, 2015); Sebastian Conrad, *What Is Global History?* (Princeton: Princeton University Press, 2016); Simon J. Potter and Jonathan Saha, "Global History, Imperial History and Connected Histories of Empire," *Journal of Colonialism and Colonial History* 16:1 (Spring 2015); and Mark Juergensmeyer, ed., *Thinking Globally: A Global Studies Reader* (Berkeley: University of California Press, 2014).

6. For a sampling, see M.L. Bush, ed., *Serfdom and Slavery: Studies in Legal Bondage* (New York: Addison Wesley Longman, 1996); David Brion Davis, *Inhuman Bondage: The Rise and Fall of Slavery in the New World* (New York: Oxford University Press, 2006); Robert Harms, Bernard K. Freamon, and David W. Blight, eds., *Indian Ocean Slavery in the Age of Abolition* (New Haven: Yale University Press, 2013); John K. Thornton, *Africa and Africans in the Making of the Atlantic World, 1400–1800* (Cambridge: Cambridge University Press, 1998); Hideaki Suzuki, ed., *Abolitions as a Global Experience* (Singapore: National University of Singapore Press, 2015); Frederick Cooper, Thomas C. Holt, and Rebecca Scott, *Beyond Slavery: Explorations of Race, Labor, and Citizenship in Postemancipation Societies* (Chapel Hill: University of North Carolina Press, 2000); and C.A. Bayly, Sven Beckert, Matthew Connelly, Isabel

Hofmeyr, Wendy Kozol, and Patricia Seed, "AHR Conversation: On Transnational History," *American Historical Review* 111 (December 2006), pp. 1440–1464.

7. The academy awaits the long-anticipated publication of Peter Kolchin's follow-up to his groundbreaking comparison of Russian serfdom and American slavery, *Unfree Labor: American Slavery and Russian Serfdom* (Cambridge: Harvard University Press, 1987), yet to be titled. Whereas his is a sweeping, macro account of emancipation in each country, mine is a micro study contextualized in the emancipation era. Amanda Brickell Bellows' study, *American Slavery and Russian Serfdom in the Post-Emancipation Imagination* (Chapel Hill: University of North Carolina Press, 2020), addresses the representation of emancipated serfs and slaves by elites in the post-emancipation period, as well as the ways in which the freed people sought to challenge them.

8. For a variety of examples on this historiographical topic, see Daniel Field, *The End of Serfdom: Nobility and Bureaucracy in Russia, 1855–1861* (Cambridge: Harvard University Press, 1976); Peter A. Zaionchkovskiy, *The Abolition of Serfdom in Russia*, edited and translated from the third (1968) Russian edition by Susan Wobst (Gulf Breeze, FL: Academic International Press, 1978); I.A. Khristoforov, "The Fate of Reform: The Russian Peasantry in Government Policy and Public Opinion from the Late 1860s to the Early 1880s," *Russian Studies in History* 46:1 (Summer 2007), pp. 24–42; and David Moon, *The Abolition of Serfdom in Russia, 1762–1902* (Harlow, UK: Longman, 2001). See also Theodore Taranovski, "Nobility in the Russian Empire: Some Problems of Definition and Interpretation," *Slavic Review* 47:2 (Summer 1988), pp. 314–318. For an example of a classic debate, see Seymour Becker, *Nobility and Privilege in Late Imperial Russia* (DeKalb: Northern Illinois University Press, 1986) and Roberta T. Manning, *The Crisis of the Old Order in Russia: Gentry and Government* (Princeton: Princeton University Press, 1982). While overall landholdings may well have contracted after emancipation, Becker argues that this process did not translate to the nobles' declension.

9. For a sampling, see Katherine Pickering

Antonova, *An Ordinary Marriage: The World of a Gentry Family in Provincial Russia* (New York: Oxford University Press, 2013); Susan Smith-Peter, *Imagining Russian Regions: Civil Society and Subnational Identity in Nineteenth Century Russia* (Leiden, Netherlands: Brill, 2018); Mary W. Cavender, *Nests of the Gentry: Family, Estate, and Local Loyalties in Provincial Russia* (Newark: University of Delaware Press, 2007) and "Provincial Nobles, Elite History, and the Imagination of Everyday Life," in *Everyday Life in Russia Past and Present*, edited by Choi Chatterjee, David L. Ransel, Mary Cavender, and Karen Petrone (Bloomington: Indiana University Press, 2015); Alexa von Winning, "The Empire as Family Affair: The Mansurovs and Noble Participation in Imperial Russia, 1850–1917," *Geschichte und Gesellschaft* 40 (January–March 2014), pp. 94–116; and Catherine Evtuhov, *Portrait of a Russian Province: Economy, Society, and Civilization in Nineteenth-Century Nizhnii Novgorod* (Pittsburgh: University of Pittsburgh Press, 2011).

10. Indeed, this requires the author to quote the infamous statements issued by Lenin himself: "The year 1861 gave birth to 1905" and "1905 was the dress rehearsal for 1917." However, I make this point with caution since it is a sweeping generalization and one that has been challenged in recent decades. Notwithstanding the suspension of liberalizing, reformist policies by Russia's last two tsars, as well as the pressures that the war with Japan in 1904 and World War I put on the country (both of which far more directly led to the revolutions of 1905 and 1917, respectively), the "peasant question" or the "agrarian problem" persisted up until the end of the autocracy in 1917 and beyond. See Stephen F. Williams, *Liberal Reform in an Illiberal Regime: The Creation of Private Property in Russia, 1906–1915* (Stanford, CA: Hoover Institution Press, 2006); Alexander Polunov, *Russia in the Nineteenth Century: Autocracy, Reform, and Social Change, 1814–1914*, edited by Thomas C. Owen and Larissa G. Zakharova (New York: M.E. Sharpe, 2005), especially chapters 4, 5, and 6; George Yaney, *The Urge to Mobilize: Agrarian Reform in Russia, 1861–1930* (Urbana: University of Illinois Press, 1982); David A.J. Macey, *Government and Peasant in Russia, 1861–1906: The Prehistory of the Stolypin Reforms* (DeKalb: Northern Illinois University Press, 1987); Lazar Volin, *A Century of Russian Agriculture: From Alexander II to Khrushchev (Russian Research Center Studies, Number 63)* (Cambridge: Harvard University Press, 1970); Francis William Wcislo, *Reforming Rural Russia: State, Local Society, and National Politics, 1855–1914* (Princeton: Princeton University Press, 1990); and David Moon, "Reassessing Russian Serfdom," *European History Quarterly* 26:4 (1996), pp. 483–526.

11. For recent examples of this debate and related issues, see Tracy K. Dennison, *The Institutional Framework of Russian Serfdom* (New York: Cambridge University Press, 2011); and

Khristoforov, "The Fate of Reform," pp. 24–42, and *"Sud'ba reformy: russkoe krest'i anstvo v pravitel'stvennoĭ politike do i posle otmeny krepostnogo prava (1830–1890-e gg.)"* (Moskva, Rossiya: Sobranie, 2011). Dennison and Kristoforov examine the institutional frameworks that influenced peasant initiatives with respect to land usage and productivity. While the former argues, among other things, that the peasants were not market averse, Khristoforov holds that the reforms exacerbated underdevelopment. Utilizing a micro case study of Voronezh and analyzing household budgets, Elvira M. Wilbur argued in "Was Russian Peasant Agriculture Really That Impoverished? New Evidence from a Case Study from the 'Impoverished Center' at the End of the Nineteenth Century," *Journal of Economic History* 43:1 (March 1983), pp. 137–144, that, either because of incorrect equations and interpretations or due to misinterpretations of peasant leasing (that it was not because of "land hunger" or efforts to ward off disaster, but rather prosperity and opportunity), the province was not impoverished. But her study pertains to the period after the focus in this book. Steven Hoch has argued that the peasants were not terribly adversely impacted; see his "Did Russia's Emancipated Serfs Really Pay Too Much for Too Little Land? Statistical Anomalies and Long-Tailed Distributions," *Slavic Review* 63:2 (Summer 2004), pp. 247–274. In "The Economic Effects of the Abolition of Serfdom: Evidence from the Russian Empire," *American Economic Review* 108:4–5 (2018), pp. 1074–1117 (especially pp. 1074, 1079–1080, and 1101), Andrei Markevich and Ekaterina Zhuravskaya argue that there was substantial agricultural productivity and industrial output, as well as an increase in peasant nutrition after emancipation, one of the centerpieces of the analysis being that the edict ended a ratchet effect operating during the times of serfdom—meaning that the more that serfs produced, the higher the share of that produce the noble landlords would demand. Hence serfdom repressed productivity. Illustrating a turn in historiography in general, which asserts complexity, nuance, and flexibility, and rejects classical generalizations, Alessandro Stanziani, in "Russian Serfdom: A Reappraisal," *Ab Imperio* 2 (2014), pp. 71–99, suggests that serf well-being and productivity were not as harsh and fixed as has been thought and that the condition of the freed people after emancipation did not improve greatly.

12. I address this topic in chapter 5.

13. Although he does not use this specific phrase, per se, it is one of the main themes in Steven Hahn's important and provocative book *The Political Worlds of Slavery and Freedom* (Cambridge: Harvard University Press, 2009). (It is cited in Tobias C. Van Veen's review of the book; see "Insurrection & Slave Rebellion in Civil War America," http://fugitive.quadrantcrossing.org/2010/07/insurrection-slave-rebellion-in-civil-war-america, accessed July 15, 2012.) Hahn argues in this slim volume that

the Civil War was in fact the greatest slave rebellion in modern history; that emancipation did not begin with the Civil War, but rather as early as 1777; and that free blacks in America were never secure in their freedom. Of course, "resistance theory" is to a great extent the result of James C. Scott's work in *Weapons of the Weak: Everyday Forms of Peasant Resistance* (New Haven: Yale University Press, 1987) and *Domination and the Arts of Resistance: Hidden Transcripts* (New Haven: Yale University Press, 1992).

14. This "tragic era" paradigm is summarized in Bernard A. Weisberger, "The Dark and Bloody Ground of Reconstruction Historiography," *Journal of Southern History* 25:4 (November 1959), pp. 427–447, and exemplified in William A. Dunning, *Reconstruction: Political and Economic, 1865–1877* (New York: Harper and Bros., 1907); Claude G. Bowers, *The Tragic Era: The Revolution after Lincoln* (New York: Houghton Mifflin, 1929); and George Fort Milton, *The Age of Hate: Andrew Johnson and the Radicals* (New York: Coward-McCann, 1930).

15. For a sampling, see Gavin Wright, *Old South, New South: Revolutions in the Southern Economy Since the Civil War* (New York: Basic Books, 1986); Michael S. Wayne, *The Reshaping of Plantation Society: The Natchez District, 1860–80* (Baton Rouge: Louisiana State University Press, 1990); especially John C. Willis, *Forgotten Time: The Yazoo-Mississippi Delta after the Civil War* (Charlottesville: University Press of Virginia, 2000); and the following by Peter Kolchin: "After Serfdom: Russian Emancipation in Comparative Perspective," in *The Terms of Labor: Slavery, Serfdom, and Free Labor*, edited by Stanley Engerman (Stanford: Stanford University Press, 1999), pp. 87–115; "Some Controversial Questions Concerning Nineteenth-Century Emancipation from Slavery and Serfdom," in *Serfdom and Slavery: Studies in Legal Bondage*, edited by M.L. Bush (New York: Addison Wesley Longman, 1996), pp. 42–67; "Some Thoughts on Emancipation in Comparative Perspective: Russia and the United States South," *Slavery and Abolition* 11 (December 1990), pp. 351–368; and "The Tragic Era? Interpreting Southern Reconstruction in Comparative Perspective," in *The Meaning of Freedom: Economics, Politics, and Culture after Slavery*, edited by Frank McGlynn and Seymour Drescher (Pittsburgh: University of Pittsburgh Press, 1992), pp. 291–311.

16. See Sven Beckert, "Emancipation and Empire: Reconstructing the Worldwide Web of Cotton Production in the Age of the American Civil War," *American Historical Review* 109:5 (December 2004), pp. 1405–1438, and *Empire of Cotton: A Global History* (New York: Penguin Random House, 2014), as well as Dale W. Tomich's *Through the Prism of Slavery: Labor, Capital, and World Economy* (Lanham, MD: Rowman & Littlefield, 2004).

17. Janet Sharp Hermann, *The Pursuit of a Dream* (New York: Oxford University Press, 1981), p. 173. See also Lawrence N. Powell, *New Masters: Northern Planters during the Civil War and Reconstruction* (New Haven: Yale University Press, 1980), chapters 1, 5, and 7; and James L. Roark, *Masters Without Slaves: Southern Planters in the Civil War and Reconstruction* (New York: W.W. Norton, 1977). While Hermann holds that the new post-emancipation planters adopted a "time is money" approach, Powell rejects this view. See Hermann, *Pursuit*, p. 173; Powell, *New Masters*, p. 126.

18. See Eric Foner, *Reconstruction: America's Unfinished Revolution, 1863–1877* (New York: Harper & Row, 1988), *A Short History of Reconstruction, 1863–1877* (New York: Harper & Row, 1990), especially pages 254–260, and *Nothing but Freedom: Emancipation and Its Legacy* (Baton Rouge: Louisiana State University Press, 1983); and Amy Dru Stanley, *From Bondage to Contract: Wage Labor, Marriage, and the Market in the Age of Slave Emancipation* (Cambridge: Cambridge University Press, 1998).

19. One benchmark study in this historiographical trend was John Blassingame, *The Slave Community: Plantation Life in the Antebellum South* (New York: Oxford University Press, 1979). For post-emancipation community studies, see Kolchin, *First Freedom*, and Herbert G. Gutman, *The Black Family in Slavery and Freedom, 1750–1925* (New York: Vintage, 1976). More recent studies include Sharon Holt, *Making Freedom Pay: North Carolina Freedpeople Working for Themselves, 1865–1900* (Athens: University of Georgia Press, 2003); Karen Cook Bell, *Claiming Freedom: Race, Kinship, and Land in Nineteenth-Century Georgia* (Columbia: University of South Carolina Press, 2018); and Dylan C. Penningroth, *The Claims of Kinfolk: African American Property and Community in the Nineteenth Century South* (Chapel Hill: University of North Carolina Press, 2003).

20. See Willis, *Forgotten Time*.

21. Boris B. Gorshkov, *Peasants in Russia from Serfdom to Stalin: Accommodation, Survival, Resistance* (New York: Bloomsbury Academic, 2018), pp. 37 and 139.

22. I explain this concept in further detail in chapter 5.

23. See V. Egorov, redaktor, "Ėkonomika i Torgovlia" v sbornike *"Simbirsko-Ulyanovskiĭ kraĭ v prodvizhenie istorii Rossii"* (Ulyanovsk, Rossiya, Korporatsiia tekhnologii, 2007), str. 222–287; and V. Egorov, and N. Rakov, "Yazykovskiĭ park," stat'ia v *Ulyanovskoĭ-Simbirskoĭ Ėntsiklopedii*, T.2 (Ulyanovsk, Simbirskaia kniga 2004), str. 473.

24. I discuss this concern in further detail in chapter 3.

25. See Alessandro Stanziani, *Bondage, Labor and Rights in Eurasia from the Sixteenth to the Early Twentieth Centuries* (New York: Berghahn [International Studies in Social History, 24], 2014). See especially introduction and chapters 4–1.

Introduction

1. D. Clayton James, *Antebellum Natchez* (Baton Rouge: Louisiana State University Press, 1968), p. 136. The term originated from the European who made his fortune in the Orient, especially India. There is also evidence that its source is found in a Native American term, *nawab*, for great wealth and power, or a great governor or leader. Regarding Natchez, a nabob was a member of a close-knit, pseudo-aristocratic group, numbering about forty families in the area, and related in an intricate web through marriage and/or business ventures. In general, nabobs were generally of Whiggish principles—that is, pro-union and "federalist," as opposed to a "states' rights" leaning type. Obviously, as a secessionist, John Quitman was an exception to this prototype. In his early years, because he held rather elitist views, he was certainly not a Democrat. Although he fought for the Union in the Mexican-American War, he soon became a Southern nationalist and filibusterer—one who promoted the acquisition of Cuba.

2. Robert E. May, *John A. Quitman: Old South Crusader* (Baton Rouge: Louisiana State University Press, 1985), pp. 130–140.

3. Of course, interpreting emancipation in each country as part of a larger modernization project is a historiographical mainstay. For example, see W.E. Mosse, *Alexander II and the Modernization of Russia* (New York: St. Martin's Press, 1992); Francis William Wcislo, *Reforming Rural Russia: State, Local Society, and National Politics, 1855–1914*, Alexander Polunov, *Russia in the Nineteenth Century: Autocracy, Reform, and Social Change, 1814–1914*, edited by Thomas C. Owen and Larissa G. Zakharova (New York: M.E. Sharpe, 2005); Eric Foner, *The Story of American Freedom* (New York: W.W. Norton, 1998); and Sven Beckert, *Empire of Cotton: A Global History* (New York: Penguin Random House, 2014).

4. Caroline Couper Lovell to Tonie Quitman Lovell, February 11, 1894, Lovell Family Papers, Box 1, Folder 11, University of the South, Sewanee, TN.

5. It is worth noting that, like American slavery, serfdom not only was a crucial component of Russia's economy but also played a role in the country's expansionist policies. That is, whereas serf populations were relocated and fixed to the land as Moscow set in motion policies for Russia's expansion, the extension of slavery created increasingly bitter contention between the pro- and anti-slavery sections in the years leading up to the Civil War.

6. For the quotes in this paragraph and further discussion of this topic, see Peter Kolchin, *Unfree Labor: American Slavery and Russian Serfdom*, pp. 170–173 and 184–191; David Hecht, "Russian Intelligentsia and American Slavery," *Phylon (1940–1956)* 9:3 (3rd Quarter 1948), pp. 265–269; and Cathy A. Frierson, *Peasant Icons: Representations of Rural People in Late Nineteenth-Century Russia* (New York: Oxford University Press,

1993). For a discussion of how elites in the American South enlisted the notion of difference to justify and rationalize their own efforts to control the labor and subordination of black Americans, as well as how subalterns identify collectively with each other because they are exploited, or as a way of resisting exploitation, see Jaqueline Jones, "Labor and the Idea of Race in the American South," *Journal of Southern History* 75:3 (August 2009), pp. 613–626. Amanda Brickell Bellows has compared advertising in Russia and the United States after emancipation and has found that racial and ethnic physiognomies were utilized in order to distinguish between various social groups in each country. See *American Slavery and Russian Serfdom in the Post-Emancipation Imagination*, p. 171.

7. See Joseph C.G. Kennedy, ed., *Population of the United States in 1860: Compiled from the Original Returns of the Eighth Census, under the Direction of the Secretary of the Interior* (Washington, D.C.: Government Printing Office, 1864).

8. For a discussion of the "tiers" of Russian nobility and their role in society, see John P. LeDonne, *Absolutism and the Ruling Class: The Formation of the Russian Political Order, 1700–1825* (New York: Oxford University Press, 1991), p. 22; and Lee A. Farrow, *Between Clan and Crown: The Struggle to Define Noble Property Rights in Imperial Russia* (Newark: University of Delaware Press, 2004), pp. 187–202.

9. For a helpful explanation of master/serf ratios and relationships, see the introduction to Boris B. Gorshkov, ed., *A Life Under Russian Serfdom: The Memoirs of Savva Dmitrievich Purlevskii, 1800–1868* (New York: Central European University Press, 2005), pp. 1–19; for master/slave ratios and relationships, see Charles S. Sydnor, *Slavery in Mississippi* (Columbia: University of South Carolina Press, 2013).

10. See chapters 5 and 6 for the numbers after the family's recovery of Palmyra.

11. For quote, see Johnson's chapter "Agency: A Ghost Story," in *Slavery's Ghost: The Problem of Freedom in the Age of Emancipation*, by Richard Follette, Eric Foner, and Walter Johnson (Baltimore: Johns Hopkins University Press, 2011), pp. 8–32. See also Walter Johnson, "On Agency," *Journal of Social History* 37:1 (Fall 2003), pp. 113–124.

Chapter 1

1. William Alexander Percy, *Lanterns on the Levee: Recollections of a Planter's Son* (Baton Rouge: Louisiana State University Press, 1973), pp. 3–5.

2. M. Sudarev, "Nachalo," *Zhurnal "Monomakh"* Nomer 2 (2003), str. 8–12.

3. *Ibid.*

4. Sudarev, "Nachalo"; S. Gusev, "Selo Yazykovo," Karsunskiĭ Vestnik (10 aprelia 2001), str. 18.

5. See Sudarev, "Nachalo"; and Mary Matossian, "The Peasant Way of Life," in *The Peasant in Nineteenth-Century Russia*, edited by Wayne Vucinich (Stanford: Stanford University Press, 1968), pp. 1–40.

6. Sudarev, "Nachalo"; V. Egorov, N. Rakov, "Yazykovskiĭ park," stat'ia v *Ulyanovskoĭ-Simbirskoĭ Ėntsiklopedii*, T.2 (Ulyanovsk, Simbirskaia kniga 2004), str. 473; and Rex A. Wade, *Politics and Society in Provincial Russia: Saratov, 1590–1917* (Columbus: Ohio State University Press, 1989), pp. 18–19.

7. The Decembrist uprising occurred in December 1825 when a collection of noblemen and members of the military tried to launch a rebellion to establish a constitutional monarchy. It failed before it began, and the ringleaders were either executed or banished to Siberia. Other outcomes of the uprising included driving members of the nobility to quietly seek other, more discreet forms of association such as freemasonry.

8. Slavophilism was an intellectual impulse that emerged over the course of the 19th century that lauded Russian history and culture as unique and exceptional.

9. Wade, *Politics and Society*, p. 1.

10. P. Martynov, *"Gorod Simbirsk za 250 let ego sushchestvovaniia: sistematicheskiĭ sbornik istoricheskikh svedeniĭ o g. Simbirske"* (Simbirsk, Rossiya: Tipografiia gubernskogo pravleniia, 1898), str. 50, 74, 130, and 156.

11. Richard Middleton and Anne Lombard, *Colonial America: A History to 1763*, fourth edition (Malden, MA: Blackwell, 2011), pp. 20–23 and 410.

12. D. Clayton James, *Antebellum Natchez* (Baton Rouge: Louisiana State University Press, 1968), chapter 1, "Inauspicious Beginnings," pp. 3–30.

13. *Ibid.*, pp. 55 and 63.

14. Joyce Appleby, *Inheriting the Revolution: The First Generation of Americans* (Cambridge: Belknap Press of Harvard University Press, 2000), p. 10, and *passim*.

15. Robert E. May, *John A. Quitman: Old South Crusader* (Baton Rouge: Louisiana State University Press, 1985), pp. 5–6.

16. *Ibid.*, pp. 12 and 19.

17. James, *Antebellum*, p. 136.

18. The American Whig Party existed from 1834 to 1858. But "Whiggish" characteristics included pro-business, -manufacturing, -commercial and -financial interests; economic protectionism; the rule of law; and anti-Jacksonian sentiment (as in the Jacksonian Democrat Party).

19. James, *Antebellum*, pp. 78–101 and 136.

20. May, *Quitman*, pp. 130–146.

21. James T. Currie, *Enclave: Vicksburg and Her Plantations, 1863–1870* (Jackson: University Press of Mississippi, 1980), p. 85.

22. May, *Quitman*, p. 131; Caroline Couper Lovell, *The Bend of the River* (Unpublished Manuscript, 1935), pp. 1–2, 6, 32, and 35–36 (p. 36 for quote).

23. James C. Cobb, *The Most Southern Place on Earth: The Mississippi Delta and the Roots of Regional Identity* (Oxford: Oxford University Press, 1992), p. vii; Marq de Villiers, *Down the Volga in a Time of Troubles: A Journey Revealing the People and Heartland of Post-Perestroika Russia* (Toronto: HarperCollins, 1991), p. xv; and Janet M. Hartley, *The Volga: A History of Russia's Greatest River* (New Haven: Yale University Press, 2021), p. 193, and *passim*.

24. Mikhail Epstein, "Materialism, Sophiology, and the Soul of Russia: Daniel Andreev and Russian Feminine Mysticism," *Urania* 4 (1993), pp. 19–22. And see his chapter "Daniil Andreev and the Mysticism of Femininity," in *The Occult in Russian and Soviet Culture*, edited by Bernice Glatzer Rosenthal (Ithaca: Cornell University Press, 1997), pp. 325–355. Also see the introduction, conclusion, and p. xv in particular in Joanna Hubbs, *Mother Russia: The Feminine Myth in Russian Culture* (Bloomington: Indiana University Press, 1993).

25. See James L. Shaffer and John T. Tigges, *The Mississippi River: Father of Waters* (Mount Pleasant, SC: Arcadia, 2000); and Dorothy Zeisler-Vralsted, "African Americans and the Mississippi River: Race, History and the Environment," *Thesis Eleven: Critical Theory and Historical Sociology* 150:1 (January 7, 2019), pp. 81–101.

26. See this history documented in Richard Hellie, *Slavery in Russia, 1450–1725* (Chicago: University of Chicago Press, 1984); Elise Kimerling Wirtschafter, *Russia's Age of Serfdom, 1649–1861* (Hoboken: Wiley-Blackwell, 2008); and David Moon, *Abolition of Serfdom in Russia, 1762–1907* (Harlow, UK: Longman, 2001).

27. For a concise explanation of the rise of both serfdom and slavery, see Peter Kolchin, *Unfree Labor: American Slavery and Russian Serfdom* (Cambridge: Belknap Press of Harvard University Press, 1987), 1–46.

28. Barbara Bigham, "Colonists in Bondage: Indentured Servants in America," *Early American Life* 10:5 (October 1979), pp. 30–33 and 83–84; Kolchin, *Unfree Labor*, introduction; and Middleton and Lombard, *Colonial America*, chapters 10 and 11.

29. Kolchin, *Unfree Labor*, p. 7; David Moon, "Peasant Migration and the Settlement of Russia's Frontiers, 1550–1897," *Historical Journal* 40:4 (December 1997), pp. 859–893, especially pp. 862–868; Cathy A. Frierson, "Letting Loose the Red Rooster: Arson in Rural Russia," in *All Russia Is Burning! A Cultural History of Fire and Arson in Late Imperial Russia* (Seattle: University of Washington Press, 2002), pp. 101–174; and Hugh D. Hudson, Jr., "A Rhetorical War of Fire: The Middle Volga Arson Panic of 1839 as Contested Legitimacy in Prereform Russia," *Canadian Slavonic Papers* 43:1 (March 2001), pp. 29–48. Quoting the foremost 19th-century Russian historian of the peasantry, V.I. Semevskii, Hudson notes that peasant petitions rarely resulted in favorable improvements for peasants (p. 30).

30. The quote is attributed to the national historian Nikolai Karamzin.

31. Hudson, in "A Rhetorical War of Fire," p. 29, argues this tactic evidenced rational thinking. Teodor Shanin, *The Awkward Class: The Political Sociology of the Peasantry in a Developing Society: Russia 1910–1925* (Oxford: Oxford University Press, 1972), who drew heavily on the Russian agricultural economist A.V. Chaianov, was one of the first to argue for the peasant as a rational economic actor.

32. Wade, *Politics and Society*, p. 200.

33. Boris N. Mironov, "The Russian Peasant Commune after the Reforms of the 1860s," *Slavic Review* 44:3 (Fall 1985), pp. 438–467.

34. Orlando Figes, *Natasha's Dance: A Cultural History of Russia* (New York: Picador, 2002), p. 39. Avenir Korelin has explained that the emancipation decrees of 1762 and 1785, while liberating the nobility from state service, enumerated a list of delegated obligations, duties, and functions for their respective local societies, especially with respect to the provincial and district marshals of the nobility. This requirement may well have set in motion a strong element of paternalism, at least in part. See A.P. Korelin, "The Institution of Marshals of the Nobility: On the Social and Political Position of the Nobility," *Russian Studies in History* 17:4 (Spring 1979), pp. 3–35.

35. Richard Pipes, *Russia Under the Old Regime* (New York: Penguin, 1974), p. 153.

36. Leonid Heretz, *Russia on the Eve of Modernity: Popular Religion and Traditional Culture under the Last Tsars* (Cambridge: Cambridge University Press, 2008), pp. 14 and 35. See also Chris J. Chulos, "Myths of the Pious or Pagan Peasant in Post-Emancipation Central Russia (Voronezh Province)," *Russian History* 22:2 (Summer 1995/ ETE 1995), pp. 181–216.

37. See Anthony E. Kaye, "Neighbourhoods and Solidarity in the Natchez District of Mississippi: Rethinking the Antebellum Slave Community," *Slavery and Abolition* 23:1 (April 2002), pp. 1–24.

38. Middleton and Lombard, *Colonial America*, p. 298.

39. See "Of Our Spiritual Strivings" in W.E.B. Du Bois, *The Souls of Black Folk* (New York: Cosimo, 1903), pp. 7–15.

40. Philip D. Curtin, *The Rise and Fall of the Plantation Complex: Essays in Atlantic History* (Cambridge: Cambridge University Press, 1990), pp. 149–155.

41. See Liah Greenfeld, "The Formation of the Russian National Identity: The Role of Status Insecurity and *Ressentiment*," *Comparative Studies in Society and History* 32:3 (July 1990), pp. 549–591, especially p. 562; Michael Hughes, "The Russian Nobility and the Russian Countryside: Ambivalences and Orientations," *Journal of European Studies* 36:2 (June 2006), pp. 115–137; and Susan Smith-Peter, *Imagining Russian Regions: Civil Society and Subnational Identity in Nineteenth Century Russia* (Leiden, Netherlands: Brill, 2018).

42. For a concise account of American influence in Russia in the 19th century, see Allison Blakely, "American Influences on Russian Reformist Thought in the Era of the French Revolution," *Russian Review* 52 (October 1993), pp. 451–471. See also V. Polivanov, "Selo Yazykovo," *"Istoricheskii Vestnik"* (Dekabr', 1896), str. 987–999. Perepechatano v *Zhurnale Monomakh*, Nomer 2 (2003) str. 15–16. For a brief account of Russian sympathies with the North during the Civil War, especially Radical Republicans and the idea of land distribution for former slaves, see David Hecht, "Russian Intelligentsia and American Slavery," *Phylon (1940–1956)* 9:3 (3rd Quarter 1948), pp. 265–269.

43. For an explanation of this legend, see Daniel R. Vollaro, "Lincoln, Stowe, and the 'Little Woman/Great War' Story: The Making, and Breaking, of a Great American Anecdote," *Journal of the Abraham Lincoln Association* 30:1 (Winter 2009), pp. 18–34. See also John MacKay, *True Songs of Freedom: Uncle Tom's Cabin in Russian Culture and Society* (Madison: University of Wisconsin Press, 2013).

44. Lazar Volin, "The Russian Peasant and Serfdom," *Agricultural History* 17:1 (January 1943), pp. 41–61, especially p. 57.

45. I specifically refer here to the Hesychast Controversy, which was an acrimonious theological dispute within the Byzantine Empire in the 14th century, between the Byzantines and the Latins. Beginning around 1330, the proponents were led by a theologian and monk of Mt. Athos, Gregory Palamas (1296–1357), and the opponents were led by clergyman, Aristotelian scholar, and scholastic Barlaam of Calabria (1290–1357). In short, the dispute was over dogma, the nature of God, the filioque, the hesychast practice, and, especially, Palamas' argument that it was the "West's" use of reason that separated man from God. For an outstanding summary, see chapter 1 of Anita Strezova's *Hesychasm and Art: The Appearance of New Iconographic Trends in Byzantine and Slavic Lands in the 14th and 15th Centuries* (Canberra: Australian National University Press, 2014), pp. 9–62.

46. Figes, *Natasha's Dance*, p. 64; Thomas Marsden, *Afanasii Shchapov and the Significance of Religious Dissent in Imperial Russia, 1848–1870* (Stuttgart, Germany: Ibidem Press, 2007), p. 19.

47. Marsden, *Afanasii Shchapov*, p. 41. For a greater understanding of this subject, see also Thomas Marsden, *The Crisis of Religious Toleration in Imperial Russia: Bibikov's System for the Old Believers, 1841–1855 (Oxford Historical Monographs)* (Oxford: Oxford University Press, 2015).

48. See Susanna Rabow-Edling, *Slavophile Thought and the Politics of Cultural Nationalism* (Albany: State University of New York Press,

2006) in its entirety; James H. Billington, *The Icon and the Axe: An Interpretive History of Russian Culture* (New York: Vintage Books, 1970), pp. 313–315; Pipes, *Russia Under the Old Regime*, p. 266; Irina Paperno, "The Liberation of the Serfs as a Cultural Symbol," *Russian Review* 50:4 (October 1991), pp. 417–436; and David Gillespie, "Apocalypse Now: Village Prose and the Death of Russia," *Modern Language Review* 87:2 (April 1992), pp. 407–417. The Slavophiles extolled the East-West Schism of 1054 as salutary for Russia, for then Rome fell under the influence of classical culture that stressed rationalism, hubris, individualism, dissent, and central consolidated power. The Orthodox Church retained the traditional Christian features of communalism, a federated organization, and an emphasis on the mystical connection to God. Furthermore, Russia did not experience the Reformation or the Enlightenment.

49. Thomas P. Abernethy, *The South in the New Nation, 1789–1819*, Vol. 4, *A History of the South* (Baton Rouge: Louisiana State University Press, 1989), pp. 400–442; John L. Brook, "Cultures of Nationalism, Movements of Reform, and the Composite-Federal Polity: From Revolutionary Settlement to Antebellum Crisis," *Journal of the Early Republic* 29:1 (Spring 2009), pp. 1–33; and Michael T. Bernath, *The Struggle for Intellectual Independence in the Civil War South* (Chapel Hill: University of North Carolina Press, 2010).

50. David Brion Davis, *The Problem of Slavery in the Age of Emancipation* (New York: Alfred A. Knopf, 2004); see chapters 3, 4, 8, and especially 10.

51. See Vernon Louis Parrington, *The Romantic Revolution in America, 1800–1860: Main Currents in American Thought*, Vol. II (London: Routledge, 2012); William R. Taylor, *Cavalier and Yankee: The Old South and American National Character* (New York: Oxford University Press, 1993); Rabow Edling, *Slavophile Thought*; Peter K. Christoff, *An Introduction to Nineteenth-Century Russian Slavophilism: Iu. F. Samarin*, Vol. 4 (Princeton: Princeton University Press, 1991); Edward C. Thaden, "The Beginnings of Romantic Nationalism in Russia," *American Slavic and East European Review* 1:4 (December 1954), pp. 500–521; and Michael O'Brien, "The Lineaments of Antebellum Southern Romanticism," *Journal of American Studies* 20:2 (August 1986), pp. 165–188, and his opus *Conjectures of Order: Intellectual Life and the American South, 1810–1860* (Chapel Hill: University of North Carolina Press, 2004). *Conjectures of Order* is a magisterial work; the pages in this 1,000-plus-page tome are too many to cite here. For a sampling, see pp. 2–4, 10, 14, 21, 23, 28, 32, 42–43, 47, 107–108, 147, 206, 216, 222, and 285–332. In "Lineaments," O'Brien details the many meanings of the term *Romanticism* (as in "the Romantic Era"), which means different things to different historians, be they social, political, economic, or cultural. Above all, he points out, it *was* an epistemological reaction to both local and distant crises—a "doctrine

of the outsider"—and concerned a "redemptive self-consciousness."

52. For themes of civil religion and religious nationalism, see Mark A. Noll, *The Civil War as a Theological Crisis* (Chapel Hill: University of North Carolina Press, 2006); Charles Reagan Wilson, *Baptized in Blood: The Religion of the Lost Cause, 1865–1920* (Athens: University of Georgia Press, 2009); Catherine Albanese, *America: Religions and Religion* (Belmont, CA: Wadsworth, 1981), p. 284; Paul Valliere, "The Theology of Culture in Late Imperial Russia," in *Sacred Stories: Religion and Spirituality in Modern Russia*, edited by Mark D. Steinberg and Heather J. Coleman (Bloomington: Indiana University Press, 2007), pp. 377–397; and Billington, *Icon and Axe*, p. 394.

53. Greenfeld, "Formation," pp. 549, 551, 573–579, and 585. Greenfeld further explains that *ressentiment* was a term coined by Friedrich Nietzsche and later developed by Max Scheler. It refers to a "psychological state resulting from suppressed feelings of envy and hatred (existential envy) and the impossibility to satisfy these feelings (to get revenge or act them out). The ... structural condition that [is] necessary for the development of this psychological state—is ... the fundamental comparability between the subject and the object of envy." Citing Hans Rogger, Greenfeld also explains that it is an incremental development, "evolving in a series of antitheses, one element in each pair reflecting an aspect" of the subject and one reflecting an aspect of the object or model, its opposite. The sequence carries on indefinitely and one pair lays the groundwork for further comparisons that also reinforce past contrasts in comparisons. The three stages of *ressentiment* are (1) shame, (2) a rejection of any similarities that may appear between the subject and object—indeed, presenting the object as a wholly unsuitable model—and (3) *ressentiment*, alienation, and nationalism.

54. Indeed, as Rabow-Edling and O'Brien (and history) have taught, the Slavophile and Southern nationalist thinkers were basically "communities of discourse," which revealed disagreements and dialogues about their respective countries' place in the world. Above all, they sought unity (in the Slavophile case) and coherence and order (in the Southern one), and both looked to God as the answer. See Susanna Rabow-Edling, "The Role of 'Europe' in Russian Nationalism: Reinterpreting the Relationship between Russia and the West in Slavophile Thought," in *Russia in the European Context, 1879–1914: A Member of the Family*, edited by Susan P. McCaffray and Michael Melancon (New York: Palgrave Macmillan, 2005), pp. 97–112; and O'Brien, *Conjectures*, p. 1028. For "communities of discourse," see O'Brien's *Rethinking the South: Essays in Intellectual History* (Athens: University of Georgia Press, 1988), p. 46, where he is quoting Rollin G. Osterweis' *Romanticism and Nationalism in the Old South* (New Haven: Yale University Press, 1949).

55. See Peter Kolchin, "Some Controversial Questions Concerning Nineteenth-Century Emancipation from Slavery and Serfdom," in *Serfdom and Slavery: Studies in Legal Bondage*, edited by M.L. Bush (New York: Addison Wesley Longman, 1996), pp. 42–67. Of course, the Beckert and Stanziani theses, which I discuss in the preface and especially in the introduction to chapter 6, challenge this interpretation. For a broad overview, see Boris B. Gorshkov, *Peasants in Russia from Serfdom to Stalin: Accommodation, Survival, Resistance* (New York: Bloomsbury Academic, 2018), chapter 9, "Peasants and the End of Serfdom," pp. 121–133. Gorshkov stresses that it is a matter of looking at the event in economic versus political versus cultural terms. Something that he adds to this conversation is that emancipation in Russia did not occur in a vacuum. Rather, many changes occurred over the course of the 19th century that moved the country toward it. Of course, while the same points can be made about emancipation in the United States, clearly, because it was such a charged issue between the regions, the phrase "irreconcilable differences" is apropos.

56. For quotes, see Alexander Gerschenkron, "Agrarian Policies and Industrialization: Russia 1861–1917," *The Cambridge Economic History of Europe*, Vol. 6:2, *The Industrial Revolutions and After: Incomes, Population and Technological Change* (Cambridge: Cambridge University Press, 1965), pp. 706–800; Alexander Polunov, *Russia in the Nineteenth Century: Autocracy, Reform, and Social Change, 1814–1914*, edited by Thomas C. Owen and Larissa G. Zakharova (New York: M.E. Sharpe, 2005), pp. 110–111; and W. Bruce Lincoln, *The Great Reforms: Autocracy, Bureaucracy, and the Politics of Change in Imperial Russia* (DeKalb: Northern Illinois University Press, 1990), pp. 36–60, and *The Romanovs: Autocrats of All the Russias* (New York: Doubleday, 1981), p. 575.

57. James McPherson, *Battle Cry of Freedom: The Civil War Era* (New York: Oxford University Press, 1988), p. 510; Ira Berlin et al., *Slaves No More: Three Essays on Emancipation and the Civil War* (Cambridge: Cambridge University Press, 1992); Steven Hahn, *A Nation Under Our Feet: Black Political Struggles in the Rural South from Slavery to the Great Migration* (New York: Belknap Press, 2003); and Enrico Dal Lago, "'States of Rebellion': Civil War, Rural Unrest, and the Agrarian Question in the American South and the Italian Mezzogiorno, 1861–1865," *Comparative Studies in Society and History* 47:2 (April 2005), pp. 403–432.

Chapter 2

1. See Roxanne Easley, *The Emancipation of the Serfs in Russia: Peace Arbitrators and the Development of Civil Society* (New York: Routledge, 2008), pp. 104–118.

2. Literature on the emancipation of the serfs is vast. For a brief overview, see Peter Kolchin, "Some Thoughts on Emancipation in Comparative Perspective: Russia and the United States South," *Slavery and Abolition* 11 (December 1990), pp. 351–368, as well as "Some Controversial Questions Concerning Nineteenth-Century Emancipation from Slavery and Serfdom," in *Serfdom and Slavery: Studies in Legal Bondage*, edited by M.L. Bush (New York: Addison Wesley Longman, 1996), pp. 42–67, and "After Serfdom: Russian Emancipation in Comparative Perspective," in *The Terms of Labor: Slavery, Serfdom, and Free Labor*, edited by Stanley Engerman (Stanford: Stanford University Press, 1999), pp. 87–115. For greater detail, see Daniel Field, *The End of Serfdom: Nobility and Bureaucracy in Russia, 1855–1861* (Cambridge: Harvard University Press, 1976); W. Bruce Lincoln, *The Great Reforms: Autocracy, Bureaucracy, and the Politics of Change in Imperial Russia* (DeKalb: Northern Illinois University Press, 1990); Terrence Emmons, *Emancipation of the Russian Serfs* (Geneva, IL: Holt McDougal, 1970); Ben Eklof and Stephen Frank, eds., *The World of the Russian Peasants: Post-Emancipation Culture and Society* (Boston: Unwin Hyman, 1990); David Moon, *Abolition of Serfdom in Russia, 1762–1907* (Harlow, UK: Longman, 2001); Ben Eklof, John Bushnell, and Larissa Zakharova, *Russia's Great Reforms, 1855–1881* (Bloomington: Indiana University Press, 1994); Peter A. Zaionchkovskiy, *The Abolition of Serfdom in Russia*, edited and translated from the third (1968) Russian edition by Susan Wobst (Gulf Breeze, FL: Academic International Press, 1978), and "Provedenie v zhizn' krest'ianskoĭ reformy 1861 g." (Moskva: Izdatel'stvo sotsial'no-ėkonomicheskoĭ literatury, 1958); and L.G. Zakharova, *Autocracy and the Abolition of Serfdom in Russia, 1856–1861*, translated and edited by Gary M. Hamburg (Armonk, NY: M.E. Sharpe, 1987).

3. *Mississippi Slave Narratives from the Federal Writers' Project, 1936–1938* (Bedford, MA: Applewood Books, 2006), p. 52.

4. Similarly, historical literature on the emancipation of the slaves is immense. For a brief discussion, see Kolchin's "Some Thoughts on Emancipation." For greater detail, refer to Eric Foner, *Reconstruction: America's Unfinished Revolution, 1863–1877* (New York: Harper & Row, 1988); Ira Berlin et al., *Slaves No More: Three Essays on Emancipation and the Civil War* (Cambridge: Cambridge University Press, 1992); Leon Litwack, *Been in the Storm So Long: The Aftermath of Slavery* (New York: Vintage Boks, 1980); Steven Hahn, *The Political Worlds of Slavery and Freedom* (Cambridge: Harvard University Press, 2009); and James Oakes, *Freedom National: The Destruction of Slavery in the United States, 1861–1865* (New York: W.W. Norton, 2013).

5. Although President Johnson vetoed the 1866 Civil Rights Act, Congress overrode his veto.

6. For more information about the freedwomen's experiences, see Mary Farmer-Kaiser,

Freedwomen and the Freedmen's Bureau: Race, Gender, and Public Policy in the Age of Emancipation (New York: Fordham University Press, 2010); Noralee Frankel, *Freedom's Women: Black Women and Families in Civil War Era Mississippi (Blacks in the Diaspora)* (Bloomington: Indiana University Press, 1999); Christine D. Worobec, *Peasant Russia: Family and Community in the Post-Emancipation Period* (DeKalb: Northern Illinois University Press, 1995), pp. 69–70; and Beatrice Farnsworth, "The Litigious Daughter-in-Law: Family Relations in Rural Russia in the Second Half of the Nineteenth Century," in *Russian Peasant Women*, edited by Beatrice Farnsworth and Lynne Viola (New York: Oxford University Press, 1992), pp. 91 and 94–98.

7. James T. Currie, *Enclave: Vicksburg and Her Plantations, 1863–1870* (Jackson: University Press of Mississippi, 1980), p. xx.

8. Frankel, *Freedom's Women*, pp. 31–32.

9. See Frankel, *Freedom's Women*; and Farmer-Kaiser, *Freedwomen and the Freedmen's Bureau*, pp. 64–95 (p. 68 for quote).

10. Robert E. May, "Southern Elite Women, Sectional Extremism and the Male Political Sphere: The Case of John A. Quitman's Wife and Female Descendants, 1847–1931," *Journal of Mississippi History* 50 (November 1988), pp. 251–285.

11. See Dunbar Rowland, ed., *Encyclopedia of Mississippi History: Comprising Sketches of Counties, Towns, Events, Institutions and Persons*, Vol. II (Madison, WI: Selwyn A. Brant, 1907), pp. 133–34; and Ezra J. Warner, *Generals in Gray: Lives of the Confederate Commanders* (Baton Rouge: Louisiana State University Press, 1959), pp. 77 and 194.

12. John B. Jones, *A Rebel War Clerk's Diary*, Vol. I (Philadelphia: J.B. Lippincott & Co., 1866), entry for June 25, 1862, pp. 135–136. Mansfield Lovell had been in charge of defending New Orleans when it fell. He never ceased to defend his actions thereafter. See Charles L. Dufour, *The Night the War Was Lost* (New York: Doubleday Press, 1960), where Mansfield is completely exonerated, and even more so in Daniel E. Sutherland, "Mansfield Lovell's Quest for Justice: Another Look at the Fall of New Orleans," *Louisiana History: The Journal of the Louisiana Historical Association* 24:3 (Summer 1983), pp. 233–259. Not surprisingly, Northerners viewed the Lovells as turncoats. See pp. 235 and 238–239 in Sutherland's article.

13. Indeed, by sitting on Simbirsk District's Commission for the Preparation of Emancipation of 1857, Vasili Yazykov assisted the process. That he was the director of Simbirsk District's Department of Peasant Affairs for years also demonstrates this fact.

14. May, "Southern Elite Women," p. 265.

15. Robert E. May, *John A. Quitman: Old South Crusader* (Baton Rouge: Louisiana State University Press, 1985), p. 354.

16. May, "Southern Elite Women," p. 266.

17. May, "Southern Elite Women," p. 270; Annie Rosalie Quitman Diary, August 8, 1863, Quitman Family Papers, UNC.

18. May, "Southern Elite Women," pp. 266 and 268.

19. Caroline Couper Lovell, *The Bend of the River* (Unpublished Manuscript, 1935), p. 62.

20. May, *Quitman*, pp. 352–353.

21. Thavolia Glymph, "The Second Middle Passage: The Transition from Slavery to Freedom at Davis Bend, Mississippi," PhD dissertation, Purdue University, 1994, pp. 66–70.

22. James Wilford Garner, *Reconstruction in Mississippi* (New York: Macmillan, 1901), p. 252.

23. N. Krylov, "Nakanune velikikh reform" (Tsarskii reskript dlia Osvobozhdeniia). *Istoricheskii Vestnik*, Nomer 9 (Sentiabr', 1903), str. 786–821, especially str. 787.

24. K.E.T., sostavitel, *"Spravochnaya kniga dlya uezdnykh predvoditeley dvorianstva"* (Sankt-Peterburg, Russia: tipografiia S. Volpianskago, 1887). Handbook for the Local Marshals of the Nobility. In Russia, the institution of the marshal of the nobility was two-tiered: Each province had one, a peer elected head of the noble corporation (the Noble Society), which was governed by the Provincial Assembly of the Nobility. But each district within each province also had an elected marshal of the nobility, who, in turn, answered to the provincial marshal. Each district marshal performed countless formal and informal functions. See G.M. Hamburg, "Portrait of an Elite: Russian Marshals of the Nobility, 1861–1917," *Slavic Review* 40:4 (Winter 1981), pp. 585–602. See also I. Romashin, "Krest'ianskai a reforma v Simbirskoi gubernii," Uchënye zapiski, T. XXI (Ulyanovsk, SSSR: UGPI, 1969), glava 5, str. 10–15, especially str. 15, which states that the *Polozheniia* was issued on March 5, 1861 (O.S.), in churches across Simbirsk Province.

25. Dokument "Formuliarnyi spisok o sluzhbe Simbirskogo Uezdnogo Predvoditelia dvorianstva otstavnogo poruchika ot Artillerii V.P. Yazykova" GAUO, d. 88, opis' 5, d. 92, 1.15 (Iiun', 1879).

26. Report from Gendarme Officer A.A. Essen to Alexander II, 18 March 1861 in L.M. Ivanov, "Krest'ianskoe dvizhenie v Rossii v 1861–1869 gg." Sbornik dokumentov (Moskva, SSSR, izdatel'stvo Mysl', 1964), pp. 213–214.

27. N. Krylov, "Vospominanii a Mirovogo posrednika pervogo prizyva o vvedenii v deistvie Polozheniia 19-go fevralia 1861 goda." *Russkaia starina* 74:6 (Aprel,' 1892), str. 83.

28. N. Gureev, *"Kraevedcheskii Sbornik,"* Nomer 3 (Ulyanovsk, SSSR: Obshchestvo izucheniia Ulyanovskogo kraia, 1928), str. 30. Usolie was the sprawling estate of the famed Orlov-Davidovy noble family. Although it is in a state of deterioration, the mansion at Usolie still stands overlooking the Volga River.

29. Otmena krepostnogo prava. *"Doklady Ministerstva vnutrennikh del o posledstviiakh krest'ianskoi reformy."* M.- L. (Leningrad, SSSR, Akademiya Nauk SSSR, 1950), str. 7.

Chapter 3

1. I. Romashin, "Ocherki ėkonomiki Simbirskoĭ gubernii" (Ulyanovsk, SSSR: Ulyanovskiĭ oblastnoĭ institut usovershenstvovaniia uchiteleĭ, 1961), str. 36; S.B. Okun' i K.V. Sivkov, sostaviteli, *Krest'ianskoe dvizhenie v Rossii v 1857–1861 gg.* Sbornik dokumentov.T.t. 1 i 2. (Moskva, SSSR. Izdatel'stvo Sotsial'no-ėkonomicheskoĭ literatury, 1963), str. 471, 10 May 1861 Report #178 Simbirsk Governor Izvekov to M. of Internal Affairs P.A. Valuev.

2. Leon F. Litwack, *Been in the Storm So Long: The Aftermath of Slavery* (New York: Vintage, 1980), p. 400.

3. "Ulysses S. Grant to Andrew Johnson, December 18, 1865, Washington, DC," House Divided: The Civil War Research Engine at Dickinson College, http://hd.housedivided.dickinson.edu/node/44779, accessed September 21, 2019.

4. N. Krylov, "Vospominaniia Mirovogo posrednika pervogo prizyva o vvedenii v deĭstvie Polozheniia 19-go fevralia 1861 goda," *Russkaia starina* 74:6 (Aprel',' 1892), str. 81–102, 615–641, and specifically str. 88–89.

5. *Ibid.*, str. 81–101, especially str. 90–100. In prison slang, *volia* is the word used to describe the world outside of the jail.

6. In Imperial Russia, the Revision Lists (or *Revizskie skazki*) served as the method of counting the population for the purposes of taxation and the draft (therefore sometimes referred to as a fiscal census). From 1720 to 1858, there were 10 *Revizii*. They were not intended to enumerate the entire population of Russia, but only those "subject to taxation." Thus, the nobility, titled citizens, civil servants, and soldiers (totaling 18 privileged categories) were not included. Not surprisingly, anyone who had to pay taxes and was eligible for conscription avoided being registered at all costs. The *Revizii* were notoriously incorrect. See Boris Feldblyum's "Russian Revision Lists: A History," *AVOTAYNU* 14:3 (Fall 1998), pp. 59–61 for a brief explanation. See also Daniel Field, *Rebels in the Name of the Tsar* (Boston: Houghton Mifflin, 1976), pp. 42–43.

7. Roxanne Easley, "Opening Public Space: The Peace Arbitrator and Rural Politicization, 1861–1864," *Slavic Review* 61:4 (Winter 2002), pp. 707–731 (especially p. 718); V. Ginev, *"Narodnicheskoe dvizhenie v srednem Povolzh'e: 70-e gody 19 veka"* (Moskva, SSSR: Nauka, 1966), str. 19.

8. Okun' and Sivkov, *Krest'ianskoe dvizhenie v Rossii*, str. 469–473, 12 April 1861 Report #176 from Gorskii to Dolgorukov.

9. Krylov, "Vospominaniia," str. 91, and 96. Throughout this account, Krylov, the estate manager at Murasa, detailed the cornucopia of anecdotes that vividly portray the variety of interpretations, nuance, rumors, confusion, and literal incredulity as to the meaning of the Statutes. The noble family there, the Yermolevs, were Vasili Yazykov's maternal aunt and uncle. Murasa was just a short distance north of Yazykovo Selo. For the best source in English, see Field, *Rebels*. Of note, in Russian Bezdna means "abyss."

10. An Old Believer was someone who tenaciously opposed the 17th-century Russian Orthodox Church Liturgical Reforms, which, in general, were intended at the time to bring church practices in Russia into line with those of the Greek Orthodox Church. Mainstream Russia (and certainly the state) perceived Old Believers as extremely independent, defiant, fanatical, nonconformist, and opposed to change. Throughout Russian history they were repressed to varying degrees. Indeed, the Crimean War greatly contributed to the belief that Old Believers were a "fifth column" when rumors had it that they collaborated with the enemy in that war—namely, the Ottoman Empire. For a succinct description, see Geoffrey Hosking, *Russia: People and Empire, 1552–1917* (Boston: Harvard University Press, 1998), p. 214. For a full discussion, see Thomas Marsden, *The Crisis of Religious Toleration in Imperial Russia: Bibikov's System for the Old Believers, 1841–1855 (Oxford Historical Monographs)* (Oxford: Oxford University Press, 2015), especially chapter 6, "The Crimean War and the Domestic Enemy," pp. 169–189.

11. E. Morokhovets, redaktor,*"Krest'ianskoe dvizhenie v 1861 godu posle otmeny krepostnogo prava"* (Moskva—Leningrad, SSSR: izdatel'stvo Akademii Nauk, 1949), str. 62–66, and 71; Krylov, "Vospominaniia," str. 81–102 and 615–641. The Russian word here, *nastoiashchiĭ*, meaning "genuine" (freedom), was used repeatedly.

12. In 1670, Cossack Stenka Razin led a peasant uprising consisting of 7,000 men against the tsar, with the goal being to establish a Cossack republic along the Volga. He also promised freedom to the oppressed. Razin was halted in Simbirsk, and the tsar's troops brutally suppressed the insurrection, with Razin executed. One hundred years later, in 1774, the largest peasant rebellion in Russian history occurred, as before, in the Middle Volga region. Led by Cossak Emelyan Pugachev, the leader promised a Cossack republic and freedom from the nobility. It, too, was brutally suppressed, and Pugachev was executed.

13. N.S. Khudekov, "Bunt v Kandeevke v 1861 g.," v sbornike "Konets krepostnichestva v Rossii. Dokumenty, pis'ma, memuary, stat'i" (Moskva: Izdatel'stvo MGU, 1994), str. 287–290. These villages were those of a number of famous noblemen in Russia at the time, including the archaeologist S.A. Uvarov and Count Sheremetev. This is purportedly the first time a "red flag" was flown in Russia, which symbolized resistance and radicalism. "Molokan" is a generic term for a member of a variety of Christian sects in Russia, which the Orthodox Church considered heretical. In general, they might be compared with the organization and beliefs of Quakers in the West. One month after the event, Yegortsev died of natural causes. In 1973, a beautiful mosaic commemorating the "red flag"

at Kandievskoe was installed. Grand Duke Konstantin was the heir and brother of Alexander I, who ruled as tsar from 1801 to 1825. For a study on the "imposter phenomenon" in Russian history, see Philip Longworth, "The Pretender Syndrome in Eighteenth-Century Russia," *Past and Present* 66:1 (February 1975), pp. 61–83.

14. For a sampling, see Sergei G. Pushkarev, "The Russian Peasants' Reaction to the Emancipation of 1861," *Russian Review* 27:2 (April 1968), pp. 199–214, who describes the disturbances as strikes; Terence Emmons, "The Peasant and the Emancipation," in *The Peasant in Nineteenth-Century Russia*, edited by Wayne S. Vucinich (Stanford: Stanford University Press, 1968), pp. 41–71; W. Bruce Lincoln, *The Great Reforms: Autocracy, Bureaucracy, and the Politics of Change in Imperial Russia* (DeKalb: Northern Illinois University Press, 1990), p. 164; and Daniel Field, "The Year of Jubilee," in *Russia's Great Reforms, 1855–1881*, edited by Ben Eklof, John Bushnell, and Larissa Zakharova (Bloomington: Indiana University Press, 1994), p. 45. P.A. Zaionchkovskiy described the disturbances as minimal. See his "Provedenie v zhizn' krest'ianskoĭ reformy 1861 g." (Moskva, SSSR, Izdatel'stvo sotsial'no-ėkonomicheskoĭ literatury, 1958), str. 131.

15. For a concise explanation of the Russian *volnenie*, see Peter Kolchin, *Unfree Labor: American Slavery and Russian Serfdom* (Cambridge: Belknap Press of Harvard University Press, 1987), pp. 257–264.

16. The elected (by his noble peers) head of the nobility of a district or province who exercised an array of public functions. Vasili P. Yazykov was the marshal of nobility for Simbirsk District.

17. Okun' and Sivkov, *Krest'ianskoe dvizhenie v Rossii*, str. 285.

18. *Ibid.*, str. 24–25.

19. While Okun' and Sivkov state that the numbers of uprisings tallied were those *only* where military units were summoned, other sources disagree. For example, one source identified roughly 900 disturbances in all of Russia for the year 1861 in which the military was used. Another listed approximately 500. See Okun' and Sivkov, *Krest'ianskoe dvizhenie v Rossii*, p. 15; L.M. Ivanov, "Krest'ianskoe dvizhenie v Rossii v 1861–1869 gg." Sbornik dokumentov (Moskva, SSSR, izdatel'stvo Mysl', 1964), str. 18; and A.M. Anfimov, "Krest'ianskoe dvizhenie v Rossii vo vtoroĭ polovine 19 veka," *"Voprosy istorii,"* 1973, Nomer 5, str. 15–19.

20. Okun' and Sivkov, *Krest'ianskoe dvizhenie v Rossii*, p. 11.

21. *Ibid.*, str. 16.

22. *Ibid.*, str. 173. The typical instrument used was a birch tree branch or rod. A severe beating could involve hundreds of lashes.

23. Morokhovets, *"Krest'ianskoe dvizhenie v 1861,"* str. 215, 29 April 1861 Report #143 Col. Essen to Alexander II; Okun' and Sivkov, *Krest'ianskoe dvizhenie v Rossii*, str. 470–471,

Report #177 Col. Gorsky to Chief of Gendarme Dolgoruky.

24. Romashin, "Ocherki ėkonomiki Simbirskoĭ gubernii," str. 36; and Okun' and Sivkov, *Krest'ianskoe dvizhenie v Rossii*, str. 471, 10 May 1861 Report #178 Simbirsk Governor Izvekov to M. of Internal Affairs P.A. Valuev.

25. Okun' and Sivkov, *Krest'ianskoe dvizhenie v Rossii*, str. 471.

26. *Ibid.*, str. 473–475, 13 May 1861 Report #179 from Gendarme Gorsky to Chief of Corps Prince Dolgorukov.

27. In 19th-century Imperial Russia, a Kantonist was typically a Jewish conscript, impressed into military service.

28. See Field, *Rebels*. The myth held that the distant tsar was the peasants' benefactor and protector.

29. On the one hand, the freed people had every reason to feel celebratory. On the other hand, as Leon Litwack explained, the "Day of Jubilee" was a myth. While it was true that African Americans were ecstatic about their liberation, it was equally true that many were fearful about what the meaning of freedom would be. They certainly had been traumatized by the social upheaval wrought by the war. See Litwack, *Been in the Storm*, pp. 212–220.

30. The phrase "good and faithful labor" was a mainstay in the collective conversation of the day. It was used by various officials to describe what free labor meant, connoting a good, honest, and decent day's work for fair pay—an arrangement that was enshrined in the labor contract. In the thousands of labor contracts signed between planters and freed people, the most "common stipulation demanded by planters was the worker's promise to provide 'good and faithful labor.'" See Ronald L.F. Davis, *Good and Faithful Labor: From Slavery to Sharecropping the Natchez District, 1860–1890* (Westport, CT: Greenwood Press, 1982), p. 9.

31. For a concise discussion of this topic, see Ronald L.F. Davis, "The U.S. Army and the Origins of Sharecropping in the Natchez District—A Case Study," *Journal of Negro History* 62:1 (January 1977), pp. 60–80; Vernon Lane Wharton, *The Negro in Mississippi: 1865–1890* (New York: Harper & Row, 1965), pp. 59 and 74–77; and William C. Harris, *Presidential Reconstruction in Mississippi* (Baton Rouge: Louisiana State University Press, 1967) p. 95. For many examples of various members of the Freedmen's Bureau stating policy vis-à-vis the freed people, and cajoling them regarding their obligations, see Mary Farmer-Kaiser, *Freedwomen and the Freedmen's Bureau: Race, Gender, and Public Policy in the Age of Emancipation* (New York: Fordham University Press, 2010), pp. 17, 55, 88–89, and 94.

32. Wharton, *The Negro in Mississippi*; see also Harris, *Presidential Reconstruction in Mississippi*, p. 94.

33. Clifton Ganus, Jr., "The Freedmen's Bureau in Mississippi," PhD dissertation, Tulane University, 1953, p. 184.

34. Peter Kolchin, "Re-Evaluating the Antebellum Slave Community: A Comparative Perspective," *Journal of American History* 70 (1983), pp. 579–601.

35. For a thorough discussion of this subject, see Dan T. Carter, "The Anatomy of Fear: The Christmas Day Insurrection Scare of 1865," *Journal of Southern History* 42:3 (August 1976), pp. 345–364; Steven Hahn, "'Extravagant Expectations' of Freedom: Rumour, Political Struggle, and the Christmas Insurrection Scare of 1865 in the American South," *Past and Present* 157 (November 1997), pp. 122–158; Walter L. Fleming, "Forty Acres and a Mule," *North American Review* 182:294 (May 1906), pp. 721–737; LaWanda Cox, "The Promise of Land for the Freedmen," *Mississippi Valley Historical Review* 45 (1958), pp. 413–440; and Wharton, *The Negro in Mississippi* (see chapter 3).

36. Oscar Zeichner, "The Transition from Slave to Free Agricultural Labor in the Southern States," *Agricultural History* 13:1 (January 1939), pp. 22–32, especially p. 23. See also Paul L. Gates, "Federal Land Policy in the South, 1866–1888," *Journal of Southern History* 6 (1940), pp. 303–330.

37. Samuel Thomas to O.O. Howard, October 12, 1865, in William S. McFeely's *Yankee Stepfather: General O.O. Howard and the Freedmen* (New York: W.W. Norton, 1968), p. 70.

38. Claude F. Oubre, *Forty Acres and a Mule: The Freedmen's Bureau and Black Land Ownership* (Baton Rouge: Louisiana State University Press, 1978), pp. 1–89.

39. Robert E. May, "'Christmas Gif,' Empty Chairs, and Confederate Defeat," *North and South: The Magazine of Civil War Conflict* 8:7 (January 2006), pp. 54–60. In terms of the workload, the similarities are striking between what May describes as the spoken and unspoken practices and symbolism associated with the Christmas season with respect to American slavery and those with the Holy Lent season in Russia (as described in chapter 1). One significant contrast between the two was the sobriety associated with the Russian Lent season and the intemperance connected to the Christmas season. However, the purposes of both the solemnity around the Russian religious holiday and the relaxation of authority during the American one had to do with the maintenance of order.

40. Harris, *Presidential Reconstruction*, pp. 94 and 98; Litwack, *Been in the Storm*, p. 435.

41. "Short Contracts," *New Orleans Tribune*, December 12, 1865. This newspaper was the first daily published by African Americans in the United States. See also Amy Dru Stanley, *From Bondage to Contract: Wage Labor, Marriage, and the Market in the Age of Slave Emancipation* (Cambridge: Cambridge University Press, 1998), pp. 40–43.

42. Dan Carter tallied about 200 references to a Christmas insurrection. See "Anatomy of Fear," p. 348.

43. Harris, *Presidential Reconstruction*, pp. 88–103; Ganus, "The Freedmen's Bureau," p. 134; and Davis, "The U.S. Army and the Origins of Sharecropping," pp. 76–77.

44. Thavolia Glymph, "The Second Middle Passage: The Transition from Slavery to Freedom at Davis Bend, Mississippi," PhD dissertation, Purdue University, 1994, p. 71.

45. Eric L. McKitrick, *Andrew Johnson and Reconstruction* (Chicago: Chicago University Press, 1960), pp. 163–166, 193–195, and 200–201. (Although Mississippi voted to ratify the Thirteenth Amendment in 1995, in January 2013 it was discovered that it had failed to notify the U.S. Archivist, a mandatory legal procedure. It corrected this oversight, and on February 7, 2013, the Office of the Federal Register made the ratification official.)

46. Louisa Quitman Lovell to Captain Joseph Lovell, Monmouth, September 21, 1861, Quitman Family Papers, UNC.

47. For a full account of this incident, see Winthrop D. Jordan, *Tumult and Silence at Second Creek: An Inquiry into a Civil War Slave Conspiracy* (Baton Rouge: Louisiana State University Press, 1993). In an important article, "Rebellious Talk and Conspiratorial Plots: The Making of a Slave Insurrection in Civil War Natchez," *Journal of Southern History* 77:1 (February 2011), pp. 17–52, Justin Behrend explains that the committee members were most concerned about "loose talk"—that is, rumors of an insurrection spreading throughout the region—for this was just as threatening as a real insurrectionary plot (see pp. 29 and 51). Natchez nabob and Quitman/Lovell relative Lemuel P. Conner was the "notetaker" of the "testimony" elicited during the extralegal trial. As for "Mr. Lovell," it is unknown which of the brothers this refers to, if at all.

48. John A. Murrell was a notorious bandit who operated with a gang in the first half of the 19th century along the Mississippi River basin; he abducted slaves and sold them to other slave owners.

49. Edwin A. Miles, "The Mississippi Slave Insurrection Scare of 1835," *Journal of Negro History* 42:1 (January 1957), p. 54. See also Christopher Morris, "An Event in Community Organization: The Mississippi Slave Insurrection Scare," *Journal of Social History* 22 (1988), pp. 93–111; and Lydia Juliette Plath, "Performances of Honour: Manhood and Violence in the Mississippi Slave Insurrection Scare of 1835," PhD dissertation, University of Warwick, 2009.

50. Ganus, "The Freedmen's Bureau," p. 188.

51. Carter, "Anatomy of Fear," p. 357.

52. Michael S. Wayne, *The Reshaping of Plantation Society: The Natchez District, 1860–80* (Baton Rouge: Louisiana State University Press, 1990), p. 47.

53. Eric Foner, *Reconstruction: America's Unfinished Revolution, 1863–1877* (New York: Harper & Row, 1988), pp. 199–200.

54. Harris, *Presidential Reconstruction*, p. 121 (see also chapters 7 and 8).

55. Wharton, *The Negro in Mississippi*, p. 84.

56. See James T. Currie, "From Slavery to Freedom in Mississippi's Legal System," *Journal of Negro History* 65:2 (Spring 1980), pp. 112–125.

57. Hence, the Thirteenth, Fourteenth, and Fifteenth Amendments were products of the period. See Eric Foner, "The Reconstruction Amendments: Official Documents as Social History," *History Now: The Journal of the Gilder Lehrman Institute*, https://www.gilderlehrman.org/history-by-era/reconstruction/essays/reconstruction-amendments-official-documents-social-history, accessed October 21, 2015.

58. William Leon Woods, "Travail of Freedom: Mississippi Blacks, 1862–1870," PhD dissertation, Princeton University, 1979, pp. 125–126; Hahn, "'Extravagant Expectations,'" p. 138.

59. For example, the *Cincinnati Daily Enquirer* headlined a story "A Negro Conspiracy Discovered in Mississippi," and the *New Orleans True Delta* cited "reliable" sources that blacks would revolt on the "night before Christmas." See Stephen Nissenbaum, *The Battle for Christmas: A Cultural History of America's Most Cherished Holiday* (New York: Vintage, 1997), p. 295.

60. Carter, "Anatomy of Fear," pp. 362–363.

61. Harris, *Presidential Reconstruction*, p. 96; Carter, "Anatomy of Fear," p. 360. Also, for example, the governor of Florida told the freed people, "The President will not give you one foot of land, nor a mule, nor a hog, nor a cow, nor even a knife or fork or spoon." And referring to a Freedman's Bureau official in Georgia who told them essentially the same thing, a freedman commented, "Dat's no yank; dat just some reb dey dressed in blue clothes and brought him here to lie to us." See Litwack, *Been in the Storm*, p. 404. William C. Harris has explained that the closest the federal government came to redistributing land to the freed people was in June 1866, when, as part of the Southern Homestead Act, it opened over three million acres of public lands in Mississippi to them. Few freedmen claimed these public lands because in order to do so, one needed a white benefactor, like John F. H. Claiborne, who aided almost two hundred blacks, many of whom were his former slaves. See Harris, *Presidential Reconstruction*, pp. 92–93.

62. Harris, *Presidential Reconstruction*, pp. 93 and 100; Glymph, "Second Middle Passage," pp. 163–164; Colonel Samuel Thomas to General O.O. Howard, October 12, 1865, Records of the Commissioner, Box 9, RG 105; Colonel Samuel Thomas, Report December 1865, Bureau of Refugees, Freedmen, and Abandoned Lands (BRFAL), Mississippi, RG 105; and Colonel Samuel Thomas to Colonel John Eaton, Vicksburg, Mississippi, June 14, 1864, in *Extracts from Reports of Superintendents of Freedmen Compiled by Rev. Joseph Warren, D.D. From the Records in the Office of Col. John Eaton, Jr. General Superintendent of Freedmen, Department of the Tennessee and State of Arkansas Second Series. June 1864* (Vicksburg, MI: Freedmen Press Print, 1864), p. 32.

63. See Meridian *Clarion*, July 19, 1865; Circular No. 2, "To the Colored People of Mississippi," January 2, 1866, Vicksburg, Mississippi, BRFAL, Senate Executive Documents, p. 36; and Order of Colonel Samuel Thomas, December 31, 1865, Vicksburg, Mississippi, Senate Executive Documents, p. 35.

64. Nissenbaum, *The Battle for Christmas*, p. 296.

65. Foner, *Reconstruction*, p. 375.

66. L.M. Ivanov, *Krest'ianskoe dvizhenie v Rossii v 1861–1869 gg.* Sbornik dokumentov (Moskva, SSSR, izdatel'stvo Mysl', 1964), str. 10, and 163.

67. Morokhovet s, *"Krest'i anskoe dvizhenie v 1861,"* str. 219 Report #145, 20 May 1861 from Col. Essen to Alexander II.

68. *Ibid.*, pp. 214–215, Report #142, 19 April 1861, Colonel Essen to Alexander II.

69. A. Rassadin, "Yazykovo" Ulyanovskaia—Simbirskaia Entsiklopediia, T. 2 (Ulyanovsk, Rossiya: "Simbirskaia kniga," 2004), str. 472–479, especially str. 472.

70. Zh. Trofimov, *"Zhil i umer dzhentl'menom-poètom: dokumental'nyĭ ocherk o D. P. Oznobishine"* (Ulyanovsk, Rossiya: Pechatnyĭ Dvor, 2005), str. 86. It was not only the use of corporal punishment that quelled such disturbances. The army's cooperation was also contingent on what was known as *obzhorno komandoĭ*—that is, the feeding and quartering of troops for a given time period. This was an old tradition, an informal agreement between the landlord and the soldiers whereby, if the former had to call on the latter to come to his estate to quell an uprising, he was obliged to pay them in the form of bountiful feasts and lodgings for a period of time. According to his uncle, Vasili Yazykov was compelled to quarter the troops at Yazykovo Selo over the summer of 1861.

71. Thomas to Montgomery et al, August 3, 1865, BRFAL, RG 105, Box 14, pp. 200–204. See also Ganus, "The Freedmen's Bureau," p. 134; James T. Currie, *Enclave: Vicksburg and Her Plantations, 1863–1870* (Jackson: University Press of Mississippi, 1980), chapter 4; Foner, *Reconstruction*, p. 376; Glymph, "Second Middle Passage," p. 94.

72. See Wharton, *The Negro in Mississippi*, pp. 58–59. Johnson was a Southerner, and his views with respect to property were typical of those in Northern society at the time: that law defined property, that it was an indivisible possession, and that it was a "sacred right" which had been corrupted by Union policy during the war through its confiscation and destruction. See Dylan C. Penningroth, *The Claims of Kinfolk: African American Property and Community in the Nineteenth-Century South* (Chapel Hill: University of North Carolina Press, 2003), pp. 132–133.

73. Application of William Storrow Lovell et al. (Miss.) in Case Files of Applications from Former Confederates for Presidential Pardons, 1865, U.S. Department of War, Records of the Adjutant

General's Office, 1780s–1917, RG 94, National Archives, Washington, D.C. The Quitman/Lovell oaths are an instructive lesson in and of themselves: President Johnson required that each application for amnesty include an explanation of the extent to which the petitioner had aided the Confederacy and, if so, that great remorse should be expressed. The president also required the petitioner pledge allegiance to the United States Constitution, which included expressing a pledge to obey all laws regarding emancipation. The Lovell brothers downplayed their participation in the war on the Confederacy's behalf, and the Quitman daughters (of whom two, Tonie and Louisa, were married to the Lovell brothers, William Storrow and Joseph, respectively) stated that they had nothing to do with the late rebellion whatsoever. Instead, the brothers stressed that they were from the North, while the Quitman daughters cited their father, General Quitman, presumably to draw attention to their pre-war status. None expressed remorse.

74. William Storrow Lovell to Major General O.O. Howard, October 23, 1865. By way of comparison, the Quitmans/Lovells' neighbors, Joseph and Jefferson Davis, indicated in late 1865 that they would "never ask for a pardon." They considered the confiscation of their property illegal, and its return was not contingent on *them*, but rather the Freedmen's Bureau. Thomas to Howard, December 22, 1865, BRFAL, M826–1 and M826–6.

75. Wharton, *The Negro in Mississippi*, p. 65.

76. Labor Contracts of Freedmen, July 1865, Roll 44, M826, BRFAL, National Archives, Washington, DC; "Palmyra Negroes 1860," Lovell Family Records, Box 3, Folder 31, University of the South, Sewanee, TN; and Eldridge to Reston, June 12, 1866, BRFAL, RG 105, Box 14, Letters Received, Assistant Adjutant General's Office. See also "Plantation Regulations, General Order No. 23," *Black Republican*, May 20, 1865.

77. Thomas to Howard, September 19, 1865, BRFAL, Davis Bend, 1865–1866, RG 105, Box 14 (Mississippi), NA, pp. 328–332.

78. Assistant Commissioner Thomas to General O.O. Howard, October 14, 1865, BRFAL, RG 105, Box 14, Letters Received, Assistant Adjutant General's Office.

79. Assistant Commissioner Thomas to General O.O. Howard, January 10, 1866, BRFAL, RG 105, Box 14, Letters Received, Assistant Adjutant General's Office.

80. Montgomery to Davis, January 8, 1866, Joseph Davis Papers, 1–8, MDAH.

81. Wharton, *The Negro in Mississippi*, p. 59; Wayne, *Reshaping of Plantation Society*, pp. 122–123.

82. With respect to both the nature and the roles of rumor and gossip, James C. Scott has informed us that, for subordinates, these simultaneously express contempt and minimize the risk of identification and reprisal. And although these are forms of character assassination, elites are not affected by them if they themselves are "beyond the reach of social sanctions." See *Weapons of the Weak: Everyday Forms of Peasant Resistance* (New Haven: Yale University Press, 1987), pp. 282 and 284–285.

83. See Abby M. Schrader, "Containing the Spectacle of Punishment: The Russian Autocracy and the Abolition of the Knout, 1817–1845," *Slavic Review* 56:4 (Winter 1997), pp. 613–644. In *Domination and the Arts of Resistance: Hidden Transcripts* (New Haven: Yale University Press, 1992), pp. 216–217, James C. Scott explains that, while open defiance on the part of subordinates depends on the severity of the indignity, elites will isolate a ringleader in order to atomize, or contain, or cauterize the situation.

84. *Ibid.* "Containing the Spectacle of Punishment."

85. See Roger L. Ransom and Richard Sutch, *One Kind of Freedom: The Economic Consequences of Emancipation* (Cambridge: Cambridge University Press, 1977), pp. 81 and 86.

86. For a discussion of this and other aspects of dialogic tactics, see Hugh D. Hudson, Jr., "A Rhetorical War of Fire: The Middle Volga Arson Panic of 1839 as Contested Legitimacy in Prereform Russia," *Canadian Slavonic Papers* 43:1 (March 2001), pp. 29–48.

Chapter 4

1. Colonel Samuel Thomas to Captain G.B. Norton, August 29, 1865; and Captain J.H. Weber to Captain G. B. Norton, September 13, 1865, BRFAL, RG 105, Roll 65.

2. Report #142, April 19, 1861, Colonel Essen to Alexander II, in E. Morokhovets, redaktor, *"Krest'ianskoe dvizhenie v 1861 godu posle otmeny krepostnogo prava"* (Moskva—Leningrad, SSSR: izdatel'stvo Akademii Nauk, 1949), str. 214–215. See also Roxanne Easley, "Opening Public Space: The Peace Arbitrator and Rural Politicization, 1861–1864," *Slavic Review* 61:4 (Winter 2002), pp. 707–731.

3. Literally translated as Statutory Charter, the *Ustavnaya Gramota* has undergone a variety of translations. See Peter Kolchin, "After Serfdom: Russian Emancipation in Comparative Perspective," in *Terms of Labor: Slavery, Serfdom, and Free Labor*, edited by Stanley Engerman (Stanford: Stanford University Press, 1999), pp. 87–115, in which he describes it as the Statutory Charter. Roxanne Easley, in *Emancipation of the Serfs in Russia: Peace Arbitrators and the Development of Civil Society* (New York: Routledge, 2008), calls it a Land Transfer Charter, while Daniel Field, in *Rebels in the Name of the Tsar* (Boston: Houghton Mifflin, 1976), calls it a Regulatory Charter. In "Blurred Lines: Land Surveying and the Creation of Landed Property in Nineteenth-Century Russia," *Cahiers du Monde Russia* 57:1 (2016),

pp. 31–54, Igor Khristoforov calls it a Settlement Charter. And Peter Zaionchkovskiy, in *The Abolition of Serfdom in Russia*, edited and translated from the third (1968) Russian edition by Susan Wobst (Gulf Breeze, FL: Academic International Press, 1978), called it the Land Charter.

4. Allan K. Wildman, "The Defining Moment: Land Charters and the Post-Emancipation Agrarian Settlement in Russia, 1861–1863," in *The Carl Beck Papers in Russian & East European Studies*, No. 1205 (Pittsburgh: Center for Russian and East European Studies, University of Pittsburgh, 1996), p. 3.

5. In 1861, there were approximately 115,000 Russian estates. Sergei G. Pushkarev cited 111,555 in "The Russian Peasants' Reaction to the Emancipation of 1861," *Russian Review* 27:2 (April 1968), p. 199. Citing A. Korelin, *"Dvori anstvo v poreformennoĭ Rossii, 1861–1904 gg.: sostav, chislennost,' korporativnaia organizatsiia"* (Moskva, SSSR: Nauka, 1979), str. 136–139 Terence Emmons reported 120,000 landed gentry families, which constituted 80–85 percent of the entire noble estate. See "The Russian Landed Gentry and Politics," *Russian Review* 33:3 (July 1974), p. 270. Illustrating the decline of rural estates owned by the nobility after emancipation, I.M. Pushkareva cited 59,000 in 1877. See her "The Rural Noble Country House in Postreform Russia (Defining the Issue)," *Russian Studies in History* 42:1 (Summer 2003), p. 81. The point is that there should have been approximately this many Statutory Charters emerging in the post-emancipation period.

6. As a result of the massive uprisings across the countryside during the 1905 revolution, the government thereafter waived all remaining payments.

7. In "The Defining Moment," pp. 6–7, Wildman explains that the term "commune" is a misnomer. Because nearly all decisions in the peasant village were made "communally," there was no legal unit called a "commune." The more accurate term "assembly," he argues, should be used. For a discussion of terminology and definitions, see Steven A. Grant, "Obshchina and Mir," *Slavic Review* 35 (1976), pp. 636–651.

8. For quotes, see Easley, "Opening Public Space," pp. 708 and 711; and Wildman, "The Defining Moment," pp. 10 and 35. Also see Easley's opus *Emancipation of the Serfs*.

9. Vasili's father, Petr Mikhailovich Yazykov, and Mikhail's mother, Praskovia Mikhailovna Bestuzheva (nee Yazykova), were siblings. Further, Mikhail's mother and father worked closely with the Slavophiles Alexander Mikhailovich Yazykov (brother of Petr M. Yazykov and Praskovia M. Bestuzheva), Dmitri Valuev (son of another Yazykov sister, Aleksandra Mikhailovna Valueva, nee Yazykova), Aleksei Khomiakov (married to another Yazykov sister, Ekaterina Mikhailovna Yazykova), and the Kireevsky brothers documenting folksongs and ethnographic history of the Middle Volga region. Over the course of the 19th century, many male members of both the Bestuzhev and the Yazykov families were marshals of the nobility in Simbirsk Province.

10. T. Zakharycheva, "Dva kniazia," Simbirskiĭ Kur'er, Nomer 36 (3204), 4 aprelia, 2009.

11. For all of 1861, only 2,403 charters were signed in all of Russia. However, under government pressure, their completion and implementation accelerated by July 1862, by which date 20,108 were registered. By February 19, 1863, the two-year anniversary of emancipation, 92,000 had been completed, which represented approximately 80 percent of the estates. Of note, numbers for Simbirsk Province showed 95.52 percent of former serfs being accounted for by January 1863. By September 1, 1866, 95.4 percent of former serfs in all of Russia were accounted for in completed charters. These official numbers make it seem as though things transpired smoothly, but they do not indicate the peasants' reception of the charters. See Easley, "Opening Public Space," p. 721; L.M. Ivanov, "Krest'ianskoe dvizhenie v Rossii v 1861–1869 gg," Sbornik dokumentov (Moskva, SSSR, izdatel'stvo Mysl', 1964), str. 10; S. Volk, sostavitel,' *"Otmena krepostnogo prava: Doklady ministru vnutrennikh del o provedenii krest'ianskoĭ reformy, 1861–62"* (Moskva—Leningrad, SSSR: Akademiia nauk SSSR, 1950), str. 95, 193, 285, and 287; Zaionchkovskiy, *Abolition of Serfdom in Russia*, pp. 132 and 177–178; and Wildman, "The Defining Moment," pp. 2, 27, and 39. Especially for Simbirsk, see detailed descriptions of obstructionism and refusal to sign charters in Otmena krepostnogo prava, *"Doklady Ministerstva vnutrennikh del o posledstviiakh krest'ianskoĭ reformy,"* M.- L. (Leningrad, SSSR, Akademiya Nauk SSSR, 1950), str. 138–140, 152, 160, 165–166, 198, 202, 231–232, and 235.

12. Boris B. Gorshkov makes the point that, arguably, the state inflated the price of land for which the freed serfs would pay their former master as a way of compensating them for their "loss" in property—that is, the serfs—which represented a kind of a "hidden payment." See *Peasants in Russia from Serfdom to Stalin: Accommodation, Survival, Resistance* (New York: Bloomsbury Academic, 2018), p. 130.

13. The actual document is signed by Vasili Yazykov and Mikhail Bestuzhev, and no peasant signatures appear on it. For this trend, see Otmena krepostnogo prava, *"Doklady Ministerstva vnutrennikh del o posledstviiakh krest'ianskoĭ reformy,"* str. 138 and 178–189; Ivanov, "Krest'ianskoe dvizhenie," str. 103; and I. Romashin, "Ocherki ékonomiki Simbirskoĭ gubernii, 17–19 veka" (Ulyanovsk, SSSR: Ulyanovskiĭ oblastnoĭ institut usovershenstvovaniia uchitelei, 1961), str. 36, and 471. As for the peasants refusing a copy of the document, on the one hand, local historians in Ulyanovsk, Larissa Yershova and Alexei Sytin, relayed this legend to me. On the other hand, this is not an idle rumor, as a number of

documented cases exist in which peasants at locations in Yazykovo Selo's neighborhood refused to sign the document. See Ivanov, "Krest'ianskoe dvizhenie," str. 103–104 and 238–239.

14. The universal measure of the individual "soul" was male gendered and replaced the anachronism of *tiaglo*, which was literally a "unit of labor," whether it be a man, woman, or horse. Associated with feudalism, *tiaglo* had been the typical unit on *barshchina* estates.

15. The charter for Yazykovo Selo indicates the maximum and minimum for Simbirsk Province was 4 and 1.3, respectively. Romashin's "Ocherki ekonomiki Simbirskoĭ gubernii," str. 34, as well as his "Krest'ianskaia reforma v Simbirskoĭ gubernii," Uchënye zapiski, T. XXI (Ulyanovsk, SSSR: UGPI, 1969), glava 5, str. 13, note this fact. However, *Prilozhenie k trudam redaktsionnoĭ komissii dlia sostavleniia Polozheniia o krest'ianakh, vykhodiashchikh iz krepostnoĭ zavisimosti: svedeniia o pomeshchich'ikh imeniiakh. T.3* (Sankt-Peterburg, Rossiya: Tipografiia V.I. Bezobrazova, 1860), translated as "Appendix to the Proceedings of the Editorial Commission's Instructions for the Implementation of the Regulations for the Serfs' Emancipation" Information regarding the Landlords' Estates, Vol. 3," indicates the maximum and minimum for Simbirsk Province were 4.5 and 2, respectively. It would be fair to infer, however, that since Vasili Yazykov allotted 4 *desiatiny* per eligible soul, he could well have understood it to be 4.

16. Richard Pipes, *Russia Under the Old Regime* (New York: Penguin, 1974), pp. 147–148. While land was allotted to the men on the estate, the custodianship of which was placed with the commune, women received no land apportionments. But they were included in work obligations. There is an interesting parallel here with the American freed people in that, typically, the male head of a household would sign a labor contract, but his "dependents," including wife and children, would thus be obligated to work.

17. This rule is cited in Wildman, "The Defining Moment," pp. 6–8. In addition, Wildman points out that if a nobleman retained more than one-third of his land (which Vasili Yazykov did), he could impose *barshchina* legally until a Redemption Agreement was made per the terms of the *Regulations*. For the *barshchina* condition intact in 1881, see the Bill of Sale, Dokument "Kupchaia Stepanova." GAUO, f.477, opis' 3, dok.71, 1.25.

18. Plus 2,162 *sazhen*. Each charter detailed the amount of land right down to the number of *sazhen*, 1 = 7 feet. I do not include these minute details in the final numbers. The number of 2,162 was a total of detailed items such as 56 *desiatiny* plowed land for personal use; 41 *desiatiny* green commons; 34 *desiatiny* hay fields; 22 *desiatiny* used for hay; 249 *desiatiny* tilled fields; 123 *desiatiny* for bushes and shrubbery; and the like.

19. Note: This was in fact a gift—it was neither mandated by the *Regulations* nor included as part of the redemption payments. However, the fact that Yazykov swapped their plots with his does not change the overall final numbers.

20. Like Vasili Yazykov, Mikhail Bestuzhev had an illustrious career of service to the tsar. He sat on the Simbirsk District Committee on "How to Improve and Establish the Everyday Life of the Estate Peasants" in 1858. In 1860, he served as a bureaucrat for the special tasks for the governor of Simbirsk. From 1862 to 1870, he was a peace mediator for Simbirsk District. In 1872, he was hired as a bureaucrat with the Ministry of Internal Affairs in St. Petersburg. Then, from 1873 to 1876, he was sent to Sakhalin Island as an aide to help improve the living conditions of labor prisoners. From 1876 to 1882, he was the vice governor of Ufa, the capital of Bashkirai. From 1882 to 1886, he was the vice governor of Tambov Province. Both his great-grandfather and great-great-grandfather had been provincial marshals of the nobility. See Dokument "Formuliarnyĭ spisok o sluzhbe M.P. Bestuzheva i nekrolog o nem" v Tambovskikh Gubernskikh Vedomostiakh, 1886, nomer. 117.

21. Sources for the Yazykov charter include Dokument "Ustavnaia Gramota Simbirskoĭ gubernii, Simbirskogo Uezda, sela Bogorodskoe (Yazykovo) vladenii a podporuchika ot Artillerii Vasiliia Petrovicha Yazykova, 1862 god." GAUO, f.85, opis' 1, d. 19, 1.1–4, 45, 46, 47 i 48 (1862); and Romashin, "Ocherki ekonomiki Simbirskoĭ gubernii," str. 33–37, and 471; and "Krest'ianskaia reforma v Simbirskoĭ gubernii," str. 10–15; and *Prilozhenie k trudam*.

22. Dokument "Spravka ot Simbirskogo Gubernskogo po Krest'ianskim delam Prisutstviia pomeshchika A.P. Yazykova," 21 iiulia 1864 g. (17 ianvaria 1881 g.) GAUO, f.85, opis' 1, d. 123,1.71 (1864–1881); M.V. Rusin, Selianin Simbirskogo uezda: Khroniki i istorii sela Voskresenskogo (ono zhe Undory): materialy dlia istorii Simbirskogo dvorianstva i chastnogo zemlevladeniia v Simbirskom uezde. Napechatano v knige: P. Martynov "Materialy dlia istorii Simbirskogo dvorianstva i chastnogo zemlevladeniia v Simbirskom uezde" (Izdanie Simbirskoĭ Gubernskoĭ Uchenoĭ Arkhivnoĭ komissii, 1903); and *Prilozhenie k trudam*. It is curious that the charter reflected no household serfs at Undory, as such an arrangement would be impossible for an estate such as Undory. Similar to his brother at Yazykovo Selo the year before, Alexander witnessed a disturbance at Undory in May 1862 associated with the implementation of the Statutory Charter. Also like Vasili, Alexander sold the estate at an auction in 1881 to local merchants.

23. As Allan Wildman has made clear, 57 percent of the charters in Russia did not have peasant signatures. See Wildman, "Defining Moment," p. 40; Otmena krepostnogo prava, *"Doklady Ministerstva vnutrennikh del o posledstviiakh krest'ianskoĭ reformy,"* str. 138–140; and Romashin, "Ocherki ekonomiki Simbirskoĭ gubernii," str. 36.

24. Ivanov, "Krest'ianskoe dvizhenie," str. 103.

25. *Ibid.*, str. 238–240 and 563.

26. For this quote, see I.A. Chukanov, L.A. Shaĭpak, I.I. TSeloval'nikova, "Otmena krepostnogo prava v Simbirskoĭ gubernii,", v élektronnom izdanii "Letopis' simbirskogo krest'ianstva (s drevneĭshikh vremën do nashikh dneĭ)," glava 9. http://els.ulspu.ru/Files/!ELS/disc/letop-simb-krest/10..html, accessed December 7, 2020.

27. Otmena krepostnogo prava. *"Doklady Ministerstva vnutrennikh del o posledstviī akh krest'ianskoĭ reformy,"* str. 138.

28. Ivanov, "Krest'ianskoe dvizhenie," str. 405–406, 563, and 580. The estates in these examples were between two and ten miles from Yazykovo Selo.

29. Wildman, "The Defining Moment," p. 43. Wildman notes that in addition to refusing to sign and accept a copy of the charter, peasants refused to tour the lands earmarked for them.

30. Wildman, "The Defining Moment," pp. 17–18 and 28; P.A. Zaionchkovskiy, redaktor, *"Krestyanskoe dvizhenie v Rossii v 1870–1880 gg."* Sbornik dokumentov (Moskva, SSSR: Nauka, 1968). Vvedeniye N.M. Druzhinina, str. 36.

31. Easley, "Opening Public Space," p. 718; Ivanov, "Krest'ianskoe dvizhenie," str. 12–13, 23–26, and 399–402; and V. Ginev, *"Narodnicheskoe dvizhenie v srednem Povolzh'e: 70-e gody 19 veka"* (Moskva, SSSR: Nauka, 1966), str. 19.

32. Ivanov, "Krest'ianskoe dvizhenie," str. 8. See also Otmena krepostnogo prava. *"Doklady Ministerstva vnutrennikh del o posledstviīakh krest'ianskoĭ reformy,"* str. 138–140, 152, 160, 165–166, 202, 321–322, and 235.

33. Easley, "Opening Public Space," p. 721.

34. Otmena krepostnogo prava. *"Doklady Ministerstva vnutrennikh del o posledstviīakh krest'ianskoĭ reformy,"* str. 4. In general, the peasants received roughly 20 percent less land than what they used before the reform. Both Soviet and subsequent Russian historians use the marker of 5–8 *desiatiny* of land needed to support a male peasant and his family. These are the most commonly cited figures. See T. Pon'ko, V. Trofimov, "Tema 11. Rossiya: pravlenie Aleksandra II: §.1. Épokha velikikh reform." Soderzhanie kursa "Obshchestvoznanie." Redaktor Sergeĭ Nizhnikov. (Moskva, Rossiya. Razrabotka instituta distant-sionnogo obrazovaniia, RUDN, 2006). Also online dated April 25, 2007, http://www.ido.rudn.ru/nfpk/hist/hist11.html, accessed June 8, 2009.

35. Wildman, "The Defining Moment," pp. 15–16, 18, and 45. Wildman's case study focuses on charters from estates in Saratov, a Middle Volga province and immediate neighbor to the south of Simbirsk.

36. *Ibid.*, p. 18.

37. See Wildman, "The Defining Moment," p. 20; Romashin, "Krest'ianskai a reforma v Simbirskoĭ gubernii," str. 10–15; Simbirskie Gubernskie Vedomosti, n. 45, Subbota (9 noiabria 1863); P. Pikman, "150 let Manifestu ob otmene krepostnogo prava," gazeta "Kaskad," Nomer 04 (376), fevral',' 2011, str. 16–18; and I. Stetsenko,

"Krest'iane," *Ulyanovskaia-Simbirskaia Éntsiklopediia*, T. 1 (Ulyanovsk, Rossiya: Simbirskaia kniga, 2004), str. 307. M. Naĭdenov argued the "severe debt" thesis well before Wildman. See *"Klassovaia bor'ba v poreformennoĭ derevne (1861–1863)"* (Moskva, SSSR: Gospolitizdat, 1955), str. 290. Here Boris B. Gorshkov makes an interesting observation that, since indebted nobles had mortgaged their serfs repeatedly, one way of accomplishing emancipation would have been for the government, acting essentially as a bank or a collections agency, to repossess the serfs in response to the nobility's failure to pay off its debt to the state. See *Peasants in Russia*, p. 126.

38. V.A. Aunovskiĭ, "Sukonnye fabriki i sherstomoĭki v Simbirskoĭ gubernii," *"Simbirskiĭ sbornik,"* T. 2 (Simbirsk, Rossiya: Simbirskiĭ gubernskiĭ statisticheskiĭ komitet, 1870), str. 82–102.

39. Seymour Becker, *Nobility and Privilege in Late Imperial Russia* (DeKalb: Northern Illinois University Press, 1986), pp. 47–51.

40. Wildman, "The Defining Moment," pp. 24–25.

41. Ivanov, "Krest'ianskoe dvizhenie," str. 23–26; A. Orlov, V. Georgiev, i drugie, *"Rossiya s drevneĭshikh vremen do nashikh dneĭ,"* Uchebnik dlia vysshikh uchebnykh zavedeniĭ (Moskva, SSSR: Prospekt, 1999), str. 270–273; and Pon'ko, "Tema 11. Rossiya: pravlenie Aleksandra II."

42. Wildman, "The Defining Moment," pp. 15–16, 18–20, and 23; Naĭdenov, *"Klassovaia bor'ba,"* str. 290.

43. Emancipation as an evolving process is one of the themes in James Oakes, *Freedom National: The Destruction of Slavery in the United States, 1861–1865* (New York: W.W. Norton, 2013).

44. James T. Currie, *Enclave: Vicksburg and Her Plantations, 1863–1870* (Jackson: University Press of Mississippi, 1980), pp. xxi.

45. *Ibid.*, p. xxii.

46. Clifton L. Ganus, Jr., "The Freedmen's Bureau in Mississippi," PhD dissertation, Tulane University, 1953, p. 134; Currie, *Enclave*, p. 143; Vernon Lane Wharton, *The Negro in Mississippi: 1865–1890* (New York: Harper & Row, 1965), p. 41; Thavolia Glymph, "The Second Middle Passage: The Transition from Slavery to Freedom at Davis Bend, Mississippi," PhD dissertation, Purdue University, 1994, pp. 48, 74, 75, 76, 85, 88–89, 102–104, and 106; and Janet Sharp Hermann, *The Pursuit of a Dream* (New York: Oxford University Press, 1981), pp. 50, 61–62, 67, and 124. Robert E. May also explained that patriarch John Quitman practiced benevolent paternalism at Palmyra during the antebellum period. See his *John A. Quitman: Old South Crusader* (Baton Rouge: Louisiana State University Press, 1985), pp. 130–146, and *passim*, and "John A. Quitman and His Slaves: Reconciling Slave Resistance with the Proslavery Defense," *Journal of Southern History* 46:4 (November 1980), pp. 551–570.

47. Currie, *Enclave*, p. 91.

48. In James T. Currie, ed., "Freedmen at Davis Bend, April 1864," *Journal of Mississippi History* 46:2 (May 1984), pp. 120–129.

49. A company typically comprised 100 men.

50. Glymph, "Second Middle Passage," pp. 79 and 84. See also Stephen Joseph Ross, "Freed Soil, Freed Labor, Freed Men: John Eaton and the Davis Bend Experiment," *Journal of Southern History* 44:2 (May 1978), pp. 215–216.

51. Hermann, *Pursuit*, p. 45.

52. *Ibid.*, p. 5.

53. *Ibid.*, p. 62.

54. *Ibid.*

55. The salary statistics cited in the above discussion are taken from Hermann, *Pursuit*, chapter 2, "The Chaos of War," pp. 37–60; Glymph, "Second Middle Passage," pp. 71–83 and 89; and Currie, *Enclave*, chapter 4, "Davis Bend," pp. 83–144. It is worth noting that these three authors quote different statistics, all of which are based on archival records.

56. See Ronald L. F. Davis, "The U.S. Army and the Origins of Sharecropping in the Natchez District—A Case Study," *Journal of Negro History* 62:1 (January 1977), p. 66.

57. Big Black Island was in the Mississippi River just south of Davis Bend, at the mouth of the Big Black River.

58. "Rules and Regulations ... for the Government of the Freedmen at Davis Bend, Mississippi," BRFAL, Davis Bend, 1865–1866, RG 105, Box 39 (Mississippi), NA.

59. Hermann, *Pursuit*, pp. 59–60; Currie, *Enclave*, p. 100; Glymph, "Second Middle Passage," pp. 101–104; and Ross, "Freed Soil, Freed Labor," p. 221. See also Chungchan Gao, *African Americans in the Reconstruction Era* (New York: Garland, 2000), p. 98.

60. "To Superintendents of Colonies, Davis Bend, Miss.," April 17, 1865, *Henry Rowntree Letter Book*, BRFAL, RG 105 (Mississippi), NA, quoted in Currie, *Enclave*, p. 107. It is worth noting that his superior instructed him to "reduce the number of people supported by the Government as low as possible." Samuel Thomas, "Special Order No. 12," July 20, 1865, BRFAL, RG 105 (Mississippi), NA.

61. For a thorough and fascinating account of freedwomen's unique experiences in Mississippi, especially vis-à-vis the Freedmen's Bureau, see Noralee Frankel, *Freedom's Women: Black Women and Families in Civil War Era Mississippi (Blacks in the Diaspora)* (Bloomington: Indiana University Press, 1999); and, in general, Mary Farmer-Kaiser, *Freedwomen and the Freedmen's Bureau: Race, Gender, and Public Policy in the Age of Emancipation* (New York: Fordham University Press, 2010).

62. Currie, *Enclave*, p. 104; Hermann, *Pursuit*, p. 53; Mississippi Census, Freedmen's Department 1863–1865, Box 36, Miscellaneous Records, RG 105, NA, quoted in Glymph, "Second Middle Passage," p. 95; and U.S. War Department, *The War of the Rebellion: A Compilation of the Official Records of the Union and Confederate Armies*, Series 3, Volume 5 (Washington, DC, 1880–1901), p. 138, quoted in Glymph, "Second Middle Passage," p. 71. Glymph notes that 17,869 African American Mississippians enlisted in the Union armies.

63. Lovell Family Papers, Box 3, Folder 31, University of the South, Sewanee, TN.

64. Frankel, *Freedom's Women*, pp. 44–55; Farmer-Kaiser, *Freedwomen and the Freedmen's Bureau*, p. 24 for quote.

65. Currie, "Freedmen at Davis Bend," pp. 120–129.

66. Frankel, *Freedom's Women*, p. 38. For a comprehensive discussion of this phenomenon (especially the smallpox epidemic at this time), see Jim Downs, *Sick from Freedom: African-American Illness and Suffering during the Civil War and Reconstruction* (Oxford: Oxford University Press, 2012), especially pp. 26–28, 36, 47, and 50. See pp. 95–119 for the smallpox epidemic.

67. Marshall Scott Legan, "Disease and the Freedmen in Mississippi during Reconstruction," *Journal of the History of Medicine and Allied Sciences* 28:3 (July 1973), pp. 257–267. Legan maintains that the preponderance of disease explains the shortage of "hands" available for labor on the plantations in the post-war period.

68. Currie, *Enclave*, pp. xxi and 64; Glymph, "Second Middle Passage," pp. 66–70; James Wilford Garner, *Reconstruction in Mississippi* (New York: Macmillan, 1901), p. 252; and May, *Quitman*, pp. 352–353.

69. "Short Contracts," *New Orleans Tribune*, December 12, 1865, p. 4. See the Bureau quote in Leon F. Litwack, *Been in the Storm So Long: The Aftermath of Slavery* (New York: Vintage Books, 1980), pp. 413–415 and 435.

Chapter 5

1. See V. Egorov, redaktor, "Ėkonomika i Torgovlīa" v sbornike *"Simbirsko-Ulyanovskiĭ kraĭ v prodvizhenie istorii Rossii"* (Ulyanovsk, Rossiya, Korporatsiīa tekhnologiĭ, 2007), str. 222; and A. Rassadin, "Yazykovo" Ulyanovskaīa—Simbirskaīa Ėntsiklopediīa, T. 2 (Ulyanovsk, Rossiya: "Simbirskaīa kniga," 2004), str. 472–479.

2. Zh. Trofimov, *"Zhil i umer dzhentl'menom-poėtom: dokumental'nyĭ ocherk o D. P. Oznobishine"* (Ulyanovsk, Rossiya: Pechatnyĭ Dvor, 2005), str. 84–85. Oznobishin was also an executive committee member of Simbirsk Province's Department of Peasant Affairs. His estate, Kitovka, was not far from Yazykovo Selo.

3. P. Martynov, *"Gorod Simbirsk za 250 let ego sushchestvovaniia: sistematicheskiĭ sbornik istoricheskikh svedeniĭ o g. Simbirske"* (Simbirsk, Rossiya: Tipografiīa gubernskogo pravleniīa, 1898), str. 22.

4. See this document source listed on the

website of the *Arkhivnye dokumenty v bibliotekakh i muzeĭakh Rossiĭskoĭ Federat͡sii, Ulyanovsk, Россия,* http://portal.rusarchives.ru/muslib/mus-lib_rf/yl4.shtml, accessed January 7, 2019; it is also described at "Yazykovo," Kraevedcheskiĭ kompas Soi͡uza kraevedov Ulyanovskoĭ oblasti. http://73history.ru/set-prroekti/1000-pos-ul/144-yazykovo, accessed October 17, 2020.

5. Robert E. May, *John A. Quitman: Old South Crusader* (Baton Rouge: Louisiana State University Press, 1985), p. 354; Lynda Lassewell Crist, ed., *The Papers of Jefferson Davis*, Vol. 7, *1861* (Baton Rouge: Louisiana State University Press, 1992), pp. 176–177.

6. May, *Quitman*, p. 345. In today's money, $1,500 a year would be approximately $43,500.

7. Robert E. May, "Southern Elite Women, Sectional Extremism, and the Male Political Sphere: The Case of John A. Quitman's Wife and Female Descendants, 1847–1931," *Journal of Mississippi History* 50 (November 1988), p. 257.

8. U.S. Census, 1860 and 1880, Agricultural Schedule, Warren County, Mississippi, MDAH; Janet Sharp Hermann, *The Pursuit of a Dream* (New York: Oxford University Press, 1981), p. 26. Hermann notes that Palmyra was valued at $200,000 in 1860.

9. Due to the decline in the price of cotton (see table 6.3), the rise in production costs, credit difficulties, and overproduction in good years, the typical rate in 1879 for the delta region was 40 cents per day for men without board or $8–$15 per month with board. See Vernon Lane Wharton, *The Negro in Mississippi: 1865–1890* (New York: Harper & Row, 1965), p. 66. Lovell insisted that he reduced the credit prices in the plantation store to help offset the drop in wages about which he said he had no choice because of the low price of cotton for that year. See Hermann, *Pursuit*, p. 209; William Storrow Lovell to Eliza Quitman, December 7 and 18, 1879, and Antonia Lovell to Eliza Quitman, 1879 (no specific date entered), Lovell Family Papers, University of the South, Sewanee, TN; and May, "Southern Elite Women," p. 277. As for the "exodus," Wharton insists that it involved a very "tiny fraction" of freed people from Mississippi and "excited far more attention than it … deserved." He also explains that the excitement about the great "exodus" in the first quarter of the 20th century is often (and incorrectly) conflated or confused with the 1879 migration to Kansas. (See Wharton, *The Negro in Mississippi*, p. 116.) Both Nudie E. Williams and Nell Irvin Painter attach far greater importance to this movement. See, respectively, "Black Newspapers and the Exodusters of 1879," *Kansas History* 8 (Winter 1985–1986), pp. 217–225, and *Exodusters: Black Migration to Kansas after Reconstruction* (New York: Alfred A. Knopf, 1977). In *Forgotten Time: The Yazoo-Mississippi Delta after the Civil War* (Charlottesville: University Press of Virginia, 2000), John C. Willis insists that while it was short lived, the Kansas migration was great and posed an imminent threat to the cotton economy. See pp. 48–49.

10. Michael Wayne has explained that by taking "to the road," the freedman "introduced the marketplace into the labor settlement." See Michael S. Wayne, *The Reshaping of Plantation Society: The Natchez District, 1860–80* (Baton Rouge: Louisiana State University Press, 1990), p. 110.

11. Indeed, cat fur was a thriving business in Simbirsk Province. The trade extended from local markets to China in the east and Europe in the west. For a description, see I. Sivopli͡as, *"Istori͡a s kartinkami"* (Ulyanovsk, Rossiya: Artishok, 2008), str. 44–45.

12. See A. Avdonin, *"Pod sen'i͡u Yazyko-vskikh Muz"* (Ulyanovsk, Rossiya: Pechatnyĭ Dvor, 1991), str. 4. In "The Banking Crisis, Peasant Reform, and Economic Development in Russia, 1857–1861," *American Historical Review* 96:3 (June 1991), pp. 795–820, Steven L. Hoch explains how nobles often depended on this practice to get by (see p. 799). For a recent, richly detailed, and nuanced account, see *Bankrupts and Usurers of Imperial Russia: Debt, Property, and the Law in the Age of Dostoyevsky and Tolstoy* (Cambridge: Harvard University Press, 2016), in which Sergei Antonov cautions against sweeping generalizations and assumptions regarding business practices in general, and borrowing and debt in particular, in late Imperial Russia. For example, alongside the legal formulae of lending and borrowing existed informal, elastic, pseudo-legal frameworks, such as giving and taking loans among kin, or within (and beyond) one's estate, the point being that fixed edicts and policies handed down by the state were accompanied by informal practices from the ground up, which emerged out of issues such as necessity, tradition, and circumvention—in essence, shadow economic behavior. Generically speaking, shadow economic behavior connotes extralegal or illicit "black market" activity. But it can also simply mean self-interested economic activity that is not officially recorded or regulated. I use the latter meaning in this context.

13. Hoch, "Banking Crisis, Peasant Reform," pp. 795–797; Nicolas Spulber, *Russia's Economic Transitions: From Late Tsarism to the New Millennium* (New York: Cambridge University Press, 2003), pp. 55–61.

14. A decree dated February 16, 1809, established Simbirsk Province as a major center of wool/textile production. The Middle Volga River region was selected as a major hub for wool production because of its proximity to sheep herders to the southeast. The roots of trade between the two regions were deep. The brand name was Simbirski Wool (*Simbirskoe Sukno*), and it specialized in camel and sheep wool from Orenburg. Factories came to be a regular feature across the rural landscape of the region. During the War of 1812, the Wool Commission of Simbirsk (*Kommissiya Sukna Simbirska*) was highly productive, benefiting from government requisitions. It is estimated that at least one-third of the army's uniforms and coats were made in Simbirsk Province. Although

productivity waned after 1812, as a result of the European wars and rebellions of 1848, there was again a spike in government requisitions. Between 1850 and 1860, 16 more wool factories opened in Simbirsk, and one of these was at Yazykovo Selo. On the eve of emancipation there were reportedly 100 large wool factories in Simbirsk Province. See P. Vereshchagin, sostavitel', *"Proshloe nashego kraia, 1648–1917: sbornik dokumentov i materialov"* (Ulyanovsk, SSSR, Ulyanovskoe otdelenie Privolzhskogo knizhnogo izdatel'stva, 1968), str. 68–126, especially str. 110, and *passim*; and V. Golovin, "Pervyĭ brend gubernii," Simbirskiĭ Kur'er (15 avgusta 2011).

15. V.A. Aunovskiĭ, "Sukonnye fabriki i sherstomoĭki v Simbirskoĭ gubernii," *"Simbirskiĭ sbornik,"* T. 2 (Simbirsk, Rossiya: Simbirskiĭ gubernskiĭ statisticheskiĭ komitet, 1870), str. 82–102.

16. John P. LeDonne, *Absolutism and Ruling Class: The Formation of the Russian Political Order, 1700–1825* (Oxford: Oxford University Press, 1991), p. 230. For a solid overview of the staggering economic realities and noble landlord and peasant *mentalités*—including freedom of movement (or lack thereof) and individual initiative (or lack thereof)—see Arcadius Kahan's "The Russian Economy, 1860–1913," in *Russian Economic History: The Nineteenth Century*, edited by Roger Weiss (Chicago: University of Chicago Press, 1989), pp. 1–90. Spulber's *Russia's Economic Transitions*, Part I, pp. 1–152, is equally informative.

17. For a sampling, see Elise Kimerling Wirtschafter, *Social Identity in Imperial Russia* (DeKalb: Northern Illinois University Press, 1997); Antonov, *Bankrupts and Usurers*; and Susan Smith-Peter, *Imagining Russian Regions: Civil Society and Subnational Identity in Nineteenth Century Russia* (Leiden, Netherlands: Brill, 2018). While acknowledging the existence of a vibrant informal and traditional market system across Russia, James L. West and Nicolas Spulber, among many historians, lean toward the "towering" state power and "command" nature of economic policies in Imperial Russia. See, respectively, West's "Old Believers and New Entrepreneurs: Old Belief and Entrepreneurial Culture in Imperial Russia," in *Commerce in Russian Urban Culture, 1861–1914*, edited by William Craft Brumfield, Boris V. Anan'ich, and Yuri A. Petrov (Baltimore: Johns Hopkins University Press, 2001), pp. 79–89; and Spulber, *Russia's Economic Transitions*.

18. D. Murashov, "Provintsial'noe dvorianstvo v kontse 50-kh—70-kh godov 19 veka. (po materialam Penzenskoĭ gubernii)." Dissertatsii a: Saratov, 2004, str. 171–172. Often, if not always, merchant economic activity during the Imperial period could be described as shadow economic activity. Although he deals with this topic in conjunction with the command economy during the Soviet period of Russian history, James Heinzen

has explained that it goes hand in hand with (and emerges because of) government controls, regulations, and inclusionary/exclusionary measures. See his *The Art of the Bribe: Corruption Under Stalin, 1943–1953 (Yale-Hoover Series on Authoritarian Regimes)* (New Haven: Yale University Press, 2016), pp. 3, 14, 37, 47, 50–51, 58, 76, 93, 116, 158, 187, 277, 293, 379, and 384. For a discussion of the European versus Asian economic orientation, see Richard Pipes, *Russia Under the Old Regime* (New York: Penguin, 1974), pp. 171, 180, 195–197, and 203–220.

19. M.V. Rusin, Selianin Simbirskogo uezda: Khroniki i istorii sela Voskresenskogo (ono zhe Undory): materialy dlia istorii Simbirskogo dvorianstva i chastnogo zemlevladeniia v Simbirskom uezde. Napechatano v knige: P. Martynov "Materialy dlia istorii Simbirskogo dvorianstva i chastnogo zemlevladeniia v Simbirskom uezde" (Izdanie Simbirskoĭ Gubernskoĭ Uchenoĭ Arkhivnoĭ komissii, 1903), str. 9.

20. Aunovskiĭ, "Sukonnye fabriki," str. 82–102. In his insightful chapter "Old Believers and New Entrepreneurs," James L. West explains that merchants were the ultimate outsiders in Imperial Russia. But that is not to suggest that they did not have connections *within* the merchant community. See Catherine Evtuhov, *Portrait of a Russian Province: Economy, Society, and Civilization in Nineteenth-Century Nizhnii Novgorod* (Pittsburgh: University of Pittsburgh Press, 2011), pp. 76–79, where she stresses the mutual support and "security network" within the merchant communities.

21. Aunovskiĭ, "Sukonnye fabriki," str. 82–102.

22. Dokument "Delo ob otmene dogovora s Mangushevym" GAUO d. 88, opis' 5, d. 92, l. 15.

23. See Wayne Dowler, "Merchants and Politics in Russia: The Guild Reform of 1824," *Slavonic and East European Review* 65:1 (January 1987), pp. 38–52. There were three guild levels in Imperial Russia, the third being the lowest. Ever since the Napoleonic Wars, the first and second had been reserved for non-service members of the nobility, and their combined total membership was eclipsed by that of the third guild. Also since the turn of the century, third guild merchants had increasingly dominated the textile industry. Vasili Yazykov was not a guild member.

24. See Alfred J. Reiber, "Businessmen and Business Culture in Imperial Russia," *Proceedings of the American Philosophical Society* 128:3 (September 1984), pp. 238–243. Not surprisingly, even though the Russian merchant class was distinguished by its strong entrepreneurial ethos and hard work ethic, historians continue to wrestle with this topic in terms of whether, or the extent to which, it was capitalist, "bourgeois," "middle class," a cohesive community, or simply, as one classic description had it, "a kind of half-way house for those moving up and down the social ladder." (See Pipes, *Russia Under the Old Regime*, p. 217.) In general, what they all seem to agree on is that the Russian merchant was influenced

by religious belief. In Simbirsk Province, it is clear the Tatar, Mordvins, and Chuvashi merchants were significant and contributed greatly to the well-being of both their communities and the province in general. For further information, see Boris V. Anan'ich, "Religious and Nationalist Aspects of Entrepreneurialism in Russia," in *Russia in the European Context, 1879–1914: A Member of the Family*, edited by Susan P. McCaffray and Michael Melancon (New York: Palgrave Macmillan, 2005), pp. 85–94; Thomas Marsden, *The Crisis of Religious Toleration in Imperial Russia: Bibikov's System for the Old Believers, 1841–1855 (Oxford Historical Monographs)* (Oxford: Oxford University Press, 2015); David L. Ransel, *A Russian Merchant's Tale: The Life and Adventures of Ivan Alekseevich Tolchenov, Based on His Diary* (Bloomington: Indiana University Press, 2009), especially the introduction, pp. xi–xxvi; and T.A. Gromova, redaktor "Simbirsk kupecheskiĭ: v 2 ch.- Vypusk 1: Ocherki o simbirskom predprinimatel'stve" (Ulyanovsk, R.G. Pelikan, 2016).

25. See N. Krylov, "Vospominaniia Mirovogo posrednika pervogo prizyva o vvedenii v deĭstvie Polozheniia 19-go fevralia 1861 goda." *Russkaia starina*, 74:6 (Aprel',' 1892), str. 81–102, i 615–641, and especially str. 86 i 90, and "Nakanune velikikh reform" (Tsarskiĭ reskript dlia Osvobozhdeniia). *Istoricheskiĭ Vestnik*, Nomer 9 (Sentiabr',' 1903), str. 786–821, especially str. 802; Serge A. Zenkovsky, "The Emancipation of the Serfs in Retrospect," *Russian Review* 20:4 (October 1961), pp. 280–293 (especially pp. 282–283); and Robert P. Geraci, *Window on the East: National and Imperial Identities in Late Tsarist Russia* (Ithaca: Cornell University Press, 2001), pp. 18–19 and 34–35. See also O. Tanatarova, "Pochemu krepostnymi byli tol"ko russkie?," "Russkaia semërka" (29 ianvaria 2018) at https://russian7.ru/post/pochemu-krepostnymi-byli-tolko-russk/, accessed October 2, 2019. While it is true that down through the ages non-Russians were enserfed, these authors discuss the phenomenon in the Middle Volga region, where minorities such as Tatars had not been enserfed *because* they were not Russian. In short, the rationale was that the Russian government did not want to antagonize these minorities by impressing them into labor service. Their acquiescence was crucial for social stability.

26. Rassadin, "Yazykovo," str. 472–3; and A. Lipinskiĭ, *"Materialy dlia geografii i statistiki Rossii, sobrannye ofitserami General'nogo Shtaba: Simbirskaia Guberniia,"* t. 2 (Sankt-Peterburg, Rossiya: Voennaia tipografiia, 1868), str. 192–202.

27. See the discussion in Jeffrey Burds, *Peasant Dreams and Market Politics: Labor Migration and the Russian Village, 1861–1905* (Pittsburgh: University of Pittsburgh Press, 1998), pp. 2–10. Boris Mironov also delineates this historiographical issue in "The Russian Peasant Commune after the Reforms of the 1860s," *Slavic Review* 44:3 (Fall 1985), pp. 438–467.

28. Mironov, "The Russian Peasant Commune after the Reforms of the 1860s." In *The Russian Peasantry: The World the Peasants Made* (London: Addison Wesley Longman, 1999), p. 343, David Moon likewise holds that the reforms reinforced the peasants' communal relations and attachment to the land. See also M. Raphael Johnson's "The Peasant Commune in Russia: Rural Anarchy and Feudal Socialism," *NAMS-UK (National-Anarchist Movement Shropshire)* (January 7, 2012).

29. May, *Quitman*, p. 111.

30. *Ibid.*

31. M. Sudarev, "Nachalo," *Zhurnal "Monomakh,"* Nomer 2 (2003), str. 8–12; Rusin, Seli anin Simbirskogo uezda, str. 9.

32. The pioneering source for the American plantation mistress, which delineated her life as harsh and restricted, is Catherine Clinton, *The Plantation Mistress: Woman's World in the Old South* (New York: Random House, 1982). In *Within the Plantation Household: Black and White Women of the Old South* (Chapel Hill: University of North Carolina Press, 1988), Elizabeth Fox-Genovese analyzed the relationship between class, race, and gender, and this paradigm's influence on shaping the identity of women, both black and white, on the plantation. Although her findings include an inversion of the Western stereotypical model of demesne management (i.e., the master as the estate/plantation manager and the mistress in charge of family affairs), see Katherine Pickering Antonova, *An Ordinary Marriage: The World of a Gentry Family in Provincial Russia* (New York: Oxford University Press, 2013), pp. 74–94, which discusses the household manageress' activities. See also Michelle Lamarche Marrese, *A Woman's Kingdom: Noblewomen and the Control of Property in Russia, 1700–1861* (Ithaca: Cornell University Press, 2002), pp. 171–204.

33. For a discussion of paternalism in the American South during the antebellum period, see Steven M. Stowe, *Intimacy and Power in the Old South: Ritual in the Lives of the Planters* (Baltimore: Johns Hopkins University Press, 1987), pp. 164–166, as well as his bibliographical essay on paternalism (pp. 295–299). For a discussion of paternalism in Imperial Russia before emancipation, see Mary W. Cavender, *Nests of the Gentry: Family, Estate, and Local Loyalties in Provincial Russia* (Newark: University of Delaware Press, 2007), pp. 90–106 and 133.

34. Eugene Genovese, *The Mind of the Planter Class: History and Faith in the Southern Slaveholders' Worldview* (New York: Cambridge University Press, 2005), pp. 337–338; James C. Scott, *The Art of Not Being Governed: An Anarchist History of Upland Southeast Asia (Yale Agrarian Studies Series)* (New Haven: Yale University Press, 2010), p. 267. Of note, in his groundbreaking study, *The Black Image in the White Mind: The Debate on Afro-American Character and Destiny, 1817–1914* (New York: Harper & Row, 1971), pp. 102–103, 111–112, 121, and 170, George

M. Fredrickson explained that racist attitudes in both the North and the South, which held that African Americans were *naturally* docile, childlike, and submissive, reinforced paternalism and condescension.

35. Here it is worth pointing out that the Russian peasants' refusal to work—indeed, "participate" in any of the emancipation protocols—was an inverse of the "desertion of the plantation" phenomenon in the American South. That is, whereas the American freed people expressed that freedom *in* mobility, the Russians did so in their immobility—they expressed a kind of literal immobility with respect to obligations for their former master.

36. May, *Quitman*, pp. 131–139.

37. *Ibid.*, p. 144.

38. See Cathy A. Frierson, *Peasant Icons: Representations of Rural People in Late Nineteenth-Century Russia* (New York: Oxford University Press, 1993). For American attitudes, see Peter Kolchin, *Unfree Labor: American Slavery and Russian Serfdom* (Cambridge: Belknap Press of Harvard University Press, 1987), pp. 170–173 and 184–191; and Jaqueline Jones, "Labor and the Idea of Race in the American South," *Journal of Southern History* 75:3 (August 2009), pp. 613–626.

39. See Alison K. Smith, "'The Freedom to Choose a Way of Life': Fugitives, Border, and Imperial Amnesties in Russia," *Journal of Modern History* 83:2 (June 2011), pp. 243–271.

40. See Ronald L.F. Davis, "The U.S. Army and the Origins of Sharecropping in the Natchez District—A Case Study," *Journal of Negro History* 62:1 (January 1977), pp. 60–80, and *Good and Faithful Labor: From Slavery to Sharecropping the Natchez District, 1860–1890* (Westport, CT: Greenwood Press, 1982), p. 5. See also "The Wartime Genesis of Free Labor, 1861–1865," in Ira Berlin et al., *Slaves No More: Three Essays on Emancipation and the Civil War* (Cambridge: Cambridge University Press, 1992), pp. 77–186; Lawrence L. Powell, *New Masters: Northern Planters during the Civil War and Reconstruction* (New Haven: Yale University Press, 1980), p. 84; and Amy Dru Stanley, *From Bondage to Contract: Wage Labor, Marriage, and the Market in the Age of Slave Emancipation* (Cambridge: Cambridge University Press, 1998), chapters 1, 2, and 3 in particular. Stanley pays close attention to the shift from dependency during slavery to dependency that wage labor established.

41. Carol S. Leonard, "Agricultural Productivity Growth in Russia, 1861–1912: From Inertia to Ferment," in *Growth and Stagnation in European Historical Agriculture (Rural History in Europe)*, edited by M. Olsson and P. Svennson (Turnhout, Belgium: Brepols, 2011), pp. 249–263, also found at http://www.rees.ox.ac.uk/__data/assets/pdf_file/0016/35053/Productivity_CSL_Jan_2010.pdf, accessed January 2, 2010, and November 8, 2012. In the first 10 pages of the article, Leonard provides an outstanding historiographical overview of the "crisis" versus "declension" versus "productivity" arguments regarding agricultural production in the post-emancipation period. See also Arcadius Kahan, *The Plow, the Hammer and the Knout: An Economic History of Eighteenth Century Russia* (Chicago: University of Chicago Press, 1985), pp. 11–12; and Moon, *Russian Peasantry*, chapter 4, pp. 118–155 (specifically p. 118). In *Russia's Economic Transitions*, Spulber concludes that although the state's efforts between 1861 and 1917 were impressive, no significant progress was made in the agricultural sphere.

42. Kahan, *The Plow, the Hammer and the Knout*, pp. 101 and 104; Lipinskiĭ, *"Materialy,"* str. 192–202. On the eve of emancipation, the entire Middle Volga River corridor could boast approximately 100 estate wool factories. These could be divided roughly into three categories. The first consisted of those factories that had emerged as part of the initial wave when the government spearheaded the plan. These constituted about 60 percent of Simbirsk's factories and 43 percent of its factory workers. For the most part, they were outmoded. The second category consisted of those of average size, representing about 17 percent of the province's factories. These were part of the wave that emerged on the eve of the Crimean War. The factory at Yazykovo Selo clearly fell into this category. Above all, the factories in groups one and two were completely dependent on requisitions. The third category consisted of the largest and newest factories and could well have been run by merchants who invested in their enterprises.

43. Even Seymour Becker makes a distinction between the nobility and the demesne, arguing that although the former did not decline after emancipation, Russia witnessed a decided shift from the rural estates to the urban centers. See *Nobility and Privilege in Late Imperial Russia* (DeKalb: Northern Illinois University Press, 1986). For a thoughtful analysis of this issue, see Michael Hughes, "The Russian Nobility and the Russian Countryside: Ambivalences and Orientations," *Journal of European Studies* 36:2 (June 2006), pp. 115–137.

44. The *Regulations (Polozhenii a)* specified that *barshchina* obligations could be retained if (1) it had been the main form of obligations before emancipation and (2) the estate owner was entitled to at least one-third of his former lands. Since Vasili Yazykov did retain well more than a third, he could legally impose *barshchina*. See Allan K. Wildman, "The Defining Moment: Land Charters and the Post-Emancipation Agrarian Settlement in Russia, 1861–1863," in *The Carl Beck Papers in Russian & East European Studies*, No. 1205 (Pittsburgh: Center for Russian and East European Studies, University of Pittsburgh, 1996), pp. 6–8 and 19.

45. For a brief synopsis of the complicated, technicality-strewn terms that the *Regulations* prescribed for *barshchina* labor, see Peter A. Zaionchkovskiy, *The Abolition of Serfdom in Russia*, edited and translated from the third (1968) Russian edition by Susan Wobst (Gulf Breeze, FL:

Academic International Press, 1978), pp. 89–90 and 96.

46. Kolchin, *Unfree Labor*, pp. 63–65; Peter Waldron, *The End of Imperial Russia, 1855–1917* (New York: St. Martin's Press, 1997), p. 43–44.

47. Hugh Seton-Watson, *The Russian Empire, 1801–1917* (Oxford: Oxford University Press, 1988), pp. 399–401; Moon, *Russian Peasantry*, chapter 4, "Production," pp. 118–155; Kahan, "The Russian Economy, 1860–1913"; and Trofimov, *"Zhil i umer dzhentl'menom-poètom,"* str. 84–85.

48. "Containment," in both de jure and de facto forms, is the subject of Gene Dattel's *Cotton and Race in the Making of America: The Human Costs of Economic Power* (Lanham, MD: Ivan R. Dee, 2009). For quote, see pp. 211–212; for a detailed discussion, see chapter 5. See also Stephen Cresswell, *Rednecks, Redeemers, and Race: Mississippi after Reconstruction, 1877–1917* (Jackson: University Press of Mississippi, 2006), chapter 3, "The Persistent Institution: Black Labor and Race Control," pp. 37–51; Powell, *New Masters*, pp. 2–3, 38, and *passim*; and Louis S. Gerteis, *From Contraband to Freedman: Federal Policy toward Southern Blacks, 1861–1865* (Westport, CT: Greenwood Press, 1973), pp. 122–123. In "The U.S. Army the Origins of Sharecropping," Ronald L.F. Davis suggests that General Lorenzo Thomas's stint in Natchez before the war explains his sympathy for the planter elite during the war and afterward. He was on a "first-name basis" with the "rebel planters." And Lawrence Powell describes the general as being very "obliging" and quotes him saying about the local planters that he was "happy" to see his "old friends and talk of days gone by," and he was ready to do anything "to help his old friends out." See Powell, *New Masters*, pp. 46–47. For the Bruce quote, see Sven Beckert, "Emancipation and Empire: Reconstructing the Worldwide Web of Cotton Production in the Age of the American Civil War," *American Historical Review* 109:5 (December 2004), pp. 1405–1438, especially p. 1419.

49. For a brief but solid understanding of this issue, refer to Anatole G. Mazour, "Economic Decline of Landlordism in Russia," *Historian* 8:2 (Spring 1946), pp. 156–162. For recent commentary on this topic, see Spulber, *Russia's Economic Transitions*, Part I, especially pp. 138–152.

50. Peter Gatrell, "The Meaning of the Great Reforms in Russian Economic History," in *Russia's Great Reforms, 1855–1881*, edited by Ben Eklof, John Bushnell, and Larissa Zakharova (Bloomington: Indiana University Press, 1994), pp. 84–101. Gatrell notes that in the 1860s and 1870s production stagnated (see pp. 88 and 90). For the Daniel Field quote, see his "The Year of Jubilee," also in Eklof et al., *Russia's Great Reforms, 1855–1881*, pp. 40–57 (specifically p. 53).

51. Murashov, "Provint sial'noe dvori anstvo," str. 178.

52. See Hoch, "Banking Crisis, Peasant Reform"; Mazour, "Economic Decline";

Murashov, "Provintsial'noe dvorianstvo," str. 181–182; and Pipes, *Russia under the Old Regime*, p. 207. Murashov's work explains the complicated and bewildering structural problems in the financial side of the Russian economy.

53. Murashov, "Provintsia'noe dvorianstvo," str. 169–181, especially str. 178.

54. See James C. Scott, *Weapons of the Weak: Everyday Forms of Peasant Resistance* (New Haven: Yale University Press, 1987).

55. Murashov, "Provint sial'noe dvorianstvo," str. 169–181. See also Rodney Bohac, "Everyday Forms of Resistance: Serf Opposition to Gentry Exactions, 1800–1861," in *Peasant Economy, Culture, and Politics of European Russia, 1800–1921*, edited by Esther Kingston-Mann and Timothy Mixter (Princeton: Princeton University Press, 1991), pp. 237–238; and Burds, *Peasant Dreams*, chapter 1, "The Roots of Ambivalence," pp. 17–39.

56. M.F. Sweetser, *King's Handbook of the United States*, edited by Moses King (Buffalo: Moses King Corporation, 1892), p. 441; Cresswell, *Rednecks*, pp. 1–13.

57. See chapter 9, "Problems of Agricultural Recovery," in William C. Harris, *Presidential Reconstruction in Mississippi* (Baton Rouge: Louisiana State University Press, 1967), pp. 154–185, which details the utter chaos with respect to cash and credit issues. See also George L. Anderson, "The South and Problems of Post–Civil War Finance," *Journal of Southern History* 9:2 (May 1943), pp. 181–195; and Theodore Saloutos, "Southern Agriculture and the Problems of Readjustment: 1865–1877," *Agricultural History* 30:2 (April 1956), pp. 58–76.

58. For a succinct overview of this subject, see chapter 11, "Restoration of the Railroads," in Harris, *Presidential Reconstruction*, pp. 194–216.

59. Cresswell, *Rednecks*, pp. 1–13; Neil R. McMillen, *Dark Journey: Black Mississippians in the Age of Jim Crow* (Champaign: University of Illinois Press, 1989), p. 150. It is true that after 1865, over time, the American South's elite contracted and wealth was concentrated in fewer hands. In this regard, this factual trend and historiographic topic is similar to the Becker thesis with respect to the Russian nobility. See Wayne, *Reshaping of Plantation Society*, and Becker, *Nobility and Privilege*.

60. See Joyce Appleby, *Inheriting the Revolution: The First Generation of Americans* (Cambridge: Belknap Press of Harvard University Press, 2000).

61. Moon, *Russian Peasantry*, p. 118. For understanding distinctions between "farmers" who are profit focused and peasants who are bound by routine and tradition, see Robert Redfield, *The Little Community and Peasant Society and Culture* (Chicago: University of Chicago Press, 1989), pp. 18–19.

62. For a description of Palmyra Plantation, see chapter 11, "Patriarch of a Plantation World," in May, *Quitman*, pp. 130–146. Yazykovo Selo was

dependent on other Yazykov properties for food and supplies. See M. Sudarev, "Nachalo," *Zhurnal "Monomakh,"* Nomer 2 (2003), str. 8–12.

63. Athar Hussain and Keith Tribe, *Marxism and the Agrarian Question* (London: Palgrave Macmillan, 1983), pp. 156–170.

64. For an excellent discussion of the origins of the *mentalité* paradigm, see Patrick H. Hutton, "The History of Mentalities: The New Map of Cultural History," *History and Theory* 20:3 (October 1981), pp. 237–259.

65. Indeed, buried in an old but well-known book to scholars of Russian history is an intriguing description of a scene that occurred well after emancipation, in which a collection of peasants at the estate's office pleaded for assistance from the noble landlord. See Donald Mackenzie Wallace, *Russia: Russia of To-day*, Vol. III (Boston, MA: J.B. Millet Company, 1910), pp. 188–190. For a fairly recent, interesting reanalysis of the Russian nobility, see Vera S. Dubina, "The 'Distinction': Russian Nobility and Russian Elites in the European Context (the 18th–19th Century)," *Social Evolution & History* 7:2 (September 2008), pp. 80–100, in which she delineates the quintessential characteristics of the Russian nobility as compared with its European counterpart.

66. Becker, *Nobility and Privilege*, pp. 30–31, 9, 171–172, and 176. To be sure, the heterogeneity of the Russian nobility increased after 1861, as Michael Hughes discusses in his thoughtful study, "The Russian Nobility and the Russian Countryside."

67. In *Unfree Labor*, pp. 60–61 and chapter 2, "Planters, Pomeshchiki, and Paternalism," pp. 103–156, Peter Kolchin explains that during serfdom, the absentee noble landlord may well have been less paternalistic than Southern planters during slavery. However, gauging the presence of paternalism in the context of emancipation, as well as in an absenteeist versus resident landlord scenario, is complicated, as there are certainly variables and exceptions to overall general findings.

68. The "Russia as one great landed estate with the tsar as its landlord" trope originated with the French historian of Russian history, Anatole Leroy-Beaulieu. See Spulber, *Russia's Economic Transitions*, p. 20.

69. This topic is discussed in great length in Burds, *Peasant Dreams*; Yanni Kotsonis, *Making Peasants Backward: Agricultural Cooperatives and the Agrarian Question in Russia, 1861–1914* (New York: St. Martin's Press, 1999); Wildman, "Defining Moment," pp. 6–7; and Waldron, *The End of Imperial Russia*, chapter 2, "Field and Factory: The Russian Economy." The "commune" thesis does not assert that Russian peasants were precluded from or incapable of individual agency or contingency. However, it does assert that any typical individual effort had to be cleared with the commune's elders and that the elders had an interest in suppressing younger commune members' initiative. Long ago, Hugh Seton-Watson observed

that, unlike the progressive, liberal, socio-political tradition in Western Europe and America (which produced historical stages in which a new group of people entered the fold of social and political privileges and participation), in Russia, barring the autocrat and the elites, the prevailing view had always been that if all cannot have the same, none should have any privileges or rights. See Seton-Watson, *Russian Empire*, p. 353. Recently, the research of Tracy Dennison and Steven Nafziger has challenged the "traditional, closed society" and "all for one and one for all" paradigms. See "Economy and Society in Rural Russia: The Serf Estate of Voshchazhnikovo, 1750–1860," *Journal of Economic History* 65:2 (June 2005), pp. 536–359, and "Micro Perspectives on Russian Living Standards, 1750–1917," *Journal of Interdisciplinary History* 42:3 (2013), pp. 397–441. The critical caveat on which their thesis hinges is that individual initiative *depended* on the extent of liberal views held by the estate owner.

70. My use of the term *anarchist* in this context is not a shorthand for what one historian has described as a stereotype of one aspect of the Russian national character. See Elena Hellberg-Hirn, *Soil and Soul: The Symbolic World of Russianness (Nationalism & Fascism in Russia)* (New York: Ashgate, 1998), p. 167. Rather, I use the term, in part, in the manner explained by James C. Scott in *The Art of Not Being Governed*, pp. ix–xiii, 211–212, and 267, as well as alluded to in his *Domination and the Arts of Resistance: Hidden Transcripts* (New Haven: Yale University Press, 1992) and *Weapons of the Weak*. See also Marsden, *The Crisis of Religious Toleration*, pp. 143–144.

71. As for the "mobility" theme, one historian has characterized this phenomenon as "scattering." See Willis, *Forgotten Time*, p. 43; and Wharton, *Negro in Mississippi*, p. 126. As for schools, churches, stores, and other sinews of community after emancipation, see Peter Kolchin, *First Freedom: The Responses of Alabama's Blacks to Emancipation and Reconstruction* (Westport, CT: Greenwood Press, 1972); Leon F. Litwack, *Been in the Storm So Long: The Aftermath of Slavery* (New York: Vintage, 1980); Eric Foner, *Reconstruction: America's Unfinished Revolution, 1863–1877* (New York: Harper & Row, 1988); and Powell, *New Masters*, pp. 119 and 135. The case could also be made that while the Russian peasants physically remained on the estate, they could possess very strong sensibilities of "separateness" vis-à-vis their former master and other authorities. Broadly speaking, with respect to the slave community on the antebellum plantation, W.E.B. Du Bois and Kenneth Stampp argued the traditional view that the institution arrested a community. John Blassingame, Eugene Genovese, and Herbert Gutman challenged this idea by identifying a thriving community on the demesne. Peter Kolchin has explained that while slavery certainly interrupted the development of a sustained cohesive community, American slaves nevertheless

fashioned one as best they could. See W.E.B. Du Bois, *The Negro American Family* (New York: Negro Universities Press, 1908); Kenneth M. Stampp, *The Era of Reconstruction, 1865–1877* (New York: Alfred A. Knopf, 1966); John Blassingame, *The Slave Community: Plantation Life in the Antebellum South* (New York: Oxford University Press, 1979); Eugene Genovese, *Roll, Jordan, Roll: The World the Slaves Made* (New York: Pantheon Books, 1974); Herbert G. Gutman, *The Black Family in Slavery and Freedom, 1750–1925* (New York: Vintage Books, 1976); and Peter Kolchin, *American Slavery, 1619–1877* (New York: Hill and Wang, 1993).

72. See "Of Our Spiritual Strivings," in W.E.B. Du Bois, *The Souls of Black Folk* (New York: Cosimo, 1903), pp. 7–15.

73. For an account of the town's founding, see chapter 7, "Mound Bayou," in Hermann, *Pursuit*, pp. 219–245.

74. C. Vann Woodward, *American Counterpoint: Slavery and Racism in the North-South Dialogue* (Boston: Little, Brown, 1971), p. 252; Wayne, *Reshaping of Plantation Society*, p. 110.

Chapter 6

1. See Nicolas Spulber, *Russia's Economic Transitions: From Late Tsarism to the New Millennium* (New York: Cambridge University Press, 2003), Part I, pp. 1–152.

2. See Sven Beckert, *Empire of Cotton: A Global History* (New York: Penguin Random House, 2014), pp. xv, 275, and 281–285. No doubt Beckert's concept of "war capitalism" is a play on "War Communism" from the civil war period after the Bolshevik Revolution in 1917. See also Beckert's article "Emancipation and Empire: Reconstructing the Worldwide Web of Cotton Production in the Age of the American Civil War," *American Historical Review* 109:5 (December 2004), pp. 1405–1438. It is worth pointing out here that Donald J. Boudreaux disagrees with the Beckert thesis that slavery fueled capitalism, arguing instead that industrial capitalism destroyed it. For an outline of his arguments, see Carole E. Scott, "The Very Different but Connected Economies of the Northeast and the South before the Civil War," pp. 16–18. https://www.westga.edu/~bquest/2015/connected2015.pdf, accessed November 8, 2020.

3. Charles E. Orser, Jr., "The Archaeological Recognition of the Squad System on Postbellum Cotton Plantations," *Southeastern Archaeology* 5:1 (Summer 1986), pp. 11–20.

4. See Markus Cerman, "Alessandro Stanziani, Bondage, Labor and Rights in Eurasia from the Sixteenth to the Early Twentieth Centuries," *Cahiers du monde russe* 55:34 (2014), pp. 384–387 (especially p. 384 for quote). And see Alessandro Stanziani, "The Abolition of Serfdom in Russia," in *Abolitions as a Global Experience*, edited by Hideaki Suzuki (Singapore: National University of Singapore Press, 2015), pp. 228–255, as well as the introduction and chapter 5, "Labor and Dependence on Russian Estates," in Stanziani's *Bondage, Labor and Rights in Eurasia from the Sixteenth to the Early Twentieth Centuries* (New York: Berghahn [International Studies in Social History, 24], 2014), pp. 1–13 and 127–144 (with pp. 7 and 140 for quotes), and his "Russian Serfdom: A Reappraisal," *Ab Imperio* 2 (2014), pp. 71–99. For other quotes, see *Bondage*, pp. 56 and 164–169. Interestingly, Cerman (pp. 384–385) notes that Stanziani disagrees with the "serfdom emerged as a result of land abundance and labor shortages" paradigm. Instead, Stanziani asserts it was caused by "market integration of agriculture," which is similar to the line of argument that Beckert utilizes. See also Steven Nafziger, "Quantification and the Economic History of Imperial Russia," *Slavic Review* 76:1 (Spring 2017), pp. 30–36, for a discussion of Stanziani's methodology.

5. Andrei Markevich and Ekaterina Zhuravskaya, "The Economic Effects of the Abolition of Serfdom: Evidence from the Russian Empire," *American Economic Review* 108:4–5 (2018), pp. 1083 and 1101. See Robert William Fogel and Stanley L. Engerman, *Time on the Cross: The Economics of American Negro Slavery* (New York: W.W. Norton, 1974), and Robert William Fogel, *Without Consent or Contract: The Rise and Fall of American Slavery* (New York: W.W. Norton, 1989). See also Andrei Markevich, "The Impact of Serfdom on Economic Development," *World Economic Forum*, March 2, 2015, https://www.weforum.org/agenda/2015/03/the-impact-of-serfdom-on-economic-development/, accessed November 14, 2020. It is worth noting that while Markevich and Zhuravskaya assert that serfdom was not profitable, other historians have found that it was, such as Steven L. Hoch, *Serfdom and Social Control in Russia: Petrovskoe, a Village in Tambov* (Chicago: University of Chicago Press, 1989); David Moon, "Reassessing Russian Serfdom," *European History Quarterly* 26:4 (1996), pp. 483–526; Tracy K. Dennison, "Did Serfdom Matter? Russian Rural Society, 1750–1860," *Historical Research* 79:203 (February 2006), pp. 74–89; and of course Stanziani, "Introduction" and "Chapter 5: Labor and Dependence on Russian Estates," in *Bondage, Labor and Rights in Eurasia from the Sixteenth to the Early Twentieth Centuries* (New York: Berghahn [International Studies in Social History, 24]) 2014), pp. 1–13, and 127–144 (with pp. 7 and 140 for quotes); and "Russian Serfdom: A Reappraisal," *Ab Imperio* 2 (2014), pp. 71–99.

6. Dokument "Delo ob otmene dogovora s Mangushevym" GAUO d. 88, opis' 5, d. 92, l. 15.

7. Indeed, long ago Donald Mackenzie Wallace observed that emancipation dealt a death blow to private factories on estates. See *Russia: Russia of To-day*, Vol. III (Boston: J.B. Millet Company, 1910), p. 204.

8. V.A. Aunovskiĭ, "Sukonnye fabriki i sherstomoĭki v Simbirskoĭ gubernii," *"Simbirskiĭ*

sbornik," T. 2 (Simbirsk, Rossiya: Simbirskiĭ gubernskiĭ statisticheskiĭ komitet, 1870), str. 82–102 and chapter 3; A. Avdonin, *"Pod sen'iu Yazykovskikh Muz"* (Ulyanovsk, Rossiya: Pechatnyĭ Dvor, 1991), str. 1–20; and P. Vereshchagin, sostavitel,' *"Proshloe nashego kraia, 1648–1917: sbornik dokumentov i materialov"* (Ulyanovsk, SSSR, Ulyanovskoe otdelenie Privolzhskogo knizhnogo izdatel'stva, 1968), str. 68–126, especially 110, and *passim.* For the reference to chapter 5, see footnotes 14 and 15.

9. V. Egorov, "Pozhar v Ulyanovske," stat'ia v *Ulyanovskoĭ-Simbirskoĭ Ėntsiklopedii,* T.2 (Ulyanovsk, Rossiya, Simbirskaia kniga 2004), str. 357–360. For nine days the fire swept through the province's capital, its course twisting and turning as a result of the winds that swept across the city on the bluff. Three-quarters of the capital was destroyed, including 12 churches and the famous Karamzin Public Library, which housed sources on the region's settlement, uprisings, nobility, and serfs. Of its roughly 3,000 homes, approximately half went up in flames. Estimates were that over 15,000 people became homeless. It took the city over fifteen years to rebuild. The Yazykov city mansion was spared because it was built of brick.

10. See Hugh Seton-Watson, *The Russian Empire, 1801–1917* (Oxford: Oxford University Press, 1988), pp. 357–358 and 368–370; and Hugh D. Hudson, Jr., "A Rhetorical War of Fire: The Middle Volga Arson Panic of 1839 as Contested Legitimacy in Prereform Russia," *Canadian Slavonic Papers* 43:1 (March 2001), pp. 29–48, especially p. 34, where Hudson mentions that rumors were widespread that noblemen were setting fires.

11. Dokument "Ves'ma sekretno." GAUO, f.855, opis' 1, d.13, 1.5–7 (maĭ 26, 1867—avgust 8, 1868). The report also noted that Yazykov was able to "get away with this lifestyle" for a number of reasons: (1) he was "married to the daughter of a close confidant of the tsar," (2) "his wife openly carries on an affair [with his first cousin]," (3) "he is a Marshal of the Nobility," and (4) "he has money and is well educated."

12. Dokument "Khodataĭstvo ot Praskov'i Yazykovoĭ." GAUO, f.32, opis' 3, dok.170. 1.1.3 i 5 (Oktiabr' 28–Noiabr' 3, 1865). "I own from my husband [2nd] Lieutenant Vasili Petrovich Yazykov a damaged stone two level mansion located in Simbirsk in the second section of the city relating to the parish of the Church of Vladimir, the Mother of God, on Spasskii Street, the purchase completed in Simbirsk Civil Court, the bill of sale on August 28, 1865." And the bill of sale reads, "I Vasili Petrovich Yazykov sell out to my wife my home which I inherited from my father 2nd Lieutenant Petr Mikhailovich Yazykov on 22 June 1853.... I was paid 3,000 rubles by Praskovia."

13. Avdonin, *"Pod sen'iu Yazykovskikh Muz,"* str. 9.

14. Yazykov was involved in many governing and philanthropic endeavors, too numerous to list here. For example, he sat on the board of the Society of Christian Compassion, he was a trustee of one of Simbirsk's orphanages, and he was chief of Simbirsk's Society of Injured and Sick Soldiers. See L. Ershova, "Kak stranno tasuetsi a koloda," *Zhurnal "Monomakh,"* Nomer 3 (2000), str. 23–25. In fact, Avenir Korelin has explained that after emancipation, the nobility's role—especially that of the district marshal of the nobility (of which Vasili Yazykov was one)—actually increased in terms of obligations, duties, and even governing. See A.P. Korelin, "The Institution of Marshals of the Nobility: On the Social and Political Position of the Nobility," *Russian Studies in History* 17:4 (Spring 1979), pp. 3–35, especially pp. 6, 10, 12, 15, and 17.

15. For a detailed list of Yazykov's official duties and services, see his logbook of service: Dokument "Formuliarnyĭ spisok o sluzhbe Simbirskogo Uezdnogo Predvoditelia dvorianstva otstavnogo poruchika ot Artillerii V.P. Yazykova" GAUO, d. 88, opis' 5, d. 92, 1.15 (Iiun', 1879). A Marshal of the Nobility was elected (by his noble peers) head of the nobility for a district or province, and exercised an array of official and private functions. For a succinct overview, see G.M. Hamburg, "Portrait of an Elite: Russian Marshals of the Nobility, 1861–1917," *Slavic Review* 40:4 (Winter 1981), pp. 585–602. See also Korelin, "The Institution of Marshals of the Nobility." *Ibid.*

16. Peter A. Zaionchkovskiy, *The Abolition of Serfdom in Russia,* edited and translated from the third (1968) Russian edition by Susan Wobst (Gulf Breeze, FL: Academic International Press, 1978), p. 96. See my explanation in note 17 of chapter 4.

17. A. Lipinskiĭ, *"Materialy dlia geografii i statistiki Rossii, sobrannye ofitserami General'nogo Shtaba: Simbirskaia Guberniia,"* t. 2 (Sankt-Peterburg, Rossiya: Voennaia tipografiia, 1868), str. 192–202; and Aunovskiĭ, "Sukonnye fabriki," str. 82–102.

18. See discussed in the section on Yazykovo Selo in chapter 5.

19. Lipinskiĭ, *"Materialy,"* str. 192–202; Aunovskiĭ, "Sukonnye fabriki," str. 82–102. See also Zaionchkovskiy, *The Abolition of Serfdom,* p. 96.

20. Lipinskiĭ, *"Materialy."* The ad was titled "Malo letnikh detei." It is an interesting point of comparison that there is similarity between Stepanov turning to hire minors from the region and the intent behind some of the Black Codes enacted by the Mississippi Legislature on November 22, 1865, which targeted young, black (and especially orphaned) children for both apprenticeships and labor. For an informative introduction to the topic of child labor and child labor laws in Russia, see Boris B. Gorshkov, "Toward a Comprehensive Law: Tsarist Factory Labor Legislation in European Context, 1830–1914," in *Russia in the European Context, 1879–1914: A Member of the Family,* edited by Susan P. McCaffray and Michael Melancon (New York: Palgrave Macmillan, 2005), pp. 49–71.

21. M. Naĭdenov, *"Klassovaia bor'ba v poreformennoĭ derevne (1861–1863)"* (Moskva, SSSR:

Gospolitizdat, 1955), str. 291. During the days of serfdom, being unloaded onto the military was the Russian equivalent of the American practice of being "sold downriver" in the days of slavery.

22. Coincidentally, this sentiment proved to retard acceptance of mechanical harvesters in the cotton industry, albeit well after emancipation in the United States. Indeed, social scientists and federal officials who were worried about unemployment, especially during the Great Depression, expressed "anti-laborsaving-machine" attitudes. See Charles S. Aiken, "The Evolution of Cotton Ginning in the Southeastern United States," *Geographical Review* 63:2 (April 1973), pp. 196–224, especially p. 212.

23. *Vedomosti Simbirskoy Gubernii.* Nomer 45 (Subbota) 9 Noyabrya 1863.

24. I use this expression deliberately. Far from being a romantic sentimentalization of the Russian peasant, Joanna Hubbs explains in her ethnographic study of the myth of "Mother Russia" that its origins are found in the agrarian conception of nature in Russia; "the deep attachment to the country as mother is everywhere to be found." See her *Mother Russia: The Feminine Myth in Russian Culture* (Bloomington: Indiana University Press, 1993), introduction, and *passim* (for quote, see p. xiii). Chris J. Chulos also notes in his study of the converging worlds of rural and urban Russia after emancipation that by 1917, peasants were not loyal to the "empire" but to the actual plots of land that gave them sustenance. See *Converging Worlds: Religion and Community in Peasant Russia, 1861–1917* (DeKalb: Northern Illinois University Press, 2003), p. 77.

25. Much has been written about this topic. For a sampling of this account, see David L. Ransel, ed., *Village Life in Late Tsarist Russia: Olga Semyonova Tian-Shanskaia* (Bloomington: Indiana University Press, 1993), pp. 139 156; and Boris B. Gorshkov, *Peasants in Russia from Serfdom to Stalin: Accommodation, Survival, Resistance* (New York: Bloomsbury Academic, 2018).

26. Long ago Donald Mackenzie Wallace made just this observation. See *Russia: Russia of To-day*, p. 205. See also Gorshkov, *Peasants in Russia*, pp. 139–140; and Jeffrey Brooks, "The Zemstvo and the Education of the People," in *The Zemstvo in Russia: An Experiment in Local Self-Government*, edited by Terrence Emmons and Wayne Vucinich (New York: Cambridge University Press, 2011), p. 243. Like the Southern freed people, former serfs participated in a variety of forms of compensated work, from wages to sharecropping (*otrabotka*) to migrant labor. S. Volk, sostavitel,' *"Otmena krepostnogo prava: Doklady ministru vnutrennikh del o provedenii krest'ianskoi reformy, 1861–62"* (Moskva—Leningrad, SSSR: Akademiya nauk SSSR, 1950), str. 294, used the word *izdol'nik* for sharecropping, while Dmitri Murashov uses two: *izdol'shchina* (land tenancy) (which the *Bol'shoĭ éntsiklopedicheskiĭ slovar'* (Moskva, Rossiya: Norint, 1999), str. 104 also uses), describing as

the estate owner paying the peasant some part of the harvest, and *ispol'shchina* (where the peasant used the land and paid the estate owner one half of the harvest). See D. Murashov, "Provint sial;-noe dvorianstvo v kontse 50-kh—70-kh godov 19 veka. (po materialam Penzenskoĭ gubernii)." Dissertatsiia: Saratov, 2004, str. 181–183.

27. Granted the most famous of these were spearheaded by certain premier noblemen at their estates in the province.

28. Indeed, regular bazaars were held at Undory. See M.V. Rusin, Selianin Simbirskogo uezda: Khroniki i istorii sela Voskresenskogo (ono zhe Undory): materialy dlia istorii Simbirskogo dvori anstva i chastnogo zemlevladeniia v Simbirskom uezde. Napechatano v knige: P. Martynov, "Materialy dlia istorii Simbirskogo dvori anstva i chastnogo zemlevladeniia v Simbirskom uezde" (Izdanie Simbirskoĭ Gubernskoĭ Uchenoĭ Arkhivnoĭ komissii, 1903), str. 217–224.

29. For this discussion, see V. Egorov, redaktor, "Ėkonomika i Torgovlia" v sbornike *"Simbirsko-Ulyanovskiĭ kraĭ v prodvizhenie istorii Rossii"* (Ulyanovsk, Rossiya, Korporatsiia tekhnologiĭ, 2007), str. 222–287, especially str. 226–229; I.V. Astrakhantseva, IU.I. Titarenko, I.A. Chukanov, D.E. IArkov, S.A. Plaksin, "Krest'ianskoe khoziaistvo Simbirskogo kraia vo vtoroi polovne XIX—nachale XX v.v.," v ėlektronnom izdanii "Letopis' simbirskogo krest'ianstva (s drevneishikh vremën do nashikh dneĭ)," glava 18. http://els.ulspu.ru/Files/!ELS/disc/letop-simb-krest/19..html, accessed December 8, 2020; I.A. Chukanov, L.A. Shaĭpak, I.I. TSeloval'nikova, "Otmena krepostnogo prava v Simbirskoĭ gubernii," v ėlektronnom izdanii "Letopis' simbirskogo krest'ianstva (s drevneĭshikh vremën do nashikh dneĭ)," glava 9. http://els.ulspu.ru/Files/!ELS/disc/letop-simb-krest/10..html, accessed December 7, 2020; A.N. Morozova, "Narodnye promysly Simbirskoĭ gubernii" v sbornike "Istorii a i kul'tura povolzhskogo sela: traditsii i sovremennost': Materialy regional'noĭ studencheskoĭ nauchnoĭ konferentsii (29–30 oktiabria 2009 g., Ulyanovsk)" (Ulyanovsk, GSKhA, 2009), str. 108–109; IU. S. Pavlova, "Sbornaia iarmarka v Simbirske" v sbornike "Istoriia i kul'tura povolzhskogo sela: traditsii i sovremennost': Materialy regional'noĭ studencheskoĭ nauchnoĭ konferentsii (29–30 oktiabria 2009 g., Ulyanovsk)" (Ulyanovsk, GSKhA, 2009), str. 109–111; and P. Martynov, *"Seleniia Simbirskogo Uezda (materialy dlia Simbirskogo dvorianstva i chastnogo zemlevladeniia v Simbirskom uezde)"* (Simbirsk, Rossiya: izdanie Simbirskoĭ gubernskoĭ uchenoĭ komissii, 1903), str. 30–32. (For the final quote, see Chukanov et al.) For helpful and concise descriptions of historiographical examinations and the economic development of peasant society before and after emancipation, see Elise Kimerling Wirtschafter, *Social Identity in Imperial Russia* (DeKalb, IL: Northern Illinois University Press, 1997), pp. 108–117; and Gorshkov, *Peasants in Russia*, pp. 33–67 and 157.

30. Indeed, this is exactly the point that Jeffrey Burds makes in "The Roots of Ambivalence: Peasant Labor Migration as a Threat to Village Security," in his *Peasant Dreams and Market Politics: Labor Migration and the Russian Village, 1861–1905* (Pittsburgh: University of Pittsburgh Press, 1998), pp. 17–40, especially pp. 27–29.

31. Arguing against the "Russian serfs as isolated, parochial, and immobile" paradigm, Boris B. Gorshkov has explained that well before emancipation, serfs were a very mobile lot. See his "Serfs on the Move: Peasant Seasonal Migration in Pre-Reform Russia, 1800–61," *Kritika: Explorations in Russian and Eurasian History* 1:4 (Fall 2000) (New Series), pp. 627–656, which considers the provinces in the Central Industrial Region, including Iaroslav, Tver, Kostroma, Kaluga, Moscow, Vladimir, Nizhnii Novgorod, Tula, and Riazan. However, to be sure, there was a marked uptick in mobility after emancipation.

32. For a solid overview, see W. Edgar's "Russia's Conflict with Hunger" and M. Halstead's "Politics of the Russian Famine," both in *American Review of Reviews* 5 (1892), pp. 572, 576, and 579; Richard G. Robbins, Jr., *Famine in Russia 1891–1892: The Imperial Government Responds to a Crisis* (New York: Columbia University Press, 1975), p. 19; and "The Famine," *Soviet Russia: A Monthly Journal of Information* 5:4 (October 1921), pp. 138–142. For the argument that this famine devastated the Middle Volga River region, see V. Ginev, *"Narodnicheskoe dvizhenie v srednem Povolzh'e: 70-e gody 19 veka"* (Moskva, SSSR: Nauka, 1966), str. 16.

33. Boris N. Mironov, *The Standard of Living and Revolutions in Imperial Russia, 1700–1917*, edited by Gregory L. Freeze (New York: Routledge, 2012), pp. 398–399.

34. Kalendar' Simbirskoĭ Gubernii (visokosnyĭ), Simbirsk, Rossiya: Izdanie Simbirskogo Gubernskogo pravleniia, 1880, str. 83.

35. Indeed, on the day of his assassination, Alexander II had signed a decree that, had his heir not cancelled it, would have set the country on a very slow course toward a constitutional monarchy.

36. For an account of this story, see my chapter "Praskovia's Redemption: A Case Study of a Russian Noblewoman's Self Cloistering," in *Cultural Identity and Civil Society in Russia and Eastern Europe: Essays in Memory of Charles E. Timberlake*, edited by Andrew Kier Wise, David M. Borgmeyer, Nicole Monnier, and Byron T. Scott (Newcastle upon Tyne, UK: Cambridge Scholars, 2012), pp. 112–124.

37. Regarding the bill of sale, see Dokument "Statskiĭ Sovetnik V.P. Yazykov, prodavshiĭ imushchestvo Simbirskomu kuptsu F.S. Stepanovu 16 dekabria." GAUO, f.477, opis' 3, dok.71.1.25, and Dokument "Yazykovskaia Sukonnaĭa fabrika" GAUO, f.137, opis' 4, d.105, 1.79 (1864–1866 gg.); Aunovskiĭ, "Sukonnye fabriki," str. 82–102; and P. Martynov, *"Gorod Simbirsk za 250 let*

ego sushchestvovaniia: sistematicheskiĭ sbornik istoricheskikh svedeniĭ o g. Simbirske" (Simbirsk, Rossiya: Tipografii a gubernskogo pravleniia, 1898), str. 22; and *"Selo Yazykovo: Yazykovskaia volost"* (Simbirsk, Rossiya, 1903), str. 69–71. In 1881, the sale to Stepanov included 3,645 *desiatiny*. Given that the Land Transfer Charter in March 1862 indicated that Vasili Yazykov was left with 5,231 *desiatiny*, this is a considerable discrepancy. Records of the village in 1903 indicate that it had 175 households, with a total population of 1,188 people (567 men and 621 women). Since we know that 422 souls (men), 160 of whom were factory workers, were listed in the 1862 Land Transfer Charter, we can surmise that there were approximately 900–1,000 people in the village in that year. Martynov argued that, although the village had grown in total numbers by approximately 200 people, this increase was negligible compared to the dramatic rise in Russia's population in the second half of the 19th century. He explained that, in addition to many leaving the village for the cities during these years, some must have succumbed to the famines that swept through the region.

38. By 1900, 18 of the province's 33 factories were still operating, and one of the *most* productive was the factory at Yazykovo Selo. See Egorov, "Ėkonomika i Torgovlia," str. 222; N. Rakov, "Yazykovskiĭ park," stat'ia v *Ulyanovskoĭ-Simbirskoĭ Ėntsiklopedii*, T.2 (Ulyanovsk, Simbirskaia kniga 2004), str. 473; and Martynov, *"Selo Yazykovo."*

39. See both Avdonin, *"Pod sen'iu Yazykovskikh Muz,"* and Aunovskiĭ, "Sukonnye fabriki."

40. Although the first general census of the Russian empire was in 1897, it is a well-known fact that between 1850 and 1900 the Russian population doubled in size. Therefore, unless Yazykovo Selo was unique and truly experienced no increase in its population between 1862 and 1881, it is plausible to infer that there was considerable out-migration during the period under review.

41. Vasili Yazykov received an award of excellence from the emperor for his swift execution of the Statutory Charter. This award (*Ukazannoe otlichie za vypolnenie osvobozhdeniia kres'ian*, translated as "The Specified Distinction of Fulfilling the Emancipation of the Peasant") was bestowed on Yazykov on April 17, 1863. See his logbook of service.

42. See both Avdonin, *"Pod sen'iu Yazykovskikh Muz,"* and Aunovskiĭ, "Sukonnye fabriki."

43. I base this statement on informal conversations I had with a number of local historians in Ulyanovsk.

44. G.R. Tairova, "Simbirskoe dvorianstvo i proekty agrarnogo preobrazovaniia Rossii," v sbornike "Istoriia i kul'tura povolzhskogo sela: traditsii i sovremennost': Materialy regiona'noĭ studencheskoĭ nauchnoĭ konferentsii (Ulyanovsk, GSKhA, 2009) str. 40–42. See also Thomas Marsden, *The Crisis of Religious Toleration in Imperial*

Russia: Bibikov's System for the Old Believers, 1841–1855 (Oxford Historical Monographs) (Oxford: Oxford University Press, 2015), p. 190, where the author points out that capitalist tendencies were often suspected of threatening national integrity.

45. E. Karamysheva, "Istoriia naselennogo punkta: Undory." Moia malaia rodina, 16 fevrali a 2011. http://rodina-portal.ru/settlements/history/id/7300100004600, accessed August 19, 2014.

46. See Tracy Dennison, "Why and How Were Russian Serfs Freed? Making Sense of the 1861 Emancipation Act (A Framework for a New Project)," meeting of the Caltech Early Modern Group, March 16, 2012, http://www.hss.caltech.edu/~jlr/events/Dennison-EMGV.pdf, accessed September 15, 2014, pp. 1–16, especially pp. 11 and 15; A. Korelin, *"Dvorianstvo v poreformennoi Rossii, 1861–1904 gg.: sostav, chislennost,' korporativnai a organizatsiia"* (Moskva, SSSR: Nauka, 1979), str. 251; Mironov, *The Standard of Living*, p. 398; and L.M. Ivanov, "Krest'ianskoe dvizhenie v Rossii v 1861–1869 gg." Sbornik dokumentov (Moskva, SSSR, izdatel'stvo Mysl', 1964), str. 11–12. See also the conclusion in Chukanov, "Otmena krepostnogo prava v Simbirskoi gubernii," as well as Gorshkov, *Peasants in Russia*, p. 136.

47. Ivanov, "Krest'ianskoe dvizhenie," str. 399–400. Ginev also makes clear that outright rejection of plots was common in the Middle Volga River region. See Ginev, *"Narodnicheskoe dvizhenie,"* str. 19. For the proverb, see Burds, *Peasant Dreams*, p. 15.

48. See Allan K. Wildman, "The Defining Moment: Land Charters and the Post-Emancipation Agrarian Settlement in Russia, 1861–1863," in *The Carl Beck Papers in Russian & East European Studies*, No. 1205 (Pittsburgh: Center for Russian and East European Studies, University of Pittsburgh, 1996), p. 2; Seton-Watson, *Russian Empire*, p. 396; Ivanov, "Krest'ianskoe dvizhenie," str. 11–12, and 41; and P.A. Zaionchkovskiy, redaktor, *"Krestyanskoe dvizhenie v Rossii v 1870–1880 gg."* Sbornik dokumentov (Moskva, SSSR: Nauka, 1968). Vvedeniye N.M. Druzhinina, str. 11. Steven Nafziger has explained that by 1877 about 80 percent of former serfs had entered into Redemption Agreements. But this progress was uneven. For example, while in the far western provinces almost all estates had agreements, in the central provinces (where Simbirsk Province was located) only about 55 percent had them. See Nafziger's paper "Russian Serfdom and Emancipation: New Empirical Evidence," http://economics.yale.edu/sites/default/files/nafziger-121210.pdf, accessed and cited with the author's permission, September 8, 2019.

49. Among others, Peter Gatrell makes this point. See his "The Meaning of the Great Reforms in Russian Economic History," in *Russia's Great Reforms, 1855–1881*, edited by Ben Eklof, John Bushnell, and Larissa Zakharova (Bloomington: Indiana University Press, 1994), p. 86 in particular.

50. Clifton L. Ganus, Jr., "The Freedmen's Bureau in Mississippi," PhD dissertation, Tulane University, 1953, pp. 184–188 and 197. Furthermore, why would they sign a contract if they expected to receive land allotments?

51. The contract was with four individuals: Lewis, Britt, Vini, and Ranson (ages forty-five, twenty-eight, twenty-five, and five, respectively). Slave Inventory, Quitman Family Papers, Box 3, Folder 31, University of the South, Sewanee, TN.

52. William Storrow Lovell Plantation Records, 1866–1887, Quitman Family Papers #616, Collection Number 00436, Folder 1, Volumes 1–3, Southern Historical Collection at the Louis Round Wilson Special Collections Library, University of North Carolina at Chapel Hill (hereafter referred to as Lovell Plantation Records, Vol. 1, 2, or 3, and page number for citation).

53. This phenomenon of elites utilizing their kin and connections to conduct professional and family business before institutions (such as banks) became the norm, as well as afterward, either to circumvent them or because it was easier, is the subject of Sergei Antonov's *Bankrupts and Usurers of Imperial Russia: Debt, Property, and the Law in the Age of Dostoyevsky and Tolstoy* (Cambridge: Harvard University Press, 2016).

54. Actually, Michael Wayne has argued that cotton was only king for those planters who could attract and maintain labor pools every year, for years. In this sense, Palmyra Plantation was, indeed, exceptional. See "Ante-Bellum Planters in the Post-Bellum South: The Natchez District, 1860–1880," PhD dissertation, Yale University, 1979, pp. 68–69.

55. Janet Sharp Hermann, *The Pursuit of a Dream* (New York: Oxford University Press, 1981), p. 173. See also Powell, *New Masters*, chapters 1 and 5, pp. 1–7 and 73–96, respectively.

56. Caroline Couper Lovell, *The Bond of the River* (Unpublished Manuscript, 1935), p. 24.

57. See table 6.3. For a description of this topic that is generally widely documented, see Beckert, *Empire of Cotton*, pp. 86, 155, 180, 286, and 335.

58. Nearly 100 miles northeast from Palmyra, Belen was roughly half the size of the former and was situated on the Yazoo River. Presumably it did not suffer from the war's ravages as did Palmyra. John Quitman named the plantation after the Belen Causeway, which connected Chapultepec and Mexico City, where he participated in the siege during the Mexican-American War. There is very little surviving material about Belen.

59. Lovell Plantation Records, Vol. 1, pp. 1–7.

60. As a result of its rerouting, the river's length in this area was shortened by 20 miles.

61. For the above discussion, see Hermann, *Pursuit*, pp. 116–119 and 132–136.

62. *Ibid.*, p. 135.

63. Powell, *New Masters*, p. 122, and *passim*.

64. See Vernon Lane Wharton, *The Negro in Mississippi: 1865–1890* (New York: Harper & Row, 1965), pp. 63 and 120.

65. John C. Rodrigue, *Reconstruction in the Cane Fields: From Slavery to Free Labor in Louisiana's Sugar Parishes, 1862–1880* (Baton Rouge: Louisiana State University Press, 2001), pp. 71–76. Rodrigue focuses on contrasting the labor patterns and forms of compensation in the sugar parishes after emancipation with the cotton plantations in the Mississippi Delta region.

66. Beckert, *Empire of Cotton*, p. 286.

67. Gerald David Jaynes, *Branches without Roots: Genesis of the Black Working Class in the American South, 1862–1882* (New York: Oxford University Press, 1986), pp. 15, 35, 244, and 313–320. Also reminiscent of both the Stanziani and the Beckert "stages" theses, in his review of *Branches without Roots*, Harold D. Woodman noted that, when talking about labor in the post-emancipation South, it is important to remember that arrangements were not uniform, and the "system" was evolving—with some plantations showing "efficient form[s] of production using modern management techniques and taking advantage of economies of scale." See *"Branches without Roots: Genesis of the Black Working Class in the American South, 1862–1882. By Gerald David Jaynes,"* *Journal of Southern History* 53:1 (February 1987), pp. 119–121 (quote on p. 120).

68. William Storrow Lovell to Joseph Lovell, January 25, 1868, Lovell Collection, Box 1, Set 57, University of the South, Sewanee, TN.

69. Hermann, *Pursuit*, p. 138. It is interesting to contrast this amount with the 790 bales produced at the Davis plantations, which together comprised approximately 2,000 acres. See Thavolia Glymph, "The Second Middle Passage: The Transition from Slavery to Freedom at Davis Bend, Mississippi," PhD dissertation, Purdue University, 1994, p. 271.

70. "Cost of Producing Cotton: The Palmyra Plantation of Col. Starr Lovell," *New Orleans Times*, March 15, 1876.

71. See Aiken, "The Evolution of Cotton Ginning," especially pp. 199–201.

72. When discussing a "cotton gin," one can mean a plant where, in a building that might resemble a barn, freshly picked cotton was delivered and processed—that is, its fiber was separated from its sticky seeds, dried, and then baled, or "pressed" in a baling machine. But this term can also mean the actual machine that separated the fiber from the seeds, which was also called a gin stand. Most pre–Civil War gin stands were around six feet wide and twelve feet long, with a sixty-saw set of "teeth" or hooks, or small spokes on the roller that pulled the cotton through the machine to clean (or separate) it. It had the capacity to gin three or four bales of cotton a day. See Aiken, "The Evolution of Cotton Ginning," p. 199.

73. Lovell Plantation Records, Vol. 1, pp. 2 and 4.

74. *De Bow's Review* XXXVIII–XXXIX (1869), p. 609; William C. Harris, *Presidential Reconstruction in Mississippi* (Baton Rouge: Louisiana State University Press, 1967), chapter 9,

"Problems of Agricultural Recovery," pp. 154–185; and John C. Willis, *Forgotten Time: The Yazoo-Mississippi Delta after the Civil War* (Charlottesville: University Press of Virginia, 2000), p. 38. See also Roger L. Ransom and Richard Sutch, *One Kind of Freedom: The Economic Consequences of Emancipation* (Cambridge: Cambridge University Press, 1977), pp. 56–105.

75. Lovell, *Bend of the River*, p. 13. On p. 205, she estimated that there were 1,500 African Americans on the entire island.

76. Lovell Plantation Records, Vol. III, p. 15.

77. Lovell Plantation Records, Vol. 1, pp. 26, 45, and 91. In the 1880s, he had "20 teams" (see Vol. III, p. 99). A careful reading of all Lovell's plantation records shows that he routinely went over to visit the Perkins Place to procure, lend, or swap laborers for short or seasonal stints. For a sampling, see Lovell Plantation Records, Vol. I, pp. 65, 69, 77, 78, 94, and 104–106; and Vol. II, pp. 8, 30, and 39. In 1850, John Perkins, Sr., was estimated to be one of the wealthiest planters in Louisiana. His plantations at "the Place" were Hapaka and Somerset. In 1857, his net worth included 250 slaves, and the property was valued at $600,000. See http://sites.rootsweb.com/~lamadiso/perkins/perkins.htm, accessed January 16, 2021.

78. Wayne, "Ante-Bellum Planters," pp. 184–185.

79. Wayne, "Ante-Bellum Planters," pp. 191–197; Willis, *Forgotten Time*, pp. 32 and 38–39; and Lovell Plantation Records, Volumes 1–3. For the 1880s and beyond, consult Lovell Plantation Records, Volumes 2–3. In 1884, Lovell did note that one of his squad leaders returned with "a good many hands ... [now] I shall have all the hands I want [need?]." See Vol. II, p. 149.

80. Note that, as I indicated in chapter 4, "sharecropping" was a generic term that could mean many things and produce many variations, such as "share wages" (that is, cash wages for a specific job, or a specific time period) or "share renting" (renting land for some or all of the crop that the renter would pay to the landowner). Sometimes victuals and supplies, including mules and equipment were provided, while at other times the renter was expected to provide some or all of these. See Ransom and Sutch, *One Kind of Freedom*, p. 88.

81. This is one of the central arguments in Willis, *Forgotten Time*.

82. For a sampling, see Lovell Plantation Records, Vol. I, pp. 9, 11–14, 22, 23, 26–27, 38, 43–46, 49–57, 62, 65, 72, 74, 76, 78, 80, 85, and 92. For an informative discussion of the factor business before and after the Civil War, see Harold D. Woodman, *King Cotton and His Retainers: Financing and Marketing the Cotton Crop of the South, 1800–1925* (Hopkins, MN: Beard Books, 2000), pp. 246–303. Speaking to one aspect of what Sven Beckert would later echo in *Empire of Cotton* (pp. 286–320), Woodman explains the adjustments that were made in the factorage

business after emancipation in order to assist the cotton industry. Advances were made and supplies were provided, all on credit, with increasingly higher interest rates. They were sellers and suppliers. Above all, it was the expansion of the railroads and communications that increasingly rendered local factorages obsolete. In addition to the local plantation "stores" (which also seem to parallel the community gins that appeared) replacing the antebellum factors, distant furnishing merchants filled the void. Thus, it is not surprising to see in Lovell's records monies sent to New York and even Toronto. See Vol. I, pp. 6 and 34.

83. Lovell Plantation Records, Vol. I, pp. 61 and 102; Vol. II, pp. 31–38, 57, 99, 104, 130, 132, and 143; and Vol. III, pp. 8, 38, and 63.

84. Hermann, *Pursuit*, p. 135. With respect to identifying how $12,000 was paid to whom and at what rates, the variables to take into consideration are great. For example, we know that between the years of 1869 and 1875, a Quitman/Lovell relative, Lemuel Connor, compensated his laborers with rolling combinations of board, rations, and cash income that ranged between $70 and $300, half of which would be retained for the end of the year. See Wharton, *Negro in Mississippi*, p. 66. These could change over the course of a season, and they could also be altered depending on whether rations and tenancy rates were factored in. As for the wages Lovell paid in 1879, given that he had three squads comprising approximately twenty hands each, this figure might be considered generous. However, the records show that, as always, labor was fluid at Palmyra Plantation: additional, temporary hands were hired for specific jobs or time periods, and, especially, work on the ditch was ongoing. Therefore, that figure may well have included many other "employees" in addition to squad hands. Finally, it could mean that this amount was paid to a labor factor, possibly correcting an overdue debt.

85. See Lovell, *Bend of the River*, pp. 24–25. See also Beckert, *Empire of Cotton*, pp. 286–320, where he describes this shift in detail. For the quote (and where Beckert cites Steven Hahn's observation), see p. 288.

86. Although sources mention and/or discuss the phenomenon of migrant labor during this period, it is difficult to know exactly who the labor agents/suppliers were since, as far as I have been able to discern, it was largely an aspect of an informal, shadow economy in this period of adjustments and adaptations. For example, see Willis, *Forgotten Time*, pp. 4, 14, 105, and 184.

87. For example, see in the following: *Soards' New Orleans City Directories*, 1866–1878 (specifically, 1875, pp. 256, 518, and 553; 1877, pp. 731–733; and 1878, pp. 183, 341, and 351). See also *Edwards Annual Directory, New Orleans*, 1870, pp. 687–690, and 1872, pp. 722–723.

88. See William G. Thomas III, Richard G. Healey, and Ian Cottingham, "Reconstructing African American Mobility after Emancipation,

1865–67," *Social Science History* 41:4 (Winter 2017), pp. 673–704. In this regard, we see a similarity to the "passport" system in the Russian context, specifically with respect to the village elders being in charge of their issuance and distribution.

89. See Wharton, *Negro in Mississippi*, pp. 107–113; Herman "Skip" Mason, Jr., *Politics, Civil Rights, and Law in Black Atlanta, 1870–1970* (Charleston, SC: Arcadia, 2000), p. 56; Story Matkin-Rawn, "'The Great Negro State of the Country': Arkansas's Reconstruction and the Other Great Migration," *Arkansas Historical Quarterly* 72:1 (Spring 2013), pp. 1–2, 8–9, and 21–24; Joseph P. Reidy, *From Slavery to Agrarian Capitalism in the Cotton Plantation: Central Georgia, 1800–1880* (Chapel Hill: University of North Carolina Press, 1992), pp. 122, 232, and 310; and William C. Harris, *The Day of the Carpetbagger in Mississippi* (Baton Rouge: Louisiana State University Press, 1979), pp. 508–510. Harris points out that the Delta River Counties census numbers support this point, quoting the population numbers of 115,298 in 1870 to 187,812 in 1880, with another great migration to Kansas beginning in 1879.

90. For a sampling, see Lovell Plantation Records, Vol. I, p. 45; Vol. II, pp. 99 and 132; and Vol. III, p. 63.

91. List of Indigenous Inhabitants, BRFAL, Davis Bend, 1865–1866, RG 105, Volume 123, Box 39 (Mississippi), M1907, Roll 16, NA, 325; Slave Inventory, Quitman Family Papers, Box 3, Folder 31, University of the South, Sewanee, TN; Lovell Plantation Records, Vol. I, pp. 26, 34, 37, 45, 62, and 74, and Vol. III, pp. 63 and 69; and U.S. Censuses, 1870, Agricultural Schedule, Warren County, Mississippi, MDAH.

92. Lovell Plantation Records, Vol. I, pp. 35–37, 39, 40–41, 45, 66, 72, and 77–78; and Vol. II, pp. 28 and 95.

93. Lovell Plantation Records, Vol. II, pp. 34, 42–45, and 91–92; and Vol. III, p. 109. "R" refers to the "Rosedale Squad." The squads were named after the plantation, Palmyra; the "house," Rosedale, at Palmyra; and the leaders or overseers, such as "Jeter Squad," "Adams Squad," and the like. For further examples of Lovell's praise, see Vol. I, pp. 39, 40–42, 45, 46, 47, 56, 61, 63, 64, 65, 66, 67, 69, 75–80, 84–86, 89, and 96–97; and Vol. II, p. 94.

94. Lovell Plantation Records, Vol. II, pp. 62, 66, 87, 135, 139, and 156.

95. Hermann, *Pursuit*, p. 151.

96. Lovell Plantation Records, Vol. I, pp. 62–64; Hermann, *Pursuit*, p. 201.

97. Lovell Plantation Records, Vol. I, pp. 63 and 68. See also table 6.5.

98. Lovell Plantation Records, Vol. II, pp. 67, 69–73, 155–156, and 162. Besides the floods and the constant search to find and secure seasonal labor, another example of the typical stressors that Lovell experienced came in September 1882, when a steamer ran aground and he lost 63 bales of cotton. Vol. II, p. 93.

99. See Wharton, *Negro in Mississippi*, p. 112; Lovell Plantation Records, Vol. II, p. 18–30.

100. For notations regarding challenging the U.S. government for compensation, see Lovell Plantation Records, Vol. I, pp. 9, 21, and 41, and see pp. 47–60 for a detailed accounting inventory for the year 1874 only, which suggests that Lovell paid out stipends or "allowances" to all the family members, of which the amounts could vary greatly. For typical examples of financial entries, suggesting payments for contracts, and credits and debits with cotton factors, see Vol. I, pp. 14, 17, 24, 43–44, 46, 57, 62, 72, 74, and 78, and Vol. II, pp. 30 and 62. For the statement borrowing the $22,550, see Quitman Family Papers, Lovell Family Papers, Box 1, Set 79, University of the South, Sewanee, TN. For other examples of financial matters, see Box 1, Set 79.

101. Lovell Plantation Records, Vol. I, pp. 49–60.

102. Lovell Plantation Records, Vol. II, pp. 32–37 and 49. William Storrow Lovell's brother Joseph was married to his wife Tonie's sister, Louisa.

103. U.S. Census, 1880, Agricultural Schedule, Warren County, Mississippi, MDAH. In today's money that would be the equivalent of $3 million.

104. See Wayne, "Ante-Bellum Planters," pp. 122–142; Seymour Becker, *Nobility and Privilege in Late Imperial Russia* (DeKalb: Northern Illinois University Press, 1986); Hermann, *Pursuit*, p. 214; and George S. Pabis, *Daily Life along the Mississippi* (Westport, CT: Greenwood Press, 2007), p. 151.

105. See Richard Follette, Eric Foner, and Walter Johnson, *Slavery's Ghost: The Problem of Freedom in the Age of Emancipation* (Baltimore: Johns Hopkins University Press, 2011), pp. 52–54.

106. For a thorough discussion of this idea, see Eric Foner, *Free Soil, Free Labor, Free Men: The Ideology of the Republican Party before the Civil War* (New York: Oxford University Press, 1995).

107. Follette, Foner, and Johnson, *Slavery's Ghost*, pp. 1. See also Lawrence W. Levine, *Black Culture and Black Consciousness: Afro-American Folk Thought from Slavery to Freedom* (New York: Oxford University Press, 2007), p. xviii.

108. See chapter 2 regarding the Lovell brothers being scapegoated and chapter 3 regarding the issue of the Quitmans/Lovells' amnesty oaths.

109. Even though Russian merchants typically dealt in cash regardless of that law, Stepanov's use of wage labor coincided with the overall trend of it making its appearance in Russia.

110. As both Russian and American history have told us, post–1880 developments in each country also presented challenges for the freed people and their descendants with respect to freedom and labor obligations. For a sampling of the American portion, see Leon F. Litwack, *Trouble in Mind: Black Southerners in the Age of Jim Crow* (New York: Vintage, 1998); Neil R. McMillen, *Dark Journey: Black Mississippians in the Age of Jim Crow* (Champaign: University of Illinois Press, 1989); and Edward Ayers, *The Promise of the New South: Life after Reconstruction* (New York: Oxford University Press, 1992). For the sampling of the Russian portion, see David Moon, *The Russian Peasantry: The World the Peasants Made* (London: Addison Wesley Longman, 1999), and Gorshkov, *Peasants in Russia*.

111. The sources for table 6.1 include the 1850 U.S. Census, Agriculture Schedule, Warren County, Mississippi; 1850 Population Schedule, Mississippi; 1860 U.S. Census, Agriculture Schedule, Warren County, Mississippi; 1860 Agriculture Schedule and Slave Population Schedule, all in the Mississippi Department of Archives and History (MDAH); and Hermann, *Pursuit*, pp. 60, 85, 134, and 138.

112. The sources for table 6.2 include the following: for each year cited Personal Tax Roll, Warren County, MDAH; 1870 and 1880 U.S. Censuses, Warren County, Mississippi; 1850 and 1860 Agriculture Schedule and Slave Population Schedule, MDAH; and Hermann, *Pursuit*, pp. 21–25 and 152.

113. For New York prices, see M. B. Hammond, *The Cotton Industry* (New York: Macmillan, 1897), reproduced in Gavin Wright, "Cotton Competition and the Post Bellum Recovery of the American South," *Journal of Economic History* 34 (September 1974), p. 611. For New Orleans prices, see Harris, *Presidential Reconstruction*, pp. 79, 166, and 181; Stephen Cresswell, *Rednecks, Redeemers, and Race: Mississippi after Reconstruction, 1877–1917* (Jackson: University Press of Mississippi, 2006), pp. 1–13; and Hermann, *Pursuit*, pp. 152 and 209. It should be pointed out that the weight in pounds per bale of cotton could vary. Some sources have the amount as 400 pounds, while others make it 500 pounds. See John S. McNeily, "War and Reconstruction in Mississippi, 1863–1900," *Publications of the Mississippi Historical Society, Centenary Series* II (1918), pp. 135–535. For a detailed table for New Orleans prices, see James E. Boyle, *Cotton and the New Orleans Cotton Exchange: A Century of Commercial Evolution* (Garden City, NJ: Country Life Press, 1934), pp. 180–181.

114. U.S. Censuses, 1870 and 1880, Agricultural Schedule, Warren County, Mississippi, MDAH.

115. Vol. I, pp. 1–7, 17, 41, 68, and 89, and Vol. III, p. 31; Hermann, *Pursuit*, pp. 116–119, 132, 136, 138, and 208.

Chapter 7

1. Caroline Couper Lovell, *The Bend of the River* (Unpublished Manuscript, 1935), pp. 83–84; and *Mississippi Slave Narratives from the Federal Writers' Project, 1936–1938* (Bedford, MA: Applewood Books, 2006), pp. 5, 60, 64, 74, 87–88, 127, 129, 167, and 170 (see p. 127 for quote). In *Long Past Slavery: Representing Race in the*

Federal Writers' Project (Chapel Hill: University of North Carolina Press, 2016), Catherine A. Stewart analyzes the majority white interviewers' techniques and formulaic questions as compared with those of the minority of African American questioners, as well as the former slaves' responses to each set of inquiries. Not surprisingly, Stewart discovered differing goals and agendas, depending on the questioner's race, even with respect to documenting the "dialect" of interviewee, with the former privileging a uniform dialect most similar to the folk stories of Joel Chandler Harris, and the latter avoiding stereotypical *patois.* In addition, the former focused on superstitions, white paternalism, and black dependence, while the latter focused on civic participation, each constructing very different accounts of black identity. The interviewees, elderly when the research took place during the years of the Great Depression, understood that their stories had value, and indeed they gained access to clothes and other needed items as a result of participating in the study. In addition, they gave different answers depending on the questioner's race. Therefore, the researcher must utilize the narratives with caution.

2. For Allen quote, see *Mississippi Slave Narratives*, p. 5. For literacy rates, see Roger L. Ransom and Richard Sutch, *One Kind of Freedom: The Economic Consequences of Emancipation* (Cambridge: Cambridge University Press, 1977), p. 15, and Janet D. Cornelius, *When I Can Read My Title Clear: Literacy, Slavery and Religion in the Antebellum South* (Columbia: University of South Carolina Press, 1992).

3. Chapter 3 addressed the peasants' suspicions with respect to emancipation's authenticity as it had been presented to them in the spring of 1861; chapter 4 considered their concerns with freedom being contingent on their signing a Statutory Charter; and chapter 6 dealt with their passive resistance to labor obligations.

4. For sources consulted, see Ben Eklof, *Russian Peasant Schools: Officialdom, Village Culture, and Popular Pedagogy, 1861–1914* (Berkeley: University of California Press, 1990), pp. 16 and 34; and "Peasants and Schools," in Ben Eklof and Stephen P. Frank, eds., *The World of the Russian Peasant: Post-Emancipation Culture and Society* (Boston: Unwin Hyman, 1990), pp. 115–132. For a sobering description of rural parish schools and peasant attitudes toward them, and education in general, see V. Nazar'ev, "Sovremennaĭa glush,'" *Zhurnal "Vestnik Evropy,"* Nomer 3 (1876), str. 10–36, which the author dedicated to Vasili Yazykov's uncle, poet Nikolai Yazykov. Nazar'ev was a colleague of Ilya Ulyanov, the inspector of public schools in Simbirsk Province (1869–1886) and the father of Vladimir Ilyich Ulyanov, otherwise known as Lenin.

5. Eklof, *Russian Peasant Schools*, pp. 16 and 34; David Moon, *The Russian Peasantry: The World the Peasants Made* (London: Addison Wesley Longman, 1999), pp. 345–346; D.

Murashov, "Provintsial'noe dvorĭanstvo v kontse 50-kh—70-kh godov 19 veka. (po materialam Penzenskoĭ gubernii)." Dissertat siĭ a: Saratov, 2004, str. 181; and A. Korelin, *"Dvorĭanstvo v poreformennoĭ Rossii, 1861–1904 gg.: sostav, chislennost,' korporativnaĭa organizat sii a"* (Moskva, SSSR: Nauka, 1979). Both Eklof and Moon maintain that peasants embraced education as long as they were in charge.

6. As part of the Great Reforms, of which emancipation was one, the *zemstvo* was the institutional framework for local governments across Russia created in 1864. It was basically a council comprising elected representatives drawn from the ranks of the noble landlords, townspeople, and peasant communes. Its purpose was to draw professionals into a governing apparatus that would be responsible for a variety of local issues such as health, education, relief for the poor, libraries, and the oversight and direction of trade, agricultural development, and industry. In a sense, local institutions that previously existed separately were combined into one system. For a thorough understanding, see Terrence Emmons and Wayne Vucinich, eds., *The Zemstvo in Russia: An Experiment in Local Self-Government* (New York: Cambridge University Press, 2011), especially chapter 4, "The Zemstvo and the Peasantry," by Dorothy Atkinson, pp. 79–132, and chapter 7, "The Zemstvo and the Education of the People," by Jeffrey Brooks, pp. 243–278. For a discussion of the zemstvos (*zemstva*) in Simbirsk Province, where it notes that the work really did not get fully underway until the turn of the century, see T.A. Kobzeva, A.V. Kobzev, "Rol' zemskikh uchrezhdeniĭ v preobrazovanii simbirskoĭ derevni," v ėlektronnom izdanii "Letopis' simbirskogo krest'ĭanstva (s drevneĭshikh vremën do nashikh dneĭ)," glava 15. http://els.ulspu.ru/Files/!ELS/disc/letop-simbkrest/16..html, accessed January 31, 2021. Eklof, in *Russian Peasant Schools*, p. 71, downplays the role of the *zemstvo* in public education.

7. Two of Lenin's sisters, Anna and Olga, would become teachers in Simbirsk Province.

8. T. Pon'ko, *"Istoriĭa Otechestvennoĭ kul'tury IX—XXI vekov"* (Moskva, Rossiya: Rossiĭskiĭ Universitet Druzhby Narodov, 2009), str. 198, 203–204, and 244–247; Eklof, *Russian Peasant Schools*, pp. 32, 35, and 65.

9. In 1863, the Russian government issued a University Statute that reorganized colleges and universities into essentially self-governing organizations and granted sweeping freedoms to faculty and students. In 1864, an Elementary School Statute set in motion the idea for public schools that would be governed and managed locally. In his chapter "Peasants and Schools" in *The World of the Russian Peasants* , Eklof cites the following figures: in 1856, 1/143; 1878, 1/77; and 1896, 1/33 (see p. 116). See p. 73 in Eklof's *Russian Peasant Schools* for the expression "comic unreality."

10. See the chapter "The Children's Crusade" in Avrahm Yarmolinsky, *Road to Revolution*

(Princeton: Princeton University Press, 1986), pp. 189–209; Cathy Frierson, *Peasant Icons: Representations of Rural People in Late Nineteenth-Century Russia* (New York: Oxford University Press, 1993), pp. 1–25 and 68; Theodore H. von Laue, "The Fate of Capitalism in Russia: The Narodnik Version," *American Slavic and East European Review* 13:1 (February 1954), pp. 11–28; and Daniel Field, "Peasants and Propagandists in the Russian Movement to the People," *Journal of Modern History* 59:3 (September 1987), pp. 415–438. The cool reception with which these intellects were met by the peasants is both notorious and evidence of their distrust of outsiders. Still, Daniel Field has made it clear that this repeated story is a tale rooted in the Danilov Affair (see p. 423).

11. L.M. Ivanov, "Krest'ianskoe dvizhenie v Rossii v 1861–1869 gg." Sbornik dokumentov (Moskva, SSSR, izdatel'stvo Mysl', 1964), str. 26–27, and footnote #54 on str. 162–165.

12. Eklof, *Russian Peasant Schools*, pp. 66, 128–129, and 135–136.

13. See Nazar'ev, "Sovremennaia glush,'" especially str. 30–33.

14. It is an overstatement to call it a hospital. More correctly, it was a kind of a health clinic with very basic medical care and attention, such as a few beds, bandages, herbs, and liquor.

15. P. Martynov, *"Gorod Simbirsk za 250 let ego sushchestvovaniia: sistematicheskiĭ sbornik istoricheskikh svedeniĭ o g. Simbirske"* (Simbirsk, Rossiya: Tipografii a gubernskogo pravleniia, 1898), str. 3–4; E. Karamysheva, "Istoriia naselennogo punkta: Undory." Moia malaia rodina, 16 fevralia 2011. http://rodina-portal.ru/settlements/history/id/7300100004600, accessed August 19, 2014.

16. A. Avdonin, *"Pod sen'iu Yazykovskikh Muz"* (Ulyanovsk, Rossiya: Pechatnyĭ Dvor, 1991), str. 13–34. The 15,000-ruble donation for books at Yazykovo Selo's library would be approximately $231,098 in today's U.S. dollars. See http://opoccuu.com/kurs.htm for the conversion calculation rate http://opoccuu.com/kurs.htmand http://www.westegg.com/inflation/%5D for the rate of inflation calculation (http://www.westegg.com/inflation/%5Dboth accessed January 17, 2019). The theater at Yazykovo Selo is still fully functioning, showcasing regular theatrical productions. Mikhail Stepanov's home, painted in a rich pale blue, remains, housing a music school in the village.

17. V. Radaev, "Po sledam velikikh poétov," *Zhurnal "Monomakh,"* Nomer 1 (48), 2007, str. 42–44, str. 43. Coincidentally, the younger Lovell generation, especially son Todd and his wife, Caroline, would become very active in the "Little Theatre Movement" after they left Palmyra and moved to Birmingham, Alabama, after the turn of the century. Ironically, the movement was influenced, in part, by Konstantin Stanislavski's Moscow Arts Theatre. See Tony Guzman, "The Little Theatre Movement: The Institutionalization of the European Art Film in America," *Film History* 17:2/3 (2005), pp. 261–284.

18. Nazar'ev, "Sovremennaia glush.'" Nina Bogdan, Nazar'ev's granddaughter and author of *The Desolation of Exile: A Russian Family's Odyssey* (North Charleston, SC: CreateSpace Independent Publishing Platform, 2012), has stressed that Nazar'ev cared deeply about the future of Russia and believed that the key to all Russians' betterment was public education. On his death he bequeathed his entire estate to public education in Simbirsk Province. See chapter 7, pp. 94–117. For an obscure, though telling, anecdote of yet another example of how bureaucratic red tape and/or petty principles inhibited education, see Donald Mackenzie Wallace, *Russia: Russia of To-day*, Vol. III (Boston: J.B. Millet Company, 1910), pp. 196–197.

19. As Ben Eklof has explained, the peasants may well have been unschooled, but they were not uneducated. Their classroom was the village and their family, where they learned the ways and mores of navigating their world successfully. The peasant child was not a *"tabula rasa*, but … a slate well marked with folklore, oral poetry, historical legend and social satire as well as nature lore." See "Peasant Sloth Reconsidered: Strategies of Education and Learning in Rural Russia before the Revolution," *Journal of Social History* 14:3 (Spring 1981), pp. 356–357.

20. See Bogdan, *Desolation of Exile*. Eklof includes the report of another inspector, S.I. Miropol'skiy, whose conclusions were essentially the same as Nazar'ev's. See Eklof, *Russian Peasant Schools*, p. 391.

21. T.A. Kobzeva, N.A. Dunaeva, "Sel'skaia krest'ianskaia shkola v nachale 20 veka," v élektronnom izdanii "Letopis' simbirskogo krest'ianstva (s drevneĭshikh vremën do nashikh dneĭ)," glava 14. http://els.ulspu.ru/Files/!ELS/disc/letopsimb-krest/15..html, accessed January 31, 2021.

22. For the above discussion, especially regarding literacy rates and statistics, see Eklof, *Russian Peasant Schools*, chapters 3 and 10, respectively titled "Who Built the Schools," pp. 70–96 (especially pp. 83–84), and "The Expansion of Schooling," 283–314; Brooks, "The Zemstvo and the Education of the People," pp. 243–244; and Jeffrey Burds, *Peasant Dreams and Market Politics: Labor Migration and the Russian Village, 1861–1905* (Pittsburgh: University of Pittsburgh Press, 1998), p. 178. Both Eklof and Brooks explain that the main sticking points delaying the development of education from 1861 to 1895 were a debate over universal education, the difficult logistical realities associated with it in the rural regions, and a lack of government money to finance public education. See also Jeffrey Brooks, *When Russia Learned to Read: Literacy and Popular Literature, 1861–1917* (Evanston, IL: Northwestern University Press, 2003).

23. Eklof, *Russian Peasant Schools*, pp. 85–86.

24. To Rev. George Whipple from S.G. Wright, March 28, 1865, American Missionary Association

Papers (AMA) (microfilm), University of Delaware. The Reverend George Whipple was the secretary of the AMA, and Reverend S.G. Wright was the chaplain of a "Colored Regiment."

25. Circular, Lt. A.W. Brobst, February 1865, AMA.

26. See Bureau of Refugees, Freedmen, and Abandoned Lands, School Reports, 1865–1870, RG 0775, Series #011, Mississippi, War Department, NA.

27. Michael S. Wayne, "Ante-Bellum Planters in the Post-Bellum South: The Natchez District, 1860–1880," PhD dissertation, Yale University, 1979, pp. 164–173.

28. J.P. Bardwell to Rev. M.E. Strieby, January 5, 1865, AMA.

29. For statistics, see *Extracts from Reports of Superintendents of Freedmen Compiled by Rev. Joseph Warren, D.D. From the Records in the Office of Col. John Eaton, Jr. General Superintendent of Freedmen, Department of the Tennessee and State of Arkansas Second Series, June 1864* (Vicksburg, MS: Freedmen Press Print, 1864), pp. 3 and 10. For Rowntree quotes, see James T. Currie, ed., "Freedmen at Davis Bend, April 1864," *Journal of Mississippi History* 46:2 (May 1984), pp. 120–129.

30. Lovell, *Bend of the River*, p. 87.

31. Clifton L. Ganus, Jr., "The Freedmen's Bureau in Mississippi," PhD dissertation, Tulane University, 1953, pp. 315–317; Vernon Lane Wharton, *The Negro in Mississippi: 1865–1890* (New York: Harper & Row, 1965), p. 243. See also J.P. Bardwell to Rev. M.E. Strieby, January 5, 1865, AMA.

32. *Extracts*, p. 6; J.P. Bardwell to Rev. M.E. Strieby, January 5, 1865, AMA.

33. Ganus, "Freedmen's Bureau," pp. 327–328.

34. See *Extracts*, as well as Janet Sharp Hermann, *The Pursuit of a Dream* (New York: Oxford University Press, 1981), pp. 54–56.

35. Wayne, "Ante-Bellum Planters," p. 172.

36. Justin Behrend, *Reconstructing Democracy: Grassroots Black Politics in the Deep South after the Civil War* (Athens: University of Georgia Press, 2015), p. 69.

37. Hermann, *Pursuit*, p. 183; Lovell, *Bend of the River*, p. 19.

38. See Hermann, *Pursuit*, p. 102; J.P. Bardwell to Rev. M.E. Strieby, January 5, 1865, AMA.

39. Rev. James I. Frazer to Rev. S. G. Wright, July 25, 1865, AMA; J.P. Bardwell to Rev. M.E. Strieby, November 20, 1865, AMA.

40. Report of S.B. Varney, July 1865, Roll 1, Target 3 Miscellaneous Reports from Subordinates and Staff Officers, December 1863–July 1865. BRFAL, RG 105 (Mississippi), M1914, Roll 1, NA. The Bend's hospital closed in April 1866. Hermann, *Pursuit*, p. 95.

41. *Extracts*, pp. 3 and 10; William C. Harris, *Presidential Reconstruction in Mississippi* (Baton Rouge: Louisiana State University Press, 1967), p. 85.

42. Wharton, *The Negro in Mississippi*, pp. 244–246.

43. See Lawrence L. Powell, *New Masters: Northern Planters during the Civil War and Reconstruction* (New Haven: Yale University Press, 1980), p. 94; Peter Kolchin, "Reexamining Southern Emancipation in Comparative Perspective," *Journal of Southern History* 81:1 (February 2015), p. 37; Ronald E. Butchart, *Schooling the Freed People: Teaching, Learning, and the Struggle for Black Freedom, 1861–1876* (Chapel Hill: University of North Carolina Press, 2010); and Christopher Span, *From Cotton Field to Schoolhouse: African American Education in Mississippi, 1862–1875* (Chapel Hill: University of North Carolina Press, 2009), pp. 32–36, and *passim*.

44. Lovell, *Bend of the River*, pp. 19 and 80.

45. *Mississippi Slave Narratives*, pp. 60 and 64.

46. See David W. Blight, *Race and Reunion: The Civil War in American Memory* (Cambridge: Belknap Press of Harvard University Press, 2001), chapters 2 and 3—respectively, "Regeneration and Reconstruction" and "Decoration Days"; John W. Blassingame, *The Slave Community: Plantation Life in the Antebellum South* (New York: Oxford University Press, 1979); Mitch Kachun, *Festivals of Freedom: Meaning and Memory in African American Emancipation Celebrations, 1808–1915* (Amherst: University of Massachusetts Press, 2006); Linda J. Ivanits, *Russian Folk Belief* (Armonk, NY: M.E. Sharpe, 1992), pp. 3–18, and *passim*; David Moon, *The Russian Peasantry: The World the Peasants Made* (London: Addison Wesley Longman, 1999), pp. 24, 183, and 290–296; Mary Matossian, "The Peasant Way of Life," in *The Peasant in Nineteenth-Century Russia*, edited by Wayne Vucinich (Stanford: Stanford University Press, 1968), pp. 31–38; and Roberta Reeder, ed., *Russian Folk Lyrics* (Bloomington: Indiana University Press, 1993), pp. 1–35.

47. I am grateful to Larissa Yershova, former director of the Literature Museum "The House of Yazykovs," 22 Sovetskaya Street, Ulyanovsk, Russia, for giving me a copy of this rare photograph, which is in the museum's archives.

48. For the quotes and an elaboration on what I have cited, see Ekaterina Emeliantseva, "Introduction: The Sacred before the Camera: Religious Representation and the Medium of Photography in Late Imperial Russia and the Soviet Union," *Jahrbucher fur Geschichte Osteuropas* 2 (2009), p. 167.

49. Hermann, *Pursuit*, pp. 56–57; *Vicksburg Daily Herald*, July 6, 1864; and Lovell, *Bend of the River*, p. 76.

50. J.P. Bardwell to Rev. M.E. Strieby, January 5, 1865, AMA. Obviously, the improvisation was for 1 John 3:7: "My little children, let no man deceive you."

51. Hermann, *Pursuit*, p. 64.

52. P. Martynov, *"Seleniia Simbirskogo Uezda (materialy dlia Simbirskogo dvorianstva i chastnogo zemlevladeniia v Simbirskom uezde)"* (Simbirsk, Rossiya: izdanie Simbirskoi gubernskoi

uchenoĭ komissii, 1903), str. 174. In the Eastern Orthodox Church, one's "angel day" is the feast day of the saint after whom an individual is named. Thus, in English it is variably referred to "angel day," or "name day," or "patronal feast day."

53. Blight, *Race and Reunion*, pp. 366–380.

54. Hermann, *Pursuit*, pp. 187–188. See also Noralee Frankel, *Freedom's Women: Black Women and Families in Civil War Era Mississippi (Blacks in the Diaspora)* (Bloomington: Indiana University Press, 1999), pp. 172–174.

55. See Lawrence W. Levine, *Black Culture and Black Consciousness: Afro-American Folk Thought from Slavery to Freedom* (New York: Oxford University Press, 2007), pp. 31–33, 59–61, 135, and *passim*.

56. Christine D. Worobec, *Peasant Russia: Family and Community in the Post-Emancipation Period* (DeKalb: Northern Illinois University Press, 1995), p. 14. See also Ivanits, *Russian Folk Belief*, pp. 5–12; and Reeder, *Russian Folk Lyrics*, pp. 2–7, for concise discussions of the numerous seasonal traditions and their accompanying rituals.

57. Ivanits, *Russian Folk Belief*; Reeder, *Russian Folk Lyrics*; and William H. Wiggins, Jr., *O Freedom! Afro-American Emancipation Celebrations* (Knoxville: University of Tennessee Press, 1987), pp. 25–26.

58. See Hermann, *Pursuit*, p. 150; Lovell, *Bend of the River*, pp. 80 and 85–89.

59. Hermann, *Pursuit*, pp. 182 and 213. It should be made clear that, regardless of the well-known myth that freed female slaves were anxious to adopt the middle-class socially prescribed role for women to "keep house," the economic realities of the time meant that they, too, went to the fields to help support their families.

60. See Mary Farmer-Kaiser, *Freedwomen and the Freedmen's Bureau: Race, Gender, and Public Policy in the Age of Emancipation* (New York: Fordham University Press, 2010), pp. 93–95.

61. See Peter Kolchin, *First Freedom: The Responses of Alabama's Blacks to Emancipation and Reconstruction* (Westport, CT: Greenwood Press, 1972), chapter 3, "Strengthening the Black Family," pp. 56–78, especially p. 46.

62. Frankel, *Freedom's Women*, pp. 123–126 and 164–172.

63. *Mississippi Slave Narratives*, p. 74.

64. J.P. Bardwell to Rev. M.E. Strieby, January 5, 1865, AMA. Frankel points out that state regulation had as much to do with ensuring morality and hygiene, and combatting promiscuity, as it did with legally honoring the sanctity of two people wanting to marry. See *Freedom's Women*, pp. 39–44, 80–84, and 129.

65. See Worobec, *Peasant Russia*, pp. 151–174.

66. Worobec, *Peasant Russia*, chapter 5, "Marriage: Family and Community Renewal," and chapter 6, "The Culture of Patriarchy," pp. 151–174 and 175–207, respectively (especially pp. 175–178). Worobec has made it clear that subordination

in Russian culture "must be understood in the context of both the general hierarchical structure of Russian society ... and that of environmental challenges" (see p. 185). See Svetlana Kruikova's short but extremely informative article "The Russian Peasant Family in the Second Half of the Nineteenth Century (Based on Riazan Province)," *Russian Studies in History* 38:2 (Fall 1999), pp. 31–47 (see especially pp. 35, 40–41, and 45).

67. Worobec, *Peasant Russia*, pp. 190–191.

68. See A. Avdeev, A. Blum, and I. Troitskaia, "Peasant Marriage in Nineteenth-Century Russia," *Population* 59:6 (2004), pp. 721–764. Conversely, one recent study with respect to African American marriage after emancipation, and especially with the advent of tenant farming, found that this economic arrangement had the effect of disincentivizing a woman who needed to flee a poor marriage, because it favored male hiring. Therefore, marriage, especially for the young and old, was buttressed. See Deirdre Bloome and Christopher Muller, "Tenancy and African American Marriage in the Postbellum South," *Demography* 52:5 (October 2015), pp. 1409–1430.

69. Nazar'ev, "Sovremennaĭa glush,'" pp. 29–30; M. Naĭdenov, *"Klassovaĭa bor'ba v poreformennoĭ derevne (1861–1863)"* (Moskva, SSSR: Gospolitizdat, 1955), str. 290–292.

70. See E. Karamysheva, "Istoriĭa naselennogo punkta: Undory." Moĭa malaĭa rodina, 16 fevralĭa 2011. http://rodina-portal.ru/settlements/history/id/7300100004600, accessed August 19, 2014; I. Sivoplĭas, *"Istoriĭa s kartinkami"* (Ulyanovsk, Rossiya: Artishok, 2008), str. 44–45.

71. *Mississippi Slave Narratives*, pp. 94, 97–98, 122, and 147; Behrend, *Reconstructing Democracy*, p. 73; and Lovell, *Bend of the River*, p. 80. ("Carpetbagger" was a derogatory name used by many Southern whites to describe Northern transplants.)

72. See Burds, *Peasant Dreams*, pp. 27–28; Levine, *Black Culture and Black Consciousness*, pp. 138–139. I would add here that this is one theme of Chris J. Chulos' *Converging Worlds: Religion and Community in Peasant Russia, 1861–1917* (DeKalb: Northern Illinois University Press, 2003). Chulos discusses the processes through which village and urban worlds converged as a result of emancipation. Thus, "new peasants," increasingly literate, came to the fore and began to challenge traditions and beliefs.

73. I.M. Pushkareva, "The Rural Noble Country House in Postreform Russia (Defining the Issue)," *Russian Studies in History* 42:1 (Summer 2003), pp. 70–71. Pushkareva uses this term, "polyphony," as it was used in the poem "Muza" by Evgeny Baratinsky.

Epilogue

1. Caroline Couper Lovell, *The Bend of the River* (Unpublished Manuscript, 1935), pp.

213–214; Caroline Couper Lovell to Antonia Quitman Lovell, February 11, 1894, Lovell Family Papers, Box 1, Folder 11, University of the South, Sewanee, TN.

2. William Storrow Lovell, Jr., to William Storrow Lovell, April 21, 1897, Lovell Family Papers, Box 1, Folder 43, University of the South, Sewanee, TN.

3. Janet Sharp Hermann, *The Pursuit of a Dream* (New York: Oxford University Press, 1981), pp. 223–224; Neil R. McMillen, *Dark Journey: Black Mississippians in the Age of Jim Crow* (Champaign: University of Illinois Press, 1989), pp. 186–190.

4. War Communism was the political and economic system in place during the civil war period (1918–1921) following the Bolshevik Revolution in 1917, which nationalized all industry and established a policy of confiscation of "surplus" grain and produce in order to feed conscripted soldiers and people in urban centers. *Sovkhoz* was an abbreviation of *Sovetskoe khoziaĭstvo*, or Soviet farm. They began appearing in the early 1920s after the Bolsheviks seized power. They were precursors to the *kolkhozy*, or collective farms.

5. L. Pekhtereva, "V starom parke," Simbirskiĭ Kur'er, Nomer 73 (9 ii uli a 2009).

6. David Moon, *Abolition of Serfdom in Russia, 1762–1907* (Harlow, UK: Longman, 2001), p. 17. For a brief summary of the Southern Gothic, see Rebecca C. McIntyre's "Promoting the Gothic South," *Southern Cultures* 11:2 (Summer 2005), pp. 33–61.

7. Allan K. Wildman, "The Defining Moment: Land Charters and the Post-Emancipation Agrarian Settlement in Russia, 1861–1863," in *The Carl Beck Papers in Russian & East European Studies*, No. 1205 (Pittsburgh: Center for Russian and East European Studies, University of Pittsburgh, 1996), p. 4.

Bibliography

English Language Archival, Museum, and Other Primary Sources

American Missionary Association Papers (AMA) (microfilm), University of Delaware.

Bureau of Refugees, Freedmen, and Abandoned Lands (BRFAL). Davis Bend, 1865–1866, Record Group (RG) 105, Volume 123, Box 39 (Mississippi), M1907, Roll 16, and M1914, Roll 1, NA.

_____. School Reports, 1865–1870, RG 0775, Series #011, Mississippi, War Department, NA.

Extracts from Reports of Superintendents of Freedmen Compiled by Rev. Joseph Warren, D.D. From the Records in the Office of Col. John Eaton, Jr. General Superintendent of Freedmen, Department of the Tennessee and State of Arkansas Second Series, June 1864 (Vicksburg, MS: Freedmen Press Print, 1864).

Kennedy, Joseph C.G., ed. *Population of the United States in 1860; Compiled from the Original Returns of the Eighth Census, Under the Direction of the Secretary of the Interior* (Washington, D.C.: Government Printing Office, 1864).

Lovell, Caroline Couper. *The Bend of the River* (Unpublished Manuscript, 1935).

_____. *The Light of Other Days* (Macon, GA: Mercer University Press, 1995).

Mississippi Slave Narratives from the Federal Writers' Project, 1936–1938 (Bedford, MA: Applewood Books, 2006).

"Mound Bayou: Jewel of the Delta" (documentary), https://vimeo.com/28054533, accessed January 21, 2019.

National Archives and Records Administration, Washington, DC. Records of the Assistant Commissioner for the State of Mississippi Bureau of Refugees, Freedmen, and Abandoned Lands, RG 105, Microfilm Publication M826.

New Orleans City Directories, 1866–1877.

Quitman Family Papers, Lovell Family Papers, University of the South, Sewanee, TN.

Records of Ante-Bellum Southern Plantations from the Revolution through the Civil War, Series J, Part 6: Mississippi and Arkansas, Reels 6–12. General Editor: Kenneth M. Stampp, University of North Carolina at Chapel Hill.

"Rules and Regulations for the Government of Freedmen at Davis Bend, Miss.," Record of Captain Norton's Business, 122: 23–24, BRFAL (Mississippi), RG 105, NA.

U.S. Censuses, 1860, 1870, 1880, Agricultural Schedule, Warren County, Mississippi, Mississippi Department of Archives and History (MDAH).

U.S. War Department. *The War of the Rebellion: A Compilation of the Official Records of the Union and Confederate Armies*, Series 3, Volume 5 (Washington, DC, 1880–1901).

William Storrow Lovell Plantation Records, 1866–1887, Quitman Family Papers #616, Collection Number 00436, Folder 1, Volumes 1–3, Southern Historical Collection at the Louis Round Wilson Special Collections Library, University of North Carolina at Chapel Hill.

English-Language Secondary Sources

Abernethy, Thomas P. *The South in the New Nation, 1789–1819*, Vol. 4, *A History of the South* (Baton Rouge: Louisiana State University Press, 1989).

Aiken, Charles S. "The Evolution of Cotton Ginning in the Southeastern United States," *Geographical Review* 63:2 (April 1973), pp. 196–224.

Albanese, Catherine. *America: Religions and Religion* (Belmont, CA: Wadsworth, 1981).

Anan'ich, Boris V. "Religious and Nationalist Aspects of Entrepreneurialism in Russia," in *Russia in the European Context, 1879–1914: A Member of the Family*, edited by Susan P. McCaffray and Michael Melancon (New York: Palgrave Macmillan, 2005), pp. 85–94.

Anderson, George L. "The South and Problems of Post–Civil War Finance," *Journal of Southern History* 9:2 (May 1943), pp. 181–195.

Antonov, Sergei. *Bankrupts and Usurers of Imperial Russia: Debt, Property, and the Law in the Age of Dostoyevsky and Tolstoy* (Cambridge: Harvard University Press, 2016).

Antonova, Katherine Pickering. *An Ordinary Marriage: The World of a Gentry Family in Provincial Russia* (New York: Oxford University Press, 2013).

Appleby, Joyce. *Inheriting the Revolution: The First Generation of Americans* (Cambridge: Belknap Press of Harvard University Press, 2000).

Aptheker, Herbert. *American Negro Slave Revolts* (New York: International Publishers, 1967).

_____. "Notes on Slave Conspiracies in Confederate Mississippi," *Journal of Negro History* 29:1 (January 1944), pp. 75–79.

Avdeev, A., A. Blum, and I. Troitskaia. "Peasant Marriage in Nineteenth-Century Russia," *Population* 59:6 (2004), pp. 721–764.

Ayers, Edward. *The Promise of the New South: Life after Reconstruction* (New York: Oxford University Press, 1992).

Bayly, C.A., Sven Beckert, Matthew Connelly, Isabel Hofmeyr, Wendy Kozol, and Patricia Seed. "AHR Conversation: On Transnational History," *American Historical Review* 111 (December 2006), pp. 1440–1464.

Becker, Seymour. *Nobility and Privilege in Late Imperial Russia* (DeKalb: Northern Illinois University Press, 1986).

Beckert, Sven. "Emancipation and Empire: Reconstructing the Worldwide Web of Cotton Production in the Age of the American Civil War," *American Historical Review* 109:5 (December 2004), pp. 1405–1438.

_____. *Empire of Cotton: A Global History* (New York: Penguin Random House, 2014).

Behrend, Justin. "Rebellious Talk and Conspiratorial Plots: The Making of a Slave Insurrection in Civil War Natchez," *Journal of Southern History* 77:1 (February 2011), pp. 17–52.

_____. *Reconstructing Democracy: Grassroots Politics in the Deep South after the Civil War* (Athens: University of Georgia Press, 2015).

Bell, Karen Cook. *Claiming Freedom: Race, Kinship, and Land in Nineteenth-Century Georgia* (Columbia: University of South Carolina Press, 2018).

Bellows, Amanda Brickell. *American Slavery and Russian Serfdom in the Post-Emancipation Imagination* (Chapel Hill: University of North Carolina Press, 2020).

Berlin, Ira. *Many Thousands Gone: The First Two Centuries of Slavery in North America* (New York: Belknap Press, 1998).

Berlin, Ira, Barbara J. Fields, Steven F. Miller, Jospeh P. Reidy, and Leslie S. Rowland. *Slaves No More: Three Essays on Emancipation and the Civil War* (Cambridge: Cambridge University Press, 1992).

Bernath, Michael T. *The Struggle for Intellectual Independence in the Civil War South* (Chapel Hill: University of North Carolina Press, 2010).

Bettersworth, John K. *Confederate Mississippi* (Baton Rouge: Louisiana State University Press, 1943).

Bigelow, Martha Mitchell. "Freedmen of the Mississippi Valley, 1862–1865," *Civil War History* 8:1 (March 1962), pp. 38–47.

Bigham, Barbara. "Colonists in Bondage: Indentured Servants in America," *Early American Life* 10:5 (October 1979), pp. 30–33 and 83–84.

Billington, James H. *The Icon and the Axe: An Interpretive History of Russian Culture* (New York: Vintage, 1970).

Blackwell, W.L. *The Beginnings of Russian Industrialization, 1800–1860* (Princeton: Princeton University Press, 1968).

Blakely, Allison. "American Influences on Russian Reformist Thought in the Era of the French Revolution," *Russian Review* 52 (October 1993), pp. 451–471.

Blassingame, John W. *The Slave Community: Plantation Life in the Antebellum South* (New York: Oxford University Press, 1979).

Blight, David W. *Race and Reunion: The Civil War in American Memory* (Cambridge: Belknap Press of Harvard University Press, 2001).

Bloome, Deirdre, and Christopher Muller. "Tenancy and African American Marriage in the Postbellum South," *Demography* 52:5 (October 2015), pp. 1409–1430.

Blum, Jerome. *Lord and Peasant in Russia: From the Ninth to the Nineteenth Century* (Princeton: Princeton University Press, 1972).

_____. "Michael Confino's *Systems Agraires et Progress Agricole*," *Journal of Modern History* 43:3 (September 1971), pp. 495–498.

Bogdan, Nina. *The Desolation of Exile: A Russian Family's Odyssey* (North Charleston, SC: CreateSpace Independent Publishing Platform, 2012).

Bohac, Rodney. "Everyday Forms of Resistance: Serf Opposition to Gentry Exactions, 1800–1861," in *Peasant Economy, Culture, and Politics of European Russia, 1800–1921*, edited by Esther Kingston-Mann and Timothy Mixter (Princeton: Princeton University Press, 1991), pp. 236–260.

Bowers, Claude G. *The Tragic Era: The Revolution after Lincoln* (New York: Houghton Mifflin, 1929).

Boyle, James E. *Cotton and the New Orleans Cotton Exchange: A Century of Commercial Evolution* (Garden City, NJ: Country Life Press, 1934).

Brook, John L. "Cultures of Nationalism, Movements of Reform, and the Composite-Federal Polity: From Revolutionary Settlement to Antebellum Crisis," *Journal of the Early Republic* 29:1 (Spring 2009), pp. 1–33.

Brooks, Jeffrey. *When Russia Learned to Read: Literacy and Popular Literature, 1861–1917* (Evanston, IL: Northwestern University Press, 2003).

_____. "The Zemstvo and the Education of the People," in *The Zemstvo in Russia: An Experiment in Local Self-Government*, edited by Terrence Emmons and Wayne Vucinich (New York: Cambridge University Press, 2011), pp. 243–278.

Burds, Jeffrey. *Peasant Dreams and Market Politics: Labor Migration and the Russian Village, 1861–1905* (Pittsburgh: University of Pittsburgh Press, 1998).

Burke, Peter. "Strengths and Weaknesses of the History of Mentalities," *History of European Ideas* 7:5 (1986), pp. 439–451.

Bush, M.L., ed. *Serfdom and Slavery: Studies in*

Legal Bondage (New York: Addison Wesley Longman, 1996).

Butchart, Ronald E. *Schooling the Freed People: Teaching, Learning, and the Struggle for Black Freedom, 1861–1876* (Chapel Hill: University of North Carolina Press, 2010).

Carroll, Joseph Cephas. *Slave Insurrections in the United States, 1800–1865* (Mineola, NY: Dover, 2004).

Carter, Dan T. "The Anatomy of Fear: The Christmas Day Insurrection Scare of 1865," *Journal of Southern History* 42:3 (August 1976), pp. 345–364.

Cavender, Mary W. *Nests of the Gentry: Family, Estate, and Local Loyalties in Provincial Russia* (Newark: University of Delaware Press, 2007).

_____. "Provincial Nobles, Elite History, and the Imagination of Everyday Life," in *Everyday Life in Russia Past and Present*, edited by Choi Chatterjee, David L. Ransel, Mary Cavender, and Karen Petrone (Bloomington: Indiana University Press, 2015).

Cerman, Markus. "Alessandro Stanziani, Bondage, Labor and Rights in Eurasia from the Sixteenth to the Early Twentieth Centuries," *Cahiers du monde russe* 55:34 (2014), pp. 384–387.

Christoff, Peter K. *An Introduction to Nineteenth-Century Russian Slavophilism: Iu. F. Samarin*, Vol. 4 (Princeton: Princeton University Press, 1991).

Chulos, Chris J. *Converging Worlds: Religion and Community in Peasant Russia, 1861–1917* (DeKalb: Northern Illinois University Press, 2003).

_____. "Myths of the Pious or Pagan Peasant in Post-Emancipation Central Russia (Voronezh Province)," *Russian History* 22:2 (Summer 1995/ETE 1995), pp. 181–216.

Cimbala, Paul, and Randall Miller, eds. *The Freedmen's Bureau and Reconstruction: Reconsiderations* (New York: Fordham University Press, 1999).

Clinton, Catherine. *The Plantation Mistress: Woman's World in the Old South* (New York: Random House, 1982).

Clowes, Edith W., Samuel D. Kassow, and James L. West, eds. *Between Tsar and People: Educated Society and the Quest for Public Identity in Late Imperial Russia* (Princeton: Princeton University Press, 1991).

Cobb, James C. *The Most Southern Place on Earth: The Mississippi Delta and the Roots of Regional Identity* (Oxford: Oxford University Press, 1992).

Conrad, Sebastian. *What Is Global History?* (Princeton: Princeton University Press, 2016).

Cooper, Frederick, Thomas C. Holt, and Rebecca Scott. *Beyond Slavery: Explorations of Race, Labor, and Citizenship in Postemancipation Societies* (Chapel Hill: University of North Carolina Press, 2000).

Cornelius, Janet D. *When I Can Read My Title Clear: Literacy, Slavery and Religion in the Antebellum South* (Columbia: University of South Carolina Press, 1992).

Cox, LaWanda. "The Promise of Land for the Freedmen," *Mississippi Valley Historical Review* 45 (1958), pp. 413–440.

Cresswell, Stephen. *Rednecks, Redeemers, and Race: Mississippi after Reconstruction, 1877–1917* (Jackson: University Press of Mississippi, 2006).

Crist, Lynda Lassewell, ed. *The Papers of Jefferson Davis*, Vol. 7, *1861* (Baton Rouge: Louisiana State University Press, 1992).

Currie, James T. "The Beginning of Congressional Reconstruction in Mississippi," *Journal of Mississippi* 35 (August 1973), pp. 267–286.

_____. *Enclave: Vicksburg and Her Plantations, 1863–1870* (Jackson: University Press of Mississippi, 1980).

_____, ed. "Freedmen at Davis Bend, April 1864," *Journal of Mississippi History* 46:2 (May 1984), pp. 120–129.

_____. "From Slavery to Freedom in Mississippi's Legal System," *Journal of Negro History* 65:2 (Spring 1980), pp. 112–125.

Curtin, Philip D. *The Rise and Fall of the Plantation Complex: Essays in Atlantic History* (Cambridge: Cambridge University Press, 1990).

Dal Lago, Enrico. "'States of Rebellion': Civil War, Rural Unrest, and the Agrarian Question in the American South and the Italian Mezzogiorno, 1861–1865," *Comparative Studies in Society and History* 47:2 (April 2005), pp. 403–432.

Dal Lago, Enrico, and Rick Halpern. *The American South and the Italian Mezzogiorno: Essays in Comparative History* (New York: Palgrave Macmillan, 2002).

Dattel, Gene. *Cotton and Race in the Making of America: The Human Costs of Economic Power* (Lanham, MD: Ivan R. Dee, 2009).

Davis, David Brion. *Inhuman Bondage: The Rise and Fall of Slavery in the New World* (New York: Oxford University Press, 2006).

_____. *The Problem of Slavery in the Age of Emancipation* (New York: Alfred A. Knopf, 2004).

Davis, Ronald L.F. *Good and Faithful Labor: From Slavery to Sharecropping in the Natchez District, 1860–1890* (Westport, CT: Greenwood Press, 1982).

_____. "The U.S. Army and the Origins of Sharecropping in the Natchez District—A Case Study," *Journal of Negro History* 62:1 (January 1977), pp. 60–80.

Dennison, Tracy K. "Did Serfdom Matter? Russian Rural Society, 1750–1860," *Historical Research* 79:203 (February 2006), pp. 74–89.

_____. "Economy and Society in Rural Russia: The Serf Estate of Voshchazhnikovo, 1750–1860," *Journal of Economic History* 65:2 (June 2005), pp. 536–359.

_____. *The Institutional Framework of Russian Serfdom* (New York: Cambridge University Press, 2011).

_____. "Why and How Were Russian Serfs Freed? Making Sense of the 1861 Emancipation Act (A Framework for a New Project)," meeting of the

Caltech Early Modern Group, March 16, 2012, http://www.hss.caltech.edu/~jlr/events/Dennison-EMGV.pdf, accessed September 15, 2014.

De Villiers, Marq. *Down the Volga in a Time of Troubles: A Journey Revealing the People and Heartland of Post-Perestroika Russia* (Toronto, Canada: HarperCollins, 1991).

Dixon, Simon. "Practice and Performance in the History of the Russian Nobility," *Kritika: Explorations in Russian and Eurasian History* 11:4 (Fall 2010) (New Series), pp. 763–770.

Domar, Evsey D. "The Causes of Slavery or Serfdom: A Hypothesis," in *Worlds of Unfree Labour: From Indentured Servitude to Slavery*, edited by Colin A. Palmer (Brookfield, VT: Ashgate, 1998), pp. 69–84.

_____. "Were Russian Serfs Overcharged for Their Land by the 1861 Emancipation? The History of One Historical Table," in *Capitalism, Socialism, and Serfdom: Essays* (Cambridge: Cambridge University Press, 1989), pp. 280–289.

Dow, Roger. "Seichas: A Comparison of Pre-Reform Russia and the Ante-Bellum South," *Russian Review* 7:1 (Autumn 1947), pp. 3–15.

Dowler, Wayne. "Merchants and Politics in Russia: The Guild Reform of 1824," *Slavonic and East European Review* 65:1 (January 1987), pp. 38–52.

Downs, Jim. *Sick from Freedom: African-American Illness and Suffering during the Civil War and Reconstruction* (Oxford: Oxford University Press, 2012).

Dubina, Vera S. "The 'Distinction': Russian Nobility and Russian Elites in the European Context (the 18th–19th Century)," *Social Evolution & History* 7:2 (September 2008), pp. 80–100.

Du Bois, W.E.B. *The Negro American Family* (New York: Negro Universities Press, 1908).

_____. *The Souls of Black Folk* (New York: Cosimo, 1903).

Dufour, Charles L. *The Night the War Was Lost* (New York: Doubleday Press, 1960).

Dunning, William A. *Reconstruction: Political and Economic, 1865–1877* (New York: Harper and Bros., 1907).

Easley, Roxanne. *The Emancipation of the Serfs in Russia: Peace Arbitrators and the Development of Civil Society* (New York: Routledge, 2008).

_____. "Opening Public Space: The Peace Arbitrator and Rural Politicization, 1861–1864," *Slavic Review* 61:4 (Winter 2002), pp. 707–731.

Eaton, John. *Grant, Lincoln, and the Freedmen: Reminiscences of the Civil War* (London: Longmans, Green, and Co., 1907).

Edgar, W. "Russia's Conflict with Hunger," *American Review of Reviews* 5 (1892).

Egerton, Douglas R. "Markets without a Market Revolution: Southern Planters and Capitalism," *Journal of the Early Republic* 16:2 (Summer 1996), pp. 207–221.

Eklof, Ben. "Peasant Sloth Reconsidered: Strategies of Education and Learning in Rural Russia before the Revolution," *Journal of Social History* 14:3 (Spring 1981), p. 355–385.

_____. *Russian Peasant Schools: Officialdom, Village Culture, and Popular Pedagogy, 1861–1914* (Berkeley: University of California Press, 1990).

Eklof, Ben, John Bushnell, and Larissa Zakharova. *Russia's Great Reforms, 1855–1881* (Bloomington: Indiana University Press, 1994).

Eklof, Ben, and Stephen Frank, eds. *The World of the Russian Peasants: Post-Emancipation Culture and Society* (Boston: Unwin Hyman, 1990).

Ely, Christopher. "The Origins of Russian Scenery: Volga River Tourism and Russian Landscape Aesthetics," *Slavic Review* 62:4 (Winter 2003), pp. 666–682.

Emeliantseva, Ekaterina. "Introduction: The Sacred before the Camera: Religious Representation and the Medium of Photography in Late Imperial Russia and the Soviet Union," *Jahrbucher fur Geschichte Osteuropas* 2 (2009), pp. 161–172.

Emmons, Terrence. *Emancipation of the Russian Serfs* (Geneva, IL: Holt McDougal, 1970).

_____. "The Peasant and the Emancipation," in *The Peasant in Nineteenth-Century Russia*, edited by Wayne S. Vucinich (Stanford: Stanford University Press, 1968), pp. 41–71.

_____. *The Russian Landed Gentry and Peasant Emancipation of 1861* (Cambridge: Cambridge University Press, 1968).

_____. "The Russian Landed Gentry and Politics," *Russian Review* 33:3 (July 1974), pp. 269–283.

Emmons, Terrence, and Wayne Vucinich, eds. *The Zemstvo in Russia: An Experiment in Local Self-Government* (New York: Cambridge University Press, 2011).

Engerman, Stanley L. *Slavery, Emancipation, and Freedom: Comparative Perspectives (Walter Lynwood Fleming Lectures in Southern History)* (Baton Rouge: Louisiana State University Press, 2007).

Epstein, Mikhail. "Daniil Andreev and the Mysticism of Femininity," in *The Occult in Russian and Soviet Culture*, edited by Bernice Glatzer Rosenthal (Ithaca: Cornell University Press, 1997), pp. 325–355.

_____. "Materialism, Sophiology, and the Soul of Russia: Daniel Andreev and Russian Feminine Mysticism," *Urania* 4 (1993), pp. 19–22.

Esper, Thomas. "The Incomes of Russian Serf Ironworkers in the Nineteenth Century," *Past and Present* 93 (November 1981), pp. 137–159.

Everett, Frank Edgar, Jr. *Brierfield: Plantation Home of Jefferson Davis* (Jackson: University Press of Mississippi, 1971).

Evtuhov, Catherine. *Portrait of a Russian Province: Economy, Society, and Civilization in Nineteenth-Century Nizhnii Novgorod* (Pittsburgh: University of Pittsburgh Press, 2011).

Farina, Gabriella. "Some Reflections on the Phenomenological Method," in *Dialogues in Philosophy, Mental and Neuro Sciences* 7:2 (2014), pp. 50–62. http://www.crossingdialogues.com/Ms-A14-07.pdf, accessed January 1, 2019.

Farmer, James O. *The Metaphysical Confederacy: James Henly Thornwell and the Synthesis of Southern Values* (Macon, GA: Mercer University Press, 1999).

Farmer-Kaiser, Mary. *Freedwomen and the Freedmen's Bureau: Race, Gender, and Public Policy in the Age of Emancipation* (New York: Fordham University Press, 2010).

Farnsworth, Beatrice. "The Litigious Daughter-in-Law: Family Relations in Rural Russia in the Second Half of the Nineteenth Century," in *Russian Peasant Women*, edited by Beatrice Farnsworth and Lynne Viola (New York: Oxford University Press, 1992), pp. 89–106.

Farrow, Lee A. *Between Clan and Crown: The Struggle to Define Noble Property Rights in Imperial Russia* (Newark: University of Delaware Press, 2004).

Feldblym, Boris. "Russian Revision Lists: A History," *AVOTAYNU* 14:3 (Fall 1998), pp. 59–61.

Field, Daniel. *The End of Serfdom: Nobility and Bureaucracy in Russia, 1855–1861* (Cambridge: Harvard University Press, 1976).

———. "Peasants and Propagandists in the Russian Movement to the People," *Journal of Modern History* 59:3 (September 1987), pp. 415–438.

———. *Rebels in the Name of the Tsar* (Boston: Houghton Mifflin, 1976).

———. "The Year of Jubilee," in *Russia's Great Reforms, 1855–1881*, edited by Ben Eklof, John Bushnell, and Larissa Zakharova (Bloomington: Indiana University Press, 1994), pp. 40–57.

Figes, Orlando. *Natasha's Dance: A Cultural History of Russia* (New York: Picador, 2002).

Fleming, Walter L. "Forty Acres and a Mule," *North American Review* 182:294 (May 1906), pp. 721–737.

Fogel, Robert William. *Without Consent or Contract: The Rise and Fall of American Slavery* (New York: W.W. Norton, 1989).

Fogel, Robert William, and Stanley L. Engerman. *Time on the Cross: The Economics of American Negro Slavery* (New York: W.W. Norton, 1974).

Follette, Richard, Eric Foner, and Walter Johnson. *Slavery's Ghost: The Problem of Freedom in the Age of Emancipation* (Baltimore: Johns Hopkins University Press, 2011).

Foner, Eric. *Free Soil, Free Labor, Free Men: The Ideology of the Republican Party before the Civil War* (New York: Oxford University Press, 1995).

———. *Nothing but Freedom: Emancipation and Its Legacy* (Baton Rouge: Louisiana State University Press, 1983).

———. *Reconstruction: America's Unfinished Revolution, 1863–1877* (New York: Harper & Row, 1988).

———. "The Reconstruction Amendments: Official Documents as Social History," *History Now: The Journal of the Gilder Lehrman Institute*, https://www.gilderlehrman.org/history-by-era/reconstruction/essays/reconstruction-amendments-official-documents-social-history, accessed October 21, 2015.

———. *A Short History of Reconstruction, 1863–1877* (New York: Harper & Row, 1990).

———. *The Story of American Freedom* (New York: W.W. Norton, 1998).

Fox-Genovese, Elizabeth. *Within the Plantation Household: Black and White Women of the Old South* (Chapel Hill: University of North Carolina Press, 1988).

Frankel, Noralee. *Freedom's Women: Black Women and Families in Civil War Era Mississippi (Blacks in the Diaspora)* (Bloomington: Indiana University Press, 1999).

Fredrickson, George M. *The Black Image in the White Mind: The Debate on Afro-American Character and Destiny, 1817–1914* (New York: Harper & Row, 1971).

———. "Comparative History," in *The Past before Us: Contemporary Historical Writings in the United States*, edited by Michael Kammen (Ithaca: Cornell University Press, 1980), pp. 457–474.

Freehling, William W. *The Road to Disunion*, Vol. I, *Secessionists at Bay, 1776–1854* (New York: Oxford University Press, 1990).

Frierson, Cathy A. "Letting Loose the Red Rooster: Arson in Rural Russia," in *All Russia Is Burning! A Cultural History of Fire and Arson in Late Imperial Russia* (Seattle: University of Washington Press, 2002), pp. 101–174.

———. *Peasant Icons: Representations of Rural People in Late Nineteenth-Century Russia* (New York: Oxford University Press, 1993).

Ganus, Clifton L., Jr. "The Freedmen's Bureau in Mississippi," PhD dissertation, Tulane University, 1953.

Gao, Chungchan. *African Americans in the Reconstruction Era* (New York: Garland, 2000).

Garner, James Wilford. *Reconstruction in Mississippi* (New York: Macmillan, 1901).

Gates, Paul L. "Federal Land Policy in the South, 1866 1888," *Journal of Southern History* 6 (1940), pp. 303–330.

Gatrell, Peter. "The Meaning of the Great Reforms in Russian Economic History," in *Russia's Great Reforms, 1855–1881*, edited by Ben Eklof, John Bushnell, and Larissa Zakharova (Bloomington: Indiana University Press, 1994), pp. 84–101.

Genovese, Eugene. *The Mind of the Planter Class: History and Faith in the Southern Slaveholders' Worldview* (New York: Cambridge University Press, 2005).

———. *Roll, Jordan, Roll: The World the Slaves Made* (New York: Pantheon Books, 1974).

———. *The Slaveholders' Dilemma: Freedom and Progress in Southern Conservative Thought, 1820–1800* (Columbia: University of South Carolina Press, 1992).

Geraci, Robert P. *Window on the East: National and Imperial Identities in Late Tsarist Russia* (Ithaca: Cornell University Press, 2001).

Gerschenkron, Alexander. "Agrarian Policies and Industrialization: Russia 1861–1917," in *The Cambridge Economic History of Europe*,

Vol. 6:2, *The Industrial Revolutions and After: Incomes, Population and Technological Change* (Cambridge: Cambridge University Press, 1965).

Gerteis, Louis S. *From Contraband to Freedman: Federal Policy toward Southern Blacks, 1861–1865* (Westport, CT: Greenwood Press, 1973).

Gillespie, David. "Apocalypse Now: Village Prose and the Death of Russia," *Modern Language Review* 87:2 (April 1992), pp. 407–417.

Glymph, Thavolia. *Out of the House of Bondage: The Transformation of the Plantation Household* (New York: Cambridge University Press, 2008).

———. "The Second Middle Passage: The Transition from Slavery to Freedom at Davis Bend, Mississippi," PhD dissertation, Purdue University, 1994.

Goldin, Claudia Dale. *Urban Slavery in the American South, 1820–1860: A Quantitative History* (Chicago: University of Chicago Press, 1976).

Gorshkov, Boris B. *A Life Under Russian Serfdom: The Memoirs of Saava Dmitrievich Purlevskii, 1800–1868* (New York: Central European University Press, 2005).

———. *Peasants in Russia from Serfdom to Stalin: Accommodation, Survival, Resistance* (New York: Bloomsbury Academic, 2018).

———. "Serfs on the Move: Peasant Seasonal Migration in Pre-Reform Russia, 1800–61," *Kritika: Explorations in Russian and Eurasian History* 1:4 (Fall 2000) (New Series), pp. 627–656.

———. "Toward a Comprehensive Law: Tsarist Factory Labor Legislation in European Context, 1830–1914," in *Russia in the European Context, 1879–1914: A Member of the Family*, edited by Susan P. McCaffray and Michael Melancon (New York: Palgrave Macmillan, 2005), pp. 49–71.

Grant, Steven A. "Obshchina and Mir," *Slavic Review* 35 (1976), pp. 636–651.

Greenfeld, Liah. "The Formation of the Russian National Identity: The Role of Status Insecurity and *Ressentiment*," *Comparative Studies in Society and History* 32:3 (July 1990), pp. 549–591.

Gutman, Herbert G. *The Black Family in Slavery and Freedom, 1750–1925* (New York: Vintage Press, 1976).

Guzman, Tony. "The Little Theatre Movement: The Institutionalization of the European Art Film in America," *Film History* 17:2/3 (2005), pp. 261–284.

Hahn, Steven. "Class and State in Postemancipation Societies: Southern Planters in Comparative Perspective," *American Historical Review* 95:1 (February 1990), pp. 75–98.

———. "'Extravagant Expectations' of Freedom: Rumour, Political Struggle, and the Christmas Insurrection Scare of 1865 in the American South," *Past and Present* 157 (November 1997), pp. 122–158.

———. *A Nation Under Our Feet: Black Political Struggles in the Rural South from Slavery to the Great Migration* (New York: Belknap Press, 2003).

———. *The Political Worlds of Slavery and Freedom* (Cambridge: Harvard University Press, 2009).

Halstead, M. "Politics of the Russian Famine," *American Review of Reviews* 5 (1892).

Hamburg, G.M. "Portrait of an Elite: Russian Marshals of the Nobility, 1861–1917," *Slavic Review* 40:4 (Winter 1981), pp. 585–602.

Harms, Robert, Bernard K. Freamon, and David W. Blight, eds. *Indian Ocean Slavery in the Age of Abolition* (New Haven: Yale University Press, 2013).

Harris, William C. *The Day of the Carpetbagger in Mississippi* (Baton Rouge: Louisiana State University Press, 1979).

———. *Presidential Reconstruction in Mississippi* (Baton Rouge: Louisiana State University Press, 1967).

Hartley, Janet M. *The Volga: A History of Russia's Greatest River* (New Haven: Yale University Press, 2021).

Hecht, David. "Russian Intelligentsia and American Slavery," *Phylon (1940–1956)* 9:3 (3rd Quarter 1948), pp. 265–269.

Heinzen, James. *The Art of the Bribe: Corruption Under Stalin, 1943–1953 (Yale-Hoover Series on Authoritarian Regimes)* (New Haven: Yale University Press, 2016).

Hellberg-Hirn, Elena. *Soil and Soul: The Symbolic World of Russianness (Nationalism & Fascism in Russia)* (New York: Ashgate, 1998).

Hellie, Richard. *Slavery in Russia, 1450–1725* (Chicago: University of Chicago Press, 1984).

Heretz, Leonid. *Russia on the Eve of Modernity: Popular Religion and Traditional Culture Under the Last Tsars* (Cambridge: Cambridge University Press, 2008).

Hermann, Janet Sharp. *The Pursuit of a Dream* (New York: Oxford University Press, 1981).

Hine, William C. "American Slavery and Russian Serfdom: A Preliminary Comparison," *Phylon (1960–)* 36:4 (4th Quarter 1975), pp. 376–384.

Hoch, Steven L. "The Banking Crisis, Peasant Reform, and Economic Development in Russia, 1857–1861," *American Historical Review* 96:3 (June 1991), pp. 795–820.

———. "Did Russia's Emancipated Serfs Really Pay Too Much for Too Little Land? Statistical Anomalies and Long-Tailed Distributions," *Slavic Review* 63:2 (Summer 2004), pp. 247–274.

———. *Serfdom and Social Control in Russia: Petrovskoe, a Village in Tambov* (Chicago: University of Chicago Press, 1989).

Holt, Sharon. *Making Freedom Pay: North Carolina Freedpeople Working for Themselves, 1865–1900* (Athens: University of Georgia Press, 2003).

Hosking, Geoffrey. *Russia: People and Empire, 1552–1917* (Boston: Harvard University Press, 1998).

Hubbs, Joanna. *Mother Russia: The Feminine Myth in Russian Culture* (Bloomington: Indiana University Press, 1993).

Hudson, Hugh D., Jr. "'Even If You Cut Off Our Heads': Russian Peasant Legal Consciousness in the First Half of the Nineteenth Century," *Canadian-American Slavic Studies* 35:1 (Spring 2001), pp. 1–17.

_____. "A Rhetorical War of Fire: The Middle Volga Arson Panic of 1839 as Contested Legitimacy in Prereform Russia," *Canadian Slavonic Papers* 43:1 (March 2001), pp. 29–48.

Hughes, Michael. "The Russian Nobility and the Russian Countryside: Ambivalences and Orientations," *Journal of European Studies* 36:2 (June 2006), pp. 115–137.

Hussain, Athar, and Keith Tribe. *Marxism and the Agrarian Question* (London: Palgrave Macmillan, 1983).

Husserl, Edmund. *The Crisis of European Sciences and Transcendental Phenomenology: An Introduction to Phenomenological Philosophy (Northwestern University Studies in Phenomenology & Existential Philosophy)*, translated by David Carr (Evanston, IL: Northwestern University Press, 1970).

Hutton, Patrick H. "The History of Mentalities: The New Map of Cultural History," *History and Theory* 20:3 (October 1981), pp. 237–259.

Irish, Bradley. "Historicism and Universals," September 20, 2016, https://literary-universals.uconn.edu/2016/09/20/literary-universals-and-historicism/, accessed May 12, 2018.

Ivanits, Linda J. *Russian Folk Belief* (Armonk, NY: M.E. Sharpe, 1992).

Ivanov, Iurii. "Have You Heard? Rumors and Fears in Rural Russia," *Russian Studies in History* 47:2 (Fall 2008), pp. 7–13.

James, D. Clayton. *Antebellum Natchez* (Baton Rouge: Louisiana State University Press, 1968).

Jaynes, Gerald David. *Branches without Roots: Genesis of the Black Working Class in the American South, 1862–1882* (New York: Oxford University Press, 1986).

Jeffrey, Katherine B. "The History and Provenance of a (Frequently Misidentified) Baton Rouge Civil War Photograph," *Louisiana History: The Journal of the Louisiana Historical Association* 57:3 (Summer 2016), pp. 349–358.

Johnson, M. Raphael. "The Peasant Commune in Russia: Rural Anarchy and Feudal Socialism," *NAMS-UK (National-Anarchist Movement Shropshire)* (January 7, 2012).

Johnson, Walter. "Agency: A Ghost Story," in *Slavery's Ghost: The Problem of Freedom in the Age of Emancipation*, by Richard Follette, Eric Foner, and Walter Johnson (Baltimore: Johns Hopkins University Press, 2011), pp. 8–32.

_____. "On Agency," *Journal of Social History* 37:1 (Fall 2003), pp. 113–124.

Jones, Jaqueline. "Labor and the Idea of Race in the American South," *Journal of Southern History* 75:3 (August 2009), pp. 613–626.

Jones, John B. *A Rebel War Clerk's Diary*, Vol. I (Philadelphia, PA: J.B. Lippincott & Co., 1866).

Jones, Robert E. *Emancipation of Russian Nobility, 1762–1785* (Princeton: Princeton University Press, 1973).

Jordan, Winthrop D. *Tumult and Silence at Second Creek: An Inquiry into a Civil War Slave Conspiracy* (Baton Rouge: Louisiana State University Press, 1993).

Juergensmeyer, Mark, ed. *Thinking Globally: A Global Studies Reader* (Berkeley: University of California Press, 2014).

Kahan, Arcadius. *The Plow, the Hammer, and the Knout: An Economic History of Eighteenth Century Russia* (Chicago: University of Chicago Press, 1985).

_____. "The Russian Economy, 1860–1913," in *Russian Economic History: The Nineteenth Century*, edited by Roger Weiss (Chicago: University of Chicago Press, 1989), pp. 1–90.

Kachun, Mitch. *Festivals of Freedom: Meaning and Memory in African American Emancipation Celebrations, 1808–1915* (Amherst: University of Massachusetts Press, 2006).

Kaye, Anthony E. "Neighbourhoods and Solidarity in the Natchez District of Mississippi: Rethinking the Antebellum Slave Community," *Slavery and Abolition* 23:1 (April 2002), pp. 1–24.

Kerr-Ritchie, Jeffrey R. *Freedom's Seekers: Essays on Comparative Emancipation (Antislavery, Abolition, and the Atlantic World)* (Baton Rouge: Louisiana State University Press, 2014).

Khristoforov, I.A. "Blurred Lines: Land Surveying and the Creation of Landed Property in Nineteenth-Century Russia," *Cahiers du Monde Russia* 57:1 (2016), pp. 31–54.

_____. "The Fate of Reform: The Russian Peasantry in Government Policy and Public Opinion from the Late 1860s to the Early 1880s," *Russian Studies in History* 46:1 (Summer 2007), pp. 24–42.

Kingston-Mann, Esther, and Timothy Mixter, eds. *Peasant Economy, Culture, and Politics of European Russia, 1800–1921* (Princeton: Princeton University Press, 1991)

Kitaev, V.A. "The Unique Liberalism of *Vestnik Evropy* (1870–1890)," *Russian Studies in History* 46 (2007), pp. 43–61.

Kolchin, Peter. "After Serfdom: Russian Emancipation in Comparative Perspective," in *The Terms of Labor: Slavery, Serfdom, and Free Labor*, edited by Stanley Engerman (Stanford: Stanford University Press, 1999), pp. 87–115.

_____. *American Slavery, 1619–1877* (New York: Hill and Wang, 1993).

_____. "Comparative Perspectives on Emancipation in the U.S. South: Reconstruction, Radicalism, and Russia," *Journal of the Civil War Era* 2:2, New Approaches to Internationalizing the History of the Civil War Era: A Special Issue (June 2012), pp. 203–232.

_____. *First Freedom: The Responses of Alabama's Blacks to Emancipation and Reconstruction* (Westport, CT: Greenwood Press, 1972).

_____. "The Process of Confrontation: Patterns of Resistance to Bondage in Nineteenth-Century Russia and the United States," *Journal of Social History* 11:4 (Summer 1978), pp. 457–490.

_____. "Re-evaluating the Antebellum Slave Community: A Comparative Perspective," *Journal of American History* 70 (1983), pp. 579–601.

_____. "Reexamining Southern Emancipation in Comparative Perspective," *Journal of Southern History* 81:1 (February 2015), pp. 2–40.

_____. "Some Controversial Questions Concerning Nineteenth-Century Emancipation from Slavery and Serfdom," in *Serfdom and Slavery: Studies in Legal Bondage*, edited by M.L. Bush (New York: Addison Wesley Longman, 1996), pp. 42–67.

_____. "Some Thoughts on Emancipation in Comparative Perspective: Russia and the United States South," *Slavery and Abolition* 11 (December 1990), pp. 351–368.

_____. *A Sphinx on the American Land: The Nineteenth-Century South in Comparative Perspective* (Baton Rouge: Louisiana State University Press, 2003).

_____. "The Tragic Era? Interpreting Southern Reconstruction in Comparative Perspective," in *The Meaning of Freedom: Economics, Politics, and Culture after Slavery*, edited by Frank McGlynn and Seymour Drescher (Pittsburgh: University of Pittsburgh Press, 1992), pp. 291–311.

_____. *Unfree Labor: American Slavery and Russian Serfdom* (Cambridge: Belknap Press of Harvard University Press, 1987).

Korelin, A.P. "The Institution of Marshals of the Nobility: On the Social and Political Position of the Nobility," *Russian Studies in History* 17:4 (Spring 1979), pp. 3–35.

Kotsonis, Yanni. *Making Peasants Backward: Agricultural Cooperatives and the Agrarian Question in Russia, 1861–1914* (New York: St. Martin's Press, 1999).

Kruikova, Svetlana. "The Russian Peasant Family in the Second Half of the Nineteenth Century (Based on Riazan Province)," *Russian Studies in History* 38:2 (Fall 1999), pp. 31–47.

Lachman, Gary. *Jung the Mystic: The Esoteric Dimensions of Carl Jung's Life and Teachings, a New Biography* (New York: Penguin, 2013).

_____. *The Secret Teachers of the Western World* (New York: Penguin, 2015).

LeDonne, John P. *Absolutism and Ruling Class: The Formation of the Russian Political Order, 1700–1825* (Oxford: Oxford University Press, 1991).

Legan, Marshall Scott. "Disease and the Freedmen in Mississippi during Reconstruction," *Journal of the History of Medicine and Allied Sciences* 28:3 (July 1973), pp. 257–267.

Leonard, Carol S. "Agricultural Productivity Growth in Russia, 1861–1912: From Inertia to Ferment," in *Growth and Stagnation in European Historical Agriculture (Rural History in Europe)*, edited by M. Olsson and P. Svennson (Turnhout, Belgium: Brepols, 2011), pp. 249–263. Online: http://www.rees.ox.ac.uk/__data/assets/pdf_file/0016/35053/Productivity_CSL_Jan_2010.pdf, accessed November 8, 2012.

Levine, Lawrence W. *Black Culture and Black Consciousness: Afro-American Folk Thought from Slavery to Freedom* (New York: Oxford University Press, 2007).

Lincoln, W. Bruce. *The Great Reforms: Autocracy, Bureaucracy, and the Politics of Change in Imperial Russia* (DeKalb: Northern Illinois University Press, 1990).

_____. *The Romanovs: Autocrats of All the Russias* (New York: Doubleday, 1981).

Lipski, Alexander. "A Russian Mystic Faces the Age of Rationalism and Revolution: Thought and Activity of Ivan Vladimirovich Lopukhin," *Church History* 36:2 (June 1967), pp. 170–188.

Litwack, Leon F. *Been in the Storm So Long: The Aftermath of Slavery* (New York: Vintage, 1980).

_____. *Trouble in Mind: Black Southerners in the Age of Jim Crow* (New York: Vintage, 1998).

Longworth, Philip. "The Pretender Syndrome in Eighteenth-Century Russia," *Past and Present* 66:1 (February 1975), pp. 61–83.

Macey, David A.J. *Government and Peasant in Russia, 1861–1906: The Prehistory of the Stolypin Reforms* (DeKalb: Northern Illinois University Press, 1987).

MacKay, John. *True Songs of Freedom: Uncle Tom's Cabin in Russian Culture and Society* (Madison: University of Wisconsin Press, 2013).

Magagna, Victor V. *Communities of Grain: Rural Rebellion in Comparative Perspective* (Ithaca: Cornell University Press, 1991).

Manning, Roberta T. *The Crisis of the Old Order in Russia: Gentry and Government* (Princeton: Princeton University Press, 1982).

Markevich, Andrei, and Ekaterina Zhuravskaya. "The Economic Effects of the Abolition of Serfdom: Evidence from the Russian Empire," *American Economic Review* 108:4–5 (2018), pp. 1074–1117.

Marrese, Michelle Lamarche. *A Woman's Kingdom: Noblewomen and the Control of Property in Russia, 1700–1861* (Ithaca: Cornell University Press, 2002).

Marsden, Thomas. *Afanasii Shchapov and the Significance of Religious Dissent in Imperial Russia, 1848–1870* (Stuttgart, Germany: Ibidem Press, 2007).

_____. *The Crisis of Religious Toleration in Imperial Russia: Bibikov's System for the Old Believers, 1841–1855 (Oxford Historical Monographs)* (Oxford: Oxford University Press, 2015).

Mason, Herman "Skip," Jr. *Politics, Civil Rights, and Law in Black Atlanta, 1870–1970* (Charleston, SC: Arcadia, 2000).

Matkin-Rawn, Story. "'The Great Negro State of the Country': Arkansas's Reconstruction and the Other Great Migration," *Arkansas Historical Quarterly* 72:1 (Spring 2013), pp. 1–41.

Matossian, Mary. "The Peasant Way of Life," in *The Peasant in Nineteenth-Century Russia,* edited by Wayne Vucinich (Stanford: Stanford University Press, 1968), pp. 1–40.

May, Robert E. "'Christmas Gif,' Empty Chairs, and Confederate Defeat," *North & South: The Magazine of Civil War Conflict* 8:7 (January 2006), pp. 54–60.

_____. *John A. Quitman: Old South Crusader* (Baton Rouge: Louisiana State University Press, 1985).

_____. "John A. Quitman and His Slaves: Reconciling Slave Resistance with the Proslavery Defense," *Journal of Southern History* 46:4 (November 1980), pp. 551–570.

_____. "Psychobiography and Secession: The Southern Radical as Maladjusted 'Outsider,'" *Civil War History* 34 (March 1988), pp. 46–69.

_____. "Southern Elite Women, Sectional Extremism and the Male Political Sphere: The Case of John A. Quitman's Wife and Female Descendants, 1847–1931," *Journal of Mississippi History* 50 (November 1988), pp. 251–285.

May, Robert E., and Shauna Bigham. "The Time o' All Times? Masters, Slaves, and Christmases in the Old South," *Journal of the Early Republic* 18:2 (Summer 1998), pp. 263–288.

Mazour, Anatole G. "Economic Decline of Landlordism in Russia," *Historian* 8:2 (Spring 1946), pp. 156–162.

McFeely, William S. *Yankee Stepfather: General O.O. Howard and the Freedmen* (New York: W.W. Norton, 1968).

McIntyre, Rebecca C. "Promoting the Gothic South," *Southern Cultures* 11:2 (2005), pp. 33–61.

McKibben, Davidson Burns. "Negro Slave Insurrections in Mississippi, 1800–1865," *Journal of Negro History* 34:1 (January 1949), pp. 73–90.

McKitrick, Eric L. *Andrew Johnson and Reconstruction* (Chicago: Chicago University Press, 1960).

McMillen, Neil R. *Dark Journey: Black Mississippians in the Age of Jim Crow* (Champaign: University of Illinois Press, 1989).

McNeily, John S. "War and Reconstruction in Mississippi, 1863–1900," *Publications of the Mississippi Historical Society, Centenary Series* II (1918), pp. 135–535.

McPherson, James. *Battle Cry of Freedom: The Civil War Era* (New York: Oxford University Press, 1988).

Melton, Edgar. "Enlightened Seigniorialism and Its Dilemmas in Serf Russia, 1750–1830," *Journal of Modern History* 62:4 (December 1990), pp. 675–708.

Middleton, Richard, and Anne Lombard. *Colonial America: A History to 1763*, fourth edition (Malden, MA: Blackwell, 2011).

Miles, Edwin A. "The Mississippi Slave Insurrection Scare of 1835," *Journal of Negro History* 42:1 (January 1957), pp. 48–60.

Milton, George Fort. *The Age of Hate: Andrew Johnson and the Radicals* (New York: Coward-McCann, 1930).

Mironov, Boris N. "The Russian Peasant Commune after the Reforms of the 1860s," *Slavic Review* 44:3 (Fall 1985), pp. 438–467.

_____. *The Standard of Living and Revolutions in Imperial Russia, 1700–1917*, edited by Gregory L. Freeze (New York: Routledge, 2012).

_____. "When and Why Was the Russian Peasantry Emancipated?" in *Serfdom and Slavery: Studies in Legal Bondage*, edited by M.L. Bush (New York: Addison Wesley Longman, 1996), pp. 323–347.

Moon, David. *Abolition of Serfdom in Russia, 1762–1907* (Harlow, UK: Longman, 2001).

_____. "Peasant Migration and the Settlement of Russia's Frontiers, 1550–1897," *Historical Journal* 40:4 (December 1997), pp. 859–893.

_____. "Reassessing Russian Serfdom," *European History Quarterly* 26:4 (1996), pp. 483–526.

_____. *The Russian Peasantry: The World the Peasants Made* (London: Addison Wesley Longman, 1999).

_____. *Russian Peasants and Tsarist Legislation on the Eve of Reform: The Interaction of the Peasantry and Official Russia, 1825–1855* (London: Macmillan, 1992).

Moore, John Hebron. *The Emergence of the Cotton Kingdom in the Old Southwest: Mississippi, 1770–1860* (Baton Rouge: Louisiana State University, 1988).

Morris, Christopher. "An Event in Community Organization: The Mississippi Slave Insurrection Scare," *Journal of Social History* 22 (1988), pp. 93–111.

Mosse, W.E. *Alexander II and the Modernization of Russia* (New York: St. Martin's Press, 1992).

Nafziger, Steven. "Communal Institutions, Resource Allocation, and Russian Economic Development, 1861–1905," *Journal of Economic History* (June 2008), pp. 570–575.

_____. "Quantification and the Economic History of Imperial Russia," *Slavic Review* 76:1 (Spring 2017), pp. 30–36.

Nafziger, Steven, and Tracy Dennnison. "Micro Perspectives on Russian Living Standards, 1750–1917," *Journal of Interdisciplinary History* 42:3 (2013), pp. 397–441.

Nahirny, Vladimir C. "The Russian Intelligentsia: From Men of Ideas to Men of Convictions," *Comparative Studies in Society and History* 4:4 (July 1962), p. 403–435.

Newlin, Thomas. "Rural Ruses: Illusion and Anxiety on the Russian Estate, 1775–1815," *Slavic Review* 57:2 (Summer 1998), pp. 295–319.

Nieman, Donald G. "The Freedmen's Bureau and the Mississippi Black Code," *Journal of Mississippi History* 40 (May 1978), pp. 91–118.

Nikitenko, Alexandr. *Up from Serfdom: My Childhood and Youth in Russia, 1804–1824* (New Haven: Yale University Press, 2002).

Nissenbaum, Stephen. *The Battle for Christmas: A Cultural History of America's Most Cherished Holiday* (New York: Vintage, 1997).

Noll, Mark A. *The Civil War as a Theological Crisis* (Chapel Hill: University of North Carolina Press, 2006).

Oakes, James. *Freedom National: The Destruction of Slavery in the United States, 1861–1865* (New York: W.W. Norton, 2013).

_____. *The Ruling Race: A History of American Slaveholders* (New York: W.W. Norton, 1998).

O'Brien, Michael. *Conjectures of Order: Intellectual Life and the American South, 1810–1860* (Chapel Hill: University of North Carolina Press, 2004).

_____. "The Lineaments of Antebellum Southern Romanticism," *Journal of American Studies* 20:2 (August 1986), pp. 165–188.

_____. *Rethinking the South: Essays in Intellectual History* (Athens: University of Georgia Press, 1988).

Olick, Jeffrey K., and Joyce Robbins. "Social Memory Studies: From 'Collective Memory' to the Historical Sociology of Mnemonic Practices," *Annual Review of Sociology* 24 (1998), pp. 105–140.

Olstein, Diego. *Thinking History Globally* (New York: Palgrave Macmillan, 2015).

Onuf, Nicholas, and Peter Onuf. *Nations, Markets, and War: Modern History and the American Civil War* (Charlottesville: University Press of Virginia, 2006).

Orser, Charles E., Jr. "The Archaeological Recognition of the Squad System on Postbellum Cotton Plantations," *Southeastern Archaeology* 5:1 (Summer 1986), pp. 11–20.

Oubre, Claude F. *Forty Acres and a Mule: The Freedmen's Bureau and Black Land Ownership* (Baton Rouge: Louisiana State University Press, 1978).

Pabis, George S. *Daily Life along the Mississippi* (Westport, CT: Greenwood Press, 2007).

Painter, Nell Irvin. *Exodusters: Black Migration to Kansas after Reconstruction* (New York: Alfred Knopf, 1977).

Paperno, Irina. "The Liberation of the Serfs as a Cultural Symbol," *Russian Review* 50:4 (October 1991), pp. 417–436.

Parrington, Vernon Louis. *The Romantic Revolution in America, 1800–1860: Main Currents in American Thought*, Vol. II (London: Routledge, 2012).

Penningroth, Dylan C. *The Claims of Kinfolk: African American Property and Community in the Nineteenth-Century South* (Chapel Hill: University of North Carolina Press, 2003).

Percy, William Alexander. *Lanterns on the Levee: Recollections of a Planter's Son* (Baton Rouge: Louisiana State University Press, 1973).

Perrie, Maureen. *Alexander II: Emancipation and Reform, 1855–81 (New Appreciations in History)* (London: Historical Association, 1993).

_____. "Folklore as Evidence of Peasant Mentalite: Social Attitudes and Values in Russian Popular Culture," *Russian Review* 48:2 (April 1989), pp. 119–143.

Phillips, Jason. "The Grape Vine Telegraph: Rumors and Confederate Persistence," *Journal of Southern History* 72 (2006), pp. 753–788.

Pipes, Richard. *Russia Under the Old Regime* (New York: Penguin, 1974).

Plath, Lydia Juliette. "Performances of Honour: Manhood and Violence in the Mississippi Slave Insurrection Scare of 1835," PhD Dissertation, University of Warwick, 2009.

Polunov, Alexander. *Russia in the Nineteenth Century: Autocracy, Reform, and Social Change, 1814–1914*, edited by Thomas C. Owen and Larissa G. Zakharova (New York: M.E. Sharpe, 2005).

Potter, Jack M., May N. Diaz, and George M. Foster. *Peasant Society: A Reader* (Boston: Little, Brown, 1967).

Potter, Simon J., and Jonathan Saha. "Global History, Imperial History and Connected Histories of Empire," *Journal of Colonialism and Colonial History* 16:1 (Spring 2015).

Powell, Lawrence L. *New Masters: Northern Planters during the Civil War and Reconstruction* (New Haven: Yale University Press, 1980).

Pushkarev, Sergei G. "The Russian Peasants' Reaction to the Emancipation of 1861," *Russian Review* 27:2 (April 1968), pp. 199–214.

Pushkareva, I.M. "The Rural Noble Country House in Postreform Russia (Defining the Issue)," *Russian Studies in History* 42:1 (Summer 2003), pp. 52–86.

Rabow-Edling, Susanna. *Slavophile Thought and the Politics of Cultural Nationalism* (Albany: State University of New York Press, 2006).

_____. "The Role of 'Europe' in Russian Nationalism: Reinterpreting the Relationship between Russia and the West in Slavophile Thought," in *Russia in the European Context, 1879–1914: A Member of the Family*, edited by Susan P. McCaffray and Michael Melancon (New York: Palgrave Macmillan, 2005), pp. 97–112.

Raeff, Marc. *Understanding Imperial Russia* (New York: Columbia University Press, 1984).

Randolph, John. *The House in the Garden: The Bakunin Family and the Romance of Russian Idealism* (Ithaca: Cornell University Press, 2007).

Ransel, David L. *A Russian Merchant's Tale: The Life and Adventures of Ivan Alekseevich Tolchenov, Based on His Diary* (Bloomington: Indiana University Press, 2009).

_____, ed. *Village Life in Late Tsarist Russia: Olga Semyonova Tian-Shanskaia* (Bloomington: Indiana University Press, 1993).

Ransom, Roger L., and Richard Sutch. *One Kind of Freedom: The Economic Consequences of Emancipation* (Cambridge: Cambridge University Press, 1977).

Rea, Michael. *Metaphysics: The Basics* (New York: Routledge, 2014).

Redfield, Robert. *The Little Community and Peasant Society and Culture* (Chicago: University of Chicago Press, 1989).

Reeder, Roberta, ed. *Russian Folk Lyrics* (Bloomington: Indiana University Press, 1993).

Reiber, Alfred J. "Businessmen and Business Culture in Imperial Russia," *Proceedings of the American Philosophical Society* 128:3 (September 1984), pp. 238–243.

_____. *Merchants and Entrepreneurs in Imperial*

Russia (Chapel Hill: University of North Carolina Press, 1982).

Reidy, Joseph P. *From Slavery to Agrarian Capitalism in the Cotton Plantation: Central Georgia, 1800–1880* (Chapel Hill: University of North Carolina Press, 1992).

Reyfman, Irina. "The Emergence of the Duel in Russia: Corporal Punishment and the Honor Code," *Russian Review* 54 (January 1995), pp. 26–43.

Roark, James L. *Masters without Slaves: Southern Planters in the Civil War and Reconstruction* (New York: W.W. Norton, 1977).

Robbins, Richard G., Jr. *Famine in Russia, 1891–92: The Imperial Government Responds to a Crisis* (New York: Columbia University Press, 1975).

_____. *The Tsar's Viceroys: Russian Provincial Governors in the Last Years of the Empire* (Ithaca: Cornell University Press, 1987).

Roberts, A. Sellew. "The Federal Government and Confederate Cotton," *American Historical Review* 32:2 (January 1927), pp. 262–275.

Rodrigue, John C. *Reconstruction in the Cane Fields: From Slavery to Free Labor in Louisiana's Sugar Parishes, 1862–1880* (Baton Rouge: Louisiana State University Press, 2001).

Roosevelt, Priscilla. *Life on the Russian Country Estate: A Social and Cultural History* (New Haven: Yale University Press, 1995).

Rosenberg, William G. "Understanding Peasant Russia: A Review Article," *Comparative Studies in Society and History* 35:4 (October 1993), pp. 840–849.

Ross, Stephen Joseph. "Freed Soil, Freed Labor, Freed Men: John Eaton and the Davis Bend Experiment," *Journal of Southern History* 44:2 (May 1978), pp. 213–232.

Rowland, Dunbar, ed. *Encyclopedia of Mississippi History: Comprising Sketches of Counties, Towns, Events, Institutions and Persons*, Vol. II (Madison, WI: Selwyn A. Brant, 1907).

Ruttenburg, Nancy. "Silence and Servitude: Bondage and Self-Invention in Russia and America, 1780–1861," *Slavic Review* 51:4 (Winter 1992), pp. 732–748.

Saloutos, Theodore. "Southern Agriculture and the Problems of Readjustment: 1865–1877," *Agricultural History* 30:2 (April 1956), pp. 58–76.

Scarborough, William Kauffman. *Masters of the Big House: Elite Slaveholders of the Mid-Nineteenth-Century South* (Baton Rouge: Louisiana State University Press, 2003).

_____. *The Overseer: Plantation Management in the Old South* (Baton Rouge: Louisiana State University Press, 1966).

Schmidt, Albert J. "Westernization as Consumption: Estate Building in the Moscow Region during the Eighteenth Century," *Proceedings of the American Philosophical Society* 139:4 (December 1995), pp. 380–419.

Schrader, Abby. "Containing the Spectacle of Punishment: The Russian Autocracy and the Abolition of the Knout, 1817–1845," *Slavic Review* 56:4 (Winter 1997), pp. 613–644.

_____. *Languages of the Lash: Corporal Punishment and Identity in Imperial Russia* (DeKalb: Northern Illinois Press, 2003).

Scott, James C. *The Art of Not Being Governed: An Anarchist History of Upland Southeast Asia (Yale Agrarian Studies Series)* (New Haven: Yale University Press, 2010).

_____. *Domination and the Arts of Resistance: Hidden Transcripts* (New Haven: Yale University Press, 1992).

_____. *Weapons of the Weak: Everyday Forms of Peasant Resistance* (New Haven: Yale University Press, 1987).

Seamon, David. "A Way of Seeing People and Place: Phenomenology in Environment-Behavior Research," in *Theoretical Perspectives in Environment-Behavior Research*, edited by S. Wapner, J. Demick, T. Yamamoto, and H. Minami (New York: Plenum, 2000), pp. 157–178.

Segal, Robert A. *Myth: A Very Short Introduction* (New York: Oxford University Press, 2004).

Seton-Watson, Hugh. *The Russian Empire, 1801–1917* (Oxford: Oxford University Press, 1988).

Shaffer, James L., and John T. Tigges. *The Mississippi River: Father of Waters* (Mount Pleasant, SC: Arcadia, 2000).

Shanin, Teodor. *The Awkward Class: Political Sociology of the Peasantry in a Developing Society: Russia 1910–1925* (Oxford: Oxford University Press, 1972).

Skinner, Quentin, ed. *The Return of Grand Theory in the Human Sciences* (New York: Cambridge University Press, 1985).

Smith, Alison K. "'The Freedom to Choose a Way of Life': Fugitives, Border, and Imperial Amnesties in Russia," *Journal of Modern History* 83:2 (June 2011), pp. 243–271.

Smith, Mark M. "Time, Slavery, and Plantation Capitalism in the Ante-Bellum American South," *Past and Present* 150 (February 1996), pp. 142–168.

Smith-Peter, Susan. *Imagining Russian Regions: Civil Society and Subnational Identity in Nineteenth Century Russia* (Leiden, Netherlands: Brill, 2018).

Span, Christopher M. *From Cotton Field to Schoolhouse: African American Education in Mississippi, 1862–1875* (Chapel Hill: University of North Carolina Press, 2009).

Spulber, Nicolas. *Russia's Economic Transitions: From Late Tsarism to the New Millennium* (New York: Cambridge University Press, 2003).

Stampp, Kenneth M. *The Era of Reconstruction, 1865–1877* (New York: Alfred A. Knopf, 1966).

_____. *Peculiar Institution: Slavery in the Ante-Bellum South* (New York: Random House, 1989).

Stanley, Amy Dru. *From Bondage to Contract: Wage Labor, Marriage, and the Market in the Age of Slave Emancipation* (Cambridge: Cambridge University Press, 1998).

Stanziani, Allesandro. "The Abolition of Serfdom in Russia," in *Abolitions as a Global Experience,* edited by Hideaki Suzuki (Singapore: National University of Singapore Press, 2015), pp. 228–255.

_____. *Bondage, Labor and Rights in Eurasia from the Sixteenth to the Early Twentieth Centuries* (New York: Berghahn [International Studies in Social History, 24], 2014).

_____. "Michael Confino (1926–2010)," *Kritika: Explorations in Russian and Eurasian History* 11:4 (Fall 2010) (New Series), pp. 930–933.

_____. "Russian Serfdom: A Reappraisal," *Ab Imperio* 2 (2014), pp. 71–99.

Stewart, Catherine A. *Long Past Slavery: Representing Race in the Federal Writers' Project* (Chapel Hill: University of North Carolina Press, 2016).

Stocksdale, Sally. "Praskovia's Redemption: A Case Study of a Russian Noblewoman's Self Cloistering," in *Cultural Identity and Civil Society in Russia and Eastern Europe: Essays in Memory of Charles E. Timberlake*, edited by Andrew Kier Wise, David M. Borgmeyer, Nicole Monnier, and Byron T. Scott (Newcastle upon Tyne, UK: Cambridge Scholars Publishing, 2012), pp. 112–124.

Stowe, Steven M. *Intimacy and Power in the Old South: Ritual in the Lives of the Planters* (Baltimore: Johns Hopkins University Press, 1987).

Strezova, Anita. *Hesychasm and Art: The Appearance of New Iconographic Trends in Byzantine and Slavic Lands in the 14th and 15th Centuries* (Canberra: Australian National University Press, 2014).

Sturrock, John. *Structuralism and Since: From Levi-Strauss to Derrida* (New York: Oxford University Press, 1979).

Sutherland, Daniel E. "Mansfield Lovell's Quest for Justice: Another Look at the Fall of New Orleans," *Louisiana History: The Journal of the Louisiana Historical Association* 24:3 (Summer 1983), pp. 233–259.

Suzuki, Hideaki, ed. *Abolitions as a Global Experience* (Singapore: National University of Singapore Press, 2015).

Sydnor, Charles S. *Slavery in Mississippi* (Columbia: University of South Carolina Press, 2013).

Taranovski, Theodore. "Nobility in the Russian Empire: Some Problems of Definition and Interpretation," *Slavic Review* 47:2 (Summer 1988), pp. 314–318.

Taylor, Paul S. "Plantation Agriculture in the United States: Seventeenth to Twentieth Centuries," *Land Economics* 30:2 (May 1954), pp. 141–152.

Taylor, William R. *Cavalier and Yankee: The Old South and American National Character* (New York: Oxford University Press, 1993).

Thaden, Edward C. "The Beginnings of Romantic Nationalism in Russia," *American Slavic and East European Review* 1:4 (December 1954), pp. 500–521.

Thomas, William G., III, Richard G. Healey, and Ian Cottingham. "Reconstructing African American Mobility after Emancipation, 1865–67," *Social Science History* 41:4 (Winter 2017), pp. 673–704.

Thornton, John K. *Africa and Africans in the Making of the Atlantic World, 1400–1800* (Cambridge: Cambridge University Press, 1998).

Tomich, Dale W. *Through the Prism of Slavery: Labor, Capital, and World Economy* (Lanham, MD: Rowman & Littlefield, 2004).

Ust'iantseva, Natalia. "Accountable Only to God and the Senate: Peace Mediators and the Great Reforms," in *Russia's Great Reforms, 1855–1881*, edited by Ben Eklof, John Bushnell, and Larissa Zakharova (Bloomington: Indiana University Press, 1994).

Valliere, Paul. "The Theology of Culture in Late Imperial Russia," in *Sacred Stories: Religion and Spirituality in Modern Russia*, edited by Mark D. Steinberg and Heather J. Coleman (Bloomington: Indiana University Press, 2007), pp. 377–397.

Victoir, Laura. *The Russian Country Estate Today: A Case Study of Cultural Politics in Post-Soviet Russia (Soviet and Post-Soviet Politics and Society 32)* (Hanover, Germany: Ibidem-Verlag, 2006).

Volin, Lazar. *A Century of Russian Agriculture: From Alexander II to Khrushchev (Russian Research Center Studies, Number 63)* (Cambridge: Harvard University Press, 1970).

_____. "The Russian Peasant and Serfdom," *Agricultural History* 17:1 (January 1943), pp. 41–61.

Vollaro, Daniel R. "Lincoln, Stowe, and the 'Little Woman/Great War' Story: The Making, and Breaking, of a Great American Anecdote," *Journal of the Abraham Lincoln Association* 30:1 (Winter 2009), pp. 18–34.

von Laue, Theodore H. "The Fate of Capitalism in Russia: The Narodnik Version," *American Slavic and East European Review* 13:1 (February 1954), pp. 11–28.

von Winning, Alexa. "The Empire as Family Affair: The Mansurovs and Noble Participation in Imperial Russia, 1850–1917," *Geschichte und Gesellschaft* 40 (January–March 2014), pp. 94–116.

Vorenberg, Michael. *Final Freedom: The Civil War, the Abolition of Slavery, and the Thirteenth Amendment* (Cambridge: Cambridge University Press, 2001).

Vucinich, Wayne, ed. *The Peasant in Nineteenth-Century Russia* (Stanford: Stanford University Press, 1968).

Wade, Rex A. *Politics and Society in Provincial Russia: Saratov, 1590–1917* (Columbus: Ohio State University Press, 1989).

Waldron, Peter. *The End of Imperial Russia, 1855–1917* (New York: St. Martin's Press, 1997).

Wallace, Donald Mackenzie. *Russia*, Vol. II (London: Cassell, Petter, and Galpin, 1877).

_____. *Russia: Russia of To-day*, Vol. III (Boston: J.B. Millet Company, 1910).

Warner, Ezra J. *Generals in Gray: Lives of Confederate Commanders* (Baton Rouge: Louisiana State University Press, 1959).

Wayne, Michael S. "Ante-Bellum Planters in the Post-Bellum South: The Natchez District, 1860–1880," PhD dissertation, Yale University, 1979.

———. *The Reshaping of Plantation Society: The Natchez District, 1860–80* (Baton Rouge: Louisiana State University Press, 1990).

Wcislo, Francis William. *Reforming Rural Russia: State, Local Society, and National Politics, 1855–1914* (Princeton: Princeton University Press, 1990).

Weber, Eugen. *Peasants into Frenchmen: The Modernization of Rural France, 1870–1914* (Redwood City: Stanford University Press, 1976).

Weisberger, Bernard A. "The Dark and Bloody Ground of Reconstruction Historiography," *Journal of Southern History* 25:4 (November 1959), pp. 427–447.

West, James L. "Old Believers and New Entrepreneurs: Old Belief and Entrepreneurial Culture in Imperial Russia," in *Commerce in Russian Urban Culture, 1861–1914*, edited by William Craft Brumfield, Boris V. Anan'ich, and Yuri A. Petrov (Baltimore: Johns Hopkins University Press, 2001), pp. 79–89.

Wharton, Vernon Lane. *The Negro in Mississippi: 1865–1890* (New York: Harper & Row, 1965).

White, Deborah Gray. *Ar'n't I a Woman? Female Slaves in the Plantation South* (New York: W.W. Norton, 1999).

Wiggins, William H., Jr. *O Freedom! Afro-American Emancipation Celebrations* (Knoxville: University of Tennessee Press, 1987).

Wilbur, Elvira M. "Was Russian Peasant Agriculture Really That Impoverished? New Evidence from a Case Study from the 'Impoverished Center' at the End of the Nineteenth Century," *Journal of Economic History* 43:1 (March 1983), pp. 137–144.

Wildman, Allan K. "The Defining Moment: Land Charters and the Post-Emancipation Agrarian Settlement in Russia, 1861–1863," in *The Carl Beck Papers in Russian & East European Studies*, No. 1205 (Pittsburgh: Center for Russian and East European Studies, University of Pittsburgh, 1996).

Wiley, Bell Irvin. *Southern Negroes, 1861–1865* (Baton Rouge: Louisiana State University Press, 1974).

———. "Vicissitudes of Early Reconstruction Farming in the Lower Mississippi Valley," *Journal of Southern History* 3 (1937), pp. 441–452.

Williams, Nudie E. "Black Newspapers and the Exodusters of 1879," *Kansas History* 8 (Winter 1985–1986), pp. 217–225.

Williams, Stephen F. *Liberal Reform in an Illiberal Regime: The Creation of Private Property in Russia, 1906–1915* (Stanford: Hoover Institution Press, 2006).

Willis, John C. *Forgotten Time: The Yazoo-Mississippi Delta after the Civil War* (Charlottesville: University Press of Virginia, 2000).

Wilson, Charles Reagan. *Baptized in Blood: The Religion of the Lost Cause, 1865–1920* (Athens: University of Georgia Press, 2009).

Wirtschafter, Elise Kimerling. *Russia's Age of Serfdom, 1649–1861* (Hoboken, NJ: Wiley-Blackwell, 2008).

———. *Social Identity in Imperial Russia* (DeKalb: Northern Illinois University Press, 1997).

Wolf, Eric R. *Peasants* (Upper Saddle River, NJ: Prentice Hall, 1966).

Woodman, Harold D. "*Branches without Roots: Genesis of the Black Working Class in the American South, 1862–1882*. By Gerald David Jaynes," *Journal of Southern History* 53:1 (February 1987), pp. 119–121.

———. *King Cotton and His Retainers: Financing and Marketing the Cotton Crop of the South, 1800–1925* (Hopkins, MN: Beard Books, 2000).

Woods, William Leon. "Travail of Freedom: Mississippi Blacks, 1862–1870," PhD dissertation, Princeton University, 1979.

Woodward, C. Vann. *American Counterpoint: Slavery and Racism in the North-South Dialogue* (Boston: Little, Brown, 1971).

Worobec, Christine D. *Peasant Russia: Family and Community in the Post-Emancipation Period* (DeKalb: Northern Illinois University Press, 1995).

Wright, Gavin. "Cotton Competition and the Post Bellum Recovery of the American South," *Journal of Economic History* 34 (September 1974), pp. 610–635.

———. *Old South, New South: Revolutions in the Southern Economy since the Civil War* (New York: Basic Books, 1986).

Yaney, George. *The Urge to Mobilize: Agrarian Reform in Russia, 1861–1930* (Urbana: University of Illinois Press, 1982).

Yarmolinsky, Avrahm. *Road to Revolution* (Princeton: Princeton University Press, 1986).

Yeatman, James. *A Report on the Condition of the Freedmen of the Mississippi Valley* (St. Louis, MO: Western Sanitary Commission Rooms, 1864)

———. *The Western Sanitary Commission: A Sketch of Its Origin by Jacob Gilbert Forman* (Bedford, MA: Applewood Books, 1864).

Zahavi, Dan. *Phenomenology: The Basics* (New York: Routledge, 2019).

Zaionchkovskiy, Peter A. *The Abolition of Serfdom in Russia*, edited and translated from the third (1968) Russian edition by Susan Wobst (Gulf Breeze, FL: Academic International Press, 1978).

Zakharova, L.G. *Autocracy and the Abolition of Serfdom in Russia, 1856–1861*, translated and edited by Gary M. Hamburg (Armonk, NY: M.E. Sharpe, 1987).

Zeichner, Oscar. "The Transition from Slave to Free Agricultural Labor in the Southern States," *Agricultural History* 13:1 (January 1939), pp. 22–32.

Zeisler-Vralsted, Dorothy. "African Americans and the Mississippi River: Race, History and the Environment," *Thesis Eleven: Critical Theory and Historical Sociology* 150:1 (January 7, 2019), pp. 81–101.

———. *Rivers, Memory, and Nation-Building: A*

History of the Volga and Mississippi Rivers (New York: Berghahn Books, 2014).

Zenkovsky, Serge A. "The Emancipation of the Serfs in Retrospect," *Russian Review* 20:4 (October 1961), pp. 280–293.

Zimmermann, Jens. *Hermeneutics: A Very Short Introduction* (Oxford: Oxford University Press, 2015).

Russian Language Archival, Museum, and Other Primary Sources

Throughout this list I have employed, whenever possible, a modified version of the Library of Congress transliteration scheme. Common English spellings for well-known Russian names, artists, and places are retained—hence Akademiya nauk instead of Akademiia nauk, Franciya instead of Frantsiia, Rossiya instead of Rossiia, Ulyanovsk instead of Ul'ianovsk, Usolye instead of Usol'e, Yatsenko instead of IAtsenko, Yazykov instead of IAzykov, Yury instead of IUrii.

Архивные, музейные и другие первоисточники на русском языке.

Arkhivnye, muzeĭnye i drugie pervoistochniki na russkom ïazyke.

Archive, museum, and other primary sources in Russian language.

Государственный Архив Ульяновской области (ГАУО)

Gosudarstvennyĭ Arkhiv Ulyanovskoĭ oblasti (GAUO)

Government Archive of Ulyanovsk Province

Дело (д.)

Delo (d.)

File (f.)

Фонд (ф.)

Fond (f.)

Record or archive group (rec.)

Журнал (ж.)

Zhurnal (zh.)

Magazine (mag.)

Лист (л.)

List (l.)

File number in folder (according to theme, date, or category)

Номер (н.)

Nomer (n.)

Number (n.)

Опись (оп.)

Opis' (op.)

Inventory, register (reg.)

(series or sub-group; description)

Страница (с.)

Stranitsa (s.)

Page number (p.)

Том (т.)

Tom (t.)

Volume (v.)

Arkhivnye dokumenty v bibliotekakh i muzeĭakh Rossiĭskoĭ Federatsii, Ulyanovsk, Россия. http://portal.rusarchives.ru/muslib/muslib_rf/y14.shtml, accessed October 7, 2020.

Vedomosti Simbirskoy Gubernii. Nomer 45 (Subbota) 9 Noyabrya 1863. *"Genealogiia sem'i Yazykovykh."* Literaturnyĭ muzeĭ "Dom Yazykovykh," filial.

Ulyanovskogo oblastnogo kraevedcheskogo muzeia. Ulyanovsk, Rossiia.

Dokument "Ves'ma sekretno." GAUO, f.855, opis' 1, d.13, 1.5–7 (maĭ 26, 1867—avgust 8, 1868).

Dokument "Delo ob otmene dogovora s Mangushevym." GAUO d. 88, opis' 5, d. 92, l.15.

Dokument "Kupchaia Stepanova." GAUO, f.477, opis' 3, dok.71, 1.25.

Dokument "Spravka ot Simbirskogo Gubernskogo po Krest'ianskim delam Prisutstvii a pomeshchika A.P. Yazykova," 21 iiulia 1864 g. (17 ianvaria 1881 g.). GAUO, f.85, opis' 1, d. 123,1.71 (1864–1881).

Dokument "Statskiĭ Sovetnik V.P. Yazykov, prodavshiĭ imushchestvo Simbirskomu kuptsu F.S. Stepanovu 16 dekabria." GAUO, f.477, opis' 3, dok.71.1.25.

Dokument "Usolye," ZhurnalSimbirskogo po Krest'ianskim delam prisutstviia (1862–1865 gg.) nomera: 20, 39, 42, 44, 45, 48, 60, 67, 106 i 110.

Dokument "Ustavnaia Gramota Simbirskoĭ gubernii, Simbirskogo Uezda, sela Bogorodskoe (Yazykovo) vladeniia podporuchika ot Artillerii Vasiliĭ a Petrovicha Yazykova, 1862 god." GAUO, f.85, opis' 1, d. 19, 1.1–4, 45, 46, 47 i 48 (1862).

Dokument "Formuliarnyĭ spisok o sluzhbe M.P. Bestuzheva i nekrolog" o nem v Tambovskikh Gubernskikh Vedomostiakh, 1886, nomer. 117.

Dokument "Formuliarnyĭ spisok o sluzhbe Simbirskogo Uezdnogo Predvoditelia dvorianstva otstavnogo poruchika ot Artillerii V.P. Yazykova" GAUO, d. 88, opis' 5, d. 92, 1.15 (Iiun', 1879).

Dokument "K Hodataĭstvo ot Praskov'i Yazykovoĭ." GAUO, f.32, opis' 3, dok.170. 1.1.3 i 5 (Oktiabr' 28 - Noiabr' 3, 1865).

Dokument "Yazykovskaia Sukonnaia fabrika" GAUO, f.137, opis' 4, d.105, 1.79 (1864–1866 gg.).

Dokumenty proizvodstva V.P. Yazykova, Literaturnyĭ muzeĭ "Dom Yazykovykh," Ulyanovsk, 1853.

Druzhinin N.M., sostavitel', "Krest'ianskoe dvizhenie v Rossii v 19 - nachale 20 veka" (Moskva, SSSR, Izdatel'stvo Sotsial'no-ėkonomicheskoĭ literatury, 1963).

Ivanov, L. M., "Krest'ianskoe dvizhenie v Rossii v 1861–1869 gg." Sbornik dokumentov (Moskva, SSSR, izdatel'stvo Mysl', 1964).

Interv'iu avtora dannoĭ dissertatsii s istorikom Alekseem Sytinym. Ulyanovsk, Rossiia, 29 iiunia 2010 g.

Interv'iu avtora dannoĭ dissertatsii s istorikom Larisoĭ Ershovoĭ, direktorom Literaturnogo muzeia "Dom Yazykovykh," filial oblastnogo Kraevedcheskogo muzeia. Ulyanovsk, Rossiia, 31 maia 2010 g.

Kalendar' Simbirskoĭ Gubernii (visokosnyĭ), Simbirsk, Rossiya: Izdanie Simbirskogo Gubernskogo pravleniĭa, 1880, str. 83.

K.E.T., sostavitel, *"Spravochnaya kniga dlya uezdnykh predvoditeley dvorianstva"* (Sankt-Peterburg, Russia: tipografiia S. Volpianskago, 1887). Posobie dlĭa predvoditeleĭ dvorianstva.

Nazar'ev, V. N., "Sovremennaĭa Glush,'" *Vestnik Evropy*, nomer 3 (1876) str. 10–36.

Okun', S.B. i Sivkov, K.V., sostaviteli, *"Krest'ianskoe dvizhenie v Rossii v 1857–1861 gg."* Sbornik dokumentov.T.t. 1 i 2. (Moskva, SSSR. Izdatel'stvo Sotsial'no-ėkonomicheskoĭ literatury, 1963).

Otmena krepostnogo prava. *"Doklady Ministerstva vnutrennikh del o posledstviĭakh krest'ianskoĭ reformy."* M.- L. (Leningrad, SSSR, Akademiya Nauk SSSR, 1950, str. 178–189).

Prilozhenie k trudam redakt͡sionnoĭ komissii dlĭa sostavleniĭa Polozheniĭa o krest'ianakh, vykhodiĭashchikh iz krepostnoĭ zavisimosti: svedeniĭa o pomeshchich'ikh imeniĭakh. T.3. (Sankt-Peterburg, Rossiya: Tipografiĭa V.I. Bezobrazova, 1860).

Rusin, M.V. Selianin Simbirskogo uezda: Khroniki i istorii sela Voskresenskogo (ono zhe Undory): materialy dlĭa istorii Simbirskogo dvorianstva i chastnogo zemlevladeniĭa v Simbirskom uezde. Napechatano v knige: P. Martynov "Materialy dlĭa istorii Simbirskogo dvorianstva i chastnogo zemlevladeniĭa v Simbirskom uezde" (Izdanie Simbirskoĭ Gubernskoĭ Uchenoĭ Arkhivnoĭ komissii, 1903).

"Sbornik pravitel'stvennykh rasporĭazheniĭ i ofit͡sial'nykh izvestiĭ po uluchsheniĭu byta pomeshchich'ikh krest'ian," Tt. 1–2 (Moskva, Rossiya: Tipografiĭa Semina, 1858 str. 17–18).

"Yazykovo," Kraevedcheskiĭ kompas Soĭuza kraevedov Ulyanovskoĭ oblasti.

Zaionchkovskiy, P.A., redaktor, *"Krest'yanskoe dvizhenie v Rossii v 1870–1880 gg."* Sbornik dokumentov (Moskva, SSSR: Nauka, 1968). Vvedeniye N.M. Druzhinina.

Russian-Language Secondary Sources

"Akshuat," *ZhurnalSporta i Turizma*, Nomer 1 (2006) (TOS).

Aleksandrov, P.A., "Muzeĭ v sele Akshuat Simbirskoĭ gubernii." *"Istoricheskiĭ vestnik"* (Sankt-Peterburg, Rossiya. Izdatel'stvo A.S. Suvorina, 1908), str. 982–986.

Alekseeva, M.P., *Russko-Angliĭskie literaturnye sviazi (18–1-ĭa polovina 19 veka).* (Moskva, SSSR, "Literaturnoe nasledstvo," 1982), osobenno str. 2–4, 247, 264–268, 293–325.

Anfimov, A.M., "Krest'ianskoe dvizhenie v Rossii vo vtoroĭ polovine 19 veka." *"Voprosy istorii,"* 1973, Nomer 5, str. 15–19.

Astrakhant͡seva, I.V., Titarenko, ĬU.I., Chukanov, I.A., ĬArkov, D.E., Plaksin, S.A., "Krest'ianskoe khozĭaĭstvo Simbirskogo kraĭa vo vtoroĭ polovne XIX - nachale XX v.v.," v ėlektronnom izdanii "Letopis' simbirskogo krest'ianstva (sdrevneĭshikh vremën do nashikh dneĭ)," glava 18. http://els.ulspu.ru/Files/!ELS/disc/letop-simb-krest/19..html accessed December 8, 2020.

Aunovskiĭ, V.A., "Sukonnye fabriki i sherstomoĭki v Simbirskoĭ gubernii." *"Simbirskiĭ sbornik,"* T. 2 (Simbirsk, Rossiya: Simbirskiĭ gubernskiĭ statisticheskiĭ komitet, 1870), str. 82–102.

Avdonin, A., *"Pod sen'ĭu Yazykovskikh Muz"* (Ulyanovsk, Rossiya: Pechatnyĭ Dvor, 1991).

Avdonin, A., "Rachitel'nyĭ Khozĭ ain." *Zhurnal "Monomakh,"* Ulyanovsk, Rossiya, Nomer 2 (2002), str. 38–42.

Baĭura, L., "Legendy i byli Akshuata." *Zhurnal "Monomakh,"* Ulyanovsk, Rossiya, Nomer 2 (2000), str. 15–18.

Baĭura, L., "Muzeĭ v Akshuate." *Al'manakh "Pamĭatnik Otechestva"* T. 42 (1998), str. 92–98.

Bespalova, E., "Dĭuk," *Zhurnal "Monomakh,"* Nomer 2 (2003), str. 46–47.

Bespalova, E., "Sestra Poėta," *"Ulyanovskaĭa pravda"* (15 avgusta 1992).

Bol'shaĭa Rossiĭskaĭa Ėnt͡siklopediĭa, T.I (Moskva, Rossiya: 1999).

Bol'shoĭ ėnt͡siklopedicheskiĭ slovar' (Moskva, Rossiya: Norint, 1999).

Chekmarëv, A.V., Slëzkin, A.V., "Samarskoe selo "Privolzh'e," *Russkaĭa Usad'ba,* Nomer 12 (28) (2006), str. 822–840.

Chukanov, I.A., Shaĭpak, L.A., T͡Seloval'nikova, I.I., "Otmena krepostnogo prava v Simbirskoĭ gubernii," v ėlektronnom izdanii "Letopis' simbirskogo krest'ianstva (s drevneĭshikh vremën do nashikh dneĭ)," glava 9. http://els.ulspu.ru/Files/!ELS/disc/letop-simb-krest/10..html accessed December 7, 2020.

Dimov, V., *"Dva giganta Rossiya i SShA v annalakh istorii i demokratii"* (Moskva, Rossiya: Moskovskiĭ universitet, 2004).

Egorov, V., "Akshuat." Stat'ia v *Ulyanovskoĭ-Simbirskoĭ Ėnt͡siklopedii (U-S. Ė),* T.1 (Ulyanovsk, Rossiya, Simbirskaĭa kniga, 2004), str. 25–26.

Egorov, V., "Goncharov, Oblomov i my," *Zhurnal "Monomakh,"* Nomer 2 (2002), str. 20–21.

Egorov, V., "Polivanov," stat'ia v *Ulyanovskoĭ-Simbirskoĭ Ėnt͡siklopedii,* T.2 (Ulyanovsk, Rossiya, Simbirskaĭa Kniga, 2004), str. 135–136.

Egorov, V., "Pozhar v Ulyanovske," stat'ia v *Ulyanovskoĭ-Simbirskoĭ Ėnt͡siklopedii,* T.2 (Ulyanovsk, Rossiya, Simbirskaĭa kniga 2004), str. 357–360.

Egorov, V., "Prekrasnoe dalëko," *Zhurnal "Monomakh,"* Nomer 4 (47) (2006), str. 62–63.

Egorov, V., Rakov, N., "Yazykovskiĭ park," stat'ia v *Ulyanovskoĭ-Simbirskoĭ Ėnt͡siklopedii,* T.2 (Ulyanovsk, Simbirskaĭa kniga 2004), str. 473.

Egorov, V., redaktor, "Ėkonomika i Torgovlĭa" v sbornike *"Simbirsko-Ulyanovskiĭ kraĭ v prodvizhenie istorii Rossii"* (Ulyanovsk,

Rossiya, Korporat͡siia,tekhnologii, 2007), str. 222–287.

Egorov, V., redaktor, "Kul'tura i iskusstvo" v sbornike *"Simbirsko-Ulyanovskiĭ kraĭ v prodvizhenie istorii Rossii"* (Ulyanovsk, Rossiya, Korporat͡siia tekhnologiĭ, 2007), str. 360–361.

Egorov, V., redaktor, "Stepanov—dukhovoĭ orkestr" v sbornike *"Simbirsko-Ulyanovskiĭ kraĭ v prodvizhenie istorii Rossii"* (Ulyanovsk, Rossiya, Korporat͡siia tekhnologiĭ, 2007), str. 379–387.

Ershova, L., "Kak stranno tasuetsi͡a koloda," *Zhurnal "Monomakh,"* Nomer 3 (2000), str. 23–25.

Ershova, L., "Mani͡a," *Zhurnal "Monomakh,"* Nomer 2 (2003), str. 44–46.

Ershova, L., "Pazukhiny," stat'i͡a v *Ulyanovskoĭ-Simbirskoĭ Ént͡siklopedii*, T.2 (Ulyanovsk, Rossiya, Simbirskai͡a Kniga, 2004), str. 80–81.

Ershova, L., "Pribezhishche russkoĭ poėzii," *Zhurnal "Monomakh,"* Nomer 2 (2003), str. 17–20.

Ershova, L., "Zolotoĭ Yazykovskiĭ vek," Simbirskiĭ Kur'er *(*22 marta 2008).

Fishman, T., "Zvuchi, orkestr dukhovoĭ," Narodnai͡a gazeta (5 ii͡uni͡a 2008).

Fomina, V., "Sokhranit' kul'turu krai͡a," *Zhurnal "Monomakh," Nomer* 2 (2000), str. 14.

Frolova, O., "Karsunskiĭ dvorianin Polivanov" Karsunskiĭ Vestnik (7 ii͡uni͡a 2001).

Ginev, V., *"Narodnicheskoe dvizhenie v srednem Povolzh'e: 70-e gody 19 veka"* (Moskva, SSSR: Nauka, 1966).

Golovin, V., "Pervyĭ brend gubernii," Simbirskiĭ Kur'er *(*15 avgusta 2011).

Gromova, T., "Begi za nim, Rossiya, on stoit li͡ubvi tvoeĭ!" *Delovoe obozrenie*, Nomer 7 (114) (18 ii͡uli͡a 2007).

Gromova, T.A., "Khozi͡aĭka Kindi͡akovskoĭ Ėkonomii," *Delovoe obozrenie (*1 marta 2005).

Gromova, T.A., redaktor "Simbirsk kupecheskiĭ: v 2 ch.- Vypusk 1: Ocherki o simbirskom predprinimatel'stve" (Ulyanovsk, R.G. Pelikan, 2016).

Gureev, N., *"Kraevedcheskiĭ Sbornik,"* Nomer 3 (Ulyanovsk, SSSR: Obshchestvo izucheni͡ia Ulyanovskogo krai͡a, 1928), str. 29–30.

Gurkin, N., "Istoricheskai͡a spravka ob osvobozhdenii krest'i͡an ot krepostnoĭ zavisimosti (selo Usolye, Syzranskogo uezda)." Kraevedcheskiĭ sbornik, vypusk III (Ulyanovsk, SSSR, 1928) osobenno str. 29–30.

Gurkin, V., "Dobryĭ geniĭ biblioteki," *Zhurnal "Monomakh,"* Nomer 2 (2003), str. 50–51.

Gurkin, V., *"Na beregakh Russkogo Nila: istorii͡a izucheni͡ia territorii Simbirskogo Povolzh'i͡a"* (Moskva, Rossiya, Rossiĭskai͡a Akademiya Nauk, 2005).

Gusev, S., "Selo Yazykovo," Karsunskiĭ Vestnik (10 apreli͡a 2001), str. 18.

Kanatov, V., "Svoeobrazie provedeni͡ia reformy 1861 goda v Srednem Povolzh'e," *Vestnik Moskovskogo universiteta* 9: 19.5 (Moskva, SSSR, Izdatel'stvo Moskovskogo universiteta, 1964), str. 37–54.

Karamysheva, E., "Istorii͡a naselennogo punkta: Undory." Moi͡a malai͡a rodina, 16 fevrali͡a 2011.

Khristoforov, I., *"Aristokraticheskai͡a oppozit͡sii͡a velikikh reform: konet͡s 1850-kh—seredina 1870-kh godov"* (Moskva, Rossiya: Russkoe slovo, 2002).

Khristoforov, I., *"Sud'ba reformy: russkoe krest'i͡anstvo v pravitel'stvennoĭ politike do i posle otmeny krepostnogo prava (1830–1890-e gg.)"* (Moskva, Rossiya: Sobranie, 2011).

Khudekov, N. S., "Bunt v Kandeevke v 1861 g.," v sbornike "Konet͡s krepostnichestva v Rossii. Dokumenty, pis'ma, memuary, stat'i" (Moskva, Izdatel'stvo MGU, 1994).

Kobzeva, T.A., Dunaeva, N.A., "Sel'skai͡a krest'iansko͡ia shkola v nachale 20 veka," v ėlektronnom izdanii "Letopis' simbirskogo krest'i͡anstva (s drevneĭshikh vremën do nashikh dneĭ)," glava 14. http://els.ulspu.ru/Files/!ELS/disc/letop-simb-krest/15..html accessed January 31, 2021.

Kobzeva, T.A., Kobzev A.V., "Rol' zemskikh uchrezhdeniĭ v preobrazovanii simbirskoĭ derevni," v ėlektronnom izdanii "Letopis' simbirskogo krest'i͡anstva (s drevneĭshikh vremën do nashikh dneĭ)," glava 15. http://els.ulspu.ru/Files/!ELS/disc/letop-simb-krest/16..html accessed January 31, 2021.

Korelin, A., *"Dvori͡anstvo v poreformennoĭ Rossii, 1861–1904 gg.: sostav, chislennost', korporativnai͡a organizat͡sii͡a"* (Moskva, SSSR: Nauka, 1979).

Krylov, N., "Nakanune velikikh reform" (T͡sarskiĭ reskript dli͡a Osvobozhdeni͡ia). *Istoricheskiĭ Vestnik*, Nomer 9 (Senti͡abr',' 1903), str. 786–821.

Krylov, N., "Vospominani͡ia Mirovogo posrednika pervogo prizyva o vvedenii v deĭstvie Polozheni͡ia 19-go fevrali͡a 1861 goda," *Russkai͡a starina*, 74:6 (Aprel',' 1892), str. 81–102 i 615–641.

Kuznet͡sov, V., "I ponyne stoit eshchë starinnyĭ barskiĭ dom," Ulyanovskai͡a pravda (24 dekabri͡a 1994).

Linkov, I͡A., *"Ocherki istorii krest'i͡anskogo dvizheni͡ia v Rossii v 1825–1861 gg."* (Moskva, SSSR: Gosudarstvennoe uchebno-pedagogicheskoe izdatel'stvo, 1952).

Lipinskiĭ, A., *"Materialy dli͡a geografii i statistiki Rossii, sobrannye ofit͡serami General'nogo Shtaba: Simbirskai͡a Guberni͡ia,"* t. 2 (Sankt-Peterburg, Rossiya: Voennai͡a tipografii͡a, 1868).

Litvak, B., *"Krest'i͡anskoe dvizhenie v Rossii v 1775–1904 gg."* (Moskva, SSSR: Nauka 1989).

Luk'i͡anchikova, E., "Neformal'nyĭ osnovatel'," Dykhanie Zemli (6 okti͡abri͡a 2004).

Marasinova, E., *"Psikhologii͡a Ėlity Rossiĭskogo dvori͡anstva posledneia treti 18 veka"* (Moskva, Rossiya: Rospressa, 1999).

Martynov, P., *"Gorod Simbirsk za 250 let ego sushchestvovanii͡a: sistematicheskiĭ sbornik istoricheskikh svedeniĭ o g. Simbirske"* (Simbirsk, Rossiya: Tipografii͡a gubernskogo pravleni͡ia, 1898).

Martynov, P., "Materialy istoricheskie i i︠u︡ridicheskie rai︠o︡na byvshego prikaza Kazanskogo Dvorts︠a︡," sm. arkhiv Aleksandra Petrovicha Yazykova (Simbirsk, Rossiya, 1904).

Martynov, P., *"Seleni︠i︡a Simbirskogo Uezda (materialy dli︠a︡ Simbirskogo dvori︠a︡nstva i chastnogo zemlevladeni︠i︡a v Simbirskom uezde)"* (Simbirsk, Rossiya: izdanie Simbirskoĭ gubernskoĭ uchenoĭ komissii, 1903).

Martynov, P., *"Selo Yazykovo: Yazykovska︠i︡a volost'"* (Simbirsk, Rossiya, 1903), str. 69–71.

Mavlenkova, T., "O chem pisali brat'i︠a︡ Yazykovy 150 let nazad?" Simbirskiĭ Kur'er (25 fevrali︠a︡ 1999).

Mel'nik, V., "Spasskiĭ Zhenskiĭ monastyr' v Simbirske," Russkai︠a︡ Lini︠i︡a (20 i︠i︡uli︠a︡ 2006).

Morokhovet︠s︡, E., redaktor, *"Krest'i︠a︡nskoe dvizhenie v 1861 godu posle otmeny krepostnogo prava"* (Moskva—Leningrad, SSSR: izdatel'stvo Akademii Nauk, 1949).

Morozova, A.N., "Narodnye promysly Simbirskoĭ gubernii" v sbornike "Istori︠i︡a i kul'tura povolzhskogo sela: tradit︠s︡ii i sovremennost': Materialy regional'noĭ studencheskoĭ nauchnoĭ konferent︠s︡ii (29–30 okti︠a︡bri︠a︡ 2009 g., Ulyanovsk)" (Uly-anovsk, GSKhA, 2009), str. 108–109.

Morozova, V., "Pod avgusteĭshim pokrovitel'stvom," Zhurnal *"Monomakh,"* Nomer 4 (2006), str. 16–17.

Murashov, D., "Provint︠s︡ial'noe dvori︠a︡nstvo v kont︠s︡e 50-kh - 70-kh godov 19 veka. (po materialam Penzenskoĭ gubernii)." Dissertat︠s︡i︠i︡a: Saratov, 2004.

Naĭdenov, M., *"Klassova︠i︡a bor'ba v poreformennoĭ derevne (1861–1863)"* (Moskva, SSSR: Gospolitizdat, 1955), str. 290–292.

Nelidova, P., "Zhili v Zolotom veke," Simbirskiĭ Kur'er (22 marta 2008).

Nizovskiĭ, A., *"Samye znamenitye usad'by Rossii"* (Moskva, Rossiya, Vekhi, 2000).

Nol'de, baron E., *"Yury Samarin: ego vremi︠a︡"* (Parizh, Franci︠i︡a: YMCA-Press, 1978).

Okun', S., Sivkov, K., redaktory, *"Krest'i︠a︡nskoe dvizhenie v Rossii v 1857–1861 gg.: sbornik dokumentov,"* T 2 (Moskva, SSSR: Sot︠s︡ Ėkonom Izdat, 1963).

Orlov, A., Georgiev, V., i drugie, *"Rossiya s drevneĭshikh vremen do nashikh dneĭ."* Uchebnik dli︠a︡ vysshikh uchebnykh zavedeniĭ. (Moskva, SSSR: Prospekt, 1999), str. 270–273.

Pavlova, I︠U︡.S., "Sborna︠i︡a i︠ ︡armarka v Simbirske" v sbornike "Istori︠i︡a i kul'tura povolzhskogo sela: tradit︠s︡ii i sovremennost': Materialy regional'noĭ studencheskoĭ nauchnoĭ konferent︠s︡ii (29–30 okti︠a︡bri︠a︡ 2009 g., Ulyanovsk)" (Ulyanovsk, GSKhA, 2009), str. 109–111.

Pazukhin, A. A., *"Rodoslovna︠i︡a Pazukhinykh i rodoslovnye materialy pazukhinskogo arkhiva"* (Simbirsk, Rossiya: "Voenna︠i︡a Akademiya," 1914).

Pazukhin, A. D., *"Sovremennoe sosto︠i︡anie Rossii i soslovnyĭ vopros"* (Moskva, Rossiya: Universitetska︠i︡a tipografi︠i︡a Katkova, 1886).

Pekhtereva, L., "V starom parke," Simbirskiĭ Kur'er, Nomer 73 (9 i︠i︡uli︠a︡ 2009).

Pikman, P., "150 let Manifestu ob otmene krepostnogo prava," gazeta "Kaskad," Nomer 04 (376), fevral,' 2011, str. 16–18.

"Poety iz Usol'ya: Usol'skoe Nasledie Grafov Orlovykh-Davydovykh," *"Mir Muzeya,"* T. 6 (171) (1999), str. 22–28.

Polivanov, V., *"Materialy k istorii Simbirskogo dvori︠a︡nstva, 1781–1900"* (Simbirsk, Rossiya: 1900).

Polivanov, V., "Muranskiĭ Mogil'nik." Arkheologicheskiĭ ocherk. *"Istoricheskiĭ Vestnik"* (Senti︠a︡br,' 1908), str. 1–14.

Polivanov, V., "Selo Yazykovo." *"Istoricheskiĭ Vestnik"* (Dekabr,' 1896), str. 987–999. Perepechatano v Zhurnale *"Monomakh,"* Nomer 2 (2003) str. 15–16.

Pon'ko, T., *"Istori︠i︡a Otechestvennoĭ kul'tury IX - XXI vekov"* (Moskva, Rossiya: Rossiĭskiĭ Universitet Druzhby Narodov, 2009).

Pon'ko, T., Trofimov, V., "Tema 11. Rossiya: pravlenie Aleksandra II: §.1. Ėpokha velikikh reform." Soderzhanie kursa "Obshchestvoznanie." Redaktor Sergeĭ Nizhnikov. (Moskva, Rossiya. Razrabotka instituta distant︠s︡ionnogo obrazovani︠i︡a, RUDN, 2006). http://www.ido.rudn.ru/nfpk/hist/hist11.html accessed June 8, 2009.

Radaev, V., "Po sledam velikikh poėtov," *Zhurnal "Monomakh,"* Nomer 1 (48), 2007, str. 42–44.

Radova, M., "Akshuatskiĭ izlom," Narodna︠i︡a gazeta (16 fevrali︠a︡ 1996).

Rassadin, A., "Li︠u︡bima︠i︡a sestra poėta," *Zhurnal "Monomakh,"* Nomer 2, 2003, str. 49.

Rassadin, A., "Yazykovo" Ulyanovska︠i︡a—Simbirska︠i︡a Ėnt︠s︡iklopedi︠i︡a, T. 2 (Ulyanovsk, Rossiya: "Simbirska︠i︡a kniga," 2004), str. 472–479.

Ri︠a︡bushkin, M., "Pribezhishche russkoĭ poėzii," *Zhurnal "Monomakh,"* Nomer 2 (2002) str. 17–18.

Ri︠a︡bushkin, M., "Sud'ba Yazykovskoĭ usad'by," v knige *"Dvori︠a︡nskie gnezda Rossii": Istori︠i︡a, Kul'tura, Arkhitektura: ocherki.* Redaktor M. Nashchokina (Moskva, Rossiya: Zhiraf, 2000).

Romashin, I., "Krest'i︠a︡nskai︠a︡ reforma v Simbirskoĭ gubernii," Uchën︠ ︡ye zapiski, T. XXI (Ulyanovsk, SSSR: UGPI, 1969), glava 5, str. 10–15.

Romashin, I., "Ocherki ėkonomiki Simbirskoĭ gubernii, 17–19 veka" (Ulyanovsk, SSSR: Ulyanovskiĭ oblastnoĭ institut usovershenstvovani︠i︡a uchiteleĭ, 1961), str. 36, 471.

Saĭmanov, A., sostavitel,' *"Sobranie narodnykh pesen P.V. Kireevskogo. Zapisi Yazykovykh v Simbirskoĭ i Orenburgskoĭ Guberni︠i︡akh,"* T. 1 (Leningrad, SSSR: Nauka, 1977).

Savich, M., "K 100-leti︠i︡u Simbirskoĭ Uchenoĭ Arkhivnoĭ komissii," Ulyanovska︠i︡a pravda (12 avgusta 1995).

Savich, M., "Khraniteli nasledi︠i︡a rodnogo kra︠i︡a," Ulyanovska︠i︡a pravda (11 aprel︠i︡a 1992).

Shabalkin, A., Sivoplīas, I., "Simbirskie guberna-
tory: Ivan Petrovich Khomutov i Nikolaĭ Iva-
novich Komarov," *Zhurnal "Monomakh,"* Nomer
2 (2004), str. 38.

Sheĭpak, O., "Dorogi bez kontsa," *Zhurnal "Monomakh,"* Nomer 2, 2008, str. 22–26.

Simbirskie Gubernskie Vedomosti, n. 45, Subbota
(9 noīabrīa 1863).

Sivoplīas, I., *"Istoriīa s kartinkami"* (Ulyanovsk,
Rossiya: Artishok, 2008).

Stetsenko, I., "Krest'iane," *Ulyanovskaīa-
Simbirskaīa Éntsiklopediīa,* T. 1 (Ulyanovsk,
Rossiya: Simbirskaīa kniga, 2004), str. 307.

Sudarev, M., "Nachalo," *Zhurnal "Monomakh,"*
Nomer 2 (2003), str. 8–12.

Sytin, A., Gromova T., "Bestuzhevy iz Rep'evki,"
"Delovoe obozrenie," Nomer 11 (10b) (1-go
noīabrīa 2006).

Tairova, G.R., "Simbirskoe dvorīanstvo i proekty
agrarnogo preobrazovaniīa Rossii," v sbornike
"Istoriīa i kul'tura povolzhskogo sela: traditsii i sovremennost': Materialy regional'noĭ studencheskoĭ nauchnoĭ konferentsii" (Ulyanovsk,
GSKhA, 2009) str. 40–42.

Tanatarova, O., "Pochemu krepostnymi byli tol'ko
russkie?," "Russkaīa semërka" (29 īanvarīa
2018). https://russian7.ru/post/pochemu-krepost-
nymi-byli-tolko-russk/ accessed October 2,
2019.

Tikhonov, ĪU., "Izmaĭlkovo," *"Mir russkoĭ usad'by:
ocherki"* (Moskva, Rossiya, "Nauka" 1995), str.
28–32.

Trofimov, Zh., "Gornyĭ inzhener Petr Yazykov,"
Zhurnal "Monomakh," Nomer 2 (2006), str.
20–21.

Trofimov, Zh., "Neizmenno stremit'sīa k vysokoĭ
tseli," Ulyanovskaīa pravda Nomer 71 (24
avgusta 2007).

Trofimov, Zh., *"Nikolaĭ Yazykov i pisateli push-
kinskoĭ pory"* (Ulyanovsk, Rossiya: Karavan,
2007).

Trofimov, Zh., *"Poèt-simbirīanin Nikolaĭ Yazykov"*
(Ulyanovsk, Rossiya: Pechatnyĭ Dvor, 1998).
Zdes' smotret' glavu: "V gushche sporov Zapad-
nikov i Slavīanofilov," str. 182–192.

Trofimov, Zh., "Polivanov," Ulyanovskaīa pravda,
Nomer 71 (24 avgusta 2007).

Trofimov, Zh., *"Simbirsk i Simbirīane."* Istoriko-
literaturnye izyskaniīa. (Ulyanovsk, Rossiya: Simbirskaīa kniga, 1997). Zdes' smotret'
glavu: "Spletenie semeĭnykh uz: Yazykovy,
Ermolovy, Davydovy, Zagrīazhskie i Pushkin."
str. 160–167.

Trofimov, Zh., *"Simbirskaīa Karamzinskaīa
Obshchestvennaīa biblioteka, istoricheskiĭ
ocherk"* (Moskva, Rossiya: Rossiya molodaīa,
1992).

Trofimov, Zh., "Yazykovy: Moskovskie
rodoslovnye." *Zhurnal Russkoĭ kul'tury*
(Moskva, Rossiya: īanvar' 1993), str. 184–192.

Trofimov, Zh., *"Zhil i umer dzhentl'menom-poètom:
dokumental'nyĭ ocherk o D.P. Oznobishine"*
(Ulyanovsk, Rossiya: Pechatnyĭ Dvor, 2005).

Tvardovskaīa, V., *"Ideologiīa poreformennogo
samoderzhaviīa: M.N. Katkov i ego izdaniīa"*
(Moskva, SSSR: Nauka, 1978), str. 232–249.

Tvardovskaīa, V., "Usad'ba v proshlom nastoīash-
chem: Akshuat," *"Stolitsa i Usad'ba,"* Nomer 8
(20 aprel' 1914), str. 11–12.

Vereshchagin, P., sostavitel', *"Proshloe nashego
kraīa, 1648–1917: sbornik dokumentov i
materialov"* (Ulyanovsk, SSSR, Ulyanovskoe
otdelenie Privolzhskogo knizhnogo izdatel'stva,
1968).

Volk, S., *"Reformy i kontrreformy v Rossii vo vtoroĭ
polovine XIX veka"* (Moskva—Leningrad,
SSSR, Gospolitizdat, 1950).

Volk, S., sostavitel', *"Otmena krepostnogo prava:
Doklady ministru vnutrennikh del o provedenii
krest'ianskoĭ reformy, 1861–62"* (Moskva—Leningrad, SSSR: Akademiya nauk SSSR, 1950).

Voropaev, V., "Net nichego torzhestvennee smerti."
Internet-zhurnal Sretenskogo monastyrīa (13
avgusta, 2008), str. 1–6.

Yatsenko, N., *"V gostīakh u Polivanova."* *Ozarënnye
radugoĭ* (Ulyanovsk, Rossiya: 1993).

Zaionchkovskiy, P.A., "Provedenie v zhizn'
krest'ianskoĭ reformy 1861 g." (Moskva, SSSR,
Izdatel'stvo sotsial'no-èkonomicheskoĭ literatury, 1958).

Zakharycheva, T., "Dva knīazīa," Simbirskiĭ
Kur'er, Nomer 36 (3204) ,4 aprelī a, 2009.

Index